PENTAGON PRESS

COMMITTED TO SERVE THE ARMED FORCES

Sustainable Development through Gender Equality

Sustainable Development through Gender Equality

Editor

Dr. Archana Chandra

PENTAGON PRESS

Sustainable Development through Gender Equality
Editor: Dr. Archana Chandra

ISBN 978-93-86618-48-1

First Published in 2018

Disclaimer: The views and opinions expressed in the book are the individual assertions of the Author. The Publisher does not take any responsibility for the same in any manner whatsoever. The same shall solely be the responsibility of the Author.

Published by
PENTAGON PRESS
206, Peacock Lane, Shahpur Jat
New Delhi-110049
Phones: 011-64706243, 26491568
Telefax: 011-26490600
email: rajan@pentagonpress.in
website: www.pentagonpress.in

Cover Designed by Ms. Akshita Chandra, Communication and Graphic Designer, Mumbai

Printed at Avantika Printers Private Limited.

Contents

Foreword

"She is like the merchant ship, bringing her food from afar, she gets up while it is still dark; she provides food for her family and portions for her servant girls. She considers a field and buys it; out of her earnings she plants a vineyard. She sets about her work vigorously; her arms are strong for her tasks. She sees that her trading is profitable, and her lamp does not go out at night (Proverbs 31:14-18) She opens her arms to the poor and extends her hands to the needy (Proverbs 31:20) She is clothed with strength and dignity; she can laugh at the days to come. She speaks with wisdom and faithful instruction on her tongue. She watches over the affairs of her household and does not eat the bread of idleness (Proverbs 31:25-27)"—Holy Bible

Sustainable development is closely linked with gender equality and women's empowerment. Issues related to gender inequality were relevant earlier, when in 1995, the Global Framework was formulated at the Beijing Platform for Action and remains an important and persistent issue even today, in the 2030 Agenda for Sustainable Development, where it has the status of a standalone goal – Goal 5.

In the modern world women across sectors and classes continue to hold disproportionate responsibilities of paid work and unpaid work at home. Moreover the work done at home i.e. the unpaid care work goes unrecognized too. The household responsibilities often prevent women from participation in the labour markets resulting in a personal loss and also a lost opportunity for economic growth and development at the national level. After all, notwithstanding, the gender ratios, women constitute 50 percent of the population and the world cannot afford to keep such large number of people economically unproductive and socially backward and diffident.

The issues related to women have definite complexities and need to be addressed and dealt with empathetically in order to achieve all the Sustainable Development Goals (SDGs); after all, participation of the entire population will yield better results.

Dr. Archana Chandra,Associate Professor& Head, Department of Commerce, SHUATS, Allahabad has done a wonderful compilation of articles and research papers on multi spectrum ideas related to sustainable development and gender equality which is a reiteration and reminder of the persistent issue and its related challenges. The novelty lies in drawing linkages between sustainable development and gender equality – two important goals that all governments seek to address. The interdisciplinary perspective of the book with wide coverage of areas like health & nutrition, education, literature, culture, entrepreneurship, rural development, agriculture and even management with respect to gender equality makes the volumean excellent reference book for scholars and practitioners and policy makers of various disciplines.

Most Rev. Prof. (Dr.) Rajendra B. Lal
Vice Chancellor
Sam Higginbottom University of Agriculture,
Technologyand Sciences,
Allahabad

Preface

Eliminating all forms of discrimination against women and girls is not merely a basic human right, but is also crucial to accelerating development – sustainable development. Recognizing this, Gender Equality ranks fifth in the list of seventeen Sustainable Development Goals of United Nations Organization and aims to end gender inequalities at the workplace, in opportunities in education, in provision and availability of health and nutrition, in recognition of unpaid care and domestic work etc. These issues and many more gender related issues still remain huge barriers in the development of the socio-economic and political fabric of our country.

The 2030 UN agenda recognizes that growth must be both inclusive and environmentally sound, to reduce poverty and to build shared prosperity for today's population and to continue to meet the needs of future generations. The global plan, agreed by leaders of all countries, established Goal 5, **'Achieve Gender Equality and Empower all Women and Girls',** which calls specifically for gender equality and the empowerment of all women and girls. This we believe will play a fundamental and a deep seated role in the achievement of all the 17 Sustainable Development Goals (SDGs).

Gender equality has a positive transformative effect while gender inequalities hold us back in every way. Women's access to education and health services has benefits for the families and communities that extend to future generations. When women participate fully in labour force, it creates opportunities and generates growth. Increasing the proportion of women in public institutions makes them more representative, improves innovation and decision making and benefits society at large. A healthy, confident, enterprising and empowered woman contributes more to the society, communities and the nation at large.

Providing women and girls with equal access to education, health care, decent work, and representation in political and economic decision-making processes will fuel sustainable economies and benefit societies and humanity at large. So, gender equality is not only a fundamental human right, but a necessary foundation for a peaceful, prosperous and sustainable world.

Feminist thinkers have significantly contributed towards the mindset required to prepare not just women, but also men to participate equally in building up the engines of growth and development particularly that of empowerment of women in our society, where challenging the tradition is still frowned upon. Tradition and culture are also constructs which need to be critically examined in the context of gender equality.

Bringing together gender equality and sustainable development calls for action at various platforms and all stakeholders. It requires different players to hold up each other's initiatives. The need of the hour in India is a union of efforts made by the Centre, the State, Corporations, public leaders, institutions, non-profit organizations, community leaders and all men and women from various walks of life to bring about catalytic and synergistic effects in gender equality and thereby achieve sustainable development

Academicians, scholars, managers, health professionals, educationists, activists and more, were invited to share their thoughts and opinion on the above issues and offer plausible solutions to move forward in the Indian context. An overwhelming response urged us to package the valuable insights, investigative and exploratory studies and research papers into a book for larger consumption.

This book is divided into five sections as follows:

Section 1: Introduction and Overview

Section 2: Sustainable Development through Gender Equality in Health and Nutrition

Section 3: Inclusion and Economic Development through Empowerment of Rural Women and Rural Development.

Section 4: Role and Status of Culture, Education and Literature in Gender Equality

Section 5: Sustainable Development through Women Entrepreneurship and Women Friendly Management Practices

This book is intended for scholars of Gender /Women's Studies, Management, Home Science, Education, Literature, Agriculture etc. Apart from academicians and scholars the book may be relevant to policy makers and managers of institutions and corporate houses. A large part of the work force both in corporate houses and agriculture, constitutes women; therefore the book may be relevant to a larger population to understand the issues and challenges of today's women. Sensitization and a positive mind-set towards the twin and interdependent objectives of sustainable development and gender equality is relevant to all and sundry in the present scenario. So the book may prove to be relevant to a large population.

Archana Chandra

Editor

Acknowledgements

With the benign grace and blessings of the Supreme Power – Lord Shiv, this work has been completed. He has given me yet another reason to be thankful to Him.

The encouragement and support of our Hon'ble Vice Chancellor, Prof. (Dr.) Rajendra B. Lal needs special mention. I am indeed grateful to Prof. (Dr.) Newman Fernandes, Dean, Joseph School of Business Studies for providing the crucial impetus required for this endeavour. Without his impulsion, it would not have been possible to undertake a venture of this magnitude.

I am indebted to all the authors and reviewers who have made this work an exceptional compilation for me. A special word of gratitude to all my colleagues, Dr Reena Mehta, Dr. Richa Sinha, Ms. Priyanka Saxena, Ms. Ipshita Peter, Dr. Enid Masih, Dr. Sneh Prabha Daniel, Dr. Amita Maxwell, Dr. Harshit Williams, Dr. Abhishek Frederick, Dr. Pradhyuman Singh Lakhawat, Mr. Aamir Abidi and all others, who stood by me despite their very busy schedules, to organize the presentation of the numerous papers and articles contributed by various authors.

I am appreciative and grateful to my very dear students for their support and unstinting love. I would like to bring on record my thankfulness to Mr. George Sarpong and Ms. Sumaiya Arshad, for their help in compiling the various articles.

Last but not the least, I appreciate and applaud the effort of the Cover Designer, Ms. Akshita Chandra, for her creative acumen and subtle depiction of the theme of this book. This work would never see the light of day without the gentle reminders of Mr. Rajan Arya.

Archana Chandra

Contributors

1. **Archana Chandra,** Associate Professor & Head, Department of Commerce, Joseph School of Business Studies, Sam Higginbottom Institute of Agriculture, Technology and Sciences, Allahabad.
2. **Sarvajit Mukherjee,** Professor, University of Allahabad, Allahabad.
3. **Bramhanand Jha,** Senior Consultant , National e-Governance Division, Ministry of Electronics and IT, New Delhi.

   Vinay Thakur, Director, National e-Governance Division, Ministry of Electronics and IT, New Delhi.
4. **Neelam Kalla,** Assistant Professor, Department of Management Studies, Jai Narain Vyas University, Jodhpur, Rajasthan.

   Hemaprabha Purohit, Junior Research Fellow, Department of Management Studies, Jai Narain Vyas University, Jodhpur, Rajasthan.
5. **Jaya Tripathi,** Senior Research Fellow, Ethelind College of Home Science, Sam Higginbottom University of Agriculture, Technology and Sciences, Allahabad.

   Ranu Prasad, Dean, Ethelind College of Home Science, Sam Higginbottom University of Agriculture, Technology and Sciences, Allahabad.

   Alka Gupta, Assistant Professor, Ethelind College of Home Science, Sam Higginbottom University of Agriculture, Technology and Sciences, Allahabad.
6. **Neerja Masih,** Isabella Thoburn College, Lucknow.
7. **Neda Shamim,** Research Scholar, Department of Food, Nutrition & Public Health, ECHS, SHUATS, Allahabad.

   Virginia Paul, Associate Professor, Department of Food, Nutrition & Public Health, ECHS, SHUATS, Allahabad.

Eloni Vida, Research Scholar, Department of Food, Nutrition & Public Health, ECHS, SHUATS, Allahabad.

8. **Pallavi Singh,** Research Scholar, Department of Foods and Nutrition, Ethelind Collage of Home Science, SHUATS, Allahabad.

   Virginia Paul, Associate Professor, Department of Foods and Nutrition, Ethelind Collage of Home Science, SHUATS, Allahabad.

9. **Vinay Kandpal,** Assistant Professor, Department of Accounting & Finance, University of Petroleum & Energy Studies, Dehradun, Uttarakhand.

10. **J.D. Aarthi Dhakshana,** Research Scholar, Periyar Maniammai University, Thanjavur, Tamil Nadu.

    K.V.R. Rajandran, Associate Professor, Periyar Maniammai University, Thanjavur, Tamil Nadu.

11. **Tinku Paul,** Assistant Professor and Post doctoral Fellow (ICSSR), Department of Economics, Ewing Christian College, Allahabad.

12. **Dipak Kr. Bose,** Associate Professor, Department of Agricultural Extension and Communication, SHUATS, Allahabad.

    Hira Bose, Assistant Professor, Department of English, SHUATS, Allahabad.

13. **Deep Mala Singh,** Research Scholar (Education), Dept. of Teacher Education, SHUATS, Allahabad.

14. **Prachi .K. Wasnik,** Ph.D Scholar, Warner College of Dairy Technology, SHUATS, Allahabad.

    A.A. Broadway, Professor & Director, Directorate of Extension, SHUATS Allahabad.

15. **Manish Kumar,** Ph.D Scholar, Department of Farm Machinery and Power Engineering, SHUATS, Allahabad.

    P.M. D'souza, Assistant Professor, Department of Farm Machinery and Power Engineering, SHUATS, Allahabad.

    Devesh Kumar, Ph.D Scholar, Department of Farm Machinery and Power Engineering, SHUATS, Allahabad.

    Ashok Tripathi, Professor & Head, Department of Farm Machinery and Power Engineering, SHUATS, Allahabad.

16. **Hina Kausher,** Research Scholar, Department of Home Science, University of Allahabad, Allahabad.

Sangita Srivastava, Prof. & Head, Department of Home Science, University of Allahabad, Allahabad.

17. **Ruchi Dubey,** Assistant Professor, University of Allahabad, Allahabad.

    Payal Agarwal, UGC JRF, Research Scholar, University of Allahabad, Allahabad.

    Anamika Tiwari, UGC JRF, Research Scholar, University of Allahabad, Allahabad.

18. **Shiv Kumar Yadav,** Junior Research Fellow, Department of Education, University of Lucknow, Lucknow.

19. **Kripashankar Verma,** Research Scholar, Department of English and Modern European Languages, University of Allahabad, Allahabad.

20. **Hira Bose,** Assistant Professor, Department of English, Sam Higginbottom University of Agriculture, Technology and Sciences, Allahabad.

21. **Laxmi Prasad Anuragi,** Research Scholar, Department of English & MEL, University of Allahabad, Allahabad.

22. **Lav Kumar,** D.Phil, Department of English and MEL, University Of Allahabad, Allahabad.

23. **C. Blessy,** Research Scholar, Department of Arts for Women, SHUATS, Allahabad.

    Priyanka Singh, Head, Department of Arts for Women, SHUATS, Allahabad.

24. **Ashish Alexander,** Head, Department of English, SHUATS, Allahabad.

25. **Shefali Nandan,** Assistant Professor, Motilal Nehru Institute of Research & Business Administration, University of Allahabad, Allahabad.

26. **Keshav Shyam,** Research Associate, Motilal Nehru Institute of Research & Business Administration, University of Allahabad, Allahabad.

    Ekta Verma, Assistant Professor, Motilal Nehru Institute of Research & Business Administration, University of Allahabad, Allahabad.

27. **Amita Maxwell,** Assistant Professor, Joseph School of Business Studies, SHUATS, Allahabad.

Archana Chandra, Associate Professor & Head, Department of Commerce, Joseph School of Business Studies, Sam Higginbottom Institute of Agriculture, Technology and Sciences, Allahabad.

Sarita Maxwell, Assistant Professor, Motilal Nehru Institute of Research & Business Administration, University of Allahabad, Allahabad.

28. **H.K. Singh,** Professor, Faculty of Commerce, Banaras Hindu University, Varanasi.

    Vineet Kumar Maurya, Research Scholar, Faculty of Commerce, Banaras Hindu University, Varanasi.

    Veenita Singh, Research Scholar, Department of Commerce and Business Administrative, University of Allahabad, Allahabad.

29. **Kalpana Sinha,** Head of Entrepreneurship IMS, Master Trainer National Entrepreneurship Network Entrepreneur, Startup Coach, Mentor and Incubation Specialist, New Delhi.

30. **Deependra Sharma,** Associate Professor, Amity Business School,, Amity University, Manesar, Haryana.

    Ms Amrita Grewal, Research Scholar, Amity University, Manesar, Haryana, Haryana.

31. **Aditi Hajela,** Associate Member (ACS), Institute of Company Secretaries of India Volunteer, Ten Thousand Villages, Ann Arbor, Michigan, USA.

32. **Archana Chandra,** Associate Professor & Head, Department of Commerce, Joseph School of Business Studies, Sam Higginbottom Institute of Agriculture, Technology and Sciences, Allahabad.

    Mr. George Sarpong, Research Scholar, Joseph School of Business Studies, SHUATS, Allahabad.

33. **Nidhi Khanna,** Research Scholar, Faculty of Commerce, Banaras Hindu University, Varanasi.

    Shubham Kesharwani, Research Scholar, Faculty of Commerce, Banaras Hindu University, Varanasi.

    Somya Arora, Research Scholar, Faculty of Commerce, Banaras Hindu University, Varanasi.

SECTION 1

INTRODUCTION AND OVERVIEW

1

Transforming India:

Sustainable Development through Gender Equality

Archana Chandra

SUSTAINABLE DEVELOPMENT

"Sustainable Development recognises that growth must be both inclusive and environmentally sound to reduce poverty and build shared prosperity for today's population, and to continue to meet the needs of future generations." (World Bank)

The term 'sustainable development' was used by the Brundtland Commission, which coined, what has become the most often-quoted definition of sustainable development as development that "meets the needs of the present without compromising the ability of future generations to meet their own needs". Alternatively, sustainability educator Michael Thomas Needham referred to sustainable development as "the ability to meet the needs of the present while contributing to the future generations' needs". There is an additional focus on the present generation's responsibility to improve the future generations' life by restoring the previous ecosystem damage, and resisting from contributing to further ecosystem damage.

Sustainable development ties together concern for the carrying capacity of natural systems with the social challenges faced by humanity. As early as the 1970s, "sustainability" was employed to describe an economy "in equilibrium with basic ecological support systems". Ecologists have pointed to The Limits to Growth, and presented the alternative of a "steady state economy" in order to address environmental concerns.

Over the past two decades, economic growth has lifted more than 660 million people out of poverty and has raised the income levels of millions more. But more often than not, it has come at the expense of the environment, poor communities and certain sections of society, including women.

Through a variety of market, policy and institutional failures, Earth's natural capital has been used in ways that are economically inefficient and wasteful, without sufficient reckoning of the true costs of resource depletion. The burning of fossil fuels supported rapid growth for decades but set up dangerous consequences, with climate change today threatening to roll back decades of development progress. At the same time, growth patterns have left hundreds of millions of people behind: 1.2 billion still lack access to electricity, 870 million are malnourished, and 780 million are still without access to clean, safe drinking water, not to forget the status of women which needs to be addressed too.

As per World Bank, sustainable development recognises that growth must be both inclusive and environmentally sound to reduce poverty and build shared prosperity for today's population and to continue to meet the needs of future generations. It is efficient with resources and carefully planned to deliver both immediate and long-term benefits for people, planet, and prosperity. The three pillars of sustainable development—economic growth, environmental stewardship, and social inclusion—carry across all sectors of development, from cities facing rapid urbanisation to agriculture, infrastructure, energy development and use, water availability, and transportation and also all sections of society—rich, poor, women, all castes, creed and tribes. Cities are embracing low-carbon growth and public transportation. Farmers are picking up the practices of climate-smart agriculture. Countries are recognising the value of their natural resources, and industries are realising how much they can save through energy and supply chain efficiency and at the same time achieve economic and social inclusion in all development endeavours. The concept of sustainable development may thus be broken out into three constituent parts: environmental sustainability, economic sustainability and socio-political sustainability.

The impending question facing countries, cities, corporations, and development organisations today is not *whether* to embrace sustainable development or not but *how to do it*. Ben Ki Moon, the former United Nations Secretary-General, observed emphatically, that "we don't have plan B because there is no planet B". This thought has guided the development of the Sustainable Development Goals (SDGs).

Sustainable Development Goals

The challenge to find answers to this looming question and to draft a plan, was taken up by the United Nations involving its 193 member States, as well as global civil society. The process culminated in a resolution which adopted the Sustainable Development Goals (SDGs), a proposed set of goals, targets and indicators that countries will use as a framework for designing their agendas and policies. The SDGs build on the principles agreed upon in Resolution A/RES/66/288, popularly known as "The Future We Want"—a non-binding document released as a result of Rio+20 Conference held in 2012.

The seventeen SDGs are: Goal 1: No poverty; Goal 2: Zero Hunger; Goal 3: Good Health and Well Being; Goal 4: Quality Education; Goal 5: Gender Equality; Goal 6: Clean Water and Sanitation; Goal 7: Affordable and Clean energy; Goal 8: Decent Work and economic Growth; Goal 9: Industry, Innovation and Infrastructure; Goal 10: Reduced Inequalities; Goal 11: Sustainable Cities and Communities; Goal 12: Responsible Consumption and Production; Goal 13: Climate Action; Goal 14: Life below Water; Goal 15: Life on Land; Goal 16: Peace Justice and Strong Institutions; Goal 17: Partnerships for the Goals. (United Nations, 2015)

These goals now serve as a road map for a comprehensive sustainable development while integrating and balancing the three dimensions of economic, social and environmental improvements in a comprehensive global vision. There is no doubt that these are challenges that need to be met for the betterment of the present generation as well as future generations. In India, Prime Minister Narendra Modi has emphasised, "These goals (SDGs) reflect our evolving understanding of the social, economic and environmental linkages that define our lives." *'Sabka Saath Sabka Vikas'* and the associated national programs initiated by the present government closely track the SDGs.

GOAL 5: ACHIEVE GENDER EQUALITY AND EMPOWER ALL WOMEN AND GIRLS

While each goal is significant, the focus in this article will be on Goal 5, which aims to 'Achieve Gender Equality and Empower all Women and Girls'. The vision is to empower women and girls to reach their full potential. This in turn requires elimination of all forms of discrimination and violence against them, including harmful practices. It seeks to ensure that they have every opportunity for sexual and reproductive health and reproductive rights; receive due recognition for their unpaid work; have full access to productive resources; and enjoy equal participation with men in political, economic and public life. Globally, the proportion of women aged 20 to 24 who reported that they were married before their eighteenth birthdays dropped from 32 per cent around 1990 to 26 per cent around 2015. In 30 countries where the practice of female genital mutilation is concentrated, more than a third of girls aged 15 to 19 have undergone the procedure. Based on time-use surveys conducted between 2000 and 2014 in 59 countries, women said they spend 19 per cent of their time each day on unpaid labour versus 8 per cent for men. The proportion of seats held by women in single or lower houses of parliament rose to 23 per cent in 2016—a rise of 6 percentage points over the last decade. (United Nations, 2015)

Since 2000, UNDP together with the UN partners and the rest of the global community has made gender equality central to our work, and we have seen some remarkable successes. More girls are now in school compared to 15 years ago, and most regions have reached gender parity in primary education. Women now make up to 41 percent of paid workers outside of agriculture, compared to 35 percent in 1990. (United Nations, 2015)

The Sustainable Development Goals aim to build on these achievements to ensure that there is an end to discrimination against women and girls everywhere. There are still gross inequalities in access to paid employment in some regions, and significant gaps between men and women in the labour market. Sexual violence and exploitation, the unequal division of unpaid care and domestic work, and discrimination in public decision making, all remain huge barriers.

Ensuring universal access to sexual and reproductive health, and affording women equal rights to economic resources such as land and property, are vital targets to realising this goal. There are now more women in public office than ever before, but encouraging more women leaders across all regions will help strengthen policies and legislation for greater gender equality.

Empowering women and promoting gender equality is crucial to accelerating sustainable development. Ending all forms of discrimination against women and girls is not only a basic human right, but it also has a multiplier effect across all other development areas. The specific targets of Goal 5 as established by United Nations, are:

- End all forms of discrimination against all women and girls everywhere.
- Eliminate all forms of violence against all women and girls in the

public and private spheres, including trafficking and sexual and other types of exploitation.
- Eliminate all harmful practices, such as child, early and forced marriage and female genital mutilation.
- Recognise and value unpaid care and domestic work through the provision of public services, infrastructure and social protection policies and the promotion of shared responsibility within the household and the family as nationally appropriate.
- Ensure women's full and effective participation and equal opportunities for leadership at all levels of decision making in political, economic and public life.
- Ensure universal access to sexual and reproductive health and reproductive rights as agreed in accordance with the Programme of Action of the International Conference on Population and Development and the Beijing Platform for Action and the outcome documents of their review conferences.
- Undertake reforms to give women equal rights to economic resources, as well as access to ownership and control over land and other forms of property, financial services, inheritance and natural resources, in accordance with national laws.
- Enhance the use of enabling technology, in particular information and communications technology, to promote the empowerment of women.
- Adopt and strengthen sound policies and enforceable legislation for the promotion of gender equality and the empowerment of all women and girls at all levels. (United Nations, 2014)

Providing women and girls with equal access to education, health care, decent work, and representation in political and economic decision-making processes will fuel sustainable economies and benefit societies and humanity at large. While a record 143 countries guaranteed equality between men and women in their Constitutions by 2014, another 52 had not taken this step. In many nations, gender discrimination is still woven through legal and social norms. Although goal 5 is the gender equality stand-alone goal, the SDG's can only be successful if women are completely integrated into each and every goal. Eliminating violence such as trafficking and sexual exploitation and abolishing harmful traditional practices against all women and girls in the public and private spheres, such as child, early and forced marriage and female genital mutilation are important issues. Adopting and strengthening sound policies and enforceable legislation for the promotion of gender equality and the empowerment of all women and girls at all levels, putting a stop to all forms of discrimination against all women and girls globally, compulsory completion of secondary education for the girl child, implementation and accessibility of the sexual and reproductive health rights to women and girls globally, aiding women and girls empowerment through technology are some issues that need to be addressed. Listening to girls cannot be undermined or overlooked as SDGs can deliver transformative change for girls only if they have been consulted and their priorities and needs have been taken into account. Girls should be viewed as agents of change and not as beneficiaries—therefore their engagement in the implementation of the SDGs is crucial. For this, the leadership potential of girls must be understood and realised. Massive contributions that girls and young women as volunteers delivered for MDGs has been witnessed. (UNDP, 2015)

INDIA, SUSTAINABLE DEVELOPMENT AND GENDER EQUALITY

Prime Minister Narendra Modi said in his speech at the United Nations Sustainable Development Summit in September 2015: *"Much of India's development agenda is mirrored in the Sustainable Development Goals. Our national plans are ambitious and purposeful. Sustainable development of one-sixth of humanity will be of great consequence to the world and our beautiful planet." Vasudeva Kutumbakam,* an ancient Indian phrase which means 'the world is one family', succinctly and concisely captures the spirit of India's approach to all aspects of life including economic, social and environmental development (the three pillars of sustainable development). The SDGs are, in fact, a part and parcel of the country's long-standing tradition and heritage.

As the fastest growing major economy of the world today, India is poised to deliver its commitments to inclusive and sustainable development. *'Sabka Saath Sabka Vikas'*, which is translated as 'Collective effort, Inclusive Development' as enunciated by Mr Narendra Modi, forms the cornerstone of India's national development agenda. Inclusive Development *(Sabka Vikas)* by default implies gender development along with other strata of the population and Collective Effort *(Sabka Saath)* reaches out to women and girls along with their male counterparts, to participate in developmental activities implying empowerment.

Reinforcing India's commitment to the national development agenda and SDGs, the country's Parliament has organised several forums to develop policy and action perspectives on elimination of poverty, promoting gender equality and addressing climate change. To expedite this agenda, the NITI Aayog, the premier think tank of the Government of India has carried out a detailed mapping of the 17 SDGs. While tracking the plans, policies and achievements of India's development and therefore the SDGs, the NITI Aayog in its Voluntary National Review Report, 2017, on the Implementation of the Sustainable Development Goals, submitted to the United Nations, High Level Political Forum, 2017; states truly that "the nature of SDGs is such, that the advancement of one global goal may lead to the progress in other goal as well. In fact, one set of SDGs effectively serves as instruments to achieve another set of SDGs". For example, SDG 1 (no poverty) helps achieve Goal 5 (gender equality) and SDG 8 (decent work and economic growth) helps achieve SDG 1 and SDG 5. A comprehensive and holistic approach is therefore more appropriate and therefore recommended.

In India, the root cause of discrimination against women and girls is the roles and responsibilities assigned to women and men, perpetuated and promoted by patriarchal social norms and practices. India has ratified the UN Convention on the Elimination of all Forms of Discrimination against Women (CEDAW), whilst gender equality is firmly established in the Constitution. Despite that, India ranked 125th on the Gender Inequality Index of 159 countries in 2015 and 87th as per Global Gender Gap Index, 2016 among 147 countries.

As per the Census data 2011, India's sex ratio is 933 females per 1000 males, with 946 females for rural, 900 for urban and 945 for Dalit women. Kerala has the highest sex ratio of 1084 females juxtaposed with Haryana state having one of the lowest with 879 per 1000 males. Female literacy rate is 53.7% far below the national average of 64.8% with the male literacy rate at 75.3%. Though literacy rate amongst the Dalit women has improved from 41.9% in 2001 to 56.5%, it continues to be below the national average. Literacy rate is lowest in Rajasthan at 52.6% followed by Bihar 53.3%. And while an increase in the enrolment of girls in primary and secondary schools is observed, safety, security, mobility, teacher's attitude, functional sanitation facilities, early marriages, extra household chores etc. lead to lower educational attainment among them. (Census of India 2011)

NFHS-4 reports women in the reproductive age are undernourished and over 53% are anaemic. Women parliamentarians in India constitute only 12%. Reservation of 33% for women in the government has improved representation of women in urban and rural areas, but their voice and participation remain tethered. Caste and cultural practices in the society add layers to discriminations among women. Dalit women face systemic and structural discrimination as poor dalits, and as women on top of that.

Violence against women is very much a concern in India. However, various legislations have been passed to address this issue. Protection of Women from Domestic Violence Act 2005, the Prohibition of Child Marriage Act 2006; the Protection of Children from Sexual Offences Act 2012; the Criminal Law (Amendment) Act 2013; Sexual Harassment of Women at Workplace (Prevention, Prohibition and Redressal) Act 2013; the Scheduled Castes and Scheduled Tribes (Prevention of Atrocities) Amendment Act 2015; and Immoral Traffic (Prevention) Act (1956), to name a few. The recent judgement of the Supreme Court in connection with 'Triple Talaq' is a significant step in the direction of women's rights.

Harmful practices such as child, early and forced marriage; witch hunting; honour killing and female genital mutilation, stemming from social and cultural norms are gross violations of human rights. Early, child and forced marriage perpetuates a culture that devalues girls and women denying them their basic rights. India has signed the United Nations Convention on the Rights of the Child.

India has abysmal participation of women in socio-economic and political spheres. India ranks 112th in women's representation in Parliament (wereform.org, 2016). Articles 14, 15, 15(3), 16, 39(a), 39(b), 39(c) and 42 (www.mospi.gov.in) of the Constitution inform the States to adopt measures for socio-economic, political emancipation of women. Article 243 D3, D4, T3 and T4 mentions reservation of one third seats for women in the panchayats and municipalities. These are reaffirmed by the Government of India through Articles 7, 8 and 9 of Part 2 of CEDAW and Part C of the Beijing Platform for Action. The Universal Periodic Review Report (2017) and CSW reports mentions India's commitment to increase women's representation in highest decision making bodies.

India is a signatory to the agreement at the International Conference on Population and Development (ICPD) that called for a reproductive health and rights approach rather than a "population control" approach, with greater attention to male responsibilities and the special needs of adolescents and youth. However, the socio-cultural norms hinder women and girls' access to Sexual and Reproductive Health and Rights (SRHR).

NFHS 4 reported that 26.8% women aged 20- 24 years married before the age of 18 years. The data for urban areas is 17.5% and 31.5% for rural areas. Also 7.9% of women in the age-group of 15-19 years were already mothers/pregnant at the time of survey; for which the data for urban areas is 5.0% and for rural areas it is 9.2%. Other concerns include repeated pregnancies (with less than a gap of three years between children), increased burden of family planning on women (36% tubectomy, only 0.3% Vasectomy, 5.6% male condom usage etc.). Overall, the total fertility rate (TFR) (children per woman) stands at 2.2%, with 1.8% for urban areas and 2.4% for rural areas. States like Bihar (TFR—3.4%; early marriage of girls-39.1%; early pregnancy-12.2%), Rajasthan (TFR-2.4%; early marriage of girls-35.4%; early pregnancy - 6.3%), Uttar Pradesh (TFR—2.7%; early marriage of girls—21.2%) fare poorly on TFR, early marriages, early pregnancies. States like Kerala (TFR—1.6%; early marriage of girls—7.6%; early pregnancy—3%, and Goa (TFR—1.7%; early marriage of girls—9.8%; early pregnancy—2.9%) are doing well on these indicators (National Family Health Survey—4 (2015-16)). Prevailing social norms, limited access to education, financial dependence, societal support etc. curtails the health and reproductive rights of women in India.

Biased social norms, customs and cultural practices, discriminatory inheritance practices, unequal access to land markets, and gender-biased land reform, etc. determine roles and responsibilities and distribution of resource to women and men in India.

Right to Fair Compensation and Transparency in Land Acquisition, Rehabilitation and Resettlement Act, 2013; and distribution of ceiling surplus land to the landless are some of the land related law and programmes. Article 46 of the Constitution places an obligation upon States to promote the interests of Scheduled Castes and Scheduled Tribes and protect from social injustice and all forms of exploitation. Forest Rights Act 2006 covers tribal and other forest dwellers. Initiatives like financial inclusion through Deendayal Antyodaya Yojana and Indira Awas Yojana and so on are there to ensure housing rights. However, NSS 68th Round Survey indicates falling labour force participation rate among women, aged 15-59 years for rural women from 52.5% in 2004-05 to 37.8% in 2011-12, and 26.1% to 22.2% for urban female. Global Wage Gap Report, 2016-17 highlights that women represented 63% of the lowest paid wage labour while only 15% of the highest wage earners were female.

As per agricultural census 2010-11, of the total operational holding of agricultural land in India, about 13% were operated by women. Around 87.3% of women are dependent on agriculture and yet not more than 10.34% own land in their name. Some progress has been made in changing laws, but the lack of adequate functionaries in the revenue and land reform department contributed towards the poor performance of the government land allocation programme. Lack of agricultural land also compels poor women to work as daily wage labourers, and exposes them to exploitation.

The 2005 amendment of the Hindu Succession Act has given equal inheritance rights to sons and daughters in all forms of property, including agricultural land. But this is not translating into "real rights" due to long-standing social norms favouring men's rights overland.

Women's holistic empowerment essentially means access to all kinds of information, be it social, economic or technological, which is often restricted by various socio-cultural and structural barriers. The Beijing Declaration and Platform for Action recommended resource needs for targeted action on promoting gender equality in science and technology. India is one of the few countries to enact IT Act 2000 to combat cyber crime. However, seldom reported cases, lack of clarity in the gender-neutral laws, are some reasons deterring effective implementation of the law. Only 27% women (UN Women) have access to the internet than men in the country, and primary data relating to access to technology by women is limited (Jain, 2014)

The NITI Aayog, claimed in its Voluntary National Review Report on implementation of SDGs, presented to United Nations, High Level Political Forum, 2017, *"while much progress remains to be made, a number of indicators pertaining to the status of women in India have moved in the right direction over the years. 68% of women were literate in 2015-6, as compared to 55.1% in 2005-06 and 53% of women were independently using bank or savings accounts in 2015-16, which is a significant improvement from 15.1% in 2005-06"*

Policies, Schemes and Interventions of the Government of India vis-à-vis SDGs

To achieve gender equality and empower all women, the present government, under the leadership of Prime Minister Narendra Modi, has initiated and lent impetus to numerous measures. Significant among them are; *'Beti Bachao Beti Padhao'* (Save The Girl Child, Educate The Girl Child), *'Sukanya Samridhi Yojana'* (Girl Child Prosperity Scheme), *'Support to Training and Employment Programme for Women'* (STEP, 2014), Janani Suraksha Yojna, *SWADHAR, 2011* (a scheme for women in difficult circumstances), *Kasturba Gandhi Balika Vidyalay* and the *Maternity Benefit Scheme* (protection of women from wage loss during the first six months after child birth).

Although a number of indicators pertaining to the status of women in India have moved in the right direction, much remains to be achieved. The percentage of women in the age group of 20-24 years, married before 18 years was 26.8 in the year 2015-16 as against 47.4 in 2005-06. Women having a bank account or a savings account which they use themselves has increased from 15.1 percent in 2005-06 to 53 percent in 2015-16. The health indicator Body Mass Index (BMI) has also shown improvement over a period of last 10 years. 35.5 percent of women were reported below normal BMI in 2005-06 as compared to 22.9 percent in 2015-16. There has been an improvement in women literacy too. In the year 2005-06, 55.1 percent women were literate, while 68.4 percent women were reportedly literate in 2015-16. (VNR report, NITI Aayog, 2017)

The launch of the *Beti Bachao Beti Padhao* (Save the Girl Child, Educate the Girl Child) movement by the government aims to catalyse a change in mind set as well as protect and educate the girl child. It is a two pronged approach. The first consists of a Mass Communication Campaign, which links interventions at the national, state and district levels with community level action in 100 selected districts low in Child Sex Ratio, to achieve accelerated impact. The second approach is a multi-sectoral intervention, which aims to converge the initiatives of the Ministry of Health and Family Welfare as well as the Ministry of Human Resource Development for survival, protection and education of the girl child. The *'Mukhyamantri Balika Cycle Yojana'* (Chief Minister's bicycle initiative for the girl child) was launched in the state of Bihar for reducing the school dropout rates for girls. Under this scheme, a bicycle is provided to every girl child to be promoted to Class 9 or 10 to facilitate commuting to school by the girls. It is reported that following this scheme, a substantial decrease in the dropout rate of girls from school has been achieved. *'Selfie with Daughters'* campaign needs special mention here. This campaign began in a small village in Haryana where residents were encouraged by the village leader to take pictures with their daughters.

The *'Pradhan Mantri Ujjwala Yojana'* for providing clean cooking fuel in the form of Liquefied Petroleum Gas (LPG) connections allows women free time from their daily chores which they may spend by engaging in more socially and economically productive work as also in educating themselves. A study on 'Gender and Livelihoods Impacts of Clean Cook Stoves in South Asia' reveals that Indian women spend approximately 374 hours every year collecting firewood. Lighting the 'choolah' (Indian oven) and the cooking time is also considerably more in the 'choolah' as compared to LPG cook stove. The smoke arising from the 'choolah' is also not healthy. The *'Pradhan Mantri Ujjwala Yojana'* has led to a significant increase in the percentage of households having access to clean fuel; 25.5 percent in 2005-06 as against 43.8 percent in the year 2015-16. (VNR report, NITI Aayog, 2017). The scheme is being implemented with considerable gusto and the numbers appear to be on the rise.

Women face discrimination in various ways, and the lack of sanitation facilities affect women disproportionately. Moreover, the absence of adequate infrastructure for sanitation and menstrual hygiene management in schools is one of the factors responsible for girls dropping out of secondary school. This issue is being addressed through the flagship sanitation program of the government—*The Swachch Bharat Abhiyan,* which has been started with a mission to accelerate efforts to achieve universal sanitation coverage and to focus on sanitation.

A report released by the Labour Bureau reveals that female labour force participation rate in India was as low as 23.7% in 2015-16. To address this the government has launched several initiatives. (Prominent among them is the maternity benefit Act which provides 26 weeks of paid leave to working women who are pregnant. The *Mahila e-HAAT* initiative is a bilingual direct online marketing platform leveraging technology for supporting women entrepreneurs and Self-Help Groups for showcasing their products and services. It was judged as one of the top 100 projects in India. *Stand Up India,* another initiative launched in 2016, provides bank loans to women borrowers for setting up Green Field Enterprise as one of the benefits. *Mahila Shakti Kendra* is an initiative that supports establishment of Women Empowerment Centre at the village level. The Centre aims to converge action in several areas including skill development, employment, digital literacy, health and nutrition to provide a comprehensive package of services. *Women Transforming India* is an online contest launched by NITI Aayog, in partnership with United Nations, India and MyGov for crowd sourcing stories of women who are making a difference in their respective fields. The best stories are awarded. The underlying objective of these initiatives is to empower women in all possible ways.

Strengthening social protection and security for women is imperative for their empowerment and to achieve gender equality. One Stop Crisis Centres are being established across the country for providing integrated support to women affected by violence, in public and private spaces. The services include medical assistance, psychosocial counselling, legal aid, shelter as well as video conferencing provision to facilitate police and court proceedings. The Women Helpline initiative has also been integrated with the One Stop Crisis Centres. It aims to provide an immediate response to women affected by violence through a contact number that is active 24 hours a day. *Bharosa* (trust) is an initiative of the Hyderabad City Police and Telangana government, which provides in one place a range of support services to women affected by violence. The focus is on enabling women to deal with challenges they are facing with confidence and positivity.

Himmat (courage) safety solutions for women is an initiative of the Delhi Police which is a 24x7 police emergency service, providing free services including legal support. It also provides ambulance assistance to citizens. *Himmat* enables the safety of working women who travel to their homes late at night.

Various programmes are being implemented for ensuring access to education, health and nutrition security with a special focus on women and children. Drinking water and sanitation is a priority area for the government. The *Pradhan Mantri Ujjwala Yojna,* has provided clean cooking fuel (Liquefied Petroleum Gas) connections to over 22 million families (NITI Aayog, 2017), these schemes and more, create an enabling environment for women. Improved health of women and families along with some free time from the daily chores and support from the government and other agencies, improve the possibility of women participation in social, political and economic activities.

To conclude, it is only through gender-sensitive planning, (considering the multidimensional vulnerabilities women face in India) that policy making, programming and implementation can cut ice with India's commitment to gender equality and empowerment of all women and girls. This will require a reality-based planning with participation of women in decision-making from across rural and urban areas, voicing their aspirations and how they see them being achieved with government support. A step in the right direction has been initiated by Prime Minister Narendra Modi, with emphasis on *'Sabka Saath Sabka Vikas'*, which intends to leave no woman or man outside the gamut of development.

REFERENCES

1. Ulrich Grober (2007), *Deep roots—A conceptual history of "sustainable development"* (Nachhaltigkeit), Wissenschaftszentrum Berlin für Sozialforschung, 2007
2. Lynn R. Kahle, Eda Gurel-Atay, Eds (2014). Communicating Sustainability for the Green Economy. New York: M.E. Sharpe.
3. https://sustainabledevelopment.un.org/content/documents/4538pressowg13.pdf, *Press release—UN General Assembly's Open Working Group proposes sustainable development goals"* (PDF). *Sustainabledevelopment.un.org.* 19 July 2014, retrieved March, 2016
4. https://sustainabledevelopment.un.org/post2015/transformingourworld, *"Press release—UN General Assembly's Open Working Group proposes sustainable development goals" (PDF). Sustainabledevelopment.un.org. 19 July 2014. retrieved March, 2017-*
5. https://sustainabledevelopment.un.org/post2015/transformingourworld, *"Transforming our world: the 2030 Agenda for Sustainable Development". United Nations—Sustainable Development knowledge platform,* retrieved April 2017

6. https://www.un.org/sustainabledevelopment/blog/2016/11/secretary-generals-remarks-to-the-press-at-cop22/, *"Secretary-General's remarks to the press at COP22". UN. 15 November 2016, retrieved March 2017.*
7. https://www.nytimes.com/2015/09/26/world/breakdown-of-un-sustainable-development-goals.html?_r=0, *Breakdown of Sustainable Development Goals, New York Times,* September, 2015, retrieved March, 2017.
8. http://www.legrand.com/EN/sustainable-development-description_12847.html, retrieved October, 2017
9. http://www.undp.org/content/undp/en/home/sustainable-development-goals/goal-5-gender-equality.html retrieved April, 2017
10. http://www.worldbank.org/en/topic/sustainabledevelopment/overview retrieved April, 2017
11. http://www.worldbank.org/en/topic/sustainabledevelopment/overview, *UN Women—Achieve Gender Equality and Empower all Women,* retrieved April, 2017
12. http://indicators.report/goals/goal-5/, *Indicators and a monitoring framework—Launching a Data Revolution for Sustainable Development Goals, Goal 5 : Achieve Gender Equality and Empower all Women and Girls,* retrieved in March 2017.
13. http://www.globalgoals.org/global-goals/gender-equality/*The Global Goals for Sustainable Development,* retrieved November, 2017
14. http://wadanatodo.net/wp-content/uploads/2017/07/Civil-society-Report-on-SDGs.pdf, retrieved November, 2017
15. https://sustainabledevelopment.un.org/memberstates/india, retrieved October, 2017
16. https://sustainabledevelopment.un.org/content/documents/15836India.pdf, retrieved November, 2017
17. http://ncrb.nic.in/StatPublications/CII/CII2015/chapters/Chapter% retrieved November, 2017
18. http://censusindia.gov.in/2011, view details -prov-results/data_files/india/Final_PPT_2011_chapter5.pdf
19. https://treaties.un.org/pages/ViewDetails.aspx?src=IND&mtdsg_no=IV-11&chapter=4&lang=en
20. http://reports.weforum.org/feature-demonstration/files/2016/10/IND.pdf
21. http://www.mospi.gov.in/sites/default/files/reports_and_publication/statistical_publication/social_statistics/WM16ConstitutionalLegalRights.pdf
22. http://rchiips.org/NFHS/pdf/NFHS4/India.pdf, *National Family Health Survey -4 (2015-16), India Fact Sheet,* Ministry of Health and Family Welfare, Govt. Of India, retrieved November, 2017.
23. https://www.youthkiawaaz.com/2014/07/women-empowerment-technology/, Mayank Jain (2014), *Why Has The Tech Revolution Not Arrived For Indian Women Yet? Sairee Chahal Tells Us,* retrieved November, 2017

2

Women and Development: Lessons from 'Chipko'

Sarvajit Mukerji

ABSTRACT

'Development' is a slogan that helps impose many an unpalatable project on an unwilling local community. If you resist 'development', goes this argument, you harm both your own and national interests. Many local communities are wary of developmental decisions taken in distant boardrooms and corridors of power. They watch with dismay, as the hitherto enjoyed commons suddenly become inaccessible and the fenced off property of outsiders. Worldwide, women have opposed such impositions. The 'Chipko' movement of the Uttaranchal hills was one of the first such movements of resistance. The proposed paper seeks to revisit the 'Chipko' movement and to understand its dynamics and analyse the lessons learnt, if any, from it. It proposes to focus on how the agenda of development itself is gendered in the light of the insights provided by eco-feminism.

Recently a national daily reported that following the lifting of a ban on the cutting of trees on private properties in Poland, trees were massacred in thousands in that country. In a unique gesture of defiance, young Polish mothers sat down on the felled logs and nursed their babies, thereby restating the ancient link between women, nurture and nature. The parallels with the Chipko movement of Uttarakhand are obvious. 'Chipko was sparked off by the government's decision to allot a plot of hornbeam forest in the Alaknanda valley to Symonds, a sports goods company from Allahabad. A few months before this, the Dashauli Gram Swarajya Sangh had been refused permission by the forest department to fell trees from the very same forest (which they wanted for making agricultural implements). This transparent favouritism provoked the villagers to hug the trees (Chipko means hug in Hindi) and prevent them being felled by Symonds' agents' (Guha and Gadgil, pp. 196–97). This happened in 1973 and is well documented. Sunderlal Bahuguna and Chandi Prasad Bhatt emerged as leaders of the movement, and led many similar agitations across the fragile ecosystem of the Himalayas seeking to preserve the vital link between the local community, its resources and the environment. It must be noted, however, that it was the women of the region who were at the forefront in the Chipko movement. It was the women who physically hugged the trees led by the unsung heroine Gaura Devi. Deane Curtin who has researched the involvement of women in the movement, traces the beginnings of the Chipko movement even further. Curtin notes, 'The modern Chipko movement began as a response to flooding due to deforestation in the mountains above Chipko villages. The response to deforestation varied by gender. Men were attracted to wage-labour jobs in the forestry industry. Women were drawn to reforestation, since their concerns were different.' Ecological imbalance that would occur, was affecting women, since they largely carried out agricultural and herding activities. For them the forest conservation was essential for the continuation of the economic activities that were their livelihood.

The first lesson then is that the very concept of development is understood differently by men and women. In the course of interactions with the women of Reni village, Curtin found that gender difference was used to break the Chipko movement. Men were promised jobs and petty privileges if they reined in 'their' women. Many women did face violence and intimidation. Even in the matter of reforestation, a gender difference surfaced. Men wanted fruit trees as they are profitable, while women wanted trees that provide fodder and fuel. Moreover, they felt that the men would merely squander the money they earned through wage-labour once the corporate had its way, while the trees which sustained their community would be gone forever.

In fact the concept of development, as it is generally understood, has been challenged by eminent ecofeminist Maria Mies. According to Mies, development is a mere aping of the West. Western capitalist societies would like us to believe that they have achieved the acme of perfection and the rest of the world is duty bound to emulate them. This is termed 'catching up development'. We are all in a futile race to catch up with the West. Countries, are arbitrarily labelled 'underdeveloped' or 'developing' and then cajoled into borrowing astronomical amounts from West funded institutions like the World Bank. These poor countries now turn perennial debtors who are then compelled to open their doors wide and allow an unimpeded flow of their natural resources to fuel further growth of Western economies. Can you ever catch up with a competitor who has a head start and is surging ahead, while urging you to run faster and faster and catch up? The West has needed an 'underdeveloped' South to supply it with raw materials and accessible markets since the industrial revolution. This was the basic impulse behind the entire project of colonialism and imperialism and it remains an imperative of late capitalism. Shiva and Mies point out that 'development' is a word which did not appear in the lexicon of colonialism. It is as though, so long as we were ruled by White Western powers we did not need 'development'. But as soon as the Asian and African countries started achieving political independence in the first half of the 20th century, 'development' suddenly became a buzzword in Western political discourse. The newly independent countries were suddenly categorised as underdeveloped and urged to 'develop' themselves on Western lines. It is no coincidence that the Bretton Woods institutions like the World Bank started around the same time. It has been their agenda to impose neo-colonialism and safeguard Western interests now and in the future.

The next lesson to be learnt from the Chipko movement then is that 'development' is an issue that is interpreted differently by different stakeholders. This innocuous word is, in fact, fraught with implications of the appropriation of local resources at the cost of the local populace. It is clear that a GDP impelled definition of development is not divinely ordained, and may not be acceptable to everyone. It is not acceptable to our neighbour, Bhutan today, and it was not acceptable to at least one half of the population of Reni village—the women of Reni—in 1973. The idea that which cannot be bought or sold in a market has no value and is not a resource was flatly rejected by them. They hugged the trees which gave them fuel and fodder to help sustain their family and flocks. They refused to let those trees become a commodity to be bought and sold in the market.

Another factor needs to be considered too. Many environmentally concerned people in sparsely populated countries like Canada and Australia have consistently campaigned for the protection of the wilderness. Wild nature is deemed to have an intrinsic value that has nothing to do with its contribution or otherwise to the human world. However, this was not the stance of the women of the Chipko movement. They were not responding to 'Nature' as such. Rather they were seeking to protect the trees which were integrally connected with their day-to-day existence. Women are connected with nature much more integrally than men. The roles of nurturing and caring that have always been in the domain of women integrally link them with nature. It is women who are responsible for gathering fuel, fetching water, feeding animals, cooking for the family and taking care of the old, the injured and the sick. In each of these areas nature is their vital resource and support. Women also turn to nature for rituals and medicines. And yet, when a part of their natural environment is to be turned over to be converted into a commodity for the market, these very women are never consulted.

Moreover, the movement reflects the importance of feminism as a component in the struggle to conserve forests. Women were not only protecting the trees and the environment, but were also confronting their own husbands who were open to working for the logging companies and felling the trees.

More than forty years have elapsed since the Chipko movement. Several natural disasters like floods and earthquakes have shaken and destroyed parts of Uttarakhand. Mindless felling of trees, government and corporate sponsored mega projects, like dams and power installations, unplanned construction activity and tourism seem to suggest we have learnt nothing from the Chipko movement. When natural disaster strikes whole villages are washed away or reduced to rubble. The men at least have the option of migrating in search of livelihood. They may become labourers or rickshaw-pullers in Haridwar or Dehradun. But the women are left behind to pick up the pieces and start life again. Dependent on these women are children, the old and infirm, innocent animals, the ravaged fields and destroyed houses that must be rebuilt. These are the mute and invisible heroines of Uttarakhand. But all is not lost either. Forty years and more have passed. Policy makers have slowly realised that it is these women who must be empowered. Today ration cards are issued to women, recognising that it is they who ultimately selflessly provide for their family. Women are empowered through self-help groups, micro-finance and representation in panchayats. The road ahead is rough and the terrain steep and rocky. But from between the rocks break out ferns and flowers and perhaps the trees. The mighty deodars of Uttarakhand will shower the land with benediction again.

3

Role of Digital India in Bridging Inequalities in Society

Bramhanand Jha and *Vinay Thakur*

ABSTRACT

Unity in diversity in India is a strength. Diversity brings different ideas. It democratizes innovations. However, diversity faces its biggest challenges in terms of several kinds of inequalities in the society. These inequalities can derail the inclusive growth until and unless these are not holistically addressed. The technology per se is universal neutralizer and has power to impact the human lives in a positive manner without discrimination. One of the most democratic tools available today, which can universalize the data, information, products and services, is "Information and Communication Technology". Digital India[1] *as famously told by the Prime Minister of India is IT + IT = IT, i.e. Indian Talent and Information Technology is critical for India Tomorrow.*

Digital India, a flagship programme of Government of India, is focused on bridging the gaps in society, namely, gap between digital haves and have nots, gap between the rich and the poor, gap among man, women and transgender, gap between accessibilities and in-accessibilities, etc. The paper aims to highlight various kinds of divides prevalent in Indian societies especially the gender divide in terms of education, health and economic participation. It also points out several initiatives under Digital India that have been implemented to bridge these inequalities. The study covers the central role of ICT in bridging the divides including the gender divide. It also includes upcoming new challenges as well as the potential solutions.

Keywords: *Digital India, Digital Infrastructure, Digital Services, Digital Empowerment.*

OBJECTIVES

The aim of the study is to demonstrate the effectiveness of Digital India in neutralizing the challenges posed by various types of divides including gender inequalities prevailing in the societies.

MOTIVATION FACTOR

India is an example of unity in diversity. It is a land of the oldest civilization and the largest democracy. It has over 300 languages and dialects, diverse habits and habitats. The inspiration to undertake the case study comes from the fact that India faces a unique and complex issue, wherein, a section of Indian society is marching along with modernity at par with the developed countries and another section is a struggling middle class. There is yet another section of society that has been completely left behind in development and requires inclusion in all developmental endeavors. These diversities present an opportunity for a possible solution that will meet the aspirations of all sections of the social fabric of India and enable it to qualify as a representative of a global community.

SCOPE

The study focuses on areas of gaps and diversities prevalent in Indian societies at national level and how Digital India is addressing them.

RESEARCH METHODOLOGY

The paper is based on secondary data, focus group discussions, expert opinions and field experience.

DIVIDE ANALYSIS

Gender Gap Analysis

The Global Gender Gap Report[2,3] is referred to understand the gender gap in India as the calculation in the report is based on assumption that female section is a disadvantageous group and only measures those aspects or parameters where women are traditionally weaker than men. It is to note that the score for economic participation, education attainment and political empowerment has increased while score for health and survival has decreased over a decade.

Exhibit 1: Gender Gap Report of India[2,3]

Year	*2006*		*2016*	
Parameters	*Rank*	*Score*	*Rank*	*Score*
Global Gender Gap Index	98	0.601	87	0.683
Economic Participation & Opportunity	110	0.397	136	0.408
Education Attainment	102	0.819	113	0.950
Health and Survival	103	0.962	142	0.942
Political Empowerment	20	0.227	9	0.433
Rank Out of	115	144		

Another fact worth mentioning is comparison between India's score and the world's sample average, which matches closely on education and health but shows an interesting gap on opposite scale on economy and politics.

Exhibit 2: India vis-à-vis world[2,3]

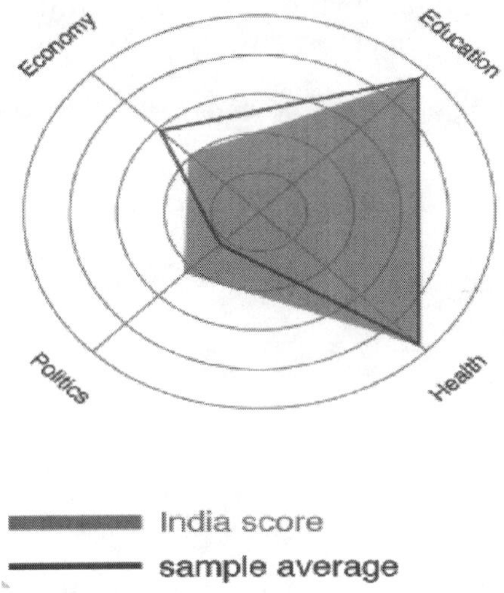

This means economic participation of Indian women is lesser but on contrary, their political participation is more than world's average.

LITERACY GAP ANALYSIS

As per the census 2011, the literacy rate in India was recorded 74.04% as against 64.84% in 2001.[4] The decadal growth stands at 9.2%. The effective literacy rate (age 7 and above) in 2011 were 65.46% for women and 82.14% for men. Digital literacy is almost non-existent among 90% of the population in the country. The data clearly shows women are more negatively impacted than men.

ECONOMIC DIVIDE ANALYSIS

Indian economy is one of the world's highest growing major economies. It is the seventh largest in the world by GDP and the third largest in the world by PPP as per Economic Freedom Index Report 2017, though Indian economy has sustained an average of about 7% growth annually, the overall development is still marred by issues like corruption, underdeveloped infrastructure and poor management of public finances.[5]

Both, extreme wealth and poverty co-exist in India as the nation modernizes rapidly and struggles to find paths to inclusive development for its large and diverse population. The IMF reported in 2016 that India's "major subsidies" (e.g. on fuels and fertilizer) dropped below 2 percent of GDP, the government is introducing a new basic food subsidy for around two-third of the population.[5]

Exhibit 3: India vis-à-vis world[5]

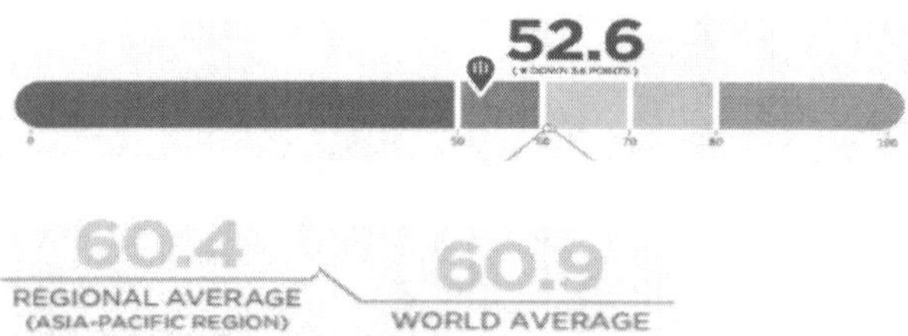

Notable Successes
Trade Freedom
Concerns
Rule of Law, Fiscal Health, and Investment Freedom

LANGUAGE DIVIDE ANALYSIS

India is a land of over 300 languages and dialects, which are said to change after an average of every 100 km in the country. Digitization of physical resources like textbooks, transcripts, official documents, records and court cases is a huge challenge. Several efforts have been made towards data digitization drive, however, absence of digital resources in native languages are norm rather than rarity. This is critical in creating an information divide in the society.

SYSTEMATIC DIVIDE ANALYSIS

Each Central as well as Government Ministry has a given mandate and domain. Almost each Ministry has notified the citizen's charter,[6] which lets people know the mandate of the concerned Ministry/Department/ Organisation, how one can get in touch with its officials, what to expect by way of services and how to seek a remedy if something goes wrong. The crux lies in the absence of mandatory electronic delivery of services, penalty provision and legal backup for citizen's charter. Moreover, from Government's perspective, there are complex challenges vis-à-vis authentication of beneficiary list, transfer of benefits to genuine beneficiary, mode of transfer and acknowledgement/feedback apart from data standard and integration.

INFORMATION GAP ANALYSIS

The root cause of all corruption is said to be borne out of either lack of information or information available with selected few. There is no dearth of data. However, the ready-to-use data is not available to large sections of stakeholders.

DIGITAL INDIA BRIDGING THE DIVIDES

Technology is a universal leveller as it does not discriminate based on case, colour, creed, income and gender. The advent of ICT has made possible

Exhibit 4: Digital India Projects Sources: Government Websites [10,11,12,13,14,15,16,17]

Digital India Programme		
Digital Infrastructure	Digital Services	Digital Empowerment
• Aadhaar - 112 Cr persons • BharatNet - OFC pipe laid for 2.25 lakh Kms (over 1 lakh GPs) • Digital Payment Tools - USSD, UPI, BHIM • Common Services Centers - ~1.5 lakh CSCs operational • Digital Locker - 47+ lakh lockers opened. 24 issuers integrated, 165 Cr documents issued • UMANG-to be launched	• e-Services - 3325 services • e-Transactions - monthly avg 120 Cr by volume • Direct Benefit Transfer - ~153 Cr Txn for Rs 66,990 Cr with saving Rs 49,560 Cr • Government e-Market - 5200+ Sellers & 167 Service Providers • National Scholarship Portal - 1.9 Cr beneficiaries for 23 schemes • Online Appointment in Hospital - 663109 appointments in 70 hospitals	• MyGov - 41+ lakh users, 1.87 lakh contributions, 37,18 lakh comments • IT for Jobs - 14,800 BPO seats • DISHA - 82 lakh trained against target of 52.5 lakh • DISHA 2.0 - target 6 Cr people • DigiGaon - to be launched • Rapid Assessment System (RAS) - 638 Services across 20+ States/UTs

to do various things in quicker, cleaner and efficient ways, which were even unthinkable in the past. This also covers the efforts towards sustainable development goals, especially those focused on inequalities like hunger, poverty, gender bias, justice, etc.[7,8,9]

Digital India being a technology-led programme has joined together all existing e-governance initiatives and started new e-initiatives into a single and comprehensive vision so that each of the e-initiative is seen as a part of larger goal of transforming India into a digitally empowered society and knowledge economy.

The vision areas of Digital India namely Digital Infrastructure as a core utility to every citizen, Digital Services on demand and Digital Empowerment has taken into consideration all the aforementioned gaps and even more.

Exhibit 5: Mapping between major inequalities in the society and major projects of Digital India

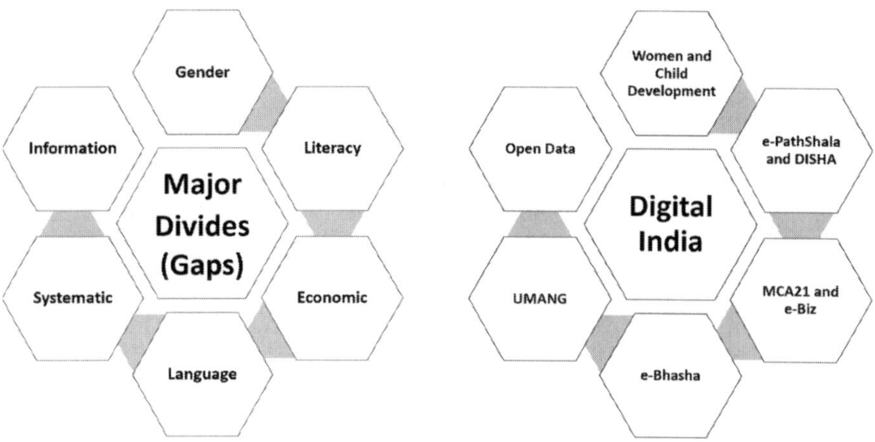

Women and Child Development Schemes like Beti Bachao Beti Padhao, UJJAWALA (a scheme to prevent trafficking and rescue victims of trafficking and sexual exploitation), Mahila e-Haat, Integrated Child Protection Scheme, Mother and Child Tracking Systems are operational and empowering women under Digital India.

e-Pathshala is providing digitized school text books from classes I to XII and Digital Shakashrta Abhiyan (DISHA) has already trained more than 80 lakh persons against a target of 52.5 lakh persons. DISHA 2.0 has been launched with a new target of training 6 crore persons in the next three years.[18]

MCA21 and e-Biz mission mode projects are focused on G2B services and thereby contributing in ease of doing business. MCA21 is providing paperless registration for companies and e-Biz is providing more than 20 G2B services at a single portal. Government e-Marketplace, a recently developed e-commerce portal, has transformed the public procurement as any male or female seller and service provider can start offering their products and services with few clicks only.

e-Bhasha MMP and Sugamya Pustakalaya[19] for divyang are the mission on language localisation. Several Government websites are made multi-lingual under language localisation initiative.[20] Divyang friendly features are also getting enabled on these websites.

Unified Mobile App for New-Age Governance (UMANG) has been developed as a single mobile platform to deliver a large number of government services. According to Mobile first policy, UMANG and various mobile apps especially related to digital payments are a kind of digital revolution witnessed in India, which has already crossed 1.05 billion mobile subscribers in December 2016.

Open data platform,[13] open standard and open software are prioritized policies of Government of India and more than 60,000 datasets have been made available in public domain for research, analysis and commercial use.

Exhibit 6: Mapping between major targets of SDG5 and major projects of Digital India

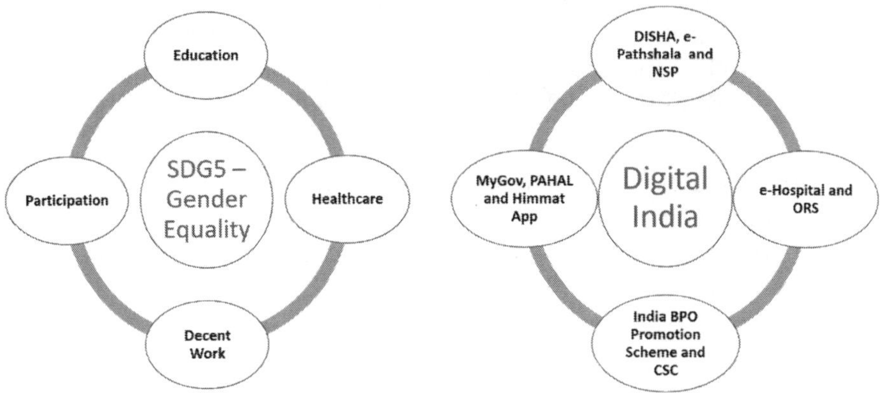

Sustainable Development Goals (SDGs) are comprehensive and focus on five Ps—people, planet, prosperity, peace and partnership. Agenda 2030 is a set of 17 specific goals to be achieved by 2030. The SDG5 (Goal 5) is about gender equality. Being initiated in 2014, India through Digital India and various other schemes are already working towards sustainable development including SDG5, i.e. elimination of gender inequality.

The four critical aspects of gender equality are access to healthcare, education, decent work and participation in decision making. Digital India initiative like e-Hospital, Online Appointment/Registration System in Hospital, Mother and Child Tracking System are assisting women to avail healthcare facilities.

e-Pathshala, National Scholarship Portal (NSP) and Digital Shakhshrta Abhiyan (DISHA) are providing equal educational opportunities to all irrespective of gender.

Indian BPO promotion scheme has earmarked special financial incentives for all Business Process Outsourcing (BPO) Agencies having 50% seats for women. It has also provisioned for extra incentives for promoting divyangs in BPO sector.

MyGov, a Government owned social platform for participatory governance, is providing equal opportunities to men and women to become active members and contribute with suggestions on Government policies right from formulation, implementation and post implementation stage.[15] DBT-PAHAL has ensured cost saving and free delivery of LPG cylinders to the poor especially rural womenfolk. Himmat App is an app for women's safety purpose.

CONCLUSION

ICT for Development (ICT4D) is crucial to achieve sustainable development goals. In this regard, Digital India is bridging gender divide, economic divide, information divide, digital divide and, thus, playing a critical role in transforming the societies through digital infrastructure, digital services and digital empowerment.

Pornography is a big challenge in the digital world, which needs continuous tracking and blocking. The challenges like data privacy, cyber security, the right to forget on digital platform, mandatory delivery of e-services and emerging technologies like digital currencies, artificial intelligence, chat-bots, etc., pose both a problem as well as opportunities, which once handled appropriately can impact and transform the societies in a positive manner.

Disclaimer

The content of the paper is the result of personal efforts and research exercise of author(s), and in no way represents the views of the organizations, they have been associated or working with.

REFERENCES

1. http://digitalindia.gov.in/content/introduction. Retrieved on 10 March 2017.
2. The World Economic Forum, 2016, *The Global Gender Gap Report*. Retrieved on 12 March 2017.
3. http://reports.weforum.org/global-gender-gap-report-2016/economies/#economy=IND. Retrieved on 12 March 2017.
4. The Census of India, 2013, *SRS Statistical Report*. Retrieved on 15 March 2017.
5. The Heritage Foundation, 2017, *Economic Freedom Index Report*. Retrieved on 15 March 2017.
6. http://goicharters.nic.in/. Retrieved on 12 March 2017
7. United Nation Summit, 2015, *The 17 Sustainable Development Goals (SDGs) of the 2030 Agenda*. Retrieved on 10 March 2017
8. International Conference on Theory and Practice of Electronic Governance, 2017, *Digital India for Sustainable Development Goals*.
9. http://www.un.org/sustainabledevelopment/gender-equality/#751f89fa361630f60.Retrieved on 10 March 2017
10. http://dbtbharat.gov.in. Retrieved on 16 March 2017.
11. http://etaal.gov.in. Retrieved on 16 March 2017.
12. http://meity.gov.in/ibps. Retrieved on 17 March 2017.
13. https://data.gov.in.Retrieved on 18 March 2017.
14. https://digilocker.gov.in. Retrieved on 15 March 2017.
15. https://www.mygov.in.Retrieved on 12 March 2017.
16. http://apna.csc.gov.in. Retrieved on 15 March 2017.
17. https://gem.gov.in. Retrieved on 15 March 2017.
18. https://www.pmgdisha.in. Retrieved on 12 April 2017.
19. Ministry of Social Justice and Empowerment, *PIB Report on Sugamya Pustakalaya – an online library for persons with visual disabilities*. Retrieved on 12 March 2017.
20. http://meity.gov.in/content/technology-development-indian-languages-tdil. Retrieved on 12 March 2017.

4

Gender Equality and Sustainable Development: The Indian Story

Neelam Kalla and *Hemaprabha Purohit*

ABSTRACT

Women represent a major part of the world's population. In spite of the fact that they can immensely contribute to the global sustainability, they struggle even for their basic rights and essentials of living. The paper is an attempt to bring out the significance of gender equality for sustainable development, and to discuss the position of India in terms of gender gap in detail, while suggesting remedies for the same. Four criteria have been employed to assess the scenario, that includes education, employment, health and political empowerment.

Keywords: *Sustainable Development, Gender Equality, Global Gender Gap*

INTRODUCTION

Women represent a major part of the world's population. According to the World Bank (2015) 48.2% of population consists of women. In spite of the fact that they can immensely contribute to the global sustainability, they are seen struggling for their basic rights and essentials of living. It has been observed across various cultures that women and girls are raised to take care of others since birth. This discerns the case of men and women or boys and girls invariably. Although several financial and social factors determine the degree of the same, and it can be seen that women on richer ends can free themselves of the unpaid work or services by employing domestic helpers. On the other hand, men assume a principal family provider's role and therefore take active part in public gatherings, and are in the capacity to dominate the life of others (Johnson-Latham, 2007). Observance of such attitudes round the globe have led to the rising debates on issues like gender equality and women rights for achieving sustainable development in past few years.

Bringing together the issues of gender equality and sustainable development is significant due to several reasons. The definition of sustainable development itself sets the stage for such enterprise. According to the highly quoted definition of sustainable development given by the Brundtland report is the "ability to make development sustainable—to ensure that it meets the needs of the present without compromising the ability of future generations to meet their own needs" (WCED, 1987). Here, both the aspects have been emphasised, i.e. satisfying the needs of the present and ensuring that the ability of future generations is not compromised., and both of which reflect the importance women carry towards achieving the ultimate aim of sustainable development. Considering the present scenario, women are fighting the battle of attaining their rights and any path to sustainable development cannot compromise on the basic human rights of women. It also reflects the harm it can cause to the ability that future generations inherit, since their predecessors are not able to make the most of their lives and talent. Besides, it is very clear that due to gender inequality, the world loses the contribution of a major pool of talent and knowledge that rests in half of the world's population.

It can be seen that, women as a part of the development process are at different levels in different parts of world. There are countries where women have chances to contribute to the process of sustainable development and also such where they have no such opportunities. On a positive note, women's lives have witnessed improvements in the past 20 years in terms of life expectancy, education, employment and legal protection. Nevertheless, the world witnesses a considerable gender gap (Hoseini, 2014). This paper is an attempt analyse the significance of gender equality for sustainable development, and the position of India in terms of gender gap.

GENDER GAP: THE INDIAN SCENARIO

In recent years, India has experienced consistent growth and steady improvement in the gender global ranking score. It is quite evident that the government is working on various indicators which are reflected in the score of the country every year. The Global Gender Gap Index is a country ranking which was introduced by World Economic Forum (WEF), that captures and tracks the progress over years of the extent of gender-based disparities assessing national gender gaps on economic, education, health and political criteria.

According to the WEF (2016) the average progress on closing the gender gaps globally stood at 0.683 considering the four sub-indexes, showing a need of 31.7% of gender gap that needs to be closed globally. Iceland was ranked as the top country amongst the 144 countries, with a score of 0.874. India reported a progress with a global ranking of 87 and an index of 0.683. India stands at a good position in terms of political empowerment showing a satisfactory representation of women in the higher levels of political decision making in the country. The country improved tremendously in terms of educational attainment sub index, on the ground of fully closing its primary and secondary education enrolment gender gaps. However, lower ranks in the area of employment and health were observed, which reflect the need of working upon these two dimensions. Particularly, its third-lowest rank in terms of Health and Survival is a clear indicator of its terrible plight, specifically in this field. Table 1, discusses the figures of sub-indexes of the global gender gap index that were observed by the forum for 2016.

Table 1: Global Gender Gap Sub Index Ranks of India

S. No.	*Sub Index*	*Global Rank*	*Global Score*
1.	Economic Participation and Opportunity	136	0.408
2.	Educational Attainment	113	0.950
3.	Health and Survival	142	0.942
4.	Political Empowerment	9	0.433

Source: World Economic Forum (2016).

DISCUSSION

The above data shows that India has definitely improved on various indicators and acquired a good position in several indicators. Nevertheless, it is still struggling to improve on some indicators. The following section discusses each sub-index in detail where both the developments over the years have been acknowledged and the root causes or some unseen problems, which might not be visible at the forefront, have been talked about.

Educational Attainment

As shown in Table 1, India scored 113th rank amongs the 144 countries. Table 2 presents the indicators of this sub-index and their ranks and scores globally.

Table 2: Indicators of Educational Attainment

S. No.	Indicator	Global Rank	Global Score	Female/Male Ratio
1.	Literacy Rate	124	0.936	0.78
2.	Enrolment in Primary Education	1	1.000	1.01
3.	Enrolment in Secondary Education	1	1.000	1.01
4.	Enrolment in Tertiary Education	99	0.936	0.94

Source: World Economic Forum (2016).

The figures above show a more than satisfactory picture of the sub-index as every indicator except literacy rate, stands at a good score and reflects tremendous efforts that have been made by the government to improve the scenario. But, there also exists a concern beyond these figures that plays a major role in keeping women away from making major contribution. The effectiveness of education that extends to the quality of teaching, time spent on learning, the number of school dropouts, etc., still remains a challenge. Education does not require enrolment merely, and enabling it to serve as a transforming mechanism that channelizes the talent towards greater benefits, further endeavours are required to be made by the government. It has been seen that the shackles of unpaid work and care services that girls are struggling with daily, hardly let them devote time towards education. Also, as mentioned earlier, the social taboos keep them away from attaining enough education throughout their lives. Besides, the section of women entering into higher education is still less and this refrains a major section of women and girls from having a say in social and economic platforms and also tapping their knowledge reservoirs to be converted to contributory elements.

Economic Participation and Opportunity

As it has been shown in Table 1 above, India scored 136th rank amongst the 144 countries. Table 3 presents the indicators of this sub-index and their ranks and scores globally.

Table 3: Indicators of Economic Participation and Opportunity

S. No.	Indicator	Global Rank	Global Score	Female/ Male Ratio
1.	Labour Force Participation	135	0.344	0.34
2.	Wage Equality For Similar Work (Survey)	103	0.573	0.57
3.	Estimated Earned Income (US$, PPP)	137	0.232	0.23
4.	Legislators, Senior Officials, and Managers	-	-	-
5.	Professional and Technical Workers	-	-	-

Source: World Economic Forum (2016).

It can be seen here that India needs to work upon the labour participation and estimated income scores. It is worth mentioning here that measures to encourage female participation in work need to be rigorous. A major chunk of women are engaged in unpaid work most of the time and such work and care service goes unacknowledged regularly. Also, their status in the labour market is far behind men, as they face problems regarding entering the markets and work conditions needed. Worsening the condition, are the social taboos, like refraining from education, child marriage, dowry, early child birth, widow dilemmas, restrictions, menace related to free mobility, etc. The capacity that rests in women and which can be utilized for improving themselves in terms of education, employment, health and a say in important decision making. Thus, this head needs efforts in multiple areas like the equal employment and wage opportunities, measures for the work–life concerns, safety and privacy measures, career advancement and employee participation opportunities.

Health and Survival

As it has been shown in Table 1, India scored 142nd rank amongst the 144 countries. Table No. 4 presents the indicators of this sub-index and their ranks and scores globally.

Table 4: Indicators of Health and Survival

S.No.	*Indicator*	*Global Rank*	*Global Score*	*Female/Male Ratio*
1.	Sex Ratio at Birth	142	0.893	0.89
2.	Healthy Life Expectancy	71	1.054	1.05

Source: World Economic Forum (2016).

The above figures reflect that the health sector improvement is the need of the hour and these indicators have proven a major setback for the sub-index. The government has been increasing the expenditure on health and related issues every year, but the results are not satisfactory. It can be said that the country has been successful in reducing famines and several diseases that were a major issue earlier but lacks a balanced development in the sector. The public sector has a plethora of operational issues and the private sector provides better services but due to cost concerns the poor category has to rely on the public healthcare. Efforts made for primary health care provided by the state, focuses on immunization, prevention of malnutrition, child birth, post natal care and treatment of common illness. Women health problems are still of major concern. The problems like malnutrition, high infant mortality, diseases, poor sanitation, and health issues in rural areas, etc., exist.

Political Empowerment

As it has been shown in Table 1, India scored 9th rank amongst the 144 countries. Table 5 presents the indicators of this sub-index and their ranks and scores globally.

Table 5: Indicators of Political Empowerment

S. No.	*Indicator*	*Global Rank*	*Global Score*	*Female/Male Ratio*
1.	Women in parliament	112	0.136	0.14
2.	Women in ministerial positions	50	0.286	0.29
3.	Years with female head of state (last 50)	2	0.723	0.72

Source: World Economic Forum (2016).

India stands at a higher position in the sub-index political empowerment. The figures clearly reflect that the country has seen both male and female leaders at higher levels of decision making and which brings us nearer to the gender gap abolishment under this head. But in order to be a contributor in totality, we also need to achieve women's participation from the lower levels of decision making. It has been observed that men play a dominant role in the families and women expressing their opinions often face violence. Also, a number of local bodies exist at the lower levels of decision making, which can contribute towards improving the situation in various areas. Thus, a number of platforms still need to be created for women to express themselves and make their voice heard.

SUGGESTIONS

Bringing together gender equality and sustainable development will require action at various platforms, and also different players to hold up each other's initiatives. The scenario requires a union of the efforts made by the centre, the state, corporations, public leaders, non-profit organisations, community leaders, and all women and men.

- First and foremost, opportunity of enrolment along with quality primary and secondary education should be provided. Here, it is to be noted that the women who are willing but not able to access such opportunities should be provided with low-cost transportation. Moreover, in rural areas, the time women spent in fetching water and lighting the 'choolah' for cooking food, etc., should be diverted to education by making these basic facilities available. Safe potable water and affordable gas connections and stoves would afford them more time for self development. The Ujjwala Yojna is an encouraging step in this direction. It is the time that we moved beyond numbers, into a more transparent and progressive scenario that embraces higher levels of content and quality.

- Secondly, it is necessary that the number of women who join higher education and other vocational programmes is increased, so that the ones who are talented and capable can be further trained, and their zest and zeal can be channelized towards development, thus rescuing them from the scenario where their talent and abilities go waste.

  Also, women should be provided enough access and knowledge on labour markets, where they can engage themselves in paid work, sell their agricultural/home-made food/creative handicraft products and make the most of their talent. Thus, proper and safe connectivity between remote areas and urban areas is essential, along with affordable means of mobility.

  Besides, equal chances of career advancement and growth should be not merely preached, but prudently practiced keeping the local community in mind. The process of entering employment and rising up the ladder should be completely left to their hard work and talent, and the hindering factors like safety and privacy issues, discrimination and glass ceiling effects should be managed by the government through a central monitoring system for the sake of greater development.
- Thirdly, the health services that are provided by the country need to be redesigned. The public sector that provides affordable health care is far from effective in most cases reported. The private sector which claims to provide a wide range of health care facilities is unaffordable and out of reach of marginal women. The problems of poor sanitation, immunization, malnutrition, child birth, post natal care, high infant mortality, and treatment of common illness are still of major concern in marginal and rural areas. It is of high importance that such issues be handed over to working committees that either initiate a public–private union on solving the matter or effective and affordable health care centres be established that work for the underprivileged.
- Fourthly, women participation needs to be encouraged and women's voice needs to be heard at various levels. It is not just the ones in the leading positions who should be able to express

themselves, it is also equally important that women at the local and community level need to be brought forward to discuss their plight. This will bring about transformation at the grassroot level.

CONCLUSION

It can be summed up that India has worked in terms of improving the scenario and it is very well reflected in the global gender gap rank it holds. But, there are indicators that the country still needs to work towards progress. There have been efforts at various levels by the government, but accountability for such measures is lacking. For attaining sustainable development through gender equality, strong democratic spaces for consideration of such issues, grassroots' voices and major accountability mechanisms at multiple levels in the country are required (Agarwal, 2010).

Women have huge potential of transforming the socio-economic and political scenario and not including them in the transformation process would be a sheer loss of opportunity of moving closer to sustainable development. Loss would be immense if we fail to capitalize on their (women's) talent and ability. Women need to be viewed as contributors and not victims. Also, this is not to add to the old debate of battle of sexes; but the sensitive issue of providing basic human rights to all with equality. The focus here is to make every individual free to grow and make the most of their talent and capabilities, so that the country moves closer towards attaining the ultimate aim of sustainable development.

REFERENCES

1. Agarwal, B. (2010). *Gender and Green Governance: The Political Economy of Women's Presence Within and Beyond Community Forestry*. Oxford: Oxford University Press.
2. Johnsson-Latham, G. (2007). A study on gender equality as a prerequisite for sustainable development. *Report to the Environment Advisory Council.*
3. The World Bank (2015). *Population Total*. Retrieved April 19, 2017, from http://data.worldbank.org/indicator/SP.POP.TOTL
4. World Commission on Environment and Development (WCED). (1987). *Our Common Future*. New York: Oxford University Press, 8.
5. World Economic Forum. (2016). *The Global Gender Gap Report 2016*. Switzerland: World Economic Forum.

SECTION 2

SUSTAINABLE DEVELOPMENT THROUGH GENDER EQUALITY IN HEALTH AND NUTRITION

5

A Study on Gender Disparity in Nutritional Status Among Children in a Rural Community of Allahabad, Uttar Pradesh

Jaya Tripathi, Ranu Prasad and Alka Gupta

ABSTRACT

Though the importance of a girl child has been stressed time and again, yet a wide level of disparity still exists, whether implicit or explicit, in nutrition and child care both in the rural and urban areas. Different underlying factors are responsible for this disparity. A girl faces discrimination from the moment she is born. The UNICEF intergenerational cycle of malnutrition stresses on the fact that the problem of malnutrition spans generations and is a vicious cycle. Therefore, this study was conducted to document the gender disparity in nutritional status with the objectives of comparing the gender disparity in nutritional status in children aged 0-5 years in rural areas and to assess the different socio-demographic factors influencing the gender disparity. A community-based cross-sectional study was conducted in Allahabad district of Uttar Pradesh. A total of 161 children were examined and their mothers interviewed. Male children were more malnourished than female children. Although the frequency of falling ill was found to be the same between both the genders, the treatment given to male children was better than that given to female children. Overall, the prevalence of disease was low in our study area. The majority of the children suffered with fever, diarrhea, and acute respiratory infection. Significant differentiation was observed between the male and female children with regard to the time lag between child falling ill and initiation of treatment and the amount spent for treatment. Male children were more malnourished than female children. This is contrary to the general and popular belief that female children are more malnourished.

Keywords: *Nutritional Status; Gender Disparity; Underweight; Illness; Malnourishment*

INTRODUCTION

Under nutrition is a serious public health problem among children in the developing countries (Nandy *et al.*, 2005). Under nutrition is one of the measures of health status that the World Health Organization (WHO) recommends for equity in health (Zere and McIntyre, 2003). It has been estimated that approximately 70% of the world's undernourished children live in Asia, giving that region the highest concentration of worldwide childhood under nutrition (Khor, 2008). Moreover, India shows the highest occurrence of childhood under nutrition in the world and it has been estimated that more than half of Indian children are undernourished (Bamji, 2003). Malnutrition impedes motor, sensory, cognitive and social development, so malnourished children will be less likely to benefit from schooling, and will consequently have lower income as adults. The most damaging effects of under-nutrition occur during pregnancy and the first two years of a child's life. These damages are irreversible. It is the right of every child to know and be cared for by his/her parents. The responsibilities for the child's well-being rest on both the parents and the society. Since the ancient times, it is the gender that determines the position of a child in the Indian society. Denial of equality, rights, opportunity and supplement in any form on the basis of gender is gender discrimination. The female subjects are more often the victims of gender discrimination. The girl child faces the neglect of the family in the form of failure to provide the basic necessities of life in terms of food, clothing, love, shelter, supervision, education, and medical care. Gender inequality exists in almost every country, but in varying degrees. A major area of concern and focus in India is the remarkable degree of variation in demographic profile, socio-economic dimensions, and cultural practices.

SCOPE

Discrimination, whether implicit or explicit, in nutrition and child care have exacerbated the plight of the girl child, which manifests in the form of excess female mortality, as has been highlighted by many studies. Girls are biologically advantageous than the boys in the perinatal and neonatal period. But this advantage is overridden by the societal practices and discrimination as the child grows. Girls face discrimination from the moment she is born. And this discrimination manifests itself in every walk of life. In other words, they are not reared as equivalent to their male counterpart. Though the importance of girl child has been stressed time and again, yet a wide level of disparity still exists both in the rural and urban areas. Different underlying factors are responsible for this disparity in the rural areas. Achieving gender equity is one of the main cornerstones for achieving universal health coverage. Therefore this study was conducted to document the gender disparity in nutritional status and to compare rural and urban differences.

OBJECTIVES OF THE STUDY

1. To compare the gender disparity in nutritional status in children aged 0-5 years.
2. To assess the different socio-demographic factors influencing the gender disparity in children aged 0-5 years.

RESEARCH METHODOLOGY

Study Design: Community based cross-sectional study.

Study Area: The present study has been carried out in Jasra block of Allahabad district.

Study Population: Children in the age group of 0-5 years.

Inclusion Criteria: Children in the age group of 0-5 years.

Exclusion Criteria: Children diagnosed with serious medical condition.

Sample Size: 161 children were selected using purposive sampling.

Data Collection Tools: Pre-designed and pre-tested schedule, weighing scale and measuring tape.

Data Collection Technique: House-to-house visit, examination and interview method.

METHODS OF MEASUREMENTS

Height: Height was measured using a measuring tape. The participants were asked to remove their footwear (shoes, slippers, sandals, etc.) and head gear (hair bows, ribbons, etc.), and then participants were told to stand with feet together, heels against the wall, knees straight, to look straight ahead and not tilt their head. It was made sure that the eyes were at the same level as the ears (Frankfurt plane). A cardboard was gradually brought down and the measurement was read to the nearest 0.1 cm. For children less than 2 years, recumbent length was measured with an infantometer.

Weight: In weighing the children less than 2 years, they were put in weighing pants and put gently on the hook of the hanging weighing scale, which was already fixed on a firm support. The beam was properly balanced and moved freely when at rest and pointer was on zero. The footwear were removed and the children were weighed with minimal clothing.

The WHO Growth Charts (2006) were used to classify the children as normal, mild to moderate, and severe type of malnutrition.

FINDINGS

Results as shown in Table 1 revealed that out of the 161, under-five children, 72 (44.7%) children were classified as underweight for their respective age. Around 40% of male children were classified as mild to moderately underweight when compared with 23.5% of female children. However, a higher percentage of female children (17.3%) were severely underweight than male children (8.8%). The association was also found to be statistically significant ($p>0.05$) Stunting was seen more in the female children (30.9% vs. 17.5%) than male children. The association was found to be statistically non-significant ($p>0.05$). On measuring the weight for height of the under-five children using the WHO Growth Charts, male children were found to be wasted than the female children. But, the association was found to be statistically non-significant ($p>0.05$).

Table 1: Socio-demographic profile of the children

		n	%
Age group (in months)			
0–12		17	10.6
13–24		43	26.7
25–36		40	24.8
37–48		37	23
48–60		24	14.9
Religion			
Hindu		126	78.3
Other religions		35	21.7
Gender			
Male		80	49.7
Female		81	50.3
Type of family			
Nuclear		45	27.8
Joint		116	72.2
Socio-economic Status			
Class 1	Above Rs. 1.5 Lakhs	11	6.8
Class 2	Rs. 88801-1,50,000	23	14.3
Class 3	Rs. 55001-88800	48	29.8
Class 4	Rs. 33001-55000	61	37.9
Class 5	Rs. 1000-33000	18	11.2

Source: National Council for Applied Economic Research (NCAER), 2013-14.

The majority of the children were between the age group of 13 and 36 months, with the majority (78.3%) belonging to Hindu religion. Equal number of boys and girls were present in the study. About 72.2% of the children belonged to joint family. Overall, 44.7% of the children were underweight, 39.7% were stunted, and 30.3% were wasted.

The median height and weight of the majority of children were within the normal range of the WHO reference data. Although, it is believed that male children are better and better-nourished than the female children, the finding in our study is contradictory, which is a positive sign. Similar kinds of results were also seen in the studies done by Ray *et al.* (2000), Pathak (2011) and Chakraborty *et al.* (2006). No such significant difference was observed between both the sexes regarding the prevalence of disease.

Table 2: Distribution of children based on weight for age

Weight for age	*Male subjects, n (%)*	*Female subjects, n (%)*	*Total*
Normal (+2 SD to –2 SD)	41 (51.2)	48 (59.3)	89 (55.3)
Underweight			
Mild to moderate (–2 SD to –3 SD)	32 (40)	19 (23.5)	51 (31.7)
Severe (less than –3 SD)	7 (8.8)	14 (17.3)	21 (13)

Table 3: Distribution of children based on height for age

Height for age	*Male subjects, n (%)*	*Female subjects, n (%)*	*Total*
Normal (+2 SD to –2 SD)	52 (65)	45 (55.5)	97 (60.2)
Stunting			
Mild to moderate (–2 SD to –3 SD)	14 (17.5)	25 (30.9)	39 (24.2)
Severe (less than –3 SD)	14 (17.5)	11 (13.6)	25 (15.5)

Table 4: Distribution of children based on weight for height

Weight for height	*Gender*		*Total*
	Male subjects, n (%)	*Female subjects, n (%)*	
Normal (+2 SD to –2 SD)	36 (60)	49 (79)	85 (69.7)
Wasting			
Mild to moderate (–2 SD to –3 SD)	17 (31.7)	14 (19.4)	31 (25.4)
Severe (less than –3 SD)	5 (8.3)	1 (1.6)	6 (4.9)

The possibilities of the recall bias do exist in this study. Unfortunately, contact very few fathers could be contacted during the researchers visit, as most of them were sole bread earners of the family and had left for the work early in the morning. Hence, information on knowledge, attitude, and practice regarding child-rearing practices and care during illness has not been analyzed completely. Nutritional status is a major determinant of health and well-being in children. This is similar to other studies done in different parts of India by various researchers like Dey and Chaudhuri (2008), Bhalani and Kotecha (2002) and Dasgupta (1987). However, in rural areas, the male child showed higher rates of being underweight and stunted as compared to the female child. This is similar to other studies as reported by Singh and Mondal (2013), and Basu *et al.* (2014).

CONCLUSION

Male children were more malnourished than female children. This is contrary to the general belief that female children are more malnourished. There was a significant association between underweight and gender in Hindu religion, caste, nuclear family, illiterate and unemployed mother and lower-income group. Gender equity is an important determinant to curb the menace of under nutrition. Though the problem of gender disparity is not as prevalent in Assam as other parts of India yet its existence can't be totally ignored. Different underlying factors play their part in the manifestation of gender discrimination. Until and unless steps are taken to deal with the social determinants of under nutrition its burden can't be lessened.

RECOMMENDATIONS

1. Percolating the message of gender equality deep into the community through IEC (Information Education and Communication) and empowerment of females in the society.
2. Special focus on creating awareness on gender equality in the minority communities and backward castes.
3. Intense awareness generation through mass media approach, stressing on female literacy, improving the overall socio-economic conditions through various income generation schemes.

REFERENCES

1. Nandy, S., Irving, M., Gordon, D., Subramanian, S.V. & Smith, G.D. (2005). Poverty, Child Under nutrition and Morbidity: New Evidences from India. *Bulletin of World Health Organization*, 83: 210–216.

2. Zere, E. & McIntyre, D. (2003). Inequities in under-five child malnutrition in South Africa, *International Journal of Equity Health*, 2:7.
3. Khor, G.L. (2008). Food-based approaches to combat the double burden among the poor: Challenges in the Asian context. *Asia Pacific Journal of Clinical Nutrition*, 17: 111–115.
4. Bamji, M.S. (2003). Early nutrition and health—Indian perspective. *Current Science*, 85(11): 37–42.
5. Ray, S.K., Biswas, A.B., Gupta, S.D., Mukherjee, D., Kumar, S. & Biswas, B.(2000). Rapid assessment of nutritional status and dietary pattern in municipal area. *Indian Journal of Community Medicine*, 25(1): 14–18.
6. Pathak, D. (2011). Gender Disparity in Health and Nutritional Status in Children under Five Years of Age in a Rural Community: A Cross-Sectional Study. *MPH Thesis*, Belgaum, KLE University.
7. Chakraborty, S., Gupta, S.B., Chaturvedi, B. & Chakraborty, S.K. (2006). A study on protein energy malnutrition (PEM) in children (0–6 years) in a rural population of Jhansi district (UP). *Indian Journal of Community Medicine*, 31(4): 291–292.
8. Census provisional population totals. (2011). Available from: http://censusindia.gov.in/2011census/censusinfodashboard/index.html
9. National Family Health Survey (NFHS-3). (2007). International Institute for Population Sciences (IIPS) and Macro International.
10. Dey, I., Chaudhuri, R.N. (2008). Gender Inequality in Nutritional Status among under Five Children in a Village in Hooghly District, West Bengal.*Indian Journal of Public Health*, 52(4): 218–220.
11. Bhalani, K.D. & Kotecha, P.V. (2002). Nutritional status and gender differences in children of age less than five years of age attending ICDS anganwadis in Vadodara city. *Indian Journal of Community Medicine*, 27(3): 124-129.
12. Gupta, M.D. (1987). Selective Discrimination against Female Children in Rural Punjab, India. *Population and Development Review*, 13: 77-100.
13. Mosley, W.H. & Chen, L.C. (1984). An analytical framework for the study of child survival in developing countries. *Population and development review (Suppl.)*, 10:25-45.
14. Singh, J. & Mondal, N. (2013). Assessment of Nutritional Status: A Case of Tribal Children in Assam, Northeast India. *Journal of Nepal Paediatrics Society*, 33(1): 1-7.
15. Debashis, B., Gulenur, I., Ratul, G., Swarupa, D. & Junumai D. (2014). Childs growth and nutritional status in two communities - Mishing tribe and Kaibarta caste of Assam, India. *International Journal of Sociology and Anthropology*,6(2):59–69.
16. United Nations Development Programmes. *Gender Inequality Index and Related Indicators. 2011.*
17. World Health Organization. Growth Charts (2006). Available at: http://www.who.int/childgrowth/standards/en/.

6

Gender Disparities in Reproductive Health and Family Planning Choices

Neerja Masih

ABSTRACT

Even in the 21st century, an age of rapid biotechnological development and globalization, women's health remains an issue. There is gender disparity in the reproductive health and the family planning choices available. Reproductive health emphasizes peoples rights to sexuality, reproduction, and family planning, and the information to actualize these rights, which have been inextricably linked to development. Women's sexual and reproductive rights became recognised as universal human right in 1994, violations of which occur in some reproductive health areas including gender concerns. The responsibility of not having unintended pregnancy or termination of such a pregnancy still rests with women. Early marriages, early pregnancies, multiple abortions, miscarriages, unwillingness of men for using any methods of contraception, myths regarding undergoing permanent method of family planning still prevail in our society. Adopting the methods of contraception becomes solely the women's responsibility and not choice, therefore she becomes the victim of side effects of these methods. As the rule of demand and supply goes, even the research agencies work only on the areas of methods of contraception for women whether it is use of Intrauterine devices (IUDs) as Long Acting Reversible Contraception (LARC) or using hormonal oral contraception. Addressing the issue of gender inequality is a collective responsibility of nations and multinational research agencies. The growing surrogacy phenomenon in which women agree to have their bodies used to undergo pregnancy and give birth to the resulting baby is becoming a major issue of the 21st century.

Keywords: *Gender disparities, reproductive health, right to sexuality, family planning, contraception methods.*

INTRODUCTION

Over the past few decades, global research has shown that gender inequalities can give rise to health inequities between men and women and between boys and girls. In developing countries of the world, differentials in morbidity and mortality between men and women arise due to utilization of reproductive health services. Again, the mortality rate amongst child-bearing women is often high in developing nations. Scholars are in agreement that there are some inevitable differences in the reproductive health needs and status of men and women in these nations. Unfortunately, many health systems and interventions have failed to respond to these different needs, typically disadvantaging women over men (Jamison, 2006) The point being made here is that gender determines production and social relations as most productive resources are controlled by men and this in turn affects health disparities between men and women (Ezeah & Achonwa, 2015). These health disparities tend to reflect the underlying distribution of roles and power between men and women in society, resulting in constraints on the ability of men and women to influence their own health outcomes, and thus are considered unfair and unjust. Therefore, promoting gender equality has become a global concern, prompting the emergence of a globally accepted strategy referred to as 'gender mainstreaming', which acts as a means to achieving gender equality (WHO, 2008). Gender mainstreaming considers the concerns and experiences of men and women as an integral dimension of all phases of programme and policy development. In the context of health, gender mainstreaming can be summarized as reducing inequities in health status and access to health care between men and women. Both men and women must have the same chances and opportunities from health policies and programmes. This is referred to as gender equality, and acts as a prerequisite for health equity (WHO, 2009), and aims to ensure equal conditions for both men and women to realize their full rights and potentials to be healthy, contribute to their community health development, and be able to benefit from the results. Sexual and reproductive health and rights are fundamental human rights and ethical imperatives that lie at the core of advancing women's empowerment and gender equality; and investing in them is central to achieving broader social, economic and sustainable development goals.

HEALTH

In the preamble of the WHO (1948, p. 100), health is defined as a state of complete physical, social and mental well-being of an individual and not merely the absence of disease or infirmity. Health is not just about one's physical health but includes the social, emotional and physical health. The social and cultural context in which, including their identities and the constraints they afford affect their health. Further, the environment from where the persons come from, their health beliefs and socio-economic status all affect their health directly and indirectly. Public health and population health is concerned with understanding health and disease occurrence in the community, and improving health and well-being. Health gains are achieved through prioritizing health approaches and addressing the inequalities in health status that exist between social groups including gender.

REPRODUCTIVE HEALTH

Reproductive health is defined as a state of physical, mental, and social well-being in all matters relating to the reproductive system, at all stages of life. Good reproductive health implies that people are able to have a satisfying and safe sex life, the capability to reproduce and the freedom to decide if, when, and how often to do so. Men and women should be informed about and have access to safe, effective, affordable, and acceptable methods of family planning of their choice, and the right to appropriate health-care services that enable women to safely go through pregnancy and childbirth.

GENDER DISPARITY AND REPRODUCTIVE HEALTH

Women's sexual and reproductive rights became recognised as universal human right, violations of which occur in some reproductive health areas including gender concerns in 1994. Since, the 1994 International Conference on Population and Development (ICPD), and the 1995 World Conference on Women, interest in men's participation in reproductive health has increased (Oyediran et al., 2002).

The responsibility of not having unintended pregnancy or termination of such a pregnancy still remains that of the women. Early marriages, early pregnancies, multiple abortions, miscarriages, unwillingness of men for using any methods of contraception, myths regarding undergoing permanent method of family planning still prevail in our society (Adinma & Adinma, 2011).

Adopting the methods of contraception becomes solely the women's responsibility and not choice therefore she becomes the victim of side effects of these methods.

The International Planned Parenthood Federation (IPPF Report) is a global service provider and a leading advocate of sexual and reproductive health and rights for all. It is felt that male or female, the individual should be free to choose parenthood or not, free to decide how many children they have and when, free to pursue healthy sexual lives without fear of unwanted pregnancies and sexually transmitted infections.

There is a link between sexual and reproductive health, and rights and gender equality. This link explores the different pathways of empowerment that girls and women experience, and analyzes how these pathways are affected by sexual and reproductive health and rights.

Policy focus and attention given to gender equality and women's empowerment has been growing over the last decade, and there are some areas where links are established more conclusively. Although there is strong documentation on the health benefits of investment in sexual and reproductive health, until recently the non-medical benefits, such as higher levels of social and political participation, have been largely ignored, partly because they are difficult to measure. While the social and economic implications of sexual and reproductive health and rights are often overlooked, they are no less real. More attention is needed to explore the links between sexual and reproductive health and rights and other critical areas relating to gender equality, such as the representation of women in political and public life. There are three focuses:

a) Sexual and reproductive health and rights and the social development of girls and women (including health, education, and freedom from sexual and gender-based violence)
b) Sexual and reproductive health and rights and women's economic participation
c) Sexual and reproductive health and rights and women's participation in political and public life

NO EQUALITY WITHOUT SEXUAL AND REPRODUCTIVE HEALTH AND RIGHTS

Gender equality and the empowerment of girls and women will not be possible without the realization of sexual and reproductive health and rights. For women and girls to lead healthy lives, and to be free to participate in social, economic and political life, they need universal access to quality services, information and education, and conditions that allow them to realize their sexual and reproductive rights.

Sexual and reproductive health and rights services are critical for women and girls to have healthy lives, address violence and power relations in their lives, and open doors to opportunities. On these grounds alone, they must be considered priority interventions. Sexual and reproductive health and rights are important rights in themselves, but can also magnify possibilities for empowering girls and women and for achieving gender equality.

SEXUAL AND REPRODUCTIVE HEALTH AND RIGHTS FREE WOMEN TO PARTICIPATE

Ensuring universal access to sexual and reproductive health and rights brings positive gains to the health and well-being of women and girls.

In some cases, it can mean the difference between life and death.

Poor sexual and reproductive health outcomes represent one-third of the total global burden of disease for women, between the ages of 15 and 44 years, with unsafe sex a major risk factor for death and disability among women and girls in low- and middle-income countries. Disabilities and ill health are experienced more by women and girls and negatively affect their survival, health and well-being. The sexual and reproductive health of women and girls is important but also affects other aspects of their lives, such as their ability to stay in school and to live free from violence.

Realizing sexual and reproductive health and rights is necessary for women and girls to stay healthy, to participate in education, and to participate in all facets of life, free from violence.

Sexual and reproductive health and rights are critical for empowering women and girls and advancing gender equality—both to realize their rights and their access to health services.

The ability of women and girls to exercise their sexual and reproductive rights to make free and informed choices about their sexual and reproductive life, and about whether and when to have children, is a central component of gender equality. At their core, sexual and reproductive health and rights mean that individuals should have the right and the means to make decisions about their reproductive lives and sexuality, free from violence, coercion and discrimination.

Larger family size exacerbates and is exacerbated by son preference, including educational preference for boys where girls are more likely to be taken out of school to care for siblings as compared to boys. It has been observed that smaller family size can also be associated with parents investing more in each child, and being less likely to discriminate on the basis of gender. As increased women's educational attainment may influence initial fertility decline, smaller family size may then increasingly influence a further investment in educating daughters

As the rule of demand and supply goes, even the research agencies work only on the areas of methods of contraception for women whether it is use of Intrauterine devices (IUDs) as Long Acting Reversible Contraception (LARC) or using hormonal oral contraception.

Socio-economic-psychological factors for the lack of availability of birth control methods for men.

On the surface, it may seem that scientific challenges are the primary barrier to excellent male birth control. A woman produces an egg only once each month, while men produce millions of sperms daily. Female fertility can be detected and timed. It starts later and ends sooner than male fertility. But those in the know say biology isn't the problem. The question is one of politics and priorities. The National Institute of Health (NIH Report) summed up the problem in direct terms over a decade ago:

The lack of progress in developing affordable, safe, effective, and reversible male contraceptives is due not to the biological complexity involved in suppressing spermatogenesis (the production of sperm), but rather to social and economic/commercial constraints.

A clinical trial of contraceptives for men was halted because of side effects—side effects that women have dealt with for decades.

For a long time, outdated perceptions have contributed to the lack of investment in birth control for men. Since women traditionally have borne the primary burden of unwanted childbearing and parenting, decision-makers have long assumed that men wouldn't be interested in contraceptives—or would have a very low tolerance for cost, side effects, or hassle. Today, though, in the age of paternity tests and child support, with fathers and mothers sharing parenting responsibility—more and more men want to be in control of their own fertility (Women Deliver).

In the past couple of decades, scientists have been slowly moving toward developing birth control for men. A recent clinical trial of an injectable hormone contraceptive for men showed super promising results: It was 96 percent effective at preventing pregnancy, by lowering sperm counts. Unfortunately, the trial was discontinued early by an independent committee, which determined that the side effects were such that "the risks to the study participants outweighed the potential benefits." The side effects in question were, "mood changes, depression, pain at the injection site, and increased libido."

If some of the possible side effects of currently available birth-control options for women are reviewed, the following is found:

- Minastrin 24 FE, a low-hormone birth control pill: Headaches, nausea, menstrual cramps, yeast infections, breast tenderness, acne, mood swings, and weight gain.
- Nuva-ring: A hormonal vaginal ring: Vaginal-tissue irritation, headaches, mood changes, nausea and vomiting, weight gain, breast pain, painful menstruation, abdominal pain, acne, and decreased libido.
- The Mirena Intrauterine Device: pelvic or abdominal pain, ovarian cysts, headaches and migraines, acne, depressed mood, "heavy or prolonged menstrual bleeding."

Intra Uterine Devices can also cause sepsis or perforate the uterus. This is very rare, but still there is risk.

All of these are FDA-approved contraceptives that are currently in the market and in women's bodies, and their side effects are just as bad as those that occurred with the injectable male birth control. Nobody halted them in their tracks, saying that perhaps the risks outweighed the benefits. Women may well decide that for themselves. It has been found that nearly 40 percent of women stop using the pill within a year of starting it.

Though men have an equal responsibility to prevent unwanted pregnancies, they don't share equally in the consequences. What's more, we're learning more about just how serious the side effects of hormonal birth control may be. A recent study of more than a million women published in *JAMA Psychiatry* found that women who used hormonal birth control were more likely to be prescribed antidepressants. The study's design has received some criticism but it nonetheless underscores that for some women, there are tradeoffs between their reproductive freedom and their mental and emotional health.

This is not so for men. Though men have an equal responsibility to prevent unwanted pregnancies, they don't share equally in the consequences, and never have. The burden of birth control has always fallen largely on women's shoulders; it is their bodies that will bear the consequences if birth control fails. Presently the only available birth-control method for men other than a vasectomy—is a condom. And because condoms are significantly less effective than IUDs, implants, contraceptive pills, and rings, it stands to reason that many will choose the more effective method.

Early versions of the hormonal birth-control pill had tons of side effects, enough that, in a trial done in Puerto Rico in the 1950s, the doctor in charge of the trial recommended against its use. However, as Bethy Squires recently reported in a history of birth control side effects for *Broadly*, a U.S. pharmaceutical company released the same formulation anyway. (Current formulations use far less hormones, but as we've seen, still have side effects.) The *Broadly* piece also notes that the same group of doctors that studied the female pill originally considered one for men, but testicle shrinkage, among other side effects, led them to abandon it. "It was believed women would tolerate side effects better than men, who demanded a better quality of life," Squires writes.

The side effects in this most recent study *were* severe in some cases: 21.6 percent of participants got mood swings or some other kind of "emotional disorder," 38 percent had an increased libido, and 23 percent felt pain at the injection site. The crazy thing, though, is that most men wanted to continue using the injectable birth control—more than 80 percent of them said they would choose to use it.* So if men in the past demanded a side-effect-free life, it seems these days many are at least open to taking on the responsibility of birth control themselves. Perhaps the hurdle that remains is that male birth control is unlikely to substantially improve a man's quality of life. He can already avoid unwanted pregnancies if his partner is on birth control; with his own he'd get the same advantages, except now he might have mood swings. But for women, birth control has been revolutionary. One-third of women's wage gains since the 1960s can be attributed to the availability of oral contraceptives, according to a report by Planned Parenthood. College enrolment has historically been higher among women who have access to the pill, and "birth control has been estimated to account for more than 30 percent of the increase in the proportion of women in skilled careers from 1970 to 1990," the report reads.

SURROGACY

The growing surrogacy phenomenon in which women agree to have their bodies used to undergo pregnancy and give birth to the resulting baby is becoming a major issue of the 21st century.

RECOMMENDATIONS

Addressing the issue of gender inequality is a collective responsibility of nations and multinational research agencies. Nations should adopt a framework hinged on three pedestals—legal, institutional and policy, employing the three recommended approaches of equal treatment, positive action, and gender mainstreaming. To promote gender equality in reproductive health in India, the following specific recommendations are put forward in this paper:

1. Free and compulsory education for the girl child must be sustained in rural India. This will help eliminate female illiteracy because good quality education is the bedrock of progress, enabling ideas and livelihoods to flourish. Sustainable development cannot be achieved when young girls' opportunities are stripped from them by not allowing them go to school.
2. Family planning service providers need to create adequate awareness through meetings, seminars and workshops with married couples, opinion and religious leaders to signify the importance of male participation in family planning.
3. Family planning services providers should develop a definite and detail work plan on the processes of male participation in family planning.
4. The government should develop policies that will reduce the disproportionate and increasing burden on women who have multiple roles including the child-bearing roles within the family by providing them with adequate support and programmes in health and social services and encourage men to share equally in child care and household work.
5. The government should offer universal access to quality, comprehensive and integrated information on reproductive health rights and services. Moreover women should be made aware of such services and encouraged to use them.
6. Education is important in equipping men with adequate knowledge regarding family planning, reduce the culture and tradition of patriarchy and also enhance the status of women.

There is need to include men in family planning programmes; for achieving this the following measures are recommended:

1. Family planning service providers need to create adequate awareness through meetings, seminars and workshops with married couples, opinion and religious leaders to signify the importance of male participation in family planning.
2. Family planning service providers should develop a definite and detail work plan on the processes of male participation in family planning.

3. Government should properly equip family planning centres with material for use by men.
4. Family planning service providers should act as both motivators of men and their confidant to enhance their participation in family planning and the myth regarding the males undergoing surgery should be eliminated.
5. Family planning service providers should provide precise information to men on the various family planning methods and how they help to prevent child birth.
6. More male-centered research on family planning should be encouraged.

REFERENCES

1. Adinma ED and Adinma BD (2011). Gender issues in reproductive health: A review. *Niger. J. Med* 2011, Jan-Mar, 201-207
2. Cohen SA (2004). The broad benefits of investing in sexual and reproductive health. *The Guttmacher Report on Public Policy*, 7(1).
3. Ezeah and Achonwa (2015). Gender inequality in reproductive health services and sustainable development in Negeria: A theoretical analysis. *International Journal of Sociology and Anthropology*, Feb 2015, Vol. 7(2), pp 46-53.
4. Jamison DT (2006). *Disease Control Priorities in Developing Countries.* (2) New York: Oxford University Press.
5. IPPF Report: Sexual and reproductive health and rights.
6. NIM Report: Socio-economic reasons for lack of research in male contraception methods.
7. Oyediran KA, Ishola GP, Feyisetan BJ (2002). "Factors affecting every married men's contraceptive knowledge and use", *Nigeria. J. Biosoc. Sci.* 34(4): 497-510. Retrieved from http/www.journals.Cambridge.org
8. *The Atlantic daily*. 1 Nov 2016, www.theatlantic.com
9. WHO (2007). "Engaging men and boys in changing gender-based inequity in health: Evidence from program interventions", in C. Barker, C. Ricardo & M. Nascimento (Eds.), *Engaging men and boys in changing gender-based inequity in health: Evidence from program interventions*, pp. 1–69. Geneva: WHO.
10. World Health Organization (2009). Integrating gender into HIV/AIDS programmes in the health sector: Tool to improve responsiveness to women's needs. Geneva, (http://whqlibdoc.who.int/publications/2009/9789241597197_eng.pdf. Accessed June 12, 2013.
11. World Health Organization (2011). Gender mainstreaming manual for health managers: A practical approach. Geneva, (http://www.who.int/gender/mainstreaming/tools/en/index1.html. Accessed June 12, 2013.
12. World Population Data Sheet (2013). Population Reference Bureau. Washington DC: The Author.
13. World Health Organization (2014). *Women and Health: 20 Years of the Beijing Declaration and Platform for Action*
14. WHO UNFPA, The World Bank (2012). *Trends in maternal mortality: 1990–2010, the maternal mortality estimation inter-agency (MMEIG).* Geneva: WHO.

7

Gender Disparity and Health Issues

Neda Shamin, Virginia Paul and Eloni Vida

ABSTRACT

The distinct roles and behaviours of men and women in a given culture, dictated by that culture's gender norms and values, give rise to gender differences. Nutrition can offer opportunities to address otherwise sensitive issues regarding gender roles. The socially constructed gender roles of men and women interact with their biological roles to affect the nutrition status of the entire family and of each gender. Until recently, 'gender in the context of health' implied a discussion on women's health. However, an inclusive approach to health should attend to the needs and differentials between men, women and other genders, along with the interaction between social and biological markers of health. In order to attain such universality in health coverage, it is essential to achieve gender equality. This may be ensured through gender equity, gender mainstreaming and empowerment. A gendered perspective would thus take into account the health needs of all categories of sexual identity; "heterosexual, homosexual, lesbian, gay, bisexual, 'queer', transgendered, transsexual, and asexual". Hence, keeping in view the health and nutrition, this paper, focuses on the burden of diseases irrespective of gender from childhood to old age, dealing with health and gender and recommendations for gender and health.

Keywords: *Gender, health care, nutrition, malnutrition.*

1. INTRODUCTION

Gender and nutrition are inextricable parts of the vicious cycle of poverty. Gender inequality can be a cause as well as an effect of hunger and malnutrition. Not surprisingly, higher levels of gender inequality are associated with higher levels of under-nutrition, both acute and chronic under-nutrition (Mucha, 2012 and UNDP, 2011). Gender and nutrition are not stand-alone issues; agriculture, nutrition, health and gender are interlinked and can be mutually reinforcing. Some experts consider women to be the nexus of the agriculture, health and nutrition sectors (IFPRI, 2011). Gender and nutrition are increasingly acknowledged by the development community as important cross-cutting issues. Recently, the reciprocal relationship between the two issues was affirmed, giving rise to various efforts that seek to mainstream gender into nutrition policy and programming.

While diverging interpretations of gender exist, there is a common understanding that women and men should have equal rights and opportunities. Women continue to face discrimination and often have less access to power and resources, including those related to nutrition. This underscores the need to apply a rights-based approach to gender programming, with opportunities to leverage complementary rights-based nutrition principles such as the Right to Food. Notwithstanding, the roles, priorities, needs and use of resources may differ between men and women. The way women and men are affected by nutrition, their actions may also differ. The tendency is to focus on women when addressing gender, yet this overlooks the instrumental role of men inbridging the gender gap. Both men and women need to be involved in this process, acknowledging their respective roles and needs, and fostering mutual awareness and partnership.

2. BURDEN OF DISEASE

A difference between the genders is apparent in risk factors and disease burdens across the lifecycle, from childhood, through adolescence and adulthood, to old age (WHO, 2008 and Kishore and Gupta, 2009). Here are some examples of these lifecycle burdens as well as those that are hidden or under-studied.

- **Childhood:** Data from NFHS-3 revealed that in 2005-06, while neonatal mortality rates were higher in boys, post-neonatal mortality rates were higher for girls, demonstrating that gender discrimination leading to inadequate care nullified the girl child's biological advantage over boys during the first few years of life (Kishore and Gupta, 2009). Gender disparities are also seen in nutrition with persistently high levels of anaemia among girls and women, and in immunization rates, where girls are significantly less likely to be fully immunized than boys.
- **Adolescence:** Complications during pregnancy are the leading cause of death among 15- to 19-year-old girls in India. Early

marriage and child-bearing can pose several additional health risks, including pregnancy-related complications, unsafe deliveries, improper prenatal and postnatal care and miscarriage (Santhya and Jejeebhoy, 2003). Mental health problems associated with puberty, identity crises, and role transitions also constitute a large proportion of the burden for adolescent girls (George, 2002). Occupational hazards due to physical labour and domestic work (especially in agricultural areas) can be particularly damaging for the underdeveloped and undernourished adolescent girls in rural areas (Malhotra and Passi, 2007). Gender differences are also apparent in tobacco use, with 33.2% of Indian boys under the age of 15 years smoking tobacco, compared to 3.8% girls under the age of 15 years in 2006.

- **Adulthood:** Studies indicate that anaemia (iron deficiency) affects 50-90% of pregnant women in India, and significantly increases the risk for maternal deaths due to haemorrhage (George, 2002). Significant health complications also arise due to unwanted pregnancies and subsequent unsafe abortions. A gender bias is seen in the way reproductive health and sexual health are considered as exclusive health needs of women and men respectively. For instance, reproductive health services are targeted towards heterosexual women who are, or will be, mothers and therefore the Reproductive Health Programme for women is required. Sexual health services, especially in relation to HIV/AIDS, are considered needs of men, and hence the National AIDS Control Programme. These kinds of gender biases need to be addressed during the sensitization and training of healthcare providers as well as while designing Essential Service Packages for men and women, including for persons of diverse sexualities.
- **Old Age:** In India, the life expectancy at birth is 66 years for women and 63 years for men. However, this longevity brings with it a considerable burden of disease for elderly women (WHO, 2011). Women over 60 years tend to have greater disability and more co-morbidities than men of the same age-group, which may be due to biological factors such as lower muscle strength and bone density in women compared to men (WHO, 2007 and WHO 2000) as well as social factors such as restricted access to nutritional food and healthcare facilities across the lifespan. Heart disease causes more deaths in older women than men; however, women are less likely to seek or receive appropriate and timely care for the condition, and are often under represented in cardiovascular risk research

(WHO, 2007). A considerable health burden for women in this age group is experienced due to neuropsychiatric conditions, especially dementia and depression. Other conditions during this period include loss of vision, cancers, osteoporosis and arthritis (WHO, 2007).

- **Hidden Burden of Disease:** Women are afflicted with a considerable hidden burden of disease which is often not accounted for in morbidity figures. Evidence indicates that there is a trend towards the growing burden of non-communicable diseases, in India and the world (Khanna, 2010 and Taylor, 2010). In a review of some Indian studies, Davar (2003) found that women are twice as likely to suffer from common mental disorders as men, which is supported by global prevalence rates (WHO, 2004). Violence against women remains high in India and a study by INCLEN (2000) reported that 40.3% of the women sampled reported at least one instance of physically abusive behaviour in their lifetime. A report by WHO-South East Asia Region Office discusses how suicide, an extreme manifestation of these hidden burdens, is now a leading cause of death among young women in India and China (WHO, 2008). Marginalization from the health system occurs in intersections, i.e. health status overlaps with social status, employment, and gender. This is the case for other vulnerable populations as well, such as those from SC/ST populations, and religious minorities. In healthcare settings in particular, transgendered Indians have had to face discrimination on the basis of transgender status, sex work status, HIV status, or a combination of the aforementioned (Raman, 2007).

3. DEALING WITH HEALTH AND GENDER

Most gender-based health differences in India can be traced back to the same underlying factors: decreasing fecundity and consequently a preference for sons, spread of the practice of dowry across most groups in the region, and the marginalization of women in agriculture. We believe that all these factors are tied to the perceived lack of economic utility of women. Current societal circumstances make the cost of having a daughter so high that families may be unwilling to invest scarce resources for their benefit. Similarly, the scarcity of resources causes society to undervalue women, who, as a rule, are not making a visible economic contribution. Attempts to address gender disparities must take into account these underlying issues. However, education and improved economic circumstances alone are likely to be insufficient to change practices that have become culturally, socially, and in some cases legally, enshrined. Programmes and policies aimed at reducing differences at the level of education and employment between men and women must enshrine gender equity as a core value. In this respect Sri Lanka might be considered a role model for the rest of South Asia—minimal gender differences in education and employment levels in Sri Lanka lead to a life expectancy and healthy life expectancy equivalent to those of industrialized countries. In this socio-cultural context, the violation of fundamental human rights, and especially reproductive rights of women, plays an important part in perpetuating gender inequity. It is therefore imperative that a rights-based approach be taken across all developmental activities in South Asian countries.

4. RECOMMENDATIONS FOR GENDER AND HEALTH

While the country's health system has a considerable distance to go in order to become truly gender sensitive, important steps need to be taken in the following core areas in the move towards Universal Health Coverage:

- Acknowledging gender diversity through the lifecycle during the conceptualization and delivery of services;
- Improving access for women and other vulnerable genders;
- Recognizing the key role that women play as formal and informal providers of health services and empowering them for that role;
- Strengthening data, analysis, and monitoring and evaluation systems in order to make them more gender sensitive; and
- Supporting and promoting the rights of girls and women to health in families and communities through programmes and policies.

5. CONCLUSION

Gender and nutrition have multiple dimensions and are highly context-specific. Ideally, the pathway towards improved food and nutrition security—for all—should be a gender-equitable process. In recent years, considerable progress has been made with regard to prioritizing gender and nutrition in policies, programmes and projects though these efforts have largely treated gender and nutrition as two distinct issues. Greater attention is needed for operationalizing opportunities to combine the two. The above recommendations are a preliminary attempt to bridge these two areas in support of gender-sensitive nutrition policies, programming and projects as a means to increasing nutritional impact.

REFERENCES

1. Davar B (2003). *Mental Health of Indian Women: A feminist Agenda.* New Delhi: Sage.
2. George A (2002). Embodying identity through heterosexual sexuality—newly married adolescent women in India. *Culture, Health, & Sexuality* 4 (2).
3. IFPRI (2011). "Agriculture, nutrition, health; exploiting the links." Washington DC.
4. INCLEN (2000). Domestic violence in India: A summary report of a multisite household survey. Washington: International Centre for Research on Women (ICRW).
5. Khanna R (2010). Policy Brief on NCDs, Gender Equality and Empowerment of Women (unpublished report) SAHAJ.
6. Kishor S and Gupta K (2009). Gender Equality and Women's Empowerment in India. National Family Health Survey (NFHS-3), India, 2005-06. Mumbai: International Institute for Population Sciences; Calverton, Maryland, USA: ICF Macro.
7. Malhotra A and Passi SJ (2007). Diet Quality and Nutritional Status of Rural Adolescent beneficiaries of ICDS in Northern India. *Asia Pacific Journal of Clinical Nutrition*16 (Suppl 1):8-16.
8. Mucha N (2012). "Enabling and equipping women to improve nutrition." Briefing Paper no. 16, Bread for the World Institute, Washington D.C.
9. Raman, PS (2007). Transsexuals want space, acceptance. *Hindustan Times* (9 February 2007). Available at: http://www.hindustantimes.com/Transsexuals-want-space-acceptance/Article1-204865.
10. Santhya KG and Jejeebhoy S (2003). Sexual and Reproductive Health Needs of Married Adolescent Girls. *Economic and Political Weekly* 38 (41): 11-17.
11. Taylor WD (2010). The Burden of Non-Communicable Diseases in India, Hamilton ON: The Cameron Institute.
12. UNDP (2011). "Human Development Report 2011. Sustainability and Equity; A Better Future for All." New York.
13. World Health Organization (2008). The Global Burden of Disease 2004 Update. Geneva, Switzerland: World Health Organization.
14. World Health Organization (2011). World Health Statistics 2011. Geneva: World Health Organization. [Internet]. Available at: http://www.who.int/whosis/whostat/2011/en/index.html
15. World Health Organization (2007). Women, Ageing and Health: A Framework for Action. Focus on Gender. Geneva: World Health Organization.
16. World Health Organization (2000). Women, ageing and health. Fact sheet. Geneva: World Health Organization. Available at: www.who.int/entity/mediacentre/factsheets/fs252/en
17. World Health Organization (2004). Gender in Mental Health Research. Geneva: Department of Gender, Women and Health, World Health Organization. Available at: http://www.who.int/gender/documents/mental_health/9241592532/en/index.html
18. World Health Organization (2008). Burden of Disease. Health in Asia and the Pacific. Geneva: World Health Organization.

8

Prevalence of Osteoporosis among the Pre- and Post-Menopausal Women of Allahabad District in Relation with their Occupation and Education

Pallavi Singh and Virginia Paul

ABSTRACT

Osteoporosis is defined as a major public health problem in developing countries like India and the data concerned with India indicates that 1 out of 3 females suffer from osteoporosis, making India one of the largest affected countries in the world. Osteoporosis is not life-threatening; and the quantitative data are scarce from developing countries like India. Considering this point, a cross-sectional study was conducted among 316 pre- and post-menopausal women of Allahabad District aged between 35 and 65 years, to determine the prevalence of osteoporosis and association of occupation, education and parity of selected female in relation with prevalence of osteoporosis. All the respondents of the study, who came to the referral hospital's outpatient department during the free BMD check-up camps by P-DEXA scan were purposively selected for this research. The P-DEXA screening reports of the respondents were classified according to the definition of osteoporosis given by World Health Organization. The results of the study revealed that the prevalence of osteoporosis was high among the post-menopausal women while the prevalence of osteopenia was high among the premenopausal women of Allahabad District. The educational Status of the respondents showed a significant association ($p<.05$) with the prevalence of osteoporosis, while occupational status of the women had no significant association ($p>.05$). So it was concluded in this study that post-menopausal status of women was a major risk factor for osteoporosis, and education status is a contributing factor in the occurrence of osteoporosis. It is recommended *that pre- and post-menopausal women go through the DEXA screening of the BMD for early detection of loss of bone mineral density and adopt healthy dietary pattern and appropriate lifestyle modifications to reduce this loss.*

Keywords: Bone Mineral Density, Osteoporosis, Osteopenia, DEXA screening, post-menopausal women

INTRODUCTION

Osteoporosis is defined as a major public health problem in developing countries, mainly in the Middle East, having high prevalence of low bone mineral density than Western Countries (Handa *et al.*, 2008). According to World Health Organization, Osteoporosis is defined as a Bone Mineral Density of 2.5 standard deviations or more below the mean peak bone mass as measured by Dual-Energy X-Ray Absorptiometry (WHO, 1994). Until recently, it was believed that osteoporosis mainly affects post-menopausal women. However, recent researches indicate that osteoporosis may occur in women aged above 40 years and even in youth. Occupation of the respondents may be associated with the occurrence of the low bone mineral density due to the absence of proper nutrition. The association of occupation with the prevalence of osteoporosis is still not well documented but some studies showed a negative impact of occupation on the osteoporosis prevention health programs (Pluskiewich *et al.*, 2014). Similarly the documented data on the relation of educational level of the population with the prevalence of osteoporosis said that improved formal education may reduce the prevalence of osteoporosis among the vulnerable population (Varenna *et al.*, 1999). Thus for the purpose of prevention and control of osteoporosis there is great interest in conducting epidemiological survey on prevalence of osteoporosis and contributing Factors like occupation and education in communities.

OBJECTIVES

1) To determine the prevalence of osteoporosis among pre- and post-menopausal women of Allahabad District.
2) To find out the association of Occupation and Educational Status of the respondents in relation with prevalence of osteoporosis.

MATERIALS AND METHODS

This study was a cross-sectional study carried out on a sample size of 316 pre- and post-menopausal women of Allahabad District. This study was conducted in one specialized hospital named Yashlok Hospital, which provides advanced health services to the community and organizes free BMD check-up camps regularly through P-DEXA machine for the general population of Allahabad district. All relatively healthy women aged between 35 and 65 years who came to the referral hospital outpatient department during the free BMD check-up camps were randomly and purposively approached to participate in the study and survey method was used for the collection of the information from the respondents. A WHO guideline for the diagnosis of osteoporosis was used to assess the prevalence of osteoporosis and osteopenia in the selected respondents (WHO, 1994). The statistical representation of the data was done with the help of statistical technique like chi-square test.

WHO Guideline for the Diagnosis of Osteoporosis

Bone mineral density value (T-Score)	*Classification*
> -1	**Normal**
-1 to -2.5	**Osteopenia**
-2.5 or lower	**Osteoporosis**

Results

Table 1: Distribution of Selected Women according to Bone Mineral Density

S. No.	*Bone Mineral Density*	*No. of Respondents*	*Percentage*
1.	T-Score (>-1) Normal	86	27.22
2.	T-Score (-1 to -2.5) Osteopenia	146	46.20
3.	T-Score ($\leq$ -2.5) Osteoporosis	84	26.58
	Total	316	100

To study the prevalence of osteoporosis was one of the prime objectives of the study. The finding after the screening of bone mineral density of selected women by using P-DEXA scan machine is presented in Table 1. The results of the study shows that among the women selected for this study, 27.22 percent women were normal, while 46.2 percent had osteopenia and 26.58 percent had osteoporosis.

In comparison, an earlier study reported that the prevalence of osteopenia and osteoporosis in the lumbar spine of the urban Indian pre- and post-menopausal women aged between 40 and 75 years was 48.4 percent and 25.8 percent respectively (Kadam *et al.*, 2010). Our estimations of prevalence of osteoporosis (26.58 percent) were similar when compared with other studies, like, in Hyderabad (29 percent) among the women in the low-income group aged between 30 and 60 years (Shatrugna *et al.*,

2005), followed by Jammu (20.25 percent) among the urban women aged between 25 and 65 years (Sharma *et al.*, 2006). It is observed that 1 in 2 women are at risk for fractures related to osteoporosis during her lifetime (US Department of Health and Human Services, 2004) and as far as India is concerned it is estimated that about 61 million Indians have osteoporosis and among them 80 percent patients are females (Joshi *et al.*, 1998). However, among the women from low-income group aged between 30 and 60 years, bone mineral density at all skeletal sites was much lower than value reported from developing countries, with a high prevalence of osteopenia (52 percent) and osteoporosis (29 percent) (International Osteoporotic Foundation Report, 2015).

Table 2: Distribution of Prevalence of Osteoporosis according to Occupation of the Respondents

S. No.	*Occupational Status*	*Osteopenic*		*Osteoporotic*		*Normal*		*Total*	
		n	*%*	*n*	*%*	*n*	*%*	*n*	*%*
1.	Professionals	48	32.88	25	29.76	29	33.72	102	32.28
2.	Self Employed	18	12.33	12	14.29	11	12.79	38	12.03
3.	Home Maker	80	54.79	47	55.95	46	53.49	176	55.69
	Total	146	100	84	100	86	100	316	100

c (cal) = 0.44 **NS****
c (tab) = 9.48 **(At 5% level of Significance)**
d.f. = 4 ****Non-Significant**

The data regarding occupational status of the respondents was gathered and represented in Table 2 and observations of the study show that majority of women (55.69 percent) were home makers and among them 55.95 percent had osteoporosis and 54.79 percent had osteopenia. Among the selected women 32.28 percent had professional occupation, while 12.03 percent were self-employed and among them 29.76 percent and 14.29 percent had osteoporosis respectively.

The statistical interpretations of the data show that there is no significant difference ($P \geq 0.05$) between the data regarding occupational status and prevalence of osteoporosis among the women. So it could be stated that the occupational status of the respondents is not positively associated with the prevalence of osteoporosis.

Similar findings were recorded in the study which estimated the influence of education and occupation on the skeletal status of the women in Poland and the data shows that occupation of the women were not positively linked with osteoporosis. But the data may suggest that occupational status of the women may have impacts on implementation of osteoporosis preventing Health Programs (Pluskiewich *et al.*, 2014). Further, in another assessment of prevalence of osteoporosis among the urban Iranian post-menopausal women, it was revealed that occupation is an independent factor for the occurrence of osteoporosis (Keramat *et al.*, 2005). The contrary data was reported among the rural and urban women of Vietnam that skeletal status (Osteoporosis) was significantly associated with life-long occupation (Vu *et al.*, 2005). As far as the Indian data is concerned, a cross sectional study among the Indian women highlighted the problem of poor bone health, who engaged in the repetitive work. Load bearing activities were not associated with better bone health probably due to the absence of adequate nutrition (Shatrugna *et al.*, 2005).

Table 3: Distribution of Prevalence of Osteoporosis according to Educational status of the Respondents

S. No.	*Educational Status*	*Osteopenic*		*Osteoporotic*		*Normal*		*Total*	
		n	*%*	*n*	*%*	*n*	*%*	*n*	*%*
1.	Illiterate	25	17.12	8	9.52	10	11.63	43	13.60
2.	High School	29	19.86	18	21.43	19	22.09	64	20.26
3.	Intermediate	13	8.90	32	38.1	16	18.60	61	19.30
4.	Graduate	47	32.2	16	19.1	25	29.07	90	28.48
5.	Post-Graduate	32	21.92	10	11.90	16	18.69	58	18.36
	Total	146	100	84	100	86	100	316	100

c (cal) = 32.60 **S***
c (tab) = 15.05 **(At 5% level of Significance)**
d.f. = 8 ***Significant**

The data in Table 3 represents distribution of osteoporosis according to the educational status of the respondents. It shows that maximum women (28.48%) were graduates while 13.60 percent were illiterate. According to the distribution with prevalence of osteoporosis, it was examined that women with no or poor education, like only high school and intermediate level, had high prevalence of osteoporosis, i.e. 9.52 percent, 21.43 percent and 38.1 percent respectively. The contrary data revealed among the women with higher education, like upto graduation and post graduate level, had lower prevalence of osteoporosis in comparison with other groups being 19.1 percent and 11.9 percent respectively.

The statistical representation of the data shows that there is significant difference ($P \leq 0.05$) between the data regarding educational status and prevalence of osteoporosis among the respondents.

Similar result was also reported in a study conducted among the Italian women that prevalence of osteoporosis varied with the educational status of the respondents and higher educational status plays a protective factor for the occurrence of osteoporosis (1999). Another study also showed a positive association of educational level and prevalence of osteoporosis among the post-menopausal women of Iran (Maddah, *et al.*, 2011). These studies recommended the importance of consideration of educational status of the respondents in the epidemiological survey related with osteoporosis. A study which was conducted among the Chinese post-menopausal women showed that higher level of education is independently associated with better BMD and lower prevalence of osteoporosis (Ho *et al.*, 2005).

CONCLUSION

The present study concluded that the prevalence of osteopenia (46.20%) was very high among the pre-menopausal women, while the prevalence of osteoporosis (26.58%) was very high among the post-menopausal women. This study revealed an alarming situation in context with bone health of pre-menopausal women as most of the women had osteopenia which may lead to osteoporosis after the menopause due to loss of hormonal control of female hormone estrogen. The findings also revealed that educational status of women showed a very strong association with the prevalence of osteoporosis and considered as a contributing risk factor for the prevalence of Osteoporosis.

RECOMMENDATION

Early detection of osteoporosis could facilitate appropriate interventions at an age when measures could maximize bone accrual and minimize loss over a much longer period after menopause. So it is recommended that pre- and post-menopausal women go through the DEXA screening of the BMD for early detection of loss of bone mineral density and adopt a healthy dietary pattern, appropriate lifestyle modifications and proper education to reduce this loss.

REFERENCES

1. Foundation No (2010). Clinician's Guide to Prevention and treatment of Osteoporosis, National Osteoporotic Foundation, Washington.
2. Facts and Statistics, International Osteoporotic Foundation, (2015)
3. Handa, R., Ali Kalla, A. and Maalouf, G. (2008). Osteoporosis in developing Countries, *Best Pract. Res. Clin. Rheumatol*, **22**:693-708.
4. Ho, S.C., Chen, Y.M., Woo, J.L. (2005). Educational level and osteoporosis risk in postmenopausal Chinese women. *Am J Epidemiol.* **161(7):** 680-90.

5. Jaipal, H.P. and Gora, M. (2015). Osteoporosis: The Emerging Silent Killer, *Indian Journal of Applied Research*, **5(2):** 423-24.
6. Joshi, V. R., Mangat, G., Balakrishnan, C., Mittal, G. (1998). Osteoporosis–approach in Indian scenario. *J Assoc Physicians India*. **46**:965–7.
7. Kadam, N., Chiplonkar, S., Khadilkar, A., Divate, U., Khadilkar, V. (2010). Low bone mass in urban Indian women above 40 years of age: prevalence and risk factors. *Gynecol Endocrinol*. **26(12)**:909-17.
8. Maddah, M., Sharami, S.H. and Karandish, M. (2011) Educational difference in the prevalence of osteoporosis in postmenopausal women: a study in northern Iran. *BMC Public Health*, **11**:845.
9. Pluskiewicz, W., Adamczyk, P., Czekajlo, A., Grzeszczak, W., Drozdzowska, B. (2014). Influence of education, marital status, occupation, and the place of living on skeletal status, fracture prevalence, and the course and effectiveness of osteoporotic therapy in women in the RAC-OST-POL Study. *J Bone Miner Metab.*, **32(1):** 89-95.
10. Shatrugna, V., Kulkarni, B., Kumar, P. A., Rani, K. U., Balakrishna, N. (2005) Bone status of Indian women from a low-income group and its relationship to the nutritional status. *Osteoporos Int*, **16:** 1827-183.
11. Sharma, S., Tandon, V. R., Mahajan, A., Kour, A., Kumar, D. (2006). Preliminary screening of osteoporosis and osteopenia in urban women from Jammu using calcaneal QUS. *Indian J Med Sci.*, **60(5)**: 183-9.
12. US Department of Health and Human Services (2004). Bone Health and Osteoporosis: A Report of the Surgeon General. Rockville, MD: US Department of Health and Human Services Office of the Surgeon General.
13. Vu, T.T., Nguyen, C.K., Nguyen, T.L., Le, B.M., Nguyen Trung, L. D., Bui, T.N., Nakamori, M., Kunii, D., Sakai, T., Yamamoto, S. (2005). Determining the prevalence of osteoporosis and related factors using quantitative ultrasound in Vietnamese adult women. *Am J Epidemiol.*; **161(9)**:824-30.
14. Varenna, M., Binelli, L., Zucchi, F., Ghiringhelli, D., Gallazzi, M., Sinigaglia, L. (1999) Prevalence of osteoporosis by educational level in a cohort of postmenopausal women. *Osteoporos Int.*: **9(3)**:236-41.
15. WHO Study Group (1994). Assessment of Fracture Risk and its Application to Screening for Post-Menopausal Osteoporosis. Assessment of fracture risk and its application it screening for post-menopausal osteoporosis: Report of a WHO study group. Geneva: WHO (WHO technical series 843.)

SECTION 3

INCLUSION AND ECONOMIC DEVELOPMENT THROUGH EMPOWERMENT OF RURAL WOMEN AND RURAL DEVELOPMENT

9

An Analysis of Financial Inclusion through Various Government Schemes in Uttarakhand, India

Vinay Kandpal

ABSTRACT

Three flagship schemes have been introduced by Prime Minister Mr. Narendra Modi which could be considered as a big initiative towards inclusive finance. This paper is an attempt to analyze the inclusive finance through various schemes of Social Security which can be a viable option for inclusive growth in India. It also studies the level of awareness about financial inclusion forces among rural households. The primary data for the research was collected using different questionnaires for people from people living in semi-urban and rural areas of Kumaun and Garhwal Region of Uttarakhand, India. In this study a sample size of 500 people from semi-urban and rural areas was taken from different districts of Uttarakhand. The data for the study also uses secondary sources of information. The majority of people do not use the banking services and are unaware of financial instruments or various social security schemes which could be used as an investment option. They generally fear to enter banks and fulfil their financial requirement or borrow money through money lenders which charges a higher rate of interest. Financial literacy is a major area that needs to be worked upon so the role of RBI has increased for spreading awareness regarding functioning of a bank and the benefits of putting money in the bank or in financial instruments. Government of India and RBI should make efforts to reach the rural population or the untouched segment of society through the expansion of banking services and with the help of financial literacy campaign which could serve the purpose of inclusive growth of every segment. The introduction of some of the schemes is good and will be beneficial for society if properly implemented. There is a need to motivate people to save and that could be possible only when their source of earning is improved. Opening of Jan Dhan or No-frill account will not by itself prove beneficial for banks as the earning of bank will improve when the people save money and put it in banks.

Keywords: *Social Security, inclusive, finance, mutual fund.*

INTRODUCTION

A strong and steady financial system is a pillar of economic growth, development and progress of an economy. A financial system, which is inherently strong, functionally mottled and displays efficiency and flexibility, is critical to our national objectives of creating a market-driven, productive and competitive economy. A mature system supports higher levels of investment and promotes growth in the economy with its depth and coverage. In the contemporary era of achieving economic power and self-reliance, it is authoritative for any regime to create congenial conditions for individuals, households and private institutions. The availability of banking facilities and strong bank branch network are the major facilitators of developmental and expansionary activities. In turn, the economic agents facilitate growth, development, investment, employment generation, infrastructure improvement. The Indian economy is the second fastest growing economy in the world. The majority of the population in India resides in rural areas. Thus, the development of rural India is a key step towards economic development of a country like ours. India has a huge network of institutional credit.

Notwithstanding the rapid increase in overall GDP and per capita income in recent years, a significant proportion of the population in both rural and urban areas still experience difficulties in accessing the formal financial system. There is currently a perception that there are a large number of people, potential entrepreneurs, small enterprises and others, who may not have acceptable access to the financial sector, which could lead to their marginalization and denial of opportunity to grow and prosper. Financial inclusion can be designated as the process of providing and confirming timely access to a range of financial products and services at reasonable costs by sound institutions in a fair and transparent manner to all sections of the society expressly to the vulnerable groups such as weaker sections and low-income groups. Inclusive financial systems allow producers and households to smoothen their production and consumption of good and services through which income is generated in an economy. Thus, financial inclusion drives income generation through increasing productive capacity, especially among those without assets to start with and facilitates inclusive growth. India has a functioning financial market/ system comprising money market, forex market, capital market, debt market to cater to financial needs and requirements of various participants and segments of society. It ensures a smooth and efficient flow of monetary resources, meeting the funding needs required for growth and prosperity.

The banking industry has shown tremendous growth in volume and complexity over the last decade or so. Despite making significant improvements in all the areas relating to financial viability, profitability and competitiveness, there are concerns that much needed banking services have not reached a vast segment of the population, especially the underprivileged sections of the society. Internationally, also efforts are being made to study the causes of financial exclusion and designing strategies to ensure financial inclusion of the poor and disadvantaged. The reasons may vary from country to country and hence the strategy could also vary, but all out efforts are being made as financial inclusion can truly lift the financial condition and standards of life of the poor and the disadvantaged. In the last twenty years, India has undergone a transformation of its economic and regulatory structures. Steps have been taken by the Government to educate the people about the banking services and financial instruments available for investment. Despite various attempts access to finance has remained infrequent in rural and semi-urban areas of India. Financial inclusion is mainly concerned with unrestricted access to public goods and services which is crucial for the growth of the economy. The unawareness about banking services and financial instruments in rural and semi-urban areas is a matter of concern. The rural and even semi-urban people are unaware about the financial instruments and banking services. They generally fear to enter banks and fulfil their financial requirement through money lenders which charge a higher rate of interest. Financial inclusion has become crucial for inclusive development of the economy. Inclusive financial system helps the deprived section of people to get access to formal credit, saving products and other services which help them to overcome poverty and to reduce income inequality existing in the Indian economy. Government of India and Reserve Bank of India should make efforts to reach the rural population through the expansion of banking services.

Prime Minister Narendra Modi announced a new scheme in his Independence Day speech on 15th Aug 2014 and called it the National Mission on Financial Inclusion (NMFI) for weaker section and low-income groups. An ambitious flagship program of financial inclusion scheme, Prime Minister Jan Dhan Scheme was launched by Prime Minister

Narendra Modi's on August 28, 2014. The major objective was to benefit the Aam Aadmi or common people of India with a lot of benefits for the Indian families. The want of conventional banking and cash are some of the toughest constraints in the rural regions of India. The Jan Dhan Scheme might be the best strategy to defeat this. Jan Dhan Scheme has made its way into the Guinness World Records for opening the highest number of bank accounts in a short period time. The success of the scheme was indeed fabulous, but still a lot of serious attempts are required in order to make financial inclusion programme a success. After Jan Dhan and providing bank accounts to 15 crore unbanked people, Prime Minister Narendra Modi launched three social security schemes. These are: Pradhan Mantri Jeevan Jyoti Bima Yojana (PMJJBY) and Pradhan Mantri Suraksha Bima Yojana (PMSBY) and Atal Pension Yojana (APY). Establishing linkages of three social security schemes with bank accounts will go a long way in expanding penetration of insurance and pension in the country and serve the cause of extending universal social security cover in most economical and efficient manner.

According to a report a massive 80% of the country's population is still outside the insurance coverage while the government estimated that merely 11% of the working population is under pension net. The new life insurance plan—the Pradhan Mantri Jeevan Jyoti Bima Yojana will offer Rs 2 lakh cover at Rs 330 premium every year. Bank account holders in the ages 18 to 50 years are eligible to avail this facility. The life risk cover will get terminated after 55 years. Pradhan Mantri Suraksha Bima Yojana will offer a renewable one year accidental death cum disability cover of Rs 2 lakh at Rs 12 premium every year. The insured will get Rs 1 lakh in case of partial permanent disability.

Atal Pension Yojana is for the people in the unorganized sector who are outside a formal pension net so far. The pension scheme would allow subscribers of ages 18 to 40. The government has promised to co-contribute 50% of the total contribution or Rs 1000 per annum, whichever is lower, for the first five years. Subscribers without any social security and who do not pay income tax will get this added benefit. However, people had to enrol themselves before December 31, 2017 to get government contribution. The financial inclusion attempt through this initiative still remains restricted to urban and semi-urban areas. The social security schemes would serve as a good option if awareness regarding its benefits is properly passed. The majority of accounts opened through this scheme are opened in public sector banks. Hence there is a need that private sector banks come forward and get involved in the activities of financial inclusion.

Literature Review

Beck and Torre (2007) suggest that expanding access to financial services should include identifying different demand and supply constraints, including both supply and demand side frictions that can lead to lower access and analyzing it. The analysis helps identify unbanked and banked population, and the binding constraint to close the gap between the two.

Beck et al. (2007a) developed indicators of access for three types of financial services, namely deposits, loas, and payments across three dimensions, viz. physical access, affordability, and eligibility. They mention that barriers such as availability of locations, minimum balance, fees, interest rates, documents requirements and procedure time vary across countries and are negatively correlated with access to financial services. These barriers have been measured by them in terms of branch and ATM penetration, by income quintile per population for physical access; number of documents required to open a checking account for eligibility; and number of days to process a SME loan application, minimum balance required to open a checking account, minimum balances and costs of transferring funds with respect to fees for affordability. These have important policy implications for expanding access to poor. They also document that barriers are lower in countries with higher income, better contractual/information systems, greater openness and competition in banking, greater transparency standards, media freedom, and greater market discipline.

Raghuram Rajan Committee (2007) views financial inclusion, broadly, "as universal access to a wide range of financial services at a reasonable cost. These include not only banking products but also other financial services such as insurance and equity products".

Mandira Sarma and Jesim Paise (2008) suggest that the issue of financial inclusion is a development policy priority in many countries. Using the index of financial inclusion developed in levels of human development and financial inclusion in a country move closely with each other, although a few exceptions exist. Among socio-economic factors, as expected, income is positively associated with the level of financial inclusion. Further physical and electronic connectivity and information availability, indicated by road network, telephone and Internet usage, also play positive role in enhancing financial inclusion.

Collins et al. (2009) show that financial activities are most often driven by a basic set of needs: daily food, illness, and other sizeable expenses including investment opportunities as they arise. None of these needs are tied to running small businesses, and yet all are equally important for everyone. Hence, access to finance has become access to financial services to provide credit, savings, payment and insurance rather than primarily delivering microcredit.

According to the Planning Commission (2009) financial inclusion refers to universal access to a wide range of financial services at a reasonable cost. These include not only banking products but also other financial services such as insurance and equity products. The household access to financial services includes access to contingency planning, credit and wealth creation. Access to contingency planning would help for future savings such as retirement savings, buffer savings and insurable contingencies and access to credit includes emergency loans, housing loans and consumption loans. On the other hand, access to wealth creation includes savings and investment based on household's level of financial literacy and risk perception.

Ellis et al. (2010) for the first time show a clear link between access to financial services and the ability of households to invest in education or a business, that can contribute to economic growth and alleviate poverty. They also evidence that semi-formal and informal financial services are very important in providing access, but formal financial services tend to be used more for investment purposes.

Joseph Massey (2010) said that role of financial institutions in a developing country is vital in promoting financial inclusion. The efforts of the government to promote financial inclusion and deepening can be further enhanced by the pro-activeness on the part of capital market players including financial institutions. Financial institutions have a very crucial and a wider role to play in fostering financial inclusion. National and international forum have recognized this and efforts are seen on domestic and global levels to encourage the financial institutions to take up larger responsibilities in including the financially excluded lot.

Honohan and King (2012) evidence that income and education is key demand/user side determinants of access to financial services. The results show that improving financial sector knowledge is associated with a significant increase in being formally banked. RBI has already taken a step in this direction by engaging Business Facilitators (BF). Summarily, even if financial institutions expand their reach, bringing credit, savings, and micro-insurance to those previously without access, potential poor often do not readily adopt the range of offerings. That's not because the services aren't needed; rather, those who would benefit most from these products often have no experience with formal financial services and often don't see them as a likely part of their lives.

King (2012) evidences the characteristics of 'unbanked' households with lower incomes, lower education, without an access to a mobile, and have lower levels of financial sector knowledge and number of formal documents in their name than the remainder of the population.

Development Research Project (2013) attempted to understand the financial needs of poor in the long-term and short-term by exploring how surplus fund is used to meet short-term, long-term and emergency requirements to develop strategies for financial inclusion and designing financial products. The rural households follow their own strategies of cash management for their daily expenditure and thereby taking advantage of this, several informal financial institutions and instruments are serving this section of society. In this context, the report examines 107 households of Ernakulum district in Kerala, as was suggested by the RBI. The aim of the study was to understand the nature of the cash flows and outflows of a sample of poor households in the district. The project also analyzed the cash flow management strategies of the poor households. Further assessment was done to analyze the structure of the financial assets and liabilities of the poor households. The project focuses on the saving patterns of the poor households and also examined factors responsible for the extent of dependence of the poor on formal and informal financial instruments/ institutions for savings and credit.

V. Ganesh Kumar (2013) noted that branch density in a state measures the opportunity for financial inclusion in India. Literacy is a prerequisite for creating investment awareness, and hence intuitively it seems to be a key tool for financial inclusion. But the above observations imply that literacy alone cannot guarantee high level financial inclusion in a state. Branch density has significant impact on financial inclusion. It is not possible to achieve financial inclusion only by creating investment awareness, without significantly improving the investment opportunities in an India.

OBJECTIVES OF STUDY

The objectives of this study are as follows:

1. To examine the level of awareness about financial inclusion forces among rural households.
2. To analyze the inclusive finance through various schemes of Social Security which can be viable option for inclusive growth in India?

3. To find out the strategies implemented by Reserve Bank of India and performance of different banks towards financial inclusion

Research Methodology

A research design is the specification of methods and procedures for acquiring the needed information. Then design adopted was descriptive as well as empirical research. The primary data was collected with the help of structured questionnaire. This study had separate questionnaires for Managers in different public and private sector banks and for people in semi-urban and rural areas. It basically seeks to extract information about financial inclusion from people living in semi-urban and rural areas of Kumaun and Garhwal Region of Uttarakhand, India. In this study a sample size of 500 people from semi-urban and rural areas were taken from different districts of Uttarakhand. The data for the study also used secondary data that was sourced from RBI bulletin, annual reports of RBI and Ministry of Finance, Government of India, Report on trends and progress of banking in India, various reputed journals, newspapers and websites of RBI, NABARD (National Bank for Agricultural and Rural Development) and Ministry of Finance, Government of India (GOI). For the purpose of analyzing the primary and secondary data and for hypothesis testing, an appropriate statistical tool was used.

Summary of Findings

Three flagships Yojna have been introduced recently by Prime Minister Narendra Modi which could be considered as a big initiative. The schemes include a life-insurance scheme named Prime Minister Accidental Insurance Scheme, an accidental death or disability insurance scheme named Prime Minister Life Insurance Scheme and a pension scheme named Prime Minister Atal Pension Scheme which have been already launched. The objective of these schemes is to give social security to the large unorganized and untouched people of the Indian society, which has largely been deprived of any such benefits and thus remain financially backward. The introduction of Jan Dhan Schemes, Atal Pension Scheme, Prime Minister Insurance Schemes are great ideas. There is a need to motivate people to save and that could be possible only when their source of earning is improved. Opening of account will not by itself prove beneficial for banks as the earning of bank will improve when the people save money and put it in banks.

ANALYSIS AND INTERPRETATIONS

Basically the households were selected from the rural and semi-urban areas of different parts of Uttarakhand and the comparison was made. The Survey carried out, covered several aspects regarding the issues of financial inclusion, micro-finance, etc. The emphasis was given on the trend followed with respect to forsavings by the villagers and poor people.

1. **Type of occupation:** As of enquired samples the figures which came out as a count of occupation can be defined as follows, as in rural areas and semi-urban areas count largely describes the huge number of farmers and labourers. In rural areas and some semi-urban areas the income ranges of people is very low so they have very less amount of savings to be kept in bank. Our study found that the average number of family members earning in a family came out to be 2 and the average number of persons in a family came out to be 5.
2. **Number of Households having A Bank Account:** Out of a sample size 500 rural and semi-urban people surveyed, 60% of household were having a bank account, whereas 40% did not even have a single bank account. This describes the belief that financial exclusion is widespread in India and much needs to be done to spread financial awareness.
3. **Number of Account in a Household:** In the analysis 50% rural households had just one account, 30% of people had 2 accounts, 10% of households had 3 accounts, 6% of households had 4 accounts and 4% of households had more than 4 accounts. The observation was made among the people who have a bank account. This analysis should be taken into consideration before we declare that 100% financial inclusion has been accomplished. It has to be ensured that there is a transparency when we are comparing the number of accounts and the number of households. It has to be guaranteed that each household has at least one bank account. In case of rural households, there exists a less number of households with more than three accounts. The accounts include savings, current, recurring as well as fixed deposit. In actual fact, we encounter a few households having double the number of accounts than the number of members in the family.
4. **Households having facility of cheque book in their bank account:** In rural areas the amount comes out after certain interpretation of data. The percentage and number of people availing the facility of cheque book comes out to be 20% and 100. The result is due to the

fact that dealings of most of these households are generally made in cash. The kind of transaction mode preferred by these people is cash exchange. The essential factor for this data would be depending upon the fact of the high illiteracy rate among these sections.

5. **Reasons behind opening a Bank account:** In rural and semi-urban households, while 50% have opened accounts for the individual purpose of receiving government payments. Twenty per cent rural households and semi urban people are inclined in availing credit from financial institutions and they depend mostly on money lenders charging higher interest. Savings are very less so only 20% of the people are putting their money in banks and rest open account s for receiving remittances.
6. **Reasons For Not Having a Bank Account:** Fifty-five per cent of the household do not have a single bank account as they do not have much money to put in the account. The barrier or problem may be about the perception of the people that the process of opening the account would be too lengthy or complicated and the charges or fees would be too high. None reported that having bank account was not important to them. As for the process, 35% of neglected people thought that the entire process of having a bank account is tedious and rest of the 10% thought that there would be too many charges in opening an account.
7. **Reasons for refusal of Bank Account to open:** As analyzed in the survey, the primary reason for the refusal on opening a bank account was the Know Your Cuctomer norms not being fulfilled. The lack of legal identity proof like identity cards, Aadhaar card, birth certificates, address proof, income proof and other formalities came out as the major reasons in the exclusion of women and, especially, migrant workers who most likely do not to an address proof. There were also people complaining that their form of applications were complete rejected without bank authorities offering any clarification. This does come as a surprise considering the indifferent attitude of officials towards the underprivileged groups whom they do not consider a sustainable business occasion.
8. **Awareness related to No-frill Accounts:** Awareness regarding these accounts was limited to a certain people of rural sections, as the No-Frill account awareness was made only in some of the regions by the bank officials and NGOs. In this account the maintenance of minimum charges is not mandatory at the end of the certain period; this type of account would be useful for the

poor and underprivileged people. As the account does not require any sort of token money at a stage the account would help the villagers to enjoy the advantages offered in these accounts. In some places the village Panchayat was also involved in the process. But during the course of the survey any poster regarding No-frill accounts was not found to create awareness of these facilities. With bank employees adopting such an insensitive and indifferent attitude towards the needs of the underprivileged groups, there is no doubt the scheme will take an indefinite period to take off in a full-driven manner.

9. **Sources for borrowing loans for household:** It was observed that requirements of urban households by financial institutions, especially banks play a major role in fulfilling the credit. In case of rural households, it happens mostly through moneylenders. When it comes to immediate and small borrowings, the mainstream prefers taking help from their friends and relatives, which is why the proportion of households in rural and urban areas remains relatively close to each other. In rural areas, households do not have a broader choice in the other category, which was seen to be controlled by the firms in which they worked. People found it much easier to approach their employers asking for loans than going to a bank, which they believed would be a complicated process. It is also easier to repay such a borrowing as the instalment is deducted from their salaries right from the source. As in case of this study the data can be analyzed as the people of rural households generally prefer relatives and friends for borrowing loan. But vast people of this segment also prefer borrowing amount from the moneylenders as that can be locally available without much pain. As compared from the past times the role of moneylender has decreased with most people exploring and approaching other possible sources like banks and regional authorities.
10. **The reasons stated for borrowing from Banks:** People generally do not approach a bank to borrow an amount of money, but as of now the time is changing and a shift has been noticed. For majority of respondents in rural as well as semi-urban households, 'bank being a trustworthy lender' and 'low rate of interest' were the primary reasons behind availing of credit facilities from banks. Most of the people were impressed by the interest rates offered by the banks for big loans. The low rate of interest of the banks attracts a lot of customers in both sectors, i.e. semi-urban and rural sections.
11. **Reasons for borrowing from other sources than banks:** In this

analyzed data it can be seen that other borrowing sources regardless of the bank, borrowing from the friends and relatives and moneylenders comes into the act. Borrowing from friends and relatives can be justified on the grounds of it being generally security free, which is also evident from the plot. Reasons for borrowing from moneylenders can be clarified only by looking at the other category in which respondents said they had no relatives or friends who could even afford to lend a relatively large amount of sum. This situation is obvious because poor households are more likely to have relatives who themselves are struck in poverty. Borrowing from the moneylenders at overpriced rates can shows the compulsions these poor people face being in a huge trap of poverty and debt. This is clearly due to illiteracy and ignorance. This also highlights how inaccessible some of our banks have become to poor households. Most of these respondents have developed a fear of stepping into a bank, which has been augmented to an extent, by the banks themselves by creating tedious procedures for those who are in terrible need of credit. Ultimately, finding no other means, these people fall into the controls of such non-institutional financial intercessors.

CONCLUSION

The majority of people do not visit banks as they perceive that lots of formalities and charges are involved in opening an account. Sixty per cent of the people from rural and semi-urban areas have a bank account. Limited amount of money to put in the bank and literacy level are also serving as constraints for people not visiting the bank. The majority of the people depend upon cash transactions. Financial inclusion has become crucial for inclusive development of the economy. Inclusive financial system helps the deprived section of people to get access to formal credit, saving products and other services that reduce poverty and income inequality existing in the Indian economy. The introduction of Jan Dhan Yojna is a great endeavour, but steps need to be initiated in the direction of financial inclusion or financial awareness program. There is a need to motivate people to save and that could be possible only when their source of earning is improved. Opening of account will not itself provide beneficial for banks as the earning of bank will improve when the people save money and put it in banks. Some people in rural and semi-urban areas are aware of social security schemes. Atal pension Yojana is not known to the majority. Recently, Government of India has taken a major step by banning Rs 500 and Rs 1000 notes which will have long-term impacts across different sectors. This will also have an impact on Financial inclusion initiatives with crores of money flowing into the banks and the untouched segment visiting bank branches for the first time. Bankers have a major role to play by setting up a better service to every customer so that those who do not have accounts are encouraged to have one, avail services and invest in financial instruments.

REFERENCES

1. 'Aadhaar' number to act as valid document to open bank account. Retrieved on April 7th, 2013, from http://www.thehindu.com/news/national/aadhaar-number-to-act-as-valid-document-to-open-bank-account/article967952.ece.
2. Agarwal, Anmol, "The need for financial inclusion with an Indian perspective", *Economic Research*, March 3, 2008, pp.1-10
3. Ashley Coutinho, 2013, "Top 15 cities still corner bulk of mutual fund assets". Retrieved April 10th, 2013, from http://www.financialexpress.com/news/top-15-cities-still-corner-bulk-of-mutual-fund-assets/1107675
4. Beck, T. H. L., and Torre, de La., (2007), "The basic analytics of access to financial services", *Financial Markets, Institutions and Instruments*, Vol. 16(2), 79-117.
5. Beck, T., Kunt, A. D., and Levine, R., (2004), "Finance, Inequality and Poverty", World Bank Policy Research Working Paper 3338.
6. Beck, T., Kunt, A.D., and Peria, M.S.M., (2007a), "Banking Services for Everyone? Barriers to Bank Access and Use around the World", Policy Research Working Paper 4079, World Bank, Washington, DC.
7. Bhandari, Amit K (2009), "Access to banking services and poverty reduction: A state wise assessment in India", IZA Discussion paper Series, pp. 1-14.
8. Chakrabarty, K.C., "Financial Inclusion: A road India needs to travel" (2011). Retrieved April 7th, 2013, from http://www.livemint.com/2011/09/21211250/Financial-Inclusion—A-road-I.html.
9. Chandan, Kumar and Srijit, Mishra. (2011) "Banking Outreach and Household level Access: Analyzing Financial Inclusion in India", M.Phil. Thesis, Indira Gandhi Institute of Development Research (IGIDR), Mumbai.
10. Collins, D., Morduch, J., Rutherford, S., and Ruthven, O. (2009), *Portfolios of the Poor: How the World's Poor Live on $2 a Day*, Princeton University Press, Princeton.
11. Financial inclusion. Retrieved April 7th, 2013, from http://en.wikipedia.org/wiki/Financial_inclusion
12. Ghatak, Sushmita, "Financial inclusion through Mutual Funds" (2011). Retrieved on April 7th, 2013, from http://www.indianexpress.com/news/financial-inclusion-through-mutual-funds/746909/0.
13. Gokaran, Subir, "Mutual Funds and Market Development in India". Retrieved on April 7th, 2013, from http://www.rbi.org.in/scripts/BS_SpeechesView.aspx?Id=584
14. King, M., (2012), "The Unbanked Four-Fifths: Barriers to Financial Services in Nigeria", IIIS Discussion Paper No.411, October 2012, Trinity College, Dublin.
15. Pandey, A. Raman, R. (2013), "Financial inclusion in Uttar Pradesh and Bihar", Prajnan-NIBM, Pune, XLI(2), pp. 125–46.
16. Pandi G. R. & Selvakumar M. (2012), "Financial Inclusion in India", *Economic*

Affairs, 57(2), pp. 119–25.

17. Ramji, Minakshi. (2009), "Financial inclusion in Gulburga: Finding usage in Access Centre for Microfinance" Institute for Financial Management and Research. Chennai. Working Paper Series No. 26, January.
18. Sangram, Panigarh and Shah, Deepak (2011), "Financial inclusion of households living below poverty line: An empirical findings from Gulbarga District of Karnataka. Growth with equity inclusion". Department of Commerce, Pondicherry University.
19. Sharma, Mandira and Pais, Jesim (2008), "Financial Inclusion and Development: A Cross Country Analysis", *Indian Council for Research on International Economic Relations*.
20. Sridhar, V. "Ring fencing banks", April 6, 2013. Retrieved on March 14, 2013, from http://www.flonnet.com/fl2419/stories/20071005502703500.html
21. Srijanani, D. (2012). "Financial inclusion: Taking banking services to the common man", *International Journal of Management and Business Studies*, 2(3), pp. 54–8.
22. NABARD (2004), "Progress of SHG-Bank Linkage in India 2003-2004", National Bank for Agriculture and Rural Development, Mumbai.

10

An Analysis of the Factors Affecting Women Marketers of Agricultural Produce

J.D. Aarthi Dhakshana and K.V.R. Rajandran

ABSTRACT

Women have been a major backbone of agricultural workforce, especially in developing countries like India. Singh and Sengupta (2009) stated that the Indian women contribute 75.38% of workforce in agriculture sector. Within agriculture sector, 94% of women are involved in crop cultivation especially cereal production and other crops. Though their effort is high, but the recognition is very low. Women participation in agriculture includes labour workforce, producing agricultural crops, tending animals, trade and marketing, etc. This paper addresses the problems of vegetable marketing among women marketers in Kumbakonam Taluk, Thanjavur district, Tamil Nadu. The data has been collected from 202 vegetable women marketers. The simple random sampling techniques was used for sample size. Structured questionnaire method was used to collect data. The collected data were statistically evaluated using SPSS reliability test, regression tool. The research findings revealed that women marketers had unsupportive husband/family; tremendous workload; and lack of credit facility, social security, transport, market information, knowledge of crops, knowledge of harvesting and adequate storage.

Keywords: *Agriculture, Marketing, Thanjavur, Tamil Nadu, Women Marketers.*

1. INTRODUCTION

The position of women in any society has an important role in improving and sustaining the development in a civilization. Women have been making vital contribution in agricultural sector in the world. Women's contribution to agriculture, whether it is in farming or commercial agriculture, when measured in number of tasks performed and time spent is greater than that of men. A micro study conducted by the Shiva Enterprise in Indian Himalayas found that on a hectare farm, a pair of bullocks work for 1064 hours, a man for 1212 hours and a woman for 3485 hours (Shiva FAO, 1991). Numbers of agricultural works done by the women were highly invisible, unnoticed and unaccounted for. Women's potential is to be recognized, and to be utilized for productivity in marketing. The development of agricultural sector of our nation depended upon women workforce. In addition, women not only participated in the agricultural labour force and production, they were also involved in marketing. Thus, there is a need to find out the issues related to women participation in agricultural products' marketing.

1.1 Objective

- To study the role of women in agricultural marketing
- To analyse the factors affecting the women in agricultural marketing

1.2 Purpose of the Study

The purpose of this study is to determine the problems encountered by the women marketers and how it affects their marketing success. This would also reflect the positive government supportive and enhancement impact on the women marketers' success.

There are enormous research studies carried out on women marketers which have provided the evidences that agricultural produce marketing is often associated with myriads of problems. Studies that have been conducted on women marketers were limited in numbers. Therefore, the overall purpose of the study was to investigate the factors affecting the women while marketing their agricultural produce.

2. LITERATURE REVIEW

Mohammed Endris Harun (2014), examined women's workload and their role in agricultural production in Ambo district, Ethiopia. The sampling size of his study was 180. The findings revealed that, while women were found with less agricultural resources and low decision making power, they spent 26 hours per week in farm activities showing high rate of involvement in agricultural production. It was also found that marital status, income and age had significant impact on women participation in agricultural production. It is recommended that women agricultural productivity should be enhanced by improving their access to agricultural resources and developing policies and technologies targeting women-related agricultural activities.

Musa, Reuben and Magaji (2013), measured problems associated with agricultural produce marketing in Nigeria: the experience of women marketers of milled rice from southern Taraba State, Nigeria. The sampling size was 60. The results indicated that the major milled rice marketing problems include inadequate credit facilities, transportation problems, and inadequate market infrastructures. Responses of the selected respondents show that they are in dire need of agricultural marketing information.

Bibhu Santosh Behera and Anama Charan Behera (2013), reviewed the gender issues: the role of women in agriculture sector in India by conceptual framework. The statement detailed that, "Women's labor power is considered inferior because of employers predetermined notion of women's primary role as homemakers". As a result of discrimination against female labor, women were found to be concentrated in the secondary sector of labor market. Their work is low paid, low status, casual, and lacks potential upward mobility. The majority of women in the rural sector work in low-paying jobs.

Tahir Munir Butt, Zakaria Yousaf Hassan, Khalid Mehmood and Sher Muhammad (2010), determined the role of rural women in agricultural development and their constraints. The sampling size was 125. The researcher used simple random sampling techniques and the descriptive statistics tool for the analysis. The findings revealed that, technical constraints were lack of female extension staff, subject matter specialist for rural women, technical training, knowledge and skills. More than 95% of the respondents confirmed this finding. It was also concluded that maximum female extension officers need to be present in the field of agriculture as suggested by majority 64.0% of the respondents.

Manas Mondal (2013), researched "The Role of Rural Women In Agriculture Sector of Sagar Island", West Bengal. 10% of the total households were surveyed. Result showed that, the discrimination against female labour, women are concentrated in the secondary sector of labour market. Their work is low paid, low status, casual and lacks potential upward mobility. Recognition of women contribution in agriculture and its allied fields are imperative for reducing the gender issues in this field.

Hemla Aggarwal, Subita Sharma and Rajni Sharma (2013) conducted a study on agricultural activities performed by rural women and problems faced by them in Jammu District of J&K State. 150 respondents participated in the study. This study revealed that majority of the agricultural women workers suffered from minor health problems, management problems, social and financial problems.

3. RESEARCH METHODOLOGY

This research has adopted a descriptive research design. The women involved in marketing their agricultural produce were the target population, and a total number of 202 respondents participated in this study.

3.1 Sampling Method

Simple random sampling has been effective for the purpose of this study.

3.2 Data Collection Method

In this study both primary and secondary data were collected.

- *Primary Data*

Primary data have been collected from women vegetable farmers, who were marketing their produce in Kumbakonam taluk, Thanjavur district with the help of personal interview schedule. The research variables were measured on the basis of five-point scale.

Rating from 5 to 1, Strongly Agree (5), Agree (4), Neutral (3), Disagree (2), Strongly Disagree (1). The questionnaire was translated to the local language, Tamil for the convenience of the respondents.

Researchers have used close-ended questions that were easier to answer by respondents and also easier for interpretation and tabulation.

- *Secondary Data*

Secondary data was collected to add the value to the primary data from relevant websites, magazines, journals, thesis, reference books, daily newspapers, etc.

3.3 Tools for Analysis

- The reliability test (Cronbach's Alpha) was used to examine the quality of questionnaire.
- The regression analysis was used to find out the high impact independent variables with dependent variable.

3.4 Hypothesis

To verify the variables, hypotheses were constructed as shown below:

H1: There is a significant relationship between the women marketers' problem and unsupportive family/husband.

H2: There is a significant relationship between the women marketers' problem and workload.

H3: There is a significant relationship between the women marketers' problem and social security.

H4: There is a significant relationship between the women marketers' problem and knowledge on harvesting.

H5: There is a significant relationship between the women marketers' problem and credit facility.

H6: There is a significant relationship between the women marketers' problem and lack of market information.

H7: There is a significant relationship between the women marketers' problem and knowledge of crops.

H8: There is a significant relationship between the women marketers' problem and lack of transport.

H9: There is a significant relationship between the women marketers' problem and inadequate storage.

4. DATA ANALYSIS AND INTERPRETATION

4.1 Reliability

Table 1: Case Processing Summary

		N	%
Cases	Valid	202	100.0
	Excluded[a]	0	0.0
	Total	202	100.0

a. Listwise deletion based on all variables in the procedure.

Table 2: Reliability of Tool used

Reliability Statistics	
Cronbach's Alpha	*N of Items*
0.984	10

The measure of internal consistency that was used in this research was Chronbach's Co-efficient Alpha. From the calculation, the Cronbach's

Alpha of the data is 0.984 and based on level of reliability it's included as a very high reliability level.

4.2 Regression

Table 3: Model Summary

Model	*R*	*R Square*	*Adjusted R Square*	*Std. Error of the Estimate*
1	.948[a]	0.898	0.893	0.426

a. Predictors: (Constant), Adequate Storage, Transport, Social Security, Knowledge of Harvesting, Unsupportive Husband, Credit Facility, Work Load, Lack of Market Information, Knowledge of Harvesting.

The analysis findings show that there is a strong positive relationship between women marketers and adequate storage, transport, social security, knowledge of harvesting, unsupportive husband, credit facility, workload, lack of market information, knowledge of harvesting as derived from the co-efficient of determination r of 0.948 and a co-relation co-efficient R – 0.898. The result of regression analysis shows that up to 89.8% of dependent variable is affected by independent variable. The more the r square the more the independent variable predict the dependent variable

Standard error of estimates tells us about the dispersion of actual values from the regression line. This model gives a low figure of standard error of estimate, i.e. 0.426 meaning that actual data is only 42% dispersed from the regression line. Co-efficient of each variable indicates that the change in dependent variable could be expected from the change in particular variable while keeping all the other variables constant.

Table 4: ANOVA

		ANOVA[a]				
Model		*Sum of Squares*	*df*	*Mean Square*	*F*	*Sig.*
1	Regression	307.961	9	34.218	188.302	.000[b]
	Residual	34.89	192	0.182		
	Total	342.851	201			

a Dependent Variable: WOMEN MARKETERS
b Predictors: (Constant), Inadequate Storage, Transport, Social Security, Knowledge of Crop, Unsupportive Husband, Credit Facility, Workload, Lack of Market Information, Knowledge of Harvesting

F–Statistics were carried out to find overall strength of the model. The value of F statistics is 188.302 shows that the model is significant shown in table co-efficient. In Table 4, sum of square of regression represents the overall experimental effect (Inadequate Storage, Transport, Social Security, Knowledge Of Crop, Unsupportive Husband, Credit Facility, Workload, Lack of Market Information, Knowledge of Harvesting), whereas the mean square of the model represents the average experimental effect. Whereas, sum of square of residual shows that there are some unsystematic errors within data due to some natural incidence. Of all the information given in ANOVA Table 4 the major concern of the researcher is to focus on the value of "Sig." Columns. This column indicates that how likely it is that F-value of that size would have occurred by chance; in this case the probability is 0.000 which shows that the chances occurrence are less than 0.05%. If the P-value given in this column is less than the critical value, i.e. 0.05, set by researcher, then the effect is said to be more significant and the greater the value of P from critical value will give insignificant results. Table 4 has shown that our P-value is much less than 0.05, meaning that there is a significance between the variables. So we can say that there is a strong problem of inadequate storage, transport, social security, knowledge of crop, unsupportive husband, credit facility, work load, lack of market information, knowledge of harvesting for women marketers. The direction of relationship can be determined from the value of sum of square of regression, which is 307.961 much larger as compared to sum of square of errors, i.e. 34.89. It shows that a relationship exists between the variables.

Table 5: Co-efficients

		Co-efficients				
Model		*Unstandardized Co-efficients*		*Standardized Co-efficients*	*t*	*Sig.*
		B	*Std. Error*	*Beta*		
1	(Constant)	0.078	0.323		-0.24	0.810
	Unsupportive husband	0.85	0.102	0.724	8.299	0.000
	Work load	-0.333	0.147	-0.25	-2.262	0.025
	Social security	0.067	0.097	0.056	0.689	0.491
	Knowledge of crop	0.488	0.095	0.543	5.121	0.000
	Credit facility	0.212	0.12	0.15	1.76	0.080
	Lack of market information	-0.381	0.12	-0.334	-3.189	0.002
	Knowledge of harvesting	0.24	0.121	0.18	1.982	0.049
	Transport	-0.109	0.094	-0.07	-1.159	0.248
	Inadequate storage	-0.045	0.126	-0.029	-0.356	0.722

a Dependent Variable: Women Marketers.

Regression Model

Women Marketers = 0.078 + 0.724 (Unsupportive husband) + (-0.25) (workload) + 0.056 (Social security) + 0.543 (Knowledge of crop) + 0.15 (Credit facility) + (-0.334) (Lack of Market Information) + 0.18 (Knowledge of harvesting) + (-0.07) (Transport) + (0.029) (Inadequate storage)

Regression equation shows the impact of one variable on another variable. It shows that how the farmers face their challenge on Women marketers. From the regression table it is shown that if the value of independent variable, i.e. Unsupportive husband is increased by 1 unit than there would be an increase in dependent variable, i.e. women marketers by 0.724 units. This shows that there is a positive impact of unsupportive husbands on women marketers. This means that if the husbands are unsupportive then more women take to marketing agricultural produce (vegetables). This could probably be ascribed to financial needs of the women and her family that are unmet by the unsupportive husbands. The results are significant because the p-value is less than the 0.05 (the significant level set by researcher).

The table shows that there is negative impact on workload and women marketers. The equation shown that the workload is increased by 1 unit then the woman marketer is going to decrease by -0.25 units. The P-value is 0.025, that is less than significant level so the result is highly significant because many women marketers face the workload challenges

The table reveals that there is positive relationship between social security and women marketers. The equation shown that the social security is increased by 1 unit then the women marketers are going to increase by 0.056 units. And the P-value is 0.05 that is more than significant level so the result is not significant because many women marketers were not facing the social security problem.

The equation shows that there is positive relationship between knowledge oft crop and women marketers. The table shows that the knowledge of crop is increased by 1 unit then the woman marketer is going to increase by 0.543 units. And the P-value is 0.05 that is less than significant level so the result is significant because knowledge of crop is a greater challenge of woman marketer.

There is a positive relation between the credit facility and women marketers. The table shows that the credit facility is increased by 1 unit then the woman marketer is going to increase by 0.15 units. The P-value is 0.080 that is greater than significant level so the result is not significant because credit facility is not a greater challenge of women marketers.

The table shows that there is negative impact on lack of market information and women marketers. The equation shows that the workload is increased by 1 unit then the woman marketer is going to decrease by -0.334 units. And the P-value is 0.002 that is less than significant level so the result is highly significant because many women marketers face the lack of market information challenges.

The equation shows that there is positive relationship between knowledge of harvesting and women marketers. The table shows that the Knowledge of harvesting is increased by 1 unit then the woman marketer is going to increase by 0.18 units. And the P-value is 0.05 that is less than significant level so the result is significant because knowledge of harvesting is a greater challenge of women marketers.

The table shows that there is negative impact on transport and women marketers. The equation shows that the workload is increased by 1 unit then the woman marketer is going to decrease by -0.07 units. And the P-value is 0.248 that is greater than significant level so the result is not significant because many women marketers face the transport challenges.

Further, the table shows that there is negative impact on inadequate storage and women marketers. The equation shows that the workload is increased by 1 unit then the woman marketer is going to decrease by -0.029 units. And the P-value is 0.722 that is greater than significant level so the result is not significant because many women marketers face the inadequate storage challenges.

5. CONCLUSION

This research study has exhibited the factors affecting women marketers is agricultural produce. In this study 9 hypotheses were verified to find out the high impact independent variables on dependent variables. The variables were chosen after revising and considered from various literature surveys. The study revealed that unsupportive husband, workload, knowledge of crop, lack of market information, knowledge of harvesting were high impact issues on the woman marketer. Thus to cope with these challenges the government should provide special subsidies to the women marketers for their enhancement. To encourage the women marketers, government needs to implement special policy for their protection.

REFERENCES

1. Bibhu Santosh Behera and Anama Charan Behera (2013), "*Gender Issues: The role of women in agriculture sector in India*", *International Journal of Marketing, Financial Services & Management Research*, Vol. 2, No. 9.

2. Hemla Aggarwal, Subita Sharma and Rajni Sharma (2013), "A Study of Agricultural Activities Performed by Rural Women and Problems Faced by them in Jammu District of J&K State", *International Journal of Scientific and Research Publications*, Volume 3, Issue 1.
3. Manas Mondal (2013), *The Role of Rural Women In Agriculture Sector Of Sagar Island, West Bengal, India", International Journal of Engineering And Science*, Volume 2, Issue 2.
4. Mohammed Endris Harun (2014), *"Women's workload and their role in agricultural production in Ambo district, Ethiopia", Journal of Development and Agricultural Economics*, Volume 6, Issue 8.
5. Musa, Reuben and Magaji (2013), "Measured Problems associated with agricultural produce marketing in Nigeria: the experience of milled rice women marketers from southern Taraba State, Nigeria", *Journal of Agricultural and Environmental management*, Volume 2, Issue 1.
6. Nyevero Maruzani (2014), *"Problems Faced by Rural Women in Buhera District of Manical and South Province of Zimbabwe", Journal of Emerging Trends in Educational Research and Policy Studies*, Volume 5, Issue 3.
7. Rajeshwari M. Shettar (2015), "A Study on Issues and Challenges of Women Empowerment in India", *Journal of Business and Management*, Volume 17, Issue 4.
8. Roopam Singh and Ranja Sengupta (2009), *"The EU India FTA in Agriculture and Likely Impact on Indian Women"*, Centre for Trade and Development and Heinrich Boell Foundation, New Delhi, December 2009
9. Shiva (1991), The state of food and agriculture—FAO, Retrieved on 08.04.2014.
10. Tahir Munir Butt, Zakaria Yousaf Hassan, Khalid Mehmood and Sher Muhammad (2010) "Role Of Rural Women In Agricultural Development and Their Constraints", *Journal of Agriculture &Social Sciences*, Vol. 6, No. 3.

11

Feminization of Agriculture:
A Trend of Concern

Tinku Paul

ABSTRACT

With employment gaining a central position in the prescriptions of poverty alleviation, it becomes imperative to study its influence on 'empowerment' *especially in the context of women, when voluminous literature have come up on* 'feminization' *of poverty and hunger. Employment has assumed central position in prescriptions for poverty reduction. Labour-intensive growth and greater economic participation by women are major policy recommendations. In this light it is imperative with changing women's share in agricultural wage employment in India to understand the implications of this feminization of agriculture. It is important to understand its' implications in light of changing women's quality of agricultural work and land ownership rights as well. Do changes in feminization of agriculture also imply changes in gender relations and patriarchal power structure or does it simply imply as a befall on women as a consequence of increased male migration and increase in female headed households? The present paper is an outcome of intensive field study conducted in the two development blocks of Allahabad district to study the implications of rural female work participation on their empowerment status. The study revisits the debate with a focus of gender relations. With constrained access and knowledge of agriculture and technical know-how, access to productive assets, illiteracy, the neo-female-headed- households struggle to grapple with changed gender relations and division of labour.*

Keywords: *feminization, agriculture, work, women, labour*

WOMEN IN AGRICULTURE

Feminization of agriculture has been taking place in Indian agriculture in two ways—'demand pull' and the other 'poverty push'. Interestingly in most places both these factors are overlapping and complimentary. Poverty in rural areas has been forcing women to supplement farm income and participate in agriculture. Thus, feminization of agriculture has been consequent to increasing poverty. Simultaneously there has been increased dearth of agricultural labour due to increasing rural-urban wage gap and resultant migration of men folk for better earnings. In this condition of migrating men, the women left behind in the villages have no choice but to take charge of agricultural activities.

Agriculture has attained an assuming position with respect to broadening and deepening of female activity especially during the post-reform period in India. With triple burden of work, rearing of children, household responsibilities and working on the farms, selling the produce etc. prove challenging for women. This trend of increased female activity in agriculture has been termed as feminization of agriculture. The Census has provided reliable data of female work participation rate in agriculture over the decades. As per Census 2011, the workforce participation rate for females is 25.51 per cent against 53.26 per cent for males. Rural sector has a better female workforce participation rate of 30.02 per cent compared with 53.03 per cent for males. In rural sector, Himachal Pradesh has the maximum female workforce participation rate (47.4%). Workforce participation is more or less equal for rural and urban males, but there is a huge gap in rural and urban female workforce participation. The percentage of rural women workers classified as agricultural labourers increased from 25.6 per cent to 43.4 per cent, compared to the increase from 16.2 per cent to 27.4 per cent for men (GoI, 2001). With a rising share, female agricultural labourers now constitute 46.9 per cent of the labour force.

With increased male migration consequent with rising urbanization and increasing rural–urban wage gap, women assume the agricultural responsibilities in all aspects including crop selection, preparation of land for cultivation, planting, weeding, pest control, irrigation, harvesting, crop storage, marketing and processing of agricultural produce. Ironically with increased participation of women in the outside sphere there has been no change in their gender roles at household sphere.

EMERGING ISSUES WITH FEMINIZATION OF AGRICULTURE

Notwithstanding the conceptual background of the data sets in encapsulating women's work, the focus is the consequential issues that emerge with growing feminization of agriculture. With rising trend of female work participation in agriculture visible from the 1960s the momentum geared up in the 1990s when the negative impact of this trend opened up interesting revelations for rethinking on the celebrations of increased FWPR (female work participation rate). With nominal size of landholdings under their control the female-headed households struggled to keep pace with changing momentum of agricultural changes and suffered massive setback revealed in the increased poverty levels. With constrained access to productive resources and technological know-how and market networks, limited mobility and additional burden of domestic responsibilities women failed to keep pace with male counterparts. Whilst the male agricultural workers preferred to reap benefits of commercial farming and export-oriented production mode the female counterparts remained constrained to their subsistence mode of production method. Adding to their ordeal are also the socio-cultural inhibitions that add to the misery of women agricultural workers. For example, certain agricultural activities like ploughing the field are restricted for women.

Empirical Understanding of the Issue

For the empirical understanding of the impact of feminization of agriculture the researcher carried out an empirical survey based on the study of 448 female respondents aged above 15 years, selected from the 6 villages of Handia (206) and Chaka blocks (242) of Allahabad District. Among the sample villages in absolute terms Kazipur reported highest number of total workers (in the Handia block) with a major proportion engaged as agricultural labourers (i.e. nearly half of the total workers) and as cultivators. Rikhipur had highest proportion of non-workers with more than 80 per cent of its population in the no-working category. Interestingly in contrast to Kazipur with highest SC population among the selected villages of Handia block and reporting highest WPR, the Rikhipur village had lowest SC population (i.e. merely 6% of its population), recorded lowest WPR. Of its (Rikhipur) working population more than 60 per cent were engaged as other workers. It is also important to note that those engaged in agriculture were mostly in the cultivator category (29%) and only a small proportion (4.3%) was engaged as agricultural labourers. This reflects that most of the agriculture is been done on own farm. Highly in contrast stands the Kanakpur village (a very interior village, far from town) that comprised very poor landless or marginal farmers and sharecroppers.

Bidi making and seasonal agriculture for subsistence forms their major occupation. This is well reflected from the data, which shows more than

Table 1: Work Participation and Category-wise Distribution of Workers of the Study Region

Village	*WPR*	*Main Workers*	*Marginal Workers*	*Non-Workers*	*Cultivators*	*Agri. Labourers*	*Hhd. Ind. Workers*	*Other Workers*
Rikhipur	15.2	10.9	4.3	84.8	28.6	4.3	1.6	65.4
Kanakpur	25.4	12.3	13.2	74.6	5.4	6.5	55.4	32.7
Kazipur	37.4	18.6	18.8	62.6	34.0	48.5	1.3	16.2
Chak Garibdas	29.9	16.4	13.5	70.1	6.0	6.7	28.2	59.1
Chak Abhaydas	41.7	33.6	8.1	58.3	10.7	59.6	4.2	25.5
Chak Kriparam	42.6	30.4	12.2	57.4	17.8	64.3	0.5	17.4

Note: Other Workers*: All workers, i.e. those who have been engaged in some economic activity during the last one-year but are not cultivators or agricultural labourers or in the household industry, are 'other workers (OW)'. The type of workers that come under this category of 'OW' include all Govt. servants, municipal employees, teachers, factory workers, plantation workers, those engaged in trade, commerce, business, transport, banking, mining, construction, political or social work, priests, entertainment artists, etc. In effect, all those workers other than cultivators or agricultural labourers or household industry workers are 'Other Workers'.

Source: UP Census Abstract, 2001.

half of the working population (55.4%) engaged in household industry. The non-working population was also very high with nearly three-fourths of its population in this category. Survey in this village reveals that a major reason for this was lack of availability of gainful work opportunity in this area. Logical reason for this could be traced from the very high illiteracy rate in this region (109%) and the very low literacy rate (25%).

In the Chaka block WPR was low in the Chak Garibdas village in comparison to over 40% WPR in the other two selected sample villages. Whereas, nearly three-fifths of the workers in the Chak Abhayram and Chak Kriparam villages were engaged as agricultural labourers, a similar proportion was engaged in the other workers category in the Chak Garibdas village.

Table 2: Village-wise Status of Employment

Village	*Status of Employment*		*Total*
	Worker	*Non-worker*	
Kazipur	26 (53.1)	23 (46.9)	49 (100.0)
Kanakpur	28 (49.1)	29 (50.9)	57 (100.0)
Rikhipur	41 (41.0)	59 (59.0)	100 (100.0)
Trans Ganga	95 (46.1)	111 (53.9)	206 (100.0)
Chak Garibdas	51 (44.0)	65 (56.0)	116 (100.0)
Chak Abhayram	46 (52.9)	41 (47.1)	87 (100.0)
Chak Kriparam	26 (66.7)	13 (33.3)	39 (100.0)
Trans Yamuna	123 (50.8)	119 (49.2)	242 (100.0)
Total	218 (48.7)	230 (51.3)	448 (100.0)

Source: Field Survey, July-September, 2005.

In our study nearly seven out of ten rural women are illiterate, followed by 12 per cent respondents with at least primary school education. Illiteracy was found more pronounced in the Trans Ganga region as compared to the Trans Yamuna region, i.e. 14 percentage points higher in the Trans Ganga region. Interestingly education beyond middle school was nil in the Trans Ganga region. This has its implications on the nature and quality of the working status of rural women.

The Work Participation Rates (WPR) of the rural women in the sample villages presents a profile of their working status. In our fieldwork in the Trans Ganga and Trans Yamuna regions of Allahabad district the nature and quality of work differed to a large extent, which has its reflection on the status of empowerment of women. For instance, the nature of economic activity in the Trans Ganga region was predominantly agriculture and was subsistence in nature.

This was observed to be especially true for the female-headed agricultural households. Though, according to secondary statistics the average FWPR is higher in the Trans Ganga Region as compared to the Trans Yamuna region, the selected villages present a contradictory profile.

STATUS AND QUALITY OF EMPLOYMENT

In the sample villages of Trans Ganga and Trans Yamuna agriculture was the backbone of the rural economy. This was more prominently visible in the Trans Ganga region. The division of rural women workers according to their work category shows that 62.3 per cent of women earned their livelihood from agriculture working as cultivators, agricultural labourers, share croppers, etc. These rural women working in the farms, participate in a wide range of farm activities by slogging alongside with men in the field as well as taking care of the home and children, thereby performing dual role that of a homemaker and of a partner in the farming activities outside the home. As is clear in the Chapter III, nearly 78 per cent of the rural female working population is engaged in agriculture either as cultivators or as agricultural labourers. ***Allahabad has the largest number of rural women workers in Uttar Pradesh which accounts to nearly five lakh*** (4, 86,248). Rural farm labourers work under severe limitations, their contribution towards agricultural production and development is noteworthy. Apart from the job they do outside the household, the unpaid activities in the domestic sphere go unnoticed and unrewarded. Women workforce outside the four walls is larger in rural areas than in urban India. For the present study, the women performing agricultural operations have been classified into four categories:

1) Women working in other's fields for cash or kind technically termed as agricultural labourers;
2) Women working in their family owned land as labourers. The research indicates that it is this section of working women who are most susceptible to underreporting. They neither own any agricultural land nor are paid any form of reward in the form of cash or kind in compensation for their hard toil;
3) Women supervising the agricultural operations performed by the labourers in family-owned lands. This category of workers is again similar to the above mentioned (third) category.
4) Women working and supervising work in their owned land, or cultivators. Share croppers have also been included in the cultivator's class.

Forty-two percent of the rural females depend on agriculture by working as labourers, who possess no land of their own. Women possessing small landholdings work in their own farm and also work as labourers for wages on others' farms, thereby, supplementing the family's income. Women who supervise the farm activities performed by the labourers generally belong to higher social strata. The study reveals that almost 70 per cent of landholdings, more than a hectare, were owned by high caste Brahmins and Thakurs, whereas 54 per cent of the landless agricultural or non-agricultural families belonged to the scheduled castes.

Table 3: Education Specific Category-wise Status of Work

Main Occupation	*Educational Status of the Respondent*				*Total*
	No Education	*Up to Primary*	*Middle School*	*Up to High School*	
Agri. Labour	77 (87.5)	9 (10.2)	0 (0.0)	2 (2.3)	88 (100.0)
Self Employed	26 (60.5)	6 (14.0)	6 (14.0)	5 (11.6)	43 (100.0)
Regular/Salaried Employed	1 (7.7)	0 (0.0)	8 (61.5)	4 (30.8)	13 (100.0)
Casual/Contractual	26 (100.0)	0 (0.0)	0 (0.0)	0 (0.0)	26 (100.0)
Cultivator	36 (75.0)	11 (22.9)	0 (0.0)	0 (0.0)	48 (100.0)
Non-Workers	149 (64.5)	43 (18.7)	229.5%	17 (7.4)	230 (100.0)
Total	315 (70.3)	69 (15.4)	368.0%	28(6.3)	448(100.0)

Source: Field Survey.

The Table 3 points out that the illiterate females were mostly engaged as agricultural labourers (88%) or as casual or contractual workers (100%). This implies that the educational standards have an implication on the quality of employment. Regular and salaried workers were mostly educated up to middle or even up to higher secondary. These included teachers in primary schools, ANMs, daais, cooks in aganwadis, and other aganwadi workers.

Table 4: Occupational Category according to Age Groups

Main Occupation	*Age of Respondent (in completed years)*						*Total*
	15-24	*25-34*	*35-44*	*45-54*	*55-59*	*60 & above*	
Agri. Labour	0(0.0)	20(22.7)	35(39.8)	19(21.6)	10(11.4)	4(4.5)	88(100.0)
Self-Employed	1(2.3)	25(58.1)	12(27.9)	1(2.30	0(0.0)	4(9.3)	43(100.0)
Regular Employed	0(0.0)	5(38.5)	0(0.0)	5(38.5)	3(23.1)	0(0.0)	13(100.0)
Casual/Contractual	0(0.0)	2(7.7)	7(26.9)	3(11.5)	4(15.40	10(38.5)	26(100.0)
Cultivator	1(0.0)	0(0.0)	7(83.3)	4(16.7)	0(0.0)	0(0.0)	12(100.00
Working on family land	0(0.0)	12(38.7)	10(32.3)	5(16.1)	3(9.7)	1(3.2)	31(100.00
Supervisory work in family land	0(0.0)	0(0.0)	1(20.0)	2(40.0)	2(40.0)	0(0.0)	5(100.0)
Non-Workers	22(9.5)	98(42.4)	32(13.9)	22(9.5)	27(11.7)	29(13.0)	230(100.0)
Total	24(5.4)	162(36.2)	104(23.2)	61(13.6)	48(10.7)	49(10.9)	448(100.0)

Source: Field Survey, July-September, 2005.

Thus, in an effort to net the contribution of these workers who are mostly under-reported, let us widen our horizons and include women working in family land and women performing supervisory work in family land. Thus, after incorporating these two categories of women (workers who are often unacknowledged as workers) the proportion of 'cultivators' to the total agricultural workers rises to 19 percent.

The study reveals that 56 per cent of the working women made contributions out of their earned income in purchasing land, buying or renovating houses, purchasing livestock, and education of children, buying durable assets of the household and even opening shops.

One out of five households was found to be female headed. With the male partners migrating in search of better income generation activities to places like Surat, Rajkot, Delhi and Mumbai, the female members with little capital assets in their control are left behind bound to hearth. Reviews on feminization of poverty reflect that female-maintained households are very often among the poorest because of wage discrimination, occupational segregation patterns in the labour market and other gender-based barriers. Family disintegration, population movements between urban and rural areas within countries and internal displacements are factors contributing to the rise of female-headed households. In nearly three-fourths of the households, husbands were heads of the households. Fifty per cent of the sample families were nuclear families.

The following was also found in this study:

1. Occupational category of the working women influences the consumption pattern of the female workers. To study this

relationship we categorized the working women into seven categories, viz. agricultural labourers, self-employed, regular and salaried, casual labourers, supervisory work on family land and women working on family land. The consumption pattern as an indicator of empowerment of working women was explained with help of proxy variables as number of times meals skipped, number of times meals taken a day, to study the variations across these work categories.

2. The status of employment, i.e. the working or non-working status of women influences positively the decision making autonomy of the women. Decision making issues have been divided into three broad groups—trivial issues, children-related issues, issues related to own self and critical issues.
3. The working status of women raises the self-esteem and self-respect of women. Self-respect and self-esteem are supposed to be very important indicators of empowerment of women and have been studied through attitude of women towards acceptance of spousal violence on several issues categorized as trivial and critical issues.
4. Category of occupation of the working women has influence on the self-esteem.
5. The working status of the respondent has negative impact on the incidence of spousal violence. To study this relationship incidence of spousal violence studied with respect to respondent's subjection to physical torture by your in-laws or husband.
6. Assertiveness level in decision making has influence on spousal violence (wife-beating). It was hypothesized that the levels to which women assert themselves (sometimes, never and always) does affect the subjection to physical torture. This has further been studied across education levels and occupational categories of women for a better understanding.
7. The status of employment of rural women has positive impact on the awareness levels. Awareness with regard to ideal age for marriage of girls, perception on early marriage of daughters, awareness on family planning methods, adoption of family planning method, awareness on child spacing, perceived level of education for daughters, decision on casting vote.
8. The occupational category of the working women affects the levels of awareness of rural women.

There have been increasing efforts to capture the process of empowerment through direct measures of decision-making, control, choice, and self-esteem. Such measures are seen as the most effective representations of the process of empowerment by many authors since they are closest to measuring agency.

Major emphasis is placed on the *agency criterion* to assess empowerment as there are several examples in the literature, of cases in which giving women *access to* resources alone does not lead to their greater *control over* resources, where changes in legal statutes have little influence on practice where political leaders do not necessarily work to promote women's interests. Thus, while resources—economic, social and political—are often critical in ensuring that women are empowered, they are not always sufficient. Without women's individual or collective ability to recognize and utilize resources in their own interests, resources cannot bring about empowerment.

Thus, 'agency' should be treated as the essence of empowerment, and resources and achievements as enabling conditions and outcomes, respectively. Thus, the indicators with 'face validity' (i.e. indicators of empowerment based on survey questions) referring to very specific, concrete actions represent power relationship and are meaningful within a particular social context.

STATUS OF EMPLOYMENT AND RESPONSIBILITY OF FINANCES

Table 5 shows very clearly that the responsibility to bear the finances to meet household needs is mostly borne by women regardless of their working status. But the burden of this responsibility is heavily borne by working women. The proportion of working women taking up this responsibility was 27 percentage points higher than that of the non-working women. With no earnings non-working women are more dependent on their spouses.

Table 5: Status of Employment and Responsibility of Finances

Status of Employment	*When money is tight who takes the responsibility that it stretches*					*Total*
	Self	*Husband*	*Both*	*Father-in-law*	*Elder Son*	
Worker	175(80.3)	25(11.5)	0(0.0)	7(3.2)	11(5.0)	218(100.0)
Non-Worker	122(53.0)	63(27.4)	8(3.5)	21(9.1)	16(7.0)	230(100.0)
Total	297(66.3)	88(19.6)	8(1.8)	28(6.3)	27(6.0)	448(100.0)

Source: Field Survey, July-September, 2005.

Unproductive saving, i.e. saving money with self at home or buying jewellery was an important indicator to assess the access to banks or institutional saving. The study reveals that the proportion of working women making unproductive savings was half that of the non-working women. The proportion of working women making institutional savings in banks, post offices, insurance companies, SHG savings, etc. was 47 per cent, 13 percentage points higher than the non-workers. Another important point to be highlighted is that almost 30 per cent of the working women revealed that they were unable to make any savings out of their meagre earnings. This was especially true for women working as agricultural labourers (51%) and casual labourers (35%) who shared that they had spent all their money income on meeting their family needs.

DEPENDENCE FOR PETTY NEEDS

Self-reliance for petty demands was also considered as a proxy for access to and control over resources. The study reveals that for petty needs 30 per cent of workers and almost double proportion of non-workers depended on husbands. This dependency among working women was found high among agricultural labourers, casual workers and women working in family land. Almost 4 out of 10 working women responded to have used their saved amount to meet their petty demands. This proportion was slightly more than two times higher for the working women than that of the non-workers. Another important fact that gets revealed from the table is that almost one-fifth of the working women had to depend on neighbours. This proportion was four times lower for non-workers. This in itself reflects the plight of these families of working women who were very poor and women fell short of their earned income to meet even their petty needs.

OWNERSHIP OF AGRICULTURAL LAND

Ownership of landholdings pattern reflects on the economic status of the respondent especially in a rural framework. The concept of ownership here is not concerned with the ownership of the land by the female respondent but concerns with the family ownership. Of the total households surveyed, 46 per cent households were landless. These landless families mostly belonged to the lower order of the social strata. Half of the sample households had access to land holdings, whereas nearly 4 per cent held land on *adhia batai* or were share croppers.

STATUS OF INDEBTEDNESS

Table 6 presents the purpose and the amount of loan taken by the sample households from various sources. The proportion of non-institutional debts (including debts taken from money lenders, thakurs or even friends and relatives) was 53 per cent and 47 per cent depended on institutional borrowing including banks or SHG funds. Nearly 6 per cent women respondents were unaware of the source of debts as they just had the idea that their spouse must have had taken some debt from somewhere. Nearly 7 out of 10 sample households were indebted. It is especially alarming to find that 68 per cent of loans were taken for unproductive purposes like marriage, illness, gambling, to fight legal cases or even to meet household needs.

Table 6: Purpose-wise Amount of Debt

Purpose	*Debt Amount (in Rs.)*				*Total*
	> 1000- 5000	*5000-20000*	*20000 or >*	*Can't say*	
Unproductive Debt	80 (38.1)	65 (31.0)	27 (12.9)	38 (18.1)	210 (68.0)
Productive Debt	10 (13.7)	54 (74.0)	1 (1.4)	8 (11.0)	73 (23.6)
Both	2 (7.7)	21 (80.8)	3 (11.5)	0 (0.0)	26 (8.4)
Total	92 (29.8)	140 (45.3)	31(10.0)	46(14.9)	309(100.0)

Note: The figures in parentheses show row percentages and the last column shows column percentages.

Source: Field Survey.

Also a very important fact to worry about was that 15 per cent or 3 out of 20 female respondents did not have the knowledge about the debt amount. More strikingly this unawareness was higher in the case of unproductive debts. This reflects on the patriarchal pattern of decision making on financial matters within the households and exclusion of women in such decisions. This fact comes out very strikingly in the discussion on women's participation or autonomy in decision making in critical issues discussed in the third section of this chapter.

WORK PARTICIPATION RATES OF RURAL WOMEN: A COMPARISON OF CENSUS AND FIELD DATA SETS

As compared to the Census 2001 the work participation rates of female sample respondents was found to be fairly high. This was due to the basic difference in the concept applied. According to Census 2001, work is defined as participation in any economically productive activity with or without compensation, wages or profit. Such participation may be physical and/or mental in nature. Work involves not only actual work but also effective supervision and direction of work. It even includes part-time help or unpaid work on farm, family enterprise or in any other economic activity. All persons engaged in 'work' as defined above are workers. ***Persons who are engaged in cultivation or milk production even solely for domestic consumption are also treated as workers.*** Though the same definition was adopted for the identification of working population, yet the proportion of female workers is high in the survey as compared to Census 2001, because of possible underreporting or other reasons to be explored. Most of the workers working in family-owned fields (both as workers or providing supervisory role) did not consider themselves as workers. It required in-depth probing and creating understanding that the real status was revealed. For example, Rikhipur, which shows comparatively higher Work Participation Rate (41 per cent) in the sample population, has a very low FWPR in the Census (1.7 per cent).

Table 7: Female Work Participation Rate of the Sample Villages (Census 2001)

Name of the Village	*Status of Employment*				*Total*
	Worker	*Work Participation Rate*	*Non-Worker*	*%age of Non-workers*	
Kazipur	147	36.3	258	63.7	405
Kanakpur	91	29.1	222	70.9	313
Rikhipur	10	1.7	569	98.3	579
Trans Ganga	*248*	*19.0*	*1049*	*81.0*	*1297*
Chak Garibdas	92	13.4	597	86.6	689
Chak Abhayram	196	36.8	336	63.2	532
Chak Kriparam	89	37.7	147	62.3	236
Trans Yamuna	*377*	*25.9*	*1080*	*74.1*	*1457*
Grand Total	625	22.7	2129	77.3	2754

Source: Uttar Pradesh Census Abstract, 2001.

During the survey it was found that most of the women worked in own (family) farms from dawn to dusk but did not consider themselves as workers. When asked are you employed? The spontaneous answer was:

> *"I don't get free time from my family responsibilities like working on farm, feeding cattle and weeding the fields, etc. I have to work and supervise in the fields from dawn to dusk."*

A comparison of the work participation rates of females as according to the Primary Census Abstract and as reflected in the primary survey shows higher participation rates in the primary survey (see Tables 7 and 8). The

Work Participation rate of the Trans Ganga region according to primary survey was 45.6 per cent. This proportion of FWPR in the Trans Yamuna region in the primary survey was nearly two times the FWPR in the Census. ***These inflated figures as reflected in the primary data point out to very important findings:***

1. The participation of women respondents has been very high in the subsistence work, home-based work or informal work. These sectors are also termed as ***'difficult to measure'*** sectors.
2. There exist gaps in the formulation of concepts and its actual gendered implementation.
3. Another plausible reason for higher FWPR could be over representation of scheduled castes. As there is a tendency among women of the lower social strata to actively support low family income, thus, participation of such women groups (which constitutes 45 per cent of the sample respondents) is high. On the other hand rural women of higher social order face stringent social restrictions, thus, with restricted mobility their participation in the labour market is low.
4. Another conceivable reason for such inflations could be because the empirical survey included a number of women who undertook milk production for household consumption.

Table 8: Work Participation Rate of the Sample Villages

Name of the Village	*Status of Employment*				*Total Female Sample Population*
	Worker	*Work Participation Rate*	*Non-Worker*	*Percentage of Non-workers*	
Kazipur	26	53.1	23	46.9	49
Kanakpur	28	49.1	29	50.9	57
Rikhipur	41	41.0	59	59.0	100
Trans Ganga	*95*	*46.1*	*111*	*53.9*	*206*
Chak Garibdas	51	44.0	65	56.0	116
Chak Abhayram	46	52.9	41	47.1	87
Chak Kriparam	26	66.7	13	33.3	39
Trans Yamuna	*123*	*50.8*	*119*	*49.2*	*242*
Total	218	48.7	230	51.3	448

Source: Field Survey.

Though this component was introduced only in 2001 Census, but in the sample villages of Chaka a number of women SHGs had not entered the second phase of funds system during the enumeration period of the Census 2001. Most of the women who were reported to be engaged in milk production in the primary survey had entered the second phase of

Chart 1: A Comparison of FWPR in Census and Primary Survey

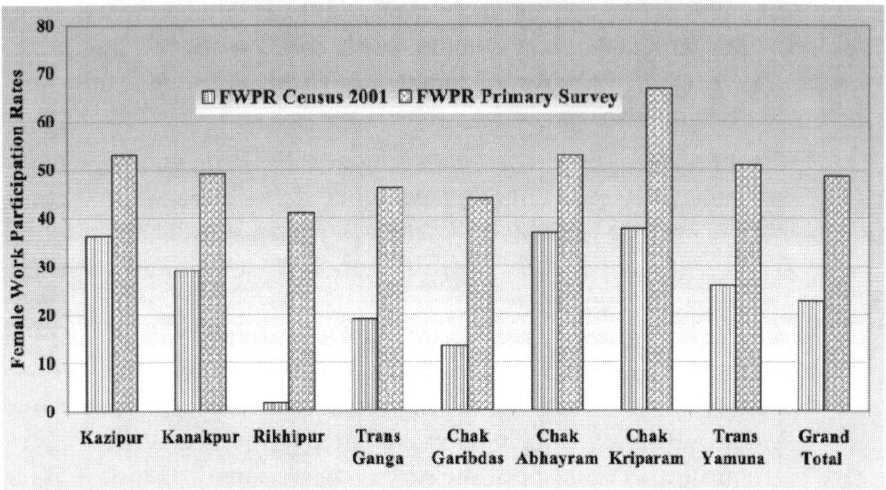

Source: Developed from the Tables 7 and 8.

funds wherein they were given credit to buy cattle to promote self employment. This lag period in the enumeration of the Census and the primary field survey could be one reason for non-reporting of a number of women who were earning from milk production captured in the field survey.

Table 8 presents the distribution of rural working women according to main and marginal categories in the Census 2001. As is clearly visible 92 per cent of the workers in the Trans Ganga region were marginal workers, i.e. working for less than 183 days of work.

OCCUPATIONAL CATEGORIZATION OF RURAL WOMEN WORKERS

Not confining to the definition of cultivators in the Census 2001 developed from the available primary data and categories restricting to the Census concepts the study adds supervisory work in family land and working on family land as separate categories. Share croppers have been merged with cultivators. This is done to demarcate the nature or pattern of female work. Confining to the definition of cultivators in the Census 2001 only 2.8 per cent of the agricultural workers in the sample were categorized as cultivators. Despite efforts made over the years to improve coverage of women's work in rural areas by proper inclusion of unpaid productive work, there have been only marginal improvements in this direction. The definition of cultivators relies on the ownership of land cultivated. This ironically eliminates women who work from dawn to dusk as workers in family land or even as supervision work in family land as they do not own land.

Leaving aside these technicalities, no one can deny the fact that women continue to be immersed in agriculture and bear heavy burden of farming tasks with less access to on-farm work than men. The rest who responded to have not been able to make so far any contributions in family assets were reported to have spent their total income in meeting the household demands and unable to make any savings out of their meagre earnings. This situation was true for 4 out of 10 respondents who were working. This validates two facts which emerge from the review of literature reinforcing the importance of female work participation.

1. Female income can necessarily alleviate state of poverty of the family, i.e. enhancing female employment is supposed to be one of the prescription to poverty alleviation. As female earnings are mostly used for meeting household needs though women work or income earned is supposed to be secondary to men's work or income.
2. The shift of agricultural responsibility on women (who lack resources for enhancing productivity or yields not satisfactory) does not make for more equitable gender relations.

With no or low economic value given to their activities, the contribution of women is seriously underestimated, and there is no adequate reward of recognition for the burden of work that women carry. In fact, the failure to value most of their work reduces women to virtual non-entities in most economic transactions-such as property ownership or offering collateral for bank loans.

WAY AHEAD

Though participation of women in workforce has been visually recognized as important in developed and developing countries yet review of various studies on female work participation and empowerment reflect on the fact that *sheer economic participation devoid of control over resources and ability to shape and make one's choices, women's empowerment seems only a myth.* Equally important factors in determining empowerment status of women are the nature and quality of work and the labour processes involved.

With changing social dynamics the gender roles in agriculture seem to changing rapidly. The government in its National Policy for Women 2016 has clearly stated that "*With increasing feminization of agriculture, women will be recognized as farmers in the agriculture and allied sectors and related value chain development. Efforts will be made to support women farmers in their livelihoods, their visibility and identity, secure their rights over resources, ensure entitlements over agricultural services, and provide social protection cover".*

According to NSSO the agricultural sector employs 80 per cent of all economically active women; they comprise 33 per cent of the agricultural labour force and 48 per cent of self-employed farmers. About 18 per cent of the farm families in India are reported to be headed by women.

Acknowledging the role of women in agriculture and changing dynamics of Indian agricultural system the government has aptly responded to the change by customizing agriculture for women, by providing targeted training for soil conservation, and develop them as Krishi Sakhis. Women have been traditionally known to conserve genetic diversity (seed banks, selection and preservation) and champion good agricultural practices. Women collectives, like SHGs, cooperatives, will be encouraged and incentivized in following sustainable agriculture practices. Agriculture for Nutrition campaign will be launched in selected districts where nutrition indicators are poor in popularizing cultivation of nutritional crops, horticulture products and traditional varieties. Skill development for forest-based, livestock-based, poultry and fisheries-based livelihoods will be encouraged as part of the inclusive strategy in agriculture. Another important move has been emphasis on provision of gender-disaggregated land ownership database. The government has also endeavoured to initiate the Mahila Kisan Sashaktikaran Pariyojana (MKSP) as a sub-component of the National Rural Livelihood Mission (NRLM). The MKSP recognizes the centrality of women in agriculture and therefore aims to provide direct and indirect support to enable them to achieve sustainable agriculture production. With the next phase of agricultural production based on greenhouse it is expected that agriculture would become less physically intensive and more of nurturing and care would be required. It is for the government to aptly respond to the changing dynamics and practically implement the women-centric policies.

REFERENCES

1. Ackerly, Brooke A, (1995), "Testing the Tools of Development: Credit Programmes, Loan Involvement, and Women's Empowerment", *IDS Bulletin* 26(3), pp. 56-68.
2. Anderson, M. L., (1988) *Thinking About Women: Sociological and Feminist Perspectives*, Second Edition, New York.
3. Beneria, L. and M. Roldan (1987), *Crossroads of Class and Gender*, Chicago, IL: University of Chicago Press.
4. Bennett, Lynn, (2002), "Using Empowerment and Social Inclusion for Pro-poor Growth: A Theory of Social Change", Working Draft of Background Paper for the Social Development Strategy Paper, Washington, DC, World Bank.

5. Bennett, Lynn, (2002), "Using Empowerment and Social Inclusion for Pro-poor Growth: A Theory of Social Change", Working Draft of Background Paper for the Social Development Strategy Paper, Washington, DC, World Bank.
6. Bhat Rashmi, (2002), "Feminization of Poverty and Empowerment of Women-An Indian Perspective & Experience", Paper presented in Townsville International Conference on "Poverty, Violence and Women's Rights: ...Setting a Global Agenda", 3-7 July 2002, at James Cook University, Australia.
7. Boserup, Esther (1970), *Women's role in Economic Development*, New York: St. Martin Press.
8. Casique, Irene, "Empowerment of Women: The Well-Being of Women and Families in Mexico irene@correo.crim.unam.mx
9. Census of India, 2001, 2011, Government of India.
10. Goetz, Anne Marie and Rina Sen Gupta, (1996), "Who takes the credit? Gender, Power, and Control over Loan Use in Rural Credit Programs in Bangladesh." *World Development* 24(1), pp. 45-63.
11. Jackson, Cecile and Palmer-Jones, Richard (1998), "Essential Matter: Work Intensity, Gender and Well-being", Geneva, Conference paper for the UNRISD Conference on Gender and Poverty in Trivandrum, Kerala, India, 1997. Now published by UNRISD, Geneva, as Occasional Paper No 10/11, 1 June 1998.
12. Kabeer, Naila, (1994), "Reversed Realities: Gender Hierarchies in Development Thought", London, Verso Publications Kumar, Prahlad and Paul, Tinku (2005), 'Empowerment of Women: Employment Trends and Market Forces', paper presented in a National Seminar Organized by Arya Kanya Degree College and Bhartiya Arthik Shodh Sansthan, during 7-8 January, 2005.
13. Kumar, Prahlad and Paul, Tinku, (2004), "Informalization and Need for Gender Sensitive Statistics", paper presented in a National Conference by Indian Political Economy Association on 'Globalization, State and the Weaker Sections' held at G.B. Pant Social Science Institute on 11-12 June, 2004.
14. NSSO, *Sarvekshana*, Report No. 458: Employment and Unemployment Situation in India, 1999-2000.
15. Uttar Pradesh Census Abstract, 2001, www.censusindia.net

12

Role of Rural Women in Agriculture in Cooch Behar District of West Bengal

Dipak Kr. Bose and Hira Bose

ABSTRACT

The study was conducted to analyze the socio-economic profile and to find out the role of rural women in agriculture. Two hundred forty rural women were selected randomly from purposively selected two blocks and twelve villages in Cooch Behar District of West Bengal. The studies revealed that majority of the respondents were middle aged, illiterate, married, marginal farmers, from low-income group. They belonged to a nuclear family system with agriculture as main occupation. It was found that rural women were largely involved in post-harvest operation, harvesting, seed cleaning and sowing, weeding and rearing activities. Age, education and income were found to be negatively and significantly correlated with different agricultural practices.

Keywords: *Role, Rural Women, Agriculture, West Bengal.*

INTRODUCTION

Rural women play a crucial role in all farm-related activities from land preparation to marketing. They are actively participating in a range of agricultural activities, including pre-harvesting and post harvesting. It was a woman who first domesticated crop plants and thereby initiated the art and science of farming. While men went hunting in search of food, women started gathering seeds from the native flora and began cultivating those of interest for food, feed, fodder, fibre and fuel (Swaminathan, 1985). It is estimated that rural women are responsible for production of more than

55 per cent grains and comprises 67 per cent of total agricultural labour force (Shivaram, FAO 1988).

Women play a significant role in agricultural development and allied fields, including in the main crop production, livestock production, horticulture, post-harvest operations, agro/social forestry, fisheries, etc. The nature and extent of women's involvement in agriculture, no doubt, varies greatly from region to region. Even within a region, their involvement varies widely among different ecological sub-zones, farming systems, castes, classes and stages in the family cycle. But regardless of these variations, there is hardly any activity in agricultural production, except ploughing, in which women are not actively involved. Studies on women in agriculture conducted in India and other developing and underdeveloped countries all point to the conclusion that women contribute far more to agricultural production than has generally been acknowledged. Recognition of their crucial role in agriculture should not obscure the fact that farm women continue to be concerned with their primary functions as wives, mothers and homemakers. Keeping the above in view the present study was conducted to analyze the socio-economic profile and to find out the role of rural women in agriculture.

METHODOLOGY

The study was conducted in purposively selected Tufanganj-I and Tufanganj-II blocks of Cooch Behar district, covering 12 villages, selected randomly. For the selection of respondents, a village-wise list of rural families who have agricultural land was prepared. From this list, 20 respondents were selected randomly from each village, thus a total of 240 respondents constituted the sample for the investigation. Data were collected using pre-tested interview schedule. The data on socio-economic aspects like age, education, family type, land holding, occupation, income, mass media exposure were collected. The information was also gathered through focused group discussion and observation methods. The collected data were coded, tabulated, classified and analysed by using frequency and percentage.

RESULTS AND DISCUSSION

Socio-economic profile of the respondents: The results of the study with respect to socio-economic profile of the respondents are presented in Table 1.

Table 1: Personal profile of the respondents

Age	*Frequency*	*Percentage*
18-30 years (Young)	69	28.75
31-45 years (Middle)	136	56.67
46-60 years (Old)	35	14.58
Education		
Illiterate	124	51.67
Literate	116	48.33
Family Type		
Joint	84	35.00
Nuclear	156	65.00
Caste		
General	46	19.17
OBC	134	55.83
SC	60	25.00
Occupation		
Agriculture	211	87.92
Agriculture + Business	19	07.92
Agriculture + Service	10	04.16
Marital Status		
Married	216	90.00
Unmarried	16	06.67
Widow	08	03.33
Annual Income		
Low	122	50.83
Medium	102	42.50
High	16	06.67
Land holding		
Marginal	130	54.17
Small	88	36.67
Large	22	09.16

Table 1 indicated that majority (56.67%) respondents were middle aged followed by young (28.75%) and old age (14.58%) in the study area. The probable reason for such distribution might be that majority of the middle aged rural women perceived agriculture as a profitable avenue. Majority of the respondents (51.67%) were illiterate while 48.33 were literate. Regarding of the type of the family majority (65.00%) of the respondents has nuclear family while 35.00 per cent lived in joint family. About the occupation, it was found that agriculture (87.92%) was the major occupation of the family followed by agriculture + business (7.92 %) and agriculture + service were only 4.16 per cent. Similar findings are also reported by Hannan (1994). The study reported that 90.00 per cent of the respondents were married while 6.67 per cent were unmarried and only

3.33 per cent were widow. It was observed that 50.83 per cent of the family had low income followed by 42.50 per cent medium and only 6.67 per cent have high income group. The study revealed that 54.17 per cent farm women families had marginal land holding followed by 36.67 per cent small farmers and only 9.16 per cent families had large land holding.

Table 2: Role of the respondents in different agricultural operations.

Ploughing/Land preparation	*Frequency*	*Percentage*
Fully participated	52	21.67
Partially participated	36	15.00
Not participated	152	63.33
Showing of seeds		
Fully participated	187	77.91
Partially participated	34	14.17
Not participated	19	07.92
Transplanting		
Fully participated	213	88.75
Partially participated	19	07.92
Not participated	08	03.33
Weeding		
Fully participated	214	89.16
Partially participated	18	07.50
Not participated	08	03.33
Irrigation		
Fully participated	163	67.92
Partially participated	48	20.00
Not participated	29	12.08
Application of insecticides and pesticides		
Fully participated	67	27.91
Partially participated	38	15.83
Not participated	135	56.25
Harvesting		
Fully participated	211	87.91
Partially participated	21	8.75
Not participated	08	3.33
Post harvest operation		
Fully participated	231	96.25
Partially participated	09	03.75
Marketing of Agricultural Produce		
Fully participated	92	38.33
Partially participated	76	31.67
Not participated	72	30.00

Table 2 depicts that 96.25 per cent women fully participated in post-harvest operation, followed by only 3.75 who partially participated. In case of harvesting 87.91 per cent fully participated, followed by 8.75 per cent partially participated and 3.33 per cent did not participate at all. It was observed that in the sowing of seeds 77.91 per cent fully participated, whereas 14.17 per cent partially and only 7.92 per cent did not participate. The findings are in the line of the findings by Damisa (2007). Majority of respondents (89.16%) fully participated in weeding, and only 38.33 per cent fully participated in the marketing of agricultural produce. It was reported that there was full participation of rural women in ploughing (21.67%), application of insecticides and pesticides (27.91%) involved comparatively less participation. A similar finding is also reported by Divya (2013). The demand for agricultural women labour in the research area fluctuates according to the seasons. Hours of work tend to be extremely long during planting and harvesting. Discrimination against women in the payment of wages is also found in the research area. Women's suggestions are not due to consideration in the decision pertaining to agricultural sector. It is because the majority of women are illiterate; they do not have the knowledge about the latest techniques of farming and have restricted mobility due to several taboos. The major causes of involvement of women in agriculture are low family income, to meet the basic family needs and the additional family requirements.

Table 3: Correlates of role in agricultural operations

Independent variables	*'r' value*
Age	-0.312
Education	-0.167
Annual income	-0.142

It is evident from Table 3 that age, education and annual income were found to be negatively and significantly correlated with different agricultural practices. It means more the age lesser the involvement. Similarly higher the education, lower the involvement in participation of agricultural activities. The probable reason may be that educated women consider these activities below dignity and prefer their involvement in other sectors.

CONCLUSION

It is concluded that rural women were found to perform almost all the activities related to agricultural operations. They spend plenty of time in different farm operations activities specially harvesting, weeding, showing of seeds, post-harvest operation, etc. It is very important for the countries like India to address the issues faced by agricultural farm women. Ignoring their role means ignoring agricultural development of the country. Rural women are the pioneers of sustainability in food production. In this regard government must formulate policies and extension strategies/programme to enhance their skills and their work should be counted in economic indicators.

REFERENCES

Chaudhury, S. (2004), Invisible Activities of Rural Women, Kurukshetra, Vol. 52, Issue 9.

Damisa, R. Samndi and M. Yohana (2007), "Women Participation in Agricultural Production: A probit Analysis", *Journal of Applied Sciences*, Vol. 7, Issue 3: 412 - 416.

Divya, Singh and Deepa Vinay (2013), "Gender Participation in Indian agriculture: An ergonomic evaluation of occupational hazard of farm and allied activities", *International Journal of Agriculture, Environment and Biotechnology*, Vol.6, Issue 1, pp.157.

Hannan, Ferocious and AKM Abdul Hannan Buiyan (2005), Role of Women in Agriculture: Some Conceptual Issues.

Rais., M. et al., (2013), "Economic Assessment of Rural Women Involved in Agriculture and Livestock Farming Activities", *Woodpecker Journal of Agricultural Research*, ISSN 2315-7259, Vol. 2, Issue 4, pp. 115–21.

Shivaram (1988), Women and food Security FAO, New Delhi.

Swaminathan, M.S. (1985), Imparting rural women perspective to agricultural research and development, Report of the Project Design Workshop on women in Rice Farming System, held at International Rice Research Institute, Los Banes, Philippines, April 10-139.

13

Role of Women in Indian Agriculture

Deep Mala Singh

ABSTRACT

The international development community has recognized that agriculture is an engine of growth and poverty reduction in countries where it is the main occupation of the poor. India is a developing country and its main occupation is agriculture, because 70 per cent of the population is involved in this occupation. Agriculture is the backbone of the Indian economy. Women play a vital role in building this economy. Over the years, there is a gradual realization of the key role of women in agricultural development and their vital contribution in the field of agriculture, food security, horticulture, processing, nutrition, sericulture, fisheries, and other allied sectors. Many women, in developing countries, are major producers of food. Nearly 63% of all economically active men are engaged in agriculture as compared to 78% of women. About 70% of farm work is performed by women. Women farmers do not have equal access to productive resources and this significantly limits their potential in enhancing productivity. The present paper shows that the contribution of women in agriculture is extremely significant. It also throws light on the obstacles faced by them in terms of less access to productive resources which do not recognize her work as active productive member.

Keywords: *Rural, Women, Production, Agriculture, Gender.*

INTRODUCTION

Women play a significant and crucial role in agricultural development and allied fields including the main crop production, livestock production, horticulture, post harvest operations, agro/social forestry, fisheries, etc. The nature and extent of women's involvement in agriculture, no doubt, varies greatly from region to region. Even within a region, their involvement varies widely among different ecological sub-zones, farming systems, castes, classes and stages in the family cycle. But regardless of these variations, there is hardly any activity in agricultural production, except ploughing in which women are not actively involved. Studies on women in agriculture conducted in India and other developing and underdeveloped countries all point to the conclusion that women contribute far more to agricultural production than has generally been acknowledged. Recognition of their crucial role in agriculture should not obscure the fact that farm women continue to be concerned with their primary functions as wives, mothers and homemakers.

Rural women form the most important productive workforce in the economy of majority of the developing nations including India. Rural women often manage complex households and pursue multiple livelihood strategies. Their activities typically include producing agricultural crops, tending animals, processing and preparing food, working for wages in agricultural or other rural enterprises, collecting fuel and water, engaging in trade and marketing, caring for family members and maintaining their homes. Many of these activities are not defined as "economically active employment" in national accounts but they are essential to the well-being of rural households. Statistical data are available regarding their participation in the agricultural sector and allied activities but their impact on the home environment has been completely ignored.

Farm women felt the impact on their children's education to a large extent, as they were able to provide them with better educational facilities as well as chances to get an education outside the village. Non-farm women only felt this impact to a medium extent; they were able to provide better educational facilities to their children by buying books and stationery but there were fewer chances to get their children educated outside the village. The impact of liberalization and globalization on women is important not only because they represent almost half of the total population, but also because they face constraints, which puts them at a disadvantage in respect of taking full benefit of the liberalization policies. Once different impacts are ascertained well-designed policy responses may aid women in taking advantage of greater openness to agriculture.

WOMEN CONTRIBUTION IN AGRICULTURE AND ALLIED ACTIVITIES

It was observed that majority of women are self-employed and work in dangerous environments. The crop farmer plants, tills, fertilizes, sprays, harvests, packs and stores the product. They are involved in activities like winnowing, weeding, grading, threshing and cleaning of field farm operations. The physical strain of female farmers in agricultural activities seems to be high because of heavy work tasks. Various activities are done by women in agriculture and allied field, such as manually handling loads/ material, threshing, transplanting, land preparation, cleaning of animals' sheds, feeding the animals and disposal of cow dung. These activities have ill-effects on women health. Due to poverty and lack of required level of nutrition most of the women have poor health.

A famous agricultural scientist, Swaminathan, describes that it was women who first domesticated crop plant and thereby initiated the art and science of farming. While men went out hunting in search of food, women started gathering seeds from the native flora and begun cultivating those of interest from the point of view of food, feed, fodder, fibre and fuel. Women have played and continue to play a key role in the conservation of basic life support systems such as land, water, flora, and fauna. They have protected the health of the oil through organic recycling and promoted crop security through the maintenance of diversity and genetic resistance.

Most of the work that women do, such as collecting fuel, fodder and water, growing vegetables and keeping poultry for domestic consumption goes unrecorded in the Census report. Many women who work on family land are not recorded as workers. Rural women engaged in agriculture from 78 per cent of all women in regular work. They are a third of all workers on the land.

During the harvesting season, utilization of women labour is maximum, carrying a bundle of harvested crop to the stop where threshing would be done is a heavy task which is performed mostly by women. Each bundle is carried as a head load by women, mostly bare footed, walking over the sharp shrubs of the harvested fields. Men rarely participated in this task.

Poultry farming is one of the major sources of rural economy. The rate of women in poultry farming at household level is central in poultry industry. Even though rural women are not using modern management techniques, such as vaccination and improved feed, but their poultry enterprise is impressive. Every year, income from poultry farming has been rising. In order to generate more and more income, rural women often sell all eggs and poultry meat and leave nothing for personal use. Due to poverty and lack of required level of nutrition most of the women have got a very poor health. Most of the women suffer from malnutrition.

CHALLENGES FACED BY FEMALE FARMERS IN AGRICULTURE SECTOR

- Women have unequal land rights. They hardly enjoy land ownership rights directly in their names. Limited rights or access to arable land further limits livelihood options and exacerbates financial strain on women, especially in women-headed households.
- Women have limited access to use of productive resources.
- Women perform all unmechanized agricultural tasks and perform multiple tasks which add more burdens to them due to lack of equipment and appropriate technology.
- Women have little control over decision making process, either inside home or outside home. Without access to capital or household decision making abilities women lack the resources that are for their labour stability and stability of their household.
- Women earn fewer wages, especially in joint, informal and private sector.
- Few women own or hold agricultural productive resources such as land, animals and machinery.
- Lack of market intelligence and inadequate information put women farmers under unfavourable situation with weak bargaining power with the buyers.
- Poor women farmers are less able to purchase technology to adapt to climate change due to lack of access to credit and agricultural services. They often have low productivity due to an inability to invest in things such as improved seeds and soil replenishment.
- Women farmers in the agricultural sector suffer from high illiteracy rates. They do not know their legal rights.

STATUS OF WOMEN IN AGRICULTURE

Globally women constitute half of the world's population and produce half of the agricultural products according to a UN report. This indicates the contribution of women in the economic prosperity of the nations, whose livelihood is agriculture, through their participation in agriculture as cultivators, agricultural labourers and casual helpers. Inspite of this, women suffer from womb to tomb in the male dominated society. Their labour plays a key role in the survival of millions of families. The problem of poverty cannot be tackled without providing opportunities of productive employment to rural women.

Women are important economic agents in India, particularly in the context of poverty. Women's income in the poverty groups is critical for household survival. Three quarter of women all over the world live in rural areas and work in agricultural sector and a wide range of related activities. In addition, a large number of women in rural areas, like their men folk depend on daily wages earned in agricultural operations. Though they work hard for long hours, they get very less money leading to indebtedness. Yet they continue to depend on the land owners for employment and loans. They are frequently tortured by the landlords for their personal interest and enrichment. They are treated as sub-servant or personal property. Thus, their dependence on agriculture makes the landlords utilize freely the services of all the members of the families. In the process of economic exploitation the female agricultural labourers even become the targets of sexual harassment. Farmers, particularly women, face high degree of economic, legal, and institutional uncertainties when investing in their land and other resources.

Employment in agriculture is thus available for fewer days per year. It is therefore becoming essential for men to migrate in cities in order to search for better-paid work. Women are filling this vacuum because in addition to working in fields, they face additional work burden that men do not. In most rural societies, women are responsible for most of the household and child-rearing activities although norms differ by culture and over time. This additional work burden is unpaid and limits women's capacity to engage in income-earning activities, which often require a minimum fixed time before being profitable.

Furthermore, the nature of tasks, such as caring for children and elderly household members requires women to stay near the home, thus limiting options to work for a wage. They are forced to work in agriculture in their own village under very bad conditions because they cannot migrate to cities as easily as men. Gender differences become clearer when looking at women's workloads. It is estimated that women provide 85 to 90 percent of the time spent on household food processing and preparation. They also have to look after the emotional needs of their families: the children, elders and husbands. The nurturing, caring and reproductive responsibilities are the dimension that have never been computed economically but are essential and significant aspects of women's work load. Women's role as food producers is related also to their role as mothers and nurturers and in sustaining their families and communities.

Their work is integral to the quality of life of people. Most of the rural women labourers are landless, homeless and belong to the socially and economically depressed classes of the society. Rural agricultural women in our society are exploited and denied their basic rights. Their inherent dignity and equal inalienable rights are not recognized in the society. Though, their socio-economic status, the nature and mode of work and the way of people's life has changed along with the new development in the society, the society, particularly rural society, is not still ready to accept any change in the women's role, work position and status because of the orthodox and conservative beliefs in villages.

NATIONAL RESEARCH CENTRE FOR WOMEN IN AGRICULTURE (NRCWA)

The National Research Centre for Women in Agriculture (NRCWA) has been functioning at Bhubaneshwar, Orissa, for developing methodologies, for identification of gender implications in farming systems approach and to develop women-specific technologies under different production systems.

There are 16 ongoing research projects in the areas of gender study on agriculture and household economy, management of coastal agro-eco system, extension methods for farm women, standardization of women-specific field practices, occupational health hazards, reducing drudgery of women in agricultural operations, improvement of farming system suited to farm women, eco-friendly pest management technologies for vegetables among farm women, evaluation of interactive learning modules, technological needs in empowering women in rural aquaculture, and improvement in storage practices of seeds and grains.

Under project on Development and testing of extension methods for farm women in eastern India, the extent of participation of farm women in different farming systems and farm enterprises and the role of change agents in that context were studied. Contrary to the situation at the coastal tract the male extension agents maintained higher contacts with farm women than the lady extension agent. The studies under Identification and improvement of farming systems suited to farm women in Eastern India project revealed that there is intense involvement of farmwomen in vegetable cultivation necessitating to take follow-up supportive activities and interventions in the area of vermi-composting, natural plant pesticides, biological control and IPM.

CONCLUSIONS AND SUGGESTIONS

Rural women are the major contributors in agriculture and its allied fields.

Her work ranges from crop production, livestock production to cottage industry. From household and family maintenance activities, to transporting water, fuel and fodder. Despite such a huge involvement, her role and dignity has yet not been recognized. Women's status is low by all social, economic, and political indicators. Women's wage work is considered a threat to the male ego and women's engagement in multiple home-based economic activities leads to under-remuneration for their work. Women spend long hours fetching water, doing laundry, preparing food, and carrying out agricultural duties. The nature and sphere of women's productivity in the labor market is largely determined by socio-cultural and economic factors. Women do not enter the labor market on equal terms when compared to men. Their occupational choices are also limited due to social and cultural constraints and lack of supportive facilities such as transport, and accommodation in the formal sector of the labor market.

Women's labor power is considered inferior because of employers' predetermined notion of women's primary role as homemakers. As a result of discrimination against female labor, women are concentrated in the secondary sector of labor market. Their work is low paid, low status, casual, and lacks potential upward mobility. The majority of women in the urban sector work in low paying jobs. These are the following suggestions for the recognition of women contribution in agriculture:

- Recognition of labor work of working women in the rural economy may be accounted in monetary terms.
- More facilities should be provided to poor rural women for land, agricultural and livestock extension services.
- Priority must be given to women in accessing credit on soft terms from banks and other financial institutions for setting up their business, for buying properties, and for house building.
- Minimum and equal wages should be fixed by state government for women agricultural labourers and the rates should be reviewed periodically.
- Women must be involved in decision-making bodies that have the potential to introduce structural changes. This action will bring some changes in the gender relations in the society.
- Women must be aware regarding their existing rights, access to judicial relief and redress, removing discrimination through legal reforms, and providing legal aid, assistance and counseling.
- Conscious efforts are needed for training of female agricultural workers in the rural areas in alternative skills.

- There is a need to make available cheap credit to needy agricultural women to start self-employment, and as a result of which our rural women may get additional opportunity for gainful employment.
- Addition to above, some alternative employment programmes and opportunities should be provided to agricultural women labour in rural areas.

To conclude, agriculture is central to economic growth where women can learn the best way to grow and cultivate their own nutritious food and sell at markets. So closing the gender gap in agriculture is imperative if we want to increase productivity and ensure food security. There is a need to examine carefully the implications of land tenure laws and regulations for women. Educational policies and funding must be changed to reflect the very high social and economic returns to women's primary education and literacy.

Agricultural extension efforts should help women improve food production while allowing them to shift more of their labour to export production. Similarly, changes in legal, financial, and educational systems must be undertaken in order to enhance women's social and economic contributions to rural development in the long term.

REFERENCES

- Chayal et al., (2013), "Involvement of Farm Women in Decision Making in Agriculture", *Stud. Home Com. Sci.* Vol. 7 Issue 1. pp.35-37.
- Dommati Devendra and Krishna Reddy Chittedi (2011) "Socio-Economic Conditions of Agricultural Women Labour in Andhra Pradesh: A Case Study of Karim Nagar District", *International Journal of Business Economics & Management Research*, Vol.2, Issue 3, pp. 1-8.
- Divya Singh and Deepa Vinay (2013), "Gender Participation in Indian agriculture: An ergonomic evaluation of occupational hazard of farm and allied activities" *International Journal of Agriculture, Environment and Biotechnology*, Vol.6, Issue. 1, p. 157.
- Krishna Rao (2006), "Role of Women in Agriculture: A Micro level study" paper presented at Nation Conference on " Empowerment of Women " organized by Sarojini Naidu Centre for women's studies of Mahatma Gandhi national Institute of research and social action, March 2006, pp. 32-41.
- Nilakshi et. al (2013), "Female participation in agriculture: A Literature Review", *International Journal of Basic Applied and Social Science* Vol. 1, Issue 1, pp. 1-8.
- Nishi Slathia (2015) "Participation of Women in Agricultural Production" *Agriculture: Towards a New Paradigm of Sustainability*, ISBN: 978-93-83083-64-0 pp. 150-157.
- Rajan Kumar Sahoo and Gyanindra Dash (2009), *Agriculture and Rural Economy* Regal Publications, New Delhi.

- Role of Women in Agriculture, prepared by Sofa Team and Cheryl Doss, *ESA working paper no. 11-02*, March 2011, pp. 2-17.
- Roshan Lal and Ashok Khurana (2011) "Gender Issues: The Role of Women in Agriculture Sector", *Zenith International Journal of Business Economics & Management Research*, Vol.1, Issue 1, pp. 32-33.
- http://agritech.tnau.ac.in/women_in_agri/pdf/index/in_agri.pdf/"Women in Agriculture" (2015), pp. 173-181

Websites:

- http://www.krishisanskriti.org
- http://www.academicjournals.org
- http://agritech.tnau.ac.in
- http://google.co.in

14

Sustainable Development through Gender Equality in Dairy Sector: Needs and Constraints

Prachi K. Wasnik and A.A. Broadway

ABSTRACT

Gender equality in dairy sector plays a major role in empowering women for achieving sustainable development. Sustainable development is impossible without women's empowerment and gender equality. The role of women across different dimensions of sustainable development is less reflected in the country. The proper use of women's labour force in the economic development of the country is minimal. The political sphere of the country is mainly reserved for men alone. Unless women are empowered and gender equality is achieved so that women can play their role in economic, social, political, and environmental areas, the country will not achieve sustainable development with the recognition of only men's participation in all these areas. Women constitute half the entire population of the country which makes empowering them to be an active part of all development initiatives in the country a compelling circumstance. Dairy is an important sector in India, providing employment opportunities, directly and indirectly, benefitting 16 million people. Dairy industry has shown the ability to sustain itself as a profitable industry in many spheres overpowering the traditional dominance exercised by agriculture. It is acknowledged as the major instrument in bringing about socio-economic transformation of rural poor in our country. Indian Dairy sector was worth 5,26,403.6 crores in 2015 having a bigger turnover than rice and sugar put together. It is also considered as the biggest employment generating and poverty alleviation activity catering largely to the unorganized sector. Approximately 1.5 crore people are employed in the dairy business. Dairy co-operatives now cover 45% of the dairy business, whereas unorganized sectors account for only 28%. Despite being the producers of milk, women have to rely on their male counterparts. Lack of exposure to markets and services prevents women from maximizing the benefits of dairy farming.

Keywords: *Dairy, gender equality, sustainable development, women's empowerment.*

INTRODUCTION

"Just as a bird cannot fly with only one wing, a nation cannot move forward when the women are left behind" were the words of Swami Vivekananda that reflect the growing concern of all those committed to development, equality and justice (Meera and Gowda, 2013). India is one among the fastest growing economies of the world and mainly depends on the agrarian sector as a tool for progress. Dairy sector is emerging as the highest contributor to the agricultural wealth of India, surpassing even cereals. India is the highest milk producing country in the world contributing 17% of the world production. The annual milk production in India has reached 121.50 million tones in 2011 against the 17 million tonnes in 1951 and the annual growth rate in this sector is 4% which is nearly three times that of the world. Sustainable dairy farming is an interaction of many factors that influence production and reproduction environment, longevity of live and input management (Kumar et al., 2012). As rightly said by Kofi Annan, "Without a gender equality revolution there can be no green revolution." Time has come when we actually accept and try to understand that without a gender equality revolution there can be no 'sustainable development in the white revolution' as well.

The Indian dairy sector has registered significant growth during the last four decades. Today, the country accounts for more than 15 per cent of world's total milk production. Approximately 70 million of 147 million rural households are engaged in dairying for their livelihoods. Unorganized sector handles around 70 per cent of the national milk volume. Of the remaining 30 per cent, dairy cooperative handle 16 per cent and large private processors handle 14 per cent milk volume. Apart from being the world's largest milk producer, India is also the largest consumer base of dairy products in the world, consuming almost all of its own milk production. While the annual milk production is growing at 3.3 per cent, consumption is growing at 5 per cent leaving a gap between demand and supply (USDA, 2014).

From the late 1980s the National Dairy Development Board (NDDB) placed a major emphasis on women's education as part of our co-operative development programme, to strengthen the role of women members in the control and governance of the dairy co-operatives. Men were educated about the role of women in dairying while women were motivated to join dairy co-operatives and to assert their rights as member, encouraged to attend meeting with extension workers and to collect the money that was paid by the society when the payments for milk were made. Women were also encouraged to stand for membership of managing committees and in some states co-operatives and unions began to reserve seats on their boards for Women's Dairy Co-operative Leadership Programme, which sets very ambitious goals to raise the percentage of active women members in dairy co-operatives, the percentage of elected leaders at every level, the numbers and status of women employees. The results of these efforts have been modestly encouraging (Patel, 1998).

Kalaivani and Bose (2015) depicted that dairy is an important sector in India, providing employment opportunities, directly and indirectly, benefiting 16 million people. Milk production and trade mainly operate as a cottage industry in the rural areas. A majority of those involved in this activity are women, for whom it provides employment and helps to supplement their family income. Traditionally, dairying and pasturing activities were done to meet the domestic requirement. Urbanization has increased the demand for milk in urban areas and this necessitated procuring, processing and distribution of milk in a scientific manner. Further, to eliminate the middlemen and to protect the interest of the producers in the villages, Milk Producers Co-operative Societies (MPCS) have been formed. This has assured a remunerative price, market support to the producers and improved the rural economy, besides catering to the needs of the consumers. Dairying has brought about socio-economic transformation in Indian states including Tamil Nadu and is playing a significant role in strengthening rural economy.

Majority of milk producers are small farmers, marginal farmers and downtrodden. Dairying has vast potential to generate employment and has helped in improving poverty in rural belt. Dairying provides definite and regular income and employment to millions of rural families throughout the year, improving the quality of their lives. The milk producers in the Co-operative sector, collectively, on an average get daily income of Rs.200 to 1,000 per day for the milk they supply to the dairy societies which show the importance of this sector in the rural economy as stated by Kalaivani and Bose (2015).

Dairy cooperatives cover about 60,000 villages all over India and only 12-14 per cent of total milk production is channelized through organized sector (Annual report, 1999). In India, 100,000 dairy co-operatives employed 12 million women which are more than that in the US, France, Italy, Brazil, Argentina, Kenya and Indonesia (ICA, 2014). Dairy industry has shown the ability to sustain itself as a profitable industry in many spheres overpowering the traditional dominance exercised by agriculture. This trend is witnessed all over the world. Fortunately, our country is blessed with vast dairy resources. Cattle and buffaloes population are the highest in India (Anon, 2000).

Dairying is acknowledged as the major instrument in bringing about socioeconomic transformation of rural poor in our country. Milk is the second largest agricultural commodity produced in our country next only to rice. India's bovine population is about 19.2 per cent of world's and 51.0 per cent of Asia's population with annual production of about 121.50 million tons of milk (Sooch, 2011). Considering the biological value of milk protein, our traditional habit of including milk in our daily diets has been one of the most important factors that saved millions of children of our country from developing malnutrition syndromes. Since, the ever-growing human population is making scarcely available land still scarcer, our aim to improve milk output should be by way of improving productivity of the animals rather than increasing the heads of bovine population (Anon, 2000).

Concerted efforts should henceforth be directed towards the dairy farmers contributing major proportion of our country's milk production to provide necessary input and make them adopt newer technologies in breeding, housing, feeding, rearing and health care to ensure substantial growth in milk output. Improved compliance to milk food legislation and conforming to international standards will also aid in improving export avenues for dairy products. Indian dairy industry is so well developed on modern lines and has acquired the technologies and engineering capabilities so well that now it is in a position to even export such technologies to other nations (Kumar et al., 2012).

PROBLEMS CONFRONTING SUSTAINABLE DAIRY PRODUCTION

There is wide variation in (i) agro-climatic condition, (ii) biodiversity and ecology, (iii) socio economic and cultural background of people, (iv) types/ breeds of dairy cattle reared, (v) Gender inequality. It is therefore necessary to plan for dairy development specific to each micro level, viz., a block, a village, a taluk and a district. This planning not only would result in optimum utilization of local resources, but will also ensure better viability of the programs and higher cost benefits ratio (Basic animal husbandary statics, 2010).

Recent estimates show that India is the third largest economy, after the US and China, in purchasing power parity terms (World Development Indicators, 2014). Despite commendable macroeconomic growth over the last decade, gender inequality indicators continue to raise concerns (UNDP, 2014). The issue of women's empowerment and gender equality is at the top of agendas across the world, as gender inequality is widespread in all cultures. In developing countries, gender disparity is highly rampant compared to the developed countries (Ahmed, 2001). Most importantly, gender-based discrimination and inequalities are very much apparent, although the government is working aggressively towards alleviating such problems. As a result, low empowerment of women and high gender gap still impede the development process of the country (Environmental Protection Authority, 2012).

Even though the country is on the path of development in various respects, the likelihood of its sustainability is in question, hence, this study reveals the need to empower women and achieve gender equality in dairy sector for the sustainable development of the country. Empowerment is central to the processes of maintaining the benefits of women at individual, household, community and broader levels (Malhotra et al., 2009) boosting the status of women through literacy, education, training and rising awareness (Alvarez and Lopez, 2013). It's a "multi-dimensional social process that helps people gain control over their own lives, fosters power in people, for use in their own lives, their communities, and in their society, by acting on issues that they define as important" (Page and Czuba, 1999). Women's empowerment refers to "women's ability to make strategic life choices where that ability had been previously denied to them" (Malhotra et al., 2009) allowing and equipping women to make life-determining choices across different issues in the country.

The ultimate goal of gender equality is the non-existence of discrimination on the basis of one's gender (Alvarez and Lopez, 2013). Gender equality is understood to mean that the "rights, responsibilities and opportunities of individuals will not depend on whether they are born male or female" (Warth and Koparanova, 2012) where all human beings are free to develop their personal abilities and make choices without the limitations set by strict gender roles; that the different aspirations and needs of women and men are considered, valued and favoured equally" (Holzner et al., 2010). To this end, empowerment of women has an indispensable role (Alvarez and Lopez, 2013) which is why the researchers prefer to use both terms together.

The concept of sustainable development arises due to the change of human perception as to what development is. In the 1950s and 1960s, the focus was on the economic growth and productive capacity of a country in the 1970s, focus shifted to equity matters, i.e. social development and income distribution [United Nations Economic Commission for Africa (ECA), 2015; Gunduz, 2004; Drexhage and Murphy, 2010]. Hence, sustainable development is perceived broadly nowadays. Sustainable development is "development which meets the needs of the present without compromising the ability of future generations to meet their own needs" (WCED, 1987).

Since milk production does not require much land, but family labour which the poor have amply, the landless poor can easily and profitably participate in the sustainable development & white revolution, deriving employment and additional income from it. Since milk is not a polluting substance in the Hindu religious ideology, people belonging to any caste, even the lowest, can and do participate in producing milk (Sheela and Ramegowda, 2013).

NEED OF GENDER EQUALITY IN DAIRY SECTOR FOR ACHIEVING SUSTAINABLE DEVELOPMENT

Sustainable development has three interrelated pillars: economic development, social development and environmental protection (Warth and Koparanova, 2012; UN, 2007; UN Women, 2014). This shows that sustainable development can be achieved if and only if these three elements are satisfied cumulatively (Stevens, 2010). Therefore, sustainable development denotes achieving a balance among the three pillars sustainably (Drexhage and Murphy, 2010; Murphy, 2012). The government is also convinced that sustainable development will be achieved in the country only when balanced development of those three areas is pursued and all citizens benefit from it (Birhanu, 2015). Economic development, as one component of sustainable development, is unthinkable without the involvement of women (Solomon and Memar, 2014; OECD, 2008). A study provided an account of empowering women in terms of increasing women's participation and their role in decision making in dairying. Women should also see dairying as their responsibility as well as an opportunity for them (Pandey *et al., 2014).*

Rural Indian women are extensively involved in agricultural activities. However the nature and extent of their involvement differs with the variations in agro-production systems. Their roles range from managers to landless labourers. In overall farm production, women's average contribution is estimated at 55 per cent to 66 per cent of the total labour with percentages much higher in certain regions, for example, in the Indian Himalayas, a pair of bullocks works 1064 hours, a man 1212 hours and a woman 3485 hours in a year on a one hectare farm, a figure that illustrates women's significant contribution to agricultural production (Shiva, 1991).

A number of studies have shown that sustainable development is impossible without women's empowerment and gender equality. Consequently, it is asserted that gender equality is both a human rights issue and a precondition for, and indicator of, sustainable development (Alvarez and Lopez, 2013). It is also affirmed that gender disparity is prevalent across the cultures of the world and that without serious steps to tackle it, sustainable development cannot be achieved (Stevens, 2010). Furthermore, UN Women (2014) rightly outlined that to create a just and sustainable world and to enhance women's roles in sustaining their families and communities, achieving gender equality is paramount. On the other hand, if gender equality is not maintained, it will retard the country's development. In line with this idea, Stevens (2010) interestingly underlines that "gender inequalities are extracting high economic costs leading to social inequities and environmental degradation around the world."

Therefore, one can understand from such explanations that without the equal inclusion of women in all areas of development initiatives, all the above-mentioned components of sustainable development cannot be achieved (UN Women, 2014). According to the 2014 Gender Inequality Index (GII) of the United Nations Development Program, India ranked at 127 out of 146 countries. India's persistently dismal performance lags behind that of other countries in the region, including countries with lower per capita gross domestic product (GDP) like Sri Lanka. Gender equality is important for sustainable economic development and empowering rural women is vital to food security and poverty reduction (UNDP, 2014).

The Indian Dairy sector is worth 5,26,403.6 crores in 2015 having a bigger turnover than rice and sugar put together. It is also considered as the biggest employment generating activity catering largely to the unorganized sector. Approximately 1.5 crore people are employed in the dairy business. Dairy co-operatives now cover 45 per cent of the dairy business, whereas unorganized sectors account for only 28 per cent (Narke, 2017).

Dairying has always been regarded as one of the activities that could contribute to poverty alleviation and employment generation, especially in drought-prone and rain-fed areas. Compared to other sectors, gender equality is more pronounced in livestock and animal husbandry sector where women constitute about 69 per cent of the workforce. To bring women into the mainstream and give them economic, social and gender equality, it is necessary to empower them on all fronts. The dairy sector with dairy co-operatives provides the right impetus in this regard (Pandey et al., 2014).

A survey based socio-personal study carried out by Rathod et al. (2011) to ascertain the role and participation of rural women in dairy farming, revealed that majority of the women were middle aged (55%) in joint families (65%) with 53.33 per cent being literates. Most of the respondent families were marginal farmers (33.33%) with low annual family income (60.83%) having agriculture (52.5%) as the major occupation. About 30 operations of dairy farming were selected in consultation with experts and were broadly categorized into six aspects as feeding, management, breeding, health care, processing, marketing and miscellaneous. The study described that women participation was maximum in caring of pregnant animals (91.66%) followed by taking animals for pregnancy diagnosis (90.83%). It concluded that 90 per cent women were involved in milking while 89.16 per cent women cared for newborn or young animals. The farm-women actively involved in cleaning of animal sheds (89.16%), feeding the animals (87%) and disposal of cow dung (86.66 %). The farm women participation was least in farm record maintenance (52.5%) and getting loans or credits from the banks (49.16%). The study explained that women participated mostly in non-financial activities and there is a need to educate farm women about scientific management practices for increasing livestock production.

Doomra et al. (2007) stated that most of the work involved in livestock management are considered as traditional responsibility of women. Dairy related task such as fodder cutting, care of animals, grazing, milking of animals, cleaning of sheds, etc., are carried out mostly by women. In spite of dual responsibility of home and farm sector, women have to perform all the dairy activities as their own 'thankless job' responsibility. Dairy farming involved back-breaking tasks as all the activities are carried out in arduous posture. Heavy load in these activities can cause muscular-skeletal disorders and disability. Therefore, improved work, worker and workplace interaction with intervention of drudgery reducing technologies and tools in dairy sector is the need of the hour. Research on ergonomics of rural women would be helpful in formulating strategies to improve the working efficiency and reducing the drudgery at home and allied fields.

Hence there is need for identifying technologies which demand less capital, less time and minimum operations; need to explore the possibilities of providing loans at the lowest interest rates with subsidies for dairy development activities; need for gradual improvement of existing indigenous breeds of animals; need for gradual removal of useless stock and replacement with high yielding superior quality animals; need to gradual manipulation in husbandry practice for improving animal productivity and adoption of biotechnological interventions in feed and fodder, reproduction and growth aspects; need for government role in improving the supply of inputs and service to dairy farmers/beneficiaries at their doorsteps with minimum cost; need for contribution from various non-governmental agencies/organization to ease the problems of farmers in association with the governmental agencies; need for developing viable farmer's cooperatives societies/federations like, milk producers cooperative societies at village and district levels, federations, boards and corporations; need for simultaneous development of cold chain storage and marketing facilities especially for milk and milk products; need for extension services from the Government, Agriculture Universities, R&D institutions, federations and corporation, besides mobilization of various input services from various agencies (Kumar et al., 2012).

Women accounted for 93 percent of total employment in dairy production (World Bank 1991). In fact, it has been observed that women perform 34 different kinds of activities throughout the day as against men who do just 22 different activities on the farm. This shows that in order to produce quality milk and farm products women put in more complex and strenuous efforts. India has 6,40,930 villages and 1,65,835 dairy co-operatives. This translates to one dairy co-operative society after every 3-4 villages. According to NDDB, the total number of women producers is 43.80 lakhs out of which 3.29 lakhs are management committee members and 354 are board members. Women are no longer on the backend of dairying but have become the vanguard of dairy development. Further, the all-women registered DCS out of 1.60 lakh village dairy cooperative society stands at 26,700. The annual growth rate of these all women DCS is about 10%. The above figures definitely make a positive statement about women empowerment in dairy industry, but unfortunately women still do not have a high level of participation in these co-operatives. The reason behind this is that men do not recognize women as separate members of the dairy co-operative. They believe the enrolment of one person (i.e. the husband farmer) is enough representation at the co-operative society level (Narke, 2017).

The Food and Agricultural Organization (FAO) estimates that if women had the same access as men to agricultural resources and services, they would produce 20-30 percent more food, and their families would enjoy better health, nutrition, and education (Food and Agriculture Organization, 2011).

Women account for 70% of the world's poor because of unequal economic opportunities (OECD, 2008). In this regard, valuing women's work is instrumental to rescuing women from a life of poverty so they might contribute to the country's economic growth. It is well known that one significant factor inhibiting poverty reduction and economic growth across the developing world is the failure to value women's work. This assertion applies even more forcibly where women are engaged in unpaid, tiresome household work, leading them to be the most impoverished section of society (Tigist, 2011). Therefore, it is highly recommended to remunerate women's domestic work in order to alleviate poverty as well as promote economic growth (OECD, 2008). Women, more than men, may also face an increased risk of harassment and abuse as they move into working situations in which they do not control their own labour, as is found in industrial livestock systems (FAO, 2006).

Active involvement of women in decision-making positions will help foster the overall quality of governance in terms of boosting accountability and transparency, reducing corruption, and protecting the interest of marginalized sections of society (OECD, 2008). If women were placed in key decision-making roles, there could be a faster move towards sustainability in the economic sphere (Stevens, 2010). Women's economic empowerment, which is a precondition for sustainable development, requires sound gender-mainstreamed policies and strategies. Women should be educated to keep their health and their families' health, so as to improve the overall social development and economic growth of the country by reducing the loss of a productive working force. Furthermore, there are gender-specific diseases as well as diseases related to reproduction, and various socio-economic factors (OECD, 2008). Gender is a socially and culturally constructed identity, to bring about social development, removing the badly socialized stereotyped perception of society towards women which is also equally important. (King and Mason, 2001).

MAJOR CONSTRAINTS IN SUSTAINABLE DEVELOPMENT THROUGH GENDER EQUALITY IN DAIRY SECTOR

According to reports of UN (2013) and OECD (2015) gender equality and women's rights are both a goal and a means of achieving sustainable development. Governments from all regions of the world have made the achievement of gender equality and the empowerment of women and girls a high priority of the Sustainable Development Goals (SDGs), but ambitious financing will be needed to turn these political aspirations into a reality. Despite an upward trend, funding is vastly insufficient to achieve gender equality. The third Millennium Development Goal (MDG 3) paves a way to promote gender equality and empower women and galvanise new resources for gender equality and women's rights. Yet financing for standalone projects on gender equality (marked "principal" according to the gender equality policy marker) is far below that of programmes in which gender equality is mainstreamed. In 2012-13, just USD 4 billion on average per year targeted gender equality as a principal objective, representing 5 per cent of the aid screened against the DAC gender marker. By comparison, USD 22 billion (25%) targeted gender equality as a secondary objective. Taken together, this means that only a small proportion of aid (30%) is responsive to women's needs and interests.

Most of the small farms are not connected to the formal marketing channels and rely on middlemen for access to the market, which leads to exploitation and poor profitability for the farmers. The situation is even worse for women, as they have minimal participation in selling of milk through formal channels due to the restrictions on their mobility (Oxfam, 2012; Munawar et al., 2013; Zia et al., 2011). Despite being the producers of milk, women have to rely on their male counterparts to have access to processor companies' collection points. This lack of exposure to markets and services prevents women from maximizing the benefits of dairy farming (Oxfam, 2012).

Lack of access and minimum understanding of the technical knowledge on feeding, animal health, milk seasonality and breeding coupled with the dearth of training institutions, are also an important productivity constraints faced by small farmers, especially for rural women in Pakistan (Oxfam, 2012; Amin, et al., 2010, Nosheen et al., 2008). Similarly women also lack an understanding of the market rules (pricing, payment conditions, quality and safety standards) making them more vulnerable to exploitation by the middlemen. Some reasons posited for this are that the low levels of literacy for women, their limited interaction with the markets and the lack of formal education on extension services to better take care of the animals (Niamir-Fuller, 1994).

Specific challenges faced by women in the dairy sector include livestock ownership, decision-making over the animals, control over the income derived from their work, as well as the environment in which they operate. Traditionally women only own the livestock that they bring as dowry, which mostly consists of small animals (Bravo-Baumann, 2000). Similarly, women's independent decision making with regards to buying and selling of livestock is inversely proportional to the material value of animal (Amin et al., 2010). This means that women might be independent decision makers over the raising of poultry, goat and sheep, but their decision making is largely constrained to large (most milk producing) animals that they rarely own (Munawar et al., 2013; Sathar and Kazi, 2000).

Women not only lack ownership of the livestock in rural area due to their limited participation in milk marketing activities, they also have little or no control over the rewards of their work. Another possible explanation for this is the low aspirations of women in rural area due to which they themselves do not demand the economic benefits of their work (Fafchamps and Quisumbing, 1999). Several factors in the enabling environment like societal and cultural norms, lack of social security, social conflicts, lack of employment opportunities, and lack of media information also inhibit the women from realizing the importance of their livestock management activities (Kazi and Raza, 1991; FAO, 2003; Taj et al., 2012; Munawar et al., 2013). Many times, due to the observance of strict 'purdah', rural women's contribution is perceived to be simply a part of her household work (Amin et al., 2010, Munawar et al., 2013).

A study concluded that farmers lack access to BDS services, which is needed to improve their production, therefore government needs to mobilize and attract investors to invest in the dairy sector and provide some of the services and equipment that farmers need. Also, there is need to create more awareness about the benefits of the dairy cooperatives to members and target mobilisation. Campaigns could be done in areas which are considered to have many unregistered members. Farmers also need to be supported to improve milk production and quality. According to the findings, farmers are constrained by poor milk quality which perhaps could be affecting the process of market acquisition. Therefore efforts should be made to help farmers improve on quality of milk so that they can be able to access market (Zeuli and Cropp, 2004).

The 4th gender equality for sustainable development conference report (2016) stated some major constraints as follows:

- **The Role of Institutions in Financial Inclusivity**: Many banks have stringent and gender insensitive lending regimes, which deprive women of opportunities to borrow capital. There is need for banks to rethink their lending approaches and requirements to enhance the numbers of women beneficiaries.

- **The Place of Technology**: Technology mediated financial services, especially money transfer platforms like M-pesa have immensely contributed to deepening the penetration of financial services to the hard-to-reach segments of the population.
- **The Limits of Policy and Legal and Regulatory Frameworks:** There is a lacuna in existing laws and policies with regard to the financial needs of women, youth and PWDs, which might partly be due to their inadequate representation in policy making organs. There are many policies and programmes in place to address financial exclusion of women, youth and PWDs, but their implementation is wanting. In addition, there is a long history of progressively abandoned policies
- **On Socio-Cultural and Other Institutions**: Patriarchal structures still hinder financial inclusivity for women and youth, sometimes slowing down the work of other institutions. It is important to create more awareness on the benefits of greater financial inclusivity.

Dairy production has been significant over the past few years. In Tamil Nadu, dairy farmers were faced with rise in cost of production of fodder (Paddy and strew); the price has gone up by cent percent. There has been constant demand by the producers to provide incentive systems. If price of milk is not raised, there would be undue decrease in production of milk in the coming years. Most of the government projects for the welfare of rural people ward turn if proper system is not formed to address this issue. Milk production issues need to be resolved in serious manner over a period of time so as to meet the rising demand (Kalaivani and Bose, 2015).

Randell and McCloskey (2014) reasoned for women facing significant barriers to participation in the development strategies: low literacy levels, weak organizational and managerial capabilities, lack of time, limited decision-making authority, ineffective public extension systems, communication barriers, unreliable funding of service providers, lack of training on gender issues among service providers, inadequate numbers of extension personnel; too few women among extension service providers, sectoral and institutional coordination weaknesses, household health and HIV/AIDS affects women's labor, income, and health.

A study illustrate Ethiopia as one of the fastest economically growing countries in the world (FDRE, 2011). However, like many developing countries, the women's labour force has not been properly utilized. Despite certain improvements following efforts from the government, the economic opportunities for and participation of Ethiopian women are still low. This is due to male-oriented development projects and the exclusion of women from the formal employment sector (Solomon and Memar, 2014), confining women to unpaid, tiresome household work. Moreover, women still suffer from lack of adequate access to training, extension and credit services, financial support and modern technology (Ministry of Agriculture and Rural Development (2008); FDRE, n.d.). Furthermore, inadequate access to education has excluded them from jobs requiring different skills and qualifications. All of this leads women to remain passive observers in the economic sector of the country.

STEPS FOR ACHIEVING SUSTAINABLE DEVELOPMENT THROUGH GENDER EQUALITY IN DAIRY SECTOR

Gerald (2011) stated that in order to achieve women's economic power in dairy sector, there is a need to start with gender analysis to understand the roles, priorities and constraints of men and women in agriculture and in value chains. He emphasized on engaging both men and women to address gender inequalities in agriculture; focusing on multiple enterprises and multiple markets; strengthening capacity especially for women to understand and engage with markets; strengthening social capital and collective action; working with women groups has been shown to be an effective mechanism to increase women's participation and benefits from markets; engaging women and men in research that helps them to respond to markets and stay competitive; increasing access to inputs, assets and services including financial services; looking beyond production: Women play important roles in production, but also in processing and as service providers for agriculture services and inputs. Strengthening their capacity in these areas has great potential for increasing their economic empowerment. Promote women that have been successful in engaging and benefiting from market-oriented agriculture at farm and at agribusiness level.

The argument of Bossel (1999) corroborates the assertion that, "sustainable development of human society has environmental, material, ecological, social, economic, legal, cultural, political and psychological dimensions that require attention". Meera and Gowda (2013) stated suggestions to enhance active participation and economic empowerment of women in dairy sector which include: Prioritization of gender mainstreaming at all levels from policies, projects to people; continued support and special incentives for women; increase margin money to fully cover the purchase of quality breed of cattle; redesign male sensitization programmes to include more effective gender sensitive modules, participatory methodology and follow-up activities at the village level towards building an enabling rural environment for women; adopt best practices and appropriate technology like direct transfer of payments to bank accounts of members through ECS which can discourage male interference and dominance of husband. It can also ensure women's financial inclusion; increase women's opportunities for financial transactions; further strengthen transparency, accountability and democratic principles of dairy cooperative societies as enshrined in the goals of cooperation.

In order to improve the performance of the cooperatives, there is need to recruit qualified staff. Thus cooperatives need to be helped to recruit qualified staff and train them to manage cooperative business. This would help to minimize on the losses and improve cooperative efficiency (Sheela and Ramegowda, 2013). According to Zeuli et al. (2004) educating co-operative members can help encourage them to become more involved and committed to the cooperatives. More training should be given to stimulate interests and commitment of members.

Sheela and Ramegowda (2013) reported that first major effort to support women's participation was funded and supported by the Ford Foundation in the states of Andhra Pradesh and Bihar to create dairy cooperative societies for women led by women and managed by women. In effect, however, women have found it difficult, if not impossible to assume a meaningful role in elected leadership or in the management of the co-operative. Therefore to support the development of all women's cooperatives a cadre of women extension workers are recruited and trained. From the late 1980s the National Dairy Development Board (NDDB) placed a major emphasis on women's education as part of our co-operative development programme, an activity designed to strengthen the role of women members in the control and governance of the dairy co-operatives. Women were encouraged to stand for membership of managing committees and in some states co-operatives and unions began to reserve seats on their boards for women. Something like 6,000 out of the 70,000 dairy co-operative societies in India are women's societies. The percentage of women members has risen from about 14 per cent a decade ago to around 20 per cent today. There have been small increases in the numbers of women serving on cooperative managing committees as well as in paid positions. But, when compared with the actual role performed by women in dairying these achievements still represent only a very small start.

Based on the findings that relate to the specific constraints faced by women in small farms, the following specific innovations are suggested by Garza et al. (2014) that are as follows:

Improve women access to mobile technology consisted of giving women pink phones to prevent the men from taking them for their use (Oxfam, 2012). The project has been piloted in India with relative success. Another alternative could be to use the SMS as a tool to engage men in the process. Currently men have no incentive to share dairy sector related information with women, as women are not responsible for selling the milk.

Reward systems for women: To ensure that women are registered as suppliers, as opposed to men, the processing companies should give women specific incentives, provision of premiums on milk prices for female providers, a strategy that is widely used with products that have a social or environmental impact. However, a big risk of any of these alternatives is that women cannot have access to all these benefits without increasing their control over income or improving their access to services and markets (Garza et al., 2014).

Mobile phones can be used to give information on milk prices to the farmers through SMS. However, the impact of this technology might have limited impact for women, as ICT penetration of women in rural Pakistan is limited (Siegmann, 2009).

The *Village Milk Collector (VMC) model* improve women's direct access to the formal markets. There should be gender neutrality while hiring VMCs as long as the he/she is able to collect milk at the farm gate ensuring that processing companies capture the benefits of women empowerment, as opposed to milk intermediaries like middlemen.

It is evident that savings accounts benefit women more than men, as it helps in maintaining control over their income (Garza et al., 2014). This savings can then be used to acquire goods and services at the MCC, an intervention that has been demonstrated to increase farmer's investment on inputs (Duvendack et al., 2011). However, as women have limited mobility, there is still a high possibility that women will have to rely on men to operate these accounts giving men control over the money.

Information and Communication Technology has been used in various countries to increase farmers' access to knowledge on best practices and market rules (International Finance Corporation, 2011; ACDI/VOCA, 2012; Miller et al., 2013; The World Bank, 2013).

The dairy market chain highlighted key points at which gender issues can be addressed, including the following (Beth, 2001): Access to, control of, and use of resources; access to production, market, and veterinary information and services; participation in decision making; change in labour and time use; mobility and access to markets; benefits and costs (social, economic, environmental). Randell and McCloskey (2014) suggested means to achieve sustainable development as follows:

Establish a structure for gender coordination, beginning with recruiting a Gender Specialist to Ministry staff; mainstream gender into all human resource and operational policies, manuals, guidelines, and procedures; establish gender focal points in key departments and programs; develop tools for extension staff and others to mainstream gender into planning for trainings, meetings, workshops, and the like; provide training to Ministry and extension staff at all levels on gender-sensitive planning and program design, and offer similar training to civil society organizations and farmers' associations; create awareness at the implementation level so that program participants understand what rights they have, and what channels they can use to address complaints or concerns; take steps to ensure specific programs focusing on crop intensification, livestock, value chain development, and others respect and promote gender equality within the household and community by seeing that women have equal access to seeds and fertilizers, are recognized as joint owners of livestock, and have equal access to agricultural credit facilities. Include women in decision-making processes and build leadership capacity and governance skills among women farmers.

DARE/ICAR Annual Report (2003–2004) provided means for achieving sustainable development by: Development of technology kits and media mixes for promoting knowledge and skill empowerment on various topics related to farming and household practices. Development of software as 'Nutriguide' based on regional foods for food and therapeutic purposes. Establishment of nutrition garden in rural households as a cost-effective solution for micronutrient malnutrition and nutritional upliftment of rural population. Development of software and a compendium on natural dyes and its subsequent use in agro and animal based fibres for textile product preparation. Development of software and a compendium on natural dye sources for use by weavers and women entrepreneurs. Organizing stimulation programmes in farms' creche for enhancing psycho-motar, mental, social and emotional development of rural children and educational interventions to rural mothers for providing conducive home environment to children. Providing supplementary feeding to infants and toddlers in farm crèche for healthy security, conducting field trials on drudgery reducing technologies for assessing ergonomic based physiological cost and work efficiency of rural women, conducting outreach programmes through radio and television talks; publication of scientific articles in newspapers, magazines. Adoption of one village by each AICRP centre and using Participatory Rural Appraisal (PRA) techniques for sustainable, self-reliant and people-centred development that is socially just, economically efficient and ecologically sound for empowering rural women. Further, low-cost ice cream freezer and fresh fish vending and display table have been fabricated under this project and the patent numbers were received. The technology has been licensed for manufacturing these two equipments for two years. Low-cost ice cream freezer (The cost of the equipment is low (Rs 3,950). No technical know-how is needed. Labour is not required as in the traditional ice cream making. Ice cream can be prepared by a layman also. Capacity per batch is 4.5-6 litres. Time required per batch is 5-7 minutes)

CONCLUSION

The concept of sustainable development is multidimensional. It is impossible without women's empowerment and gender equality. Gender equality is both, a human rights issue and a precondition for, and indicator of, sustainable development. Achieving gender equality and empowering women is far-fetched as women still struggle for occupying space in most spheres, be it at home or at work, but it is possible through dairy sector with dairy co-operatives that provide the right impetus in this regard. Women should enjoy human rights equally to be into the mainstream so that they can make great contributions to the economic, political, social and cultural arenas of dairy sector and ultimately to their country. Government needs to work hard for changing the existing vulnerable position of women which will have a positive spillover effect on the sustainable development of the country through empowering women and making full use of their labour force for economic growth; to better protect their interests and to achieve quality governance; protecting their rights to make them active participants, educating and maintaining their health to enhance productivity and social development thus providing them with fair representation across different decision-making levels.

REFERENCES

1. ACDI/VOCA. (2012). *ICT to Improve Supply Chain and Increase Profits*. Retrieved April 8, 2013, from: http://www.acdivoca.org/site/ID/FeatureICTIndiaGMED.
2. Ahmed, J. (2001). Gender Issues, Population and Development in Ethiopia: In-depth Studies from the 1994 Population and Housing Census in Ethiopia, Italian Multi-bi Research Project ETH/92/P01. Central Statistical Authority (CSA) Addis

Ababa, Ethiopia and Institute for Population Research –National Research Council (Irp-Cnr), Roma, Italy (2001).

3. Amin, H., Ali, T., Ahmad, M., & Zafar, M. I. (2010). Gender and Development: Roles of Rural Women in Livestock Production in Pakistan. *Pakistan Journal of Agriculture Science.* 47 (1), pp. 32-36.
4. Annual Report **(1999).** NABARD National Bank for Agriculture and Rural Development, Mumbai.
5. Anon **(2000).** Annual Report on National Institute of Animal Nutrition and Physiology, (ICAR), Bangalore.
6. Basic animal husbandry statics (2010). Dept. of animal husbandry, dairying and fisheries, Govt. of India.
7. Beth, A.M. (2001). Rights to Livestock: Empowering women to achieve food security. International food policy research. Retrieved from July 12, 2009 from [http://www.ifpri.org/2020/focus].
8. Birhanu, M. (2015). Global viewpoints on the state of science, technology and sustainable development: Ethiopian focus. J. *Educ. Res. Behav. Sci.*, 4 (4) (2015), pp. 135–141.
9. Bossel, H. (1999). Indicators for Sustainable Development: Theory, Method, Applications: a Report to the Balaton Group International Institute for Sustainable Development, Canada.
10. Bravo-Baumann, H. (2000). *Livestock and Gender: A Winning Pair.* Swiss Agency for Development and Cooperation. Bern: Food and Agriculture Organization.
11. Buviniæ, M., & Furst-Nichols, R. (2014). Promoting women's economic empowerment: what works? *The World Bank Research Observer,* lku 013. (http://wbro.oxfordjournals.org/content/early/2014/11/27/wbro.lku013.full.pdf)
12. Chhay, D. (2011). Women's economic empowerment through microfinance in Cambodia. *Development in Practice,* 21(8), pp. 1122–37.
13. DARE/ICAR Annual Report (2003–2004) Women in Agriculture, pp. 173-182.
14. Doomra, Z., Singh, K., Mehta, M. and Dilbagi, M (2007) Involvement of Women in Dairy Activities. *J. Dairying, Foods & H.S.* 26 (3/4),pp. 169–73.
15. Drexhage, J. and Murphy, D. (2010) Sustainable Development: from Brundtland to Rio 2012, Background Paper Prepared for Consideration by the High Level Panel on Global Sustainability at its First Meeting, 19 September 2010 United Nations Headquarters, New York.
16. Duvendack, M., Palmer-Jones, R., Copestake, J., Hooper, L., Loke, Loke, Y., et al. (2011). What is the evidence of the impact of microfinance on the well-being of poor people? University of London, Social Science Research Unit, Institute of Education. Online: EPPI Centre.
17. Fafchamps, M., & Quisumbing, A.R. (1999). Katrina Kosec, Madeeha Hameed and Stephanie Hausladen. *The Journal of Human Resources,* 34 (2), pp. 369–406.
18. FAO (2003). *Uplift and Empowerment of Rural Women (Farmers Wife).* Rome: FAO.
19. FAO/OIE/WHO (2006). "The Global Strategy for the Progressive Control of Highly Pathogenic Avian Influenza (HPAI)." Draft Report. Rome: FAO (Food and Agriculture Organization); Paris: OIE (World Organisation for Animal Health); Geneva: WHO (World Health Organization.)
20. Federal Democratic Republic of Ethiopia (FDRE) (2011). Ethiopia's Climate-resilient Green Economy: Green Economy Strategy
21. Food and Agriculture Organization. (2011). The State of Food and Agriculture:

Women in Agriculture, Closing the Gender Gap for Development. Rome: Food and Agriculture Organization.

22. Garza, M. M., Anis, A. and Bokhari, S.S.A (2014). Women Empowerment through the Dairy Sector in Pakistan, p1-24.
23. Gerald, M. (2011). Women and Dairy Farming: A Winning Pair? *East Africa Dairy Development News*, Vol. 7, pp. 3–4.
24. Gunduz, C. (2004). Human Rights and Development: the World Bank's Need for a Consistent Approach, Working Paper Series No.04-49. Development Studies Institute, London.
25. Holzner, B. (2010) (ed.), *et al.* Gender Equality and Empowerment of Women: Policy Document, Federal Ministry for European and International Affairs, Vienna.
26. ICA (2014), "Co-operative Facts & Figures" (Available at: http://ica.coop/en/whats-co-op/co-operative-facts-figures, accessed on 3rd April, 2013).
27. International Farm Comparison Network (2013). *Dairy Report 2013*. Kiel: IFCN.
28. Kalaivani, A. and Bose, A. (2015) Sustainable Development Of Dairy Farming System in Theni District of Tamilnadu. *International Journal of Commerce, Business and Management (IJCBM)*, ISSN: 2319–2828, Vol. 4, No.4, pp. 1301–11.
29. Kazi, S., & Raza, B. (1991). Duality of Female Employment in Pakistan. *The Pakistan Development Review, 30* (4), pp. 733–43.
30. King, E.M. and Mason, A.D. (2001). Engendering Development through Gender Equality in Rights, Resources, and Voice: a World Bank Policy Research Report. Oxford University Press, New York.
31. Kumar, S.S., Singh, R., Mishra U.K. and Mishra D.J. (2012). Strategies for Sustainable Dairy Farming in India: A Review. *Research Journal of Recent Sciences*. Vol (2), pp. 42–4 ISSN 2277-2502.
32. Malhotra, A. (2009) et al., Innovation for Women's Empowerment and Gender Equality. International Center for Research on Women (ICRW) (2009) North Washington, D.C.
33. Meera, M. and Gowda, K. (2013). Towards Economic Empowerment: Study of Rural Women in Dairy Cooperatives of *Heggada Devana Kote* Taluk in Mysore District. *JMSD*. pp.17–35.
34. Miller, C., Saroja, V.N. & Chris Linde (2013). ICT uses for inclusive agricultural value chains. Rome: FAO.
35. Ministry of Agriculture and Rural Development (2008). Rural capacity building project gender mainstreaming guideline.
36. Munawar, M., Safdar, U., Luqman, M., Butt, T. M., Hassan, M. Z., & Khalid, M. F. (2013). Factors Inhibiting the Participation of Rural Women in Livestock Production Activities. *J. Agric. Res., 2013*, 51(2), pp. 213–20.
37. Murphy, K (2012). The social pillar of sustainable development: a literature review and framework for policy analysis. Sustain. Sci. Pract. Policy, 8 (1), pp. 15–29.
38. Narke, A. (2017). Women Empowerment through Dairy Co-operatives. *Indian Dairyman*. 16-20.
39. Niamir-Fuller, M. (1994). *Women Livestock Managers in the Third World: a focus on technical knowledge.* IFAD.
40. Nosheen, F., Ali, T., Ahmad, M., & Nawaz, H. (2008). Exploring The Gender Involvement In Agricultural Decision Making: A Case Study of District Chakwal. *Pak. J. Agri. Sci.*, 45(3), pp. 101–6.

41. OECD (2008). Gender and sustainable development: maximizing the economic, social and environmental role of women. A Report to the United Nations Commission on Sustainable Development (UNCSD).
42. OECD (2015), Financing UN Security Council Resolution 1325: Aid in support of gender equality and women's rights in fragile contexts, OECD: Paris, France.
43. Organization for Economic Cooperation and Development (OECD) (2012) Women's Economic Empowerment. http://www.oecd.org/dac/poverty reduction/50157530.pdf
44. Oxfam, N.D. (2012). *Pink telephones—using technology to empower women in Cambodia*. Retrieved March 4, 2014, from http://policy-practice.oxfam.org.uk/blog/2012/03/pink-telephones-in-cambodia. Oxfam. (n.d.). *Value Chain Analysis Dairy Sector in Pakistan*. Great Britain: Oxfam.
45. Page, N. and Czuba, C.E. (1999). Empowerment: what is it? J. Ext., 37 (5).
46. Pandey, V., Unni, J., Modi, P and Sharma, S. (2014). Role of Indian Dairy Cooperatives in Empowering Women and Improving Gender Parity. Report on "Impact of NDP-I interventions on Women Empowerment in India's dairy sector", a study commissioned by The Project Management Unit, National Dairy Development Board (NDDB) to assess whether the National Dairy Plan Phase I (NDP-I) has improved women's inclusion and empowerment. *Institute of Rural Management, Anand (IRMA).*
47. Patel, A. (1998) Women and the White Revolution. Co-op Dialogue, ICA, Vol.8, No.1. pp. 20–5.
48. Randell, S. And Megan Mccloskey, M. (2014) Sustainable Rural Development In Rwanda: The Importance Of A Focus On Women In Agriculture. *Int. J. Agr. Ext.*, pp. 107–19.
49. Rathod, P.K., Nikam, T.R., Sariput Landge, S., Vajreshwari, S and Hatey, A. (2011) Participation of Rural Women in Dairy Farming in Karnataka, *Indian Res. J. Ext. Edu*. 11 (2), pp. 31–6.
50. Sathar, Z. A., & Kazi, S. (2000). Women's Autonomy in the Context of Rural Pakistan. *The Pakistan Development Review*, 39 (2), pp. 89–110.
51. Sheela K.S. and A Ramegowda (2013). Dairy Cooperatives and Empowerment of Women. *International Journal of Advanced Social Science and Humanities*. Vol. 2, No. 9, pp. 034-042. http://www.wrpjournals.com/V/IJRSSH.
52. Shiva, V. (1991). Most Farmers in India are Women. FAO, New Delhi, 1991.
53. Siegmann, KA. (2009) *The Gender Digital Divide in Rural Pakistan: How Wide is it and How to Bridge it?* Islamabad: SDPI.
54. Solomon, G. and Memar, A. (2014). The millennium development goals and the status of gender disparity in Ethiopia: achievements and challenges. Am. Sci. Res. J. Eng. Technol. Sci. (ASRJETS), 8 (1) (2014), pp. 56–78.
55. Sooch S.S. (2011). Value addition and promoting life style of rural masses through efficient livestock waste disposal. Proceedings of the national symposium on emerging management concepts for sustainable livestock and poultry production, ISAPMCON, Nov.2-4, Ludhiana, Punjab.
56. Taj, S., Bashi, A., Shahid, R., & Shah, H. (2012). Livestock Development Through Microcredit: A Hope For Poor Resource Women in Rural Areas of Faisalabad, Punjab. *J. Agric. Res., 50* (1).
57. The 4th gender equality for sustainable development conference report (2016). *"Financial Inclusion for Gender Justice, Women's Empowerment, and Sustainable*

Development" Conference Organised by We Effect East Africa Region in partnership with GROOTS Kenya, Men for Gender Equality Now (MEGEN) and The Alliance Africa (ICA) Nairobi, 27th–29th September 2016.

58. The Federal Democratic Republic of Ethiopia (FDRE) (n.d.) National Report on the Implementation of the Beijing Declaration and Platform for Action (1995) and The Outcome of the 23rd Special Session of the United Nations General Assembly (2000).
59. The World Bank. (2013). *Mobile Applications for Agriculture and Rural Development.* http://go.worldbank.org/TPFOHR7230.
60. Tigist, Z. (2011). The Political Participation of Women in Ethiopia: Challenges and Prospects. Women Lawyers Association, Addis Ababa.
61. U.N. Women (2014). World Survey on the Role of Women in Development 2014: Gender Equality and Sustainable Development United Nations, New York.
62. UN (2007). Indicators of Sustainable Development: Guidelines and Methodologies (third ed.) United Nations, New York.
63. UNDP (2014). http://www.in.undp.org/content/india/en/home/countryinfo/challeng.html.
64. United Nations (2013). The Millennium Development Goals Report 2013.
65. United Nations Economic Commission for Africa (ECA) (2015) Africa Regional Report on the Sustainable Development Goals: Summary. United Nations Economic Commission for Africa, Addis Ababa.
66. USDA (2014). http://gain.fas.usda.gov/Recent%20GAIN%20 Publications/Dairy% 20and% 20Products %20 Annual_New%20 Delhi_India_10-15-2014.pdf.
67. World Commission on Environment and Development (WCED) (1987) Report of the World Commission on Environment and Development: Our Common Future
68. World Development Indicators (2014) the World Bank 2014. http://data.worldbank.org/data-catalog/GDP-PPP-based-table.
69. Zeuli K, Freshwater D, Markley D, Barckley D (2004). "Cooperative in rural community development: A new framework for analysis" *Journal of the Community Development Society*, 35 (2), pp. 17–35.
70. Zeuli, Kimberly A. and Cropp, R (2004). Cooperatives: Principles and practices in the 21st century, University of Wisconsin Center for Cooperatives (UWCC), http://learningstore.uwex.edu/pdf%5CA1457.pdf
71. Zia, U. E., Mahmood, T., & Ali, M. (2011). *Dairy Development in Pakistan.* Retrieved June 20, 2013, from FAO: http://www.fao.org/docrep/014/al750e/al750e00.pdf.

15

The Role of Women in the Production of sugarcane (*Saccharum officinarum* L.)

Manish Kumar, P.M. D'souza, Devesh Kumar, Ashok Tripathi

ABSTRACT

Agriculture can be an important engine of growth and poverty reduction. But the sector is under performing in many countries in part because women, who are often a crucial resource in agriculture and the rural economy, face constraints that reduce their productivity. Sugarcane occupies a very prominent position on the agricultural map of India covering large areas in sub-tropics and tropics. It is the sole raw material for the largest agro-processing industry in the rural sector, wherein about 6.0 million growers cultivate this crop. In this paper we draw on the available empirical evidence, to study, in which areas and to what degree women participate in sugarcane farming. Aggregate data shows that women comprise about 43 percent of the agricultural labour force globally and in developing countries. But this figure masks considerable variation across regions and within countries according to age and social class. Time use surveys, which are more comprehensive but typically not nationally representative, add further insight into the substantial heterogeneity among sugarcane producing states in India and within States in women's contribution to this crop. We show that female time-use in sugarcane farming varies also by region, production cycle, age and ethnic group. A few time-use surveys have data by activity and these show that in general weeding and harvesting were predominantly female activities. Overall the labour burden of rural women exceeds that of men, and includes a higher proportion of unpaid household responsibilities related to preparing food and collecting fuel and water. The contribution of women to agricultural and food production is significant but it is impossible to verify empirically the share produced by women. Women's participation in rural labour markets varies considerably across regions, but invariably women are over represented in unpaid, seasonal and part-time work, and the available evidence suggests that women are often paid less than men, for the same work. Available data on rural and agricultural feminization shows that this is not a general trend but mainly a rural area of poor states phenomena, as well as observed in some sectors such as unskilled labour in the reaping, planting of buds and removal of unwanted plants in sugarcane sector. This paper re-affirms that women make essential contributions to agriculture and rural enterprises across the India and developing world. But there is much diversity in women's roles and over-generalization undermines policy relevance and planning. The context is important and policies must be based on sound data and gender analysis.

Keywords: *Women empowerment, Sugarcane, Irrigation, Tillage, reaping and Cane yield.*

INTRODUCTION

Women referred as 'invisible farmers' are the backbone of agricultural workforce. Be it in crop farming, animal husbandry, fisheries, forestry or any allied activities, women do the most tedious and strenuous tasks. In production agriculture, women are active partners associating in almost all unit operations of agriculture sharing work between 20-80% in certain cases and almost 100% especially in those involving arduous repetitive work. Sugarcane and beet are being produced in over 130 countries, with sugarcane accounting for 65–70 per cent of global production. Developing countries will account for nearly all future production growth raising their share from 67 per cent in the period 1998–2000 to 72 per cent by 2020 (Singh et al., 2013). The sugarcane industry in India is an important contributor to the national economy through the production of multiple products for national and international consumption as well its contribution to recent regulatory requirements for bio-ethanol to be included as a constituent of petroleum-based fuels. The production and processing of sugarcane is a major source of employment and livelihood in India. Sugarcane is an annual crop engaging around 50 million farmers of which approximately half are women. Even though women form the backbone of sugarcane cultivation, they still tend to exist as "the hidden farmers" with almost negligible access on land, resources, technologies, financial services, markets and even education. Despite their exclusive inputs in agricultural operations—like farm yard manure application, sett planting and treatments, hand weeding and detrashing, cane bundling, disposal of trash and plant protection measures—the output of the land controlled by women is drastically lesser than the male counterparts. In addition, besides the significant contribution of women in farming, considerable disparity in wages still exists between the male and female labourer (Wichterich, 2000). On an average, women labourers are paid only 50 per cent as compared to the male counterparts per day for the same work duration. Women continue to provide a large proportion of the labour that goes into agriculture, FAO's estimates show that women represent a substantial share of the total agricultural labour force, as individual food producers or as agricultural workers, and that around two-thirds of the female labour force in developing economies is engaged in agricultural work (Carr et al, 2000). Apart from direct participation in farming, women are also at the forefront of sugarcane research, cultivation and processing as researchers and academicians. Statistical projections indicate that if women have same access to resources as men have in sugarcane farming, land exploitation can increase by 20–30 per cent, raising the economy by 2.5–4.0 per cent. An increasing body of literature on gender-related aspects of trade has been emerging over the last decade. However, there is little empirical information available about women's involvement in trade expansion, and the impact of agricultural trade liberalization on women's rights and roles in agriculture and the rural economy. Therefore, a paradigm shift is required to alter the role of women in increasing sugarcane agriculture productivity and production.

Gender analysis is an approach and method which enables an analysis of the differences that exist within gender categories with respect to activities, access and control of resources and benefits. Sugarcane is an annual crop wherein more than 45 million people are engaged in various activities. We know that women play a major role in sugarcane farming but we do not know enough about what this means for technology development, adoption and further impact on productivity. Women's labour terrain is not confirmed to the farm alone. Apart from the nature of work, the measuring of time expended has rarely been addressed. Hence, issues relating to both research coverage and impact in terms of gender need careful study. Studies have shown that resources controlled by women are more likely to be used to improve family food consumption and welfare, reduce child malnutrition (Rossi Rocha et al., 2007) and increase overall well-being of the family. The necessity for thorough assessments of how trade liberalization may or may not impact on food security, nutritional status and/or access to agricultural inputs and other productive factors—from a gender-differentiated perspective—should be seen in this context. With the growing feminization of agriculture, there is need to develop specific strategies for women in agriculture. Apart from conferring land rights, it is also essential that Ministry of Women and Child Development (MWCD) work in close cooperation with Agriculture to develop their skills and strengthen their capacities as well as access to cheap finance and other inputs. This article shall provide a platform for discussing the challenges and issues faced by women that may be useful to prepare a roadmap for women empowerment in sugarcane farming by researchers, farmers, policy makers and administrators.

EMPOWERING THROUGH SKILLS TRAINING

For generations of workers in the sugarcane plantations of north-eastern Brazil, the long months between harvests have been a time of hunger. Sugarcane cutting is hard labour. Women workers rise in the early hours to prepare food for their families and leave for work before dawn, working long hours in the scorching sun. Alternatives are limited. An innovative training programme which offers participants training in non-traditional jobs is using the time between the harvests to change women's prospects, with transformational effects. There are success stories of woman sugarcane growers achieving higher productivity by adopting new improved planting techniques, best agriculture practices, irrigation, systems that reduce water consumption and integrated pest management practices. This can be achieved only through training women growers and encouraging their participation in all agricultural activities. As a part of women resource development, Vasantdada Sugar Institute annually organizes Shetty Dndyan Laxmi training programs specifically for women cane growers from the Maharashtra state on improved cane cultivation technologies. The program was initiated in the memory of Late Vasantdada Patil, Founder President of the institute, and is an appropriate forum where the women sugarcane growers from Maharashtra state get an opportunity to gather, combine, interact, share and also learn the advance practices in sugarcane farming. Open-house discussion sessions are conducted at the end of every training program. These training programs have been immensely helpful for the women trainee farmers to enhance their skill, gain knowledge and confidence (Deshmukh, 2013). Women in the sugar industry need better communication, networking and information exchange among other women. Many women working in the sector support their family and are unable to attend industry meetings, workshops or training session. It is needed to disseminate information to them via other communication means and information sharing, viz. e-mails, online networking, social networking, etc. To fulfill gender equality through several Articles of the Constitutional mandates, the government of India has taken several steps to empower women and women welfare through a series of women specific scheme and creation of National Policy for Empowerment 2001. For economic empowerment, it is necessary for women to have access to and control over productive resources for some degree of financial autonomy. Congregation of women plays a dominant role in women empowerment. Self Help Group (SHG) is a good medium to congregate women. By the end of December, 2011, 7.89 lakh women from 12,243 villages were participating in 61,072 SHGs. The total saving of these women was about Rs 176 crore and the total internal loan was Rs 493 crore. Loan received from various banks to SHGs was Rs 384 crore (Anonymous, 2004). In a nutshell, to enhance the capacity and capability of women farmer in sugarcane, they need to be given comprehensive understanding of necessity of training in each activity. In an extension programme, exclusive training programmes should be organized for women farmers on each topic/subject. Preferably, women trainers should be engaged in the initial period and once the women farmers become aware of various activities and inputs required, faculties of various discipline can be brought in training to strengthen the concept and practicability of the training.

PARTICIPATION OF MEN AND WOMEN IN DIFFERENT SUGARCANE FARMING OPERATIONS

Sugarcane farming is performed by men and women both, their practical level can differ in various activities (Table 1). Various sugarcane farming operations like ploughing, spraying, cleaning irrigation channels, earthing up, spraying plant protection chemicals and off barring are being done exclusively by men. These activities are laborious and cumbersome and hence being done by men. Activities like spreading setts in the field, sett planting and covering, hand weeding and detrashing are done exclusively by farm women. These activities are also laborious but do not demand physical energy as required by the activities done by men. In all the other activities, there exist wide variation (Shanthy, 2010).

FUTURISTIC ROLE OF WOMEN IN SUGARCANE CULTIVATION

The Prime Minister of India, Pundit Jawaharlal Nehru, Once said "In order to awaken the people, it is the women who have to be awakened, Once she is on the move, the family moves, the village moves, the nation moves". Sugarcane cultivation is a whole time engaging agricultural activity. The crop being of a sturdy nature, can absorb shocks such as water stress, lack of fertilizers, etc. However, the effect of neglect is evident on its yield and productivity. Presently, the sugarcane crop is showing day by day decrease in its cultivation of sugarcane. Considering the future need of sugar for the country, it is imperative to re-examine the issues of sugarcane cultivation right from selection of variety till harvesting at an appropriate time. Therefore, the journey of sugarcane crop invites attention at every stage of its growth. However, it must be emphasized that through sugar mills, the sugarcane crop brings out overall development in that area. The area under sugarcane has increased in our country, but the average yield and sugar recovery are low compared to their potential and remained stagnant over the years. The reasons for low sugarcane yield and average sugar recovery are as follows:

- Inadequate availability of quality seed material.
- No proper adoption of the varieties having high yield and high sugar.
- Inadequate irrigation facilities and poor water management practices.
- Poor drainage and ill-health of the soil.
- Lack of adequate and timely application.
- Inadequate farm mechanization in major farm operation.
- Inadequate efforts to control insects, diseases and weeds.
- Negligence to ratoon crop.
- Lack of participation of sugar mills in development activities.
- Lack of efficient technology transfer mechanism.
- Inadequate farm credit.

In the future, the above reasons of low sugarcane and sugar productivity will continue, in addition to the following major problems and limitations:

- Limitation to increase the area under sugarcane.
- Increasing cost of cultivation.
- Soil fertility deterioration.
- Disturbance of cyclic nature on sugar production.
- Shortage of man power.
- Shortage of electric power.
- Fragmentation of land.
- Diversion of sugarcane area to other competitive crops.

Table 1: Socio-Economic Characteristics of Sugarcane Farm Women

Variable	*Category*	*Farm women (%)*
Age	Young < 30	29.16
	Middle 31-40	48.33
	Old > 40	22.50
Education	Illiterate	31.66
	Literate	26.66
	Primary	21.66

Variable	Category	Farm women (%)
	Middle	15.83
	Graduation	4.16
Caste	General	14.16
	Other Backward Class	49.16
	Schedule Caste	36.66
Type of Family	Nuclear Family	57.50
	Joint Family	42.50
Land Holding	Marginalized	36.66
	Small	32.50
	Medium	24.16
	Large	6.66

Source: Shanthy, 2010.

MULTI DIMENSIONAL ROLE OF WOMEN IN CANE CULTIVATION

The cane cultivation, at various level of growth, needs specific attention. Women, by nature have a focused view, sincerity and commitment to work. Their sense of belongingness is of high order. If women are actively involved in the cane cultivation activity, they will carry out their role very effectively and timely. If sugarcane cultivation activities are done on time, it has a positive effect on productivity. Cleaning of the field, seed selection, de-trashing, sett treatment, sett distribution, planting, transplanting, weeding, irrigation, fertilizers applications, plant protection, harvesting, binding of the cane, transport, loading, of the cane in the vehicles in plant cane and trash mulching, stubble shaving, weeding, spraying, gap filling, and plant protection activities in ratoon crops require careful implementation of package of practices. All these activities need close supervision and monitoring. Unfortunately, all these activities though carried out, it is done in a routine manner by the growers and are not supervised or monitored properly.

Table 2 explains that in the study area, sugarcane farming is being done both by women and men; their participation levels differ in various activities. Sugarcane farming activities like spreading setts, sett planting and covering, hand weeding, cleaning channels, supply of water, mixing chemicals, rouging affected clumps, cleaning the cane, bundling, transporting the cane, collection of trash and trash disposal are exclusively done by farm women.

Table 2: Participatory Role of Women and Men in Sugarcane Farming System (N=12)

S.No.	*Activities*	*Men*	*Women*
	Land preparation		
1.	Ploughing	100	0.00
	FYM application	41.66	58.33
	Forming ridges & furrows	80.00	20.00
2.	Planting		
	Sett cutting	30.83	69.16
	Sett treatment	46.66	53.33
	Sett transport	40.00	60.00
	Spreading setts	16.66	83.33
	Sett planting & covering	24.16	75.83
3.	Weed management		
	Spraying weedicide	87.50	12.50
	Hand weeding	21.66	78.33
4.	Fertilizer application		
	Applying Super PO4	75.83	24.16
	N&K top dressing	40.83	59.16
5.	Irrigation		
	Guiding irrigation water	91.66	8.33
	Cleaning channels	21.66	78.33
6.	Earthing up	95.83	4.16
7.	Detrashing	59.16	40.83
8.	Plant protection		
	Supply of water	9.16	90.00
	Mixing chemicals	32.51	67.50
	Spraying chemicals	65.33	34.16
	Roguing affected clumps	25.83	74.16
9.	Harvesting		
	Cutting the cane	56.66	43.33
	Detopping the cane	50.83	32.50
	Cleaning the cane	8.33	91.66
	Bundling	15.83	84.16
	Transporting the cane	30.00	70.00
10.	Ratoon management		
	Collection of trash	20.83	79.16
	Trash disposal	13.33	86.66
	Off barring	64.16	35.83
11.	Miscellaneous		
	Gap filling	82.50	17.50
	Tying, wrapping and propping	89.16	10.83

Source: Shanthy, 2010.

CHALLENGES FOR WOMEN WORKERS

Poor health and malnutrition

In rural areas, women's health is grossly neglected, even if she is the main person in the household. She will try to neglect her own health, while taking care of others which reduces her capacity to work (Gore et al, 2013)

Land Ownership

The land ownership is, by and large, held by the male farmers which make women totally dependent on her husband. Thanks to the amendments brought in Hindu Succession Act and some states have taken steps to joint ownership of husband and wife and gave co-parcenory status to daughters and widow of predeceased son.

Importance of latest technology in agriculture

The women do not get an opportunity to learn latest technologies in agriculture and other means of productivity enhancements. The training and extension activities are also considered as unimportant.

Lack of Education

Women in rural areas are comparatively not educated because of sheer workload they have to carry from their childhood. Preferential treatment is given to male child in every respect such as schooling, clothing and food, whereas a female child is deprived of all these and continues work till she gets married. Even after marriage, workload and responsibilities increase manifold. Moreover, considering the small and marginal farmers, a large labour force is required to carry out agriculture operations and females from the house hold are deployed for agricultural work both on own land holding as well as labour on others' farm to earn a livelihood. The above mentioned points of handicap are only indicative but not exhaustive.

CONCLUSION

Women's increased responsibilities in the form of giving birth and maintaining the family, in most lower-income countries, have resulted in rather complex and demanding livelihood strategies. In a country like India, both men and women are equal partners in farming operations, more so in a labour-intensive long duration crop like sugarcane gender determines who has access to the local resources and what kind of access they have. These diversified livelihood strategies have to respond to the internal and external dynamics that typically influence rural families. Technology training and input support to women farmers can create a positive impact on participation of women in sugarcane agriculture. The Government of India and the state governments have taken firm and proactive actions for giving women a right role in various activities and involved them in every sphere of life as enshrined in the constitution of India.

REFERENCES

1. Anonymous (2004). International federation of agricultural producers. World Farmer (Special Issue: Women Farmers): 1–6.
2. Carr M, Chen A M and Tate J (2000). Globalization of home-based workers. World Development 6(3): 123–42.
3. Deshmukh S (2013). Potential approaches for empowering women in sugarcane industry. Proceeding of national conference on 'Women in sugarcane agriculture and industry' at IISR Lucknow, August 29-31, 2013, pp 3–7.
4. Gore H D, Singru S A, Fernandez K, Mhaske M, Babanagre S and Gore S (2013). Health profile of sugarcane harvester working in rural Maharashtra, India. *Indian Journal of Applied Research* 3(12): 451–3.
5. Joekes S (1999). A gender-analytical perspective on trade and sustainable development, UNCTAD New York and Geneva.
6. Kendre B (2011). Socio-economic background and seasonal migration of sugarcane harvesting workers. *Int J Humanit Soc Sci* 1(2):15–21.
7. Rossi Rocha F L, Palucci M M H, Cruz Robazzi M L (2007). Poverty as a predisposing factor of illness tendencies in sugarcane workers. *Rev Lat Am Enfermagem* 15:736–41.
8. ShanthY T R (2010) Gender perspectives for sustaining sugarcane based farming system. *Indian Res J Ext Edu* 10 (1): 112–116.
9. Singh R, Singh R K, Singh S, Singh V and Singh AK (2013) Participation and performance of women in sugarcane agriculture. Proceeding of national conference on 'Women in sugarcane agriculture and industry' at IISR Lucknow, August 29-31, 2013, pp 95-98.
10. Wichterich C (2000). The Globalized Woman: Reports from a Future of Inequality. London: Zed Books. Received on 12/04/2015 Accepted on 20/04/2015

SECTION 4

ROLE & STATUS OF CULTURE, EDUCATION AND LITERATURE IN GENDER EQUALITY

16

Judging Women and Defining Crime:
Men's Outlook towards Women's Modern Outfits

Hina Kausher and Sangita Srivastava

ABSTRACT

The researcher has examined the mind set of all Indian men, cutting across various religions; a data set was collected from 500 men on what they think about women's dressing up styles.

In the past 100 years, women of India have transgressed into various stages of development. With slow access to education, the socio-cultural stereotype barriers have been broken by her in the current generation. She has in today's times emerged as being educated, often financially independent or struggling to be financially independent.

Her independence has brought a basket of choices on clothing and also choosing a mate for herself. Patriarchy has been the norm in the country. Both of these major issues are now addressed by women themselves. The changes have been at a rapid pace, male counterparts still believe in age-old customs and practices. In this research an overview of men's perceptions about women's dressing up have been surveyed. The findings are intriguing.

Keywords: *socio-cultural stereotype, Patriarchy, male counterparts.*

INTRODUCTION

As history has shown, women have to follow dress codes given by society throughout the era. In ancient times, women used to wear draped dhoti which was made of pure cotton fabric. It ranged in length between 5 and 9.5 yards and is loosely tied, folded and pleated around the waist. The breasts and head are covered by the end of the dhoti. The end of the dhoti

A girls' school in Jaipur, Rajasthan, 1870.

is also pulled forward to cover the face; this is known as "ghunghat". Over the years, this "dhoti" was popularised as the "saree".

According to Oxford dictionary, veiling/purdah is defined as "the practice in certain Muslim and Hindu societies of screening women from men or strangers, especially by means of a curtain" (Olga, 1996). It is designed to hide women's figures and curves in order to prevent the unwanted attention of men (and by extension, a sexual assault), though this has not prevented millions of Indian men from bothering women over the centuries (Ghosh, 2012). Saree, with a veil, was the strict dress code for women until the middle of the nineteenth century. The veiled dhoti being the only dress code, it was also attached with imparting respect to older men and women in the in-law family. They had to adopt all imposed rules on them, if they wanted to be accepted as members of their community. Veiling, then seems to be a means of both "maintaining and creating the reputation of a women, her family and her caste and this encourages women to uphold the custom" (Tarlo 1996). This patriarchal thinking not only existed in India, but women of other countries too had to bear this. American women had to struggle for wearing trousers (Lee, Beck, 2010).

The Changing Gender Roles in Society

In early societies, most of the women were illiterate. They did household work and brought up their children. But gradually women are getting more empowered and educated, and wish to cross home boundaries and work and become financially independent. The development of women and education is taking place very rapidly. They are supporting their family financially and equally contributing as men in development and economic growth of India.

Today's women are independent. Since independence encourages people to take their own decisions, women have begun doing that. Financial independence has empowered and enabled women who are now decision makers. They are choosing their own dress code and decide what they want to wear. Today's generation dresses according to their choice, comfort and the current fashion trends. Women are adopting modern dresses; western attires such as jeans, dresses and t-shirts, besides churidar, salwar-kurta and other trendy Indian dresses have become an inseparable part of the present day women's life-style. Self-earned money and independent decision making has also impacted the choice of dress of women. They like to express varied choices in their dress and are not governed by socio-cultural stereotyping.

But has the mind set of men changed? They still want to decide what women should wear. Modern outfits of women are not getting acceptance by men. Data indicates that, if a woman is assaulted sexually then the men of patriarchal thinking say that it is the women's fault and her dress has led to such an occurrence. Many times the dressing style is held responsible for the rape of a girl, and the blame is detached from the men. This is a typically male chauvinist thinking.

LITERATURE REVIEW

Palash R. Ghosh, on the other hand, focuses on the fact that the sari was originally intended to keep teenage girls and women "both comfortable in the heat and to look 'modest'" but equates the sari's function to that of the Islamic burqa in that it was "designed to 'hide' a woman's figure and curves in order to prevent the unwanted attention of men (and, by extension, a sexual assault)," adding, though, that this has not "prevented millions of Indian men from bothering women over the centuries. (Ghosh 2012).

Women virtually and effectively take their walled courtyards with them when they venture out in a veil. It is a logical supplement to the use of enclosed living spaces and enables women to move out of these spaces in a kind of portable seclusion. If a woman must go out to work on the fields or to fetch water, her demeanour is so reserved, that it is as effective as wearing a burqa. (Purdah and Rural Housing in South Asia). This radical adjustment from daughters to wives/mothers confers Indian women a dual aspect of their identity marked by veiling restrictions. (Boolell's, "enveloppée L.F.," 1996).

Bifurcated garments named bloomers were first introduced to American women in the mid-19th century (Foote 1980). Some people criticized women in bloomers for exposing the ankles and legs. Some others referred to the Bible and said it was against the will of the God for women to adopt men's clothing. (Lee and Beck 2010). Foote (1989) suggested that American society during the period was against bloomers mainly because people were afraid of a shift in conventional gender roles and ultimate social disruption implied in women's adoption of trousers. Moreover, many women who participated in the women's rights movement adopted bloomers. Many people regarded the acceptance of bloomers and the acceptance of women's rights as a threat to the established relationship between men and women during period. (Lee and Beck, 2010). The social demands of practicality in women's day time clothes during the war offered women the experience of comfort and practicality in simple masculine garments especially pants. These experiences were not to be forgotten and contributed to the adoption of more women wearing pants after the war. (Lee and Beck, 2010).

One of the most common causes of violence against women is patriarchy which can be defined as a social system in which men are placed above women. This being so, group mentality and social practices follow suit, often resulting in the oppression and exploitation of women (Sharma 2014).

Methods and Analysis

A survey is conducted in Allahabad over 500 men between the age of 14 and 80 years through interview and structured questionnaire method by simple random sampling.

Reliability Test

The Cronbach's alpha coefficient was applied on the results obtained. Cronbach's coefficient alpha of more than 0.7 was taken as the cut off value for being acceptable.

Table 1: Why do women wear short/skinned fitting clothes

		Frequency	*Percent*	*Valid Percent*	*Cumulative Percent*
Valid	to attract opposite sex/male	253	50.6	50.8	50.8
	to feel good/confident about themselves	131	26.2	26.3	77.1
	they want to flaunt their beauty and expect to be admired in a constructive way instead of getting sexually aasaulted	51	10.2	10.2	87.3
	because girls are comfortable in these dresses to go out	63	12.6	12.7	100.0
	Total	498	99.6	100.0	
Missing	System	2	.4		
Total		500	100.0		

Table 1 shows that maximum frequency of men 253 (50.6%) out of 500 men think that women wear short/fitted clothes to attract opposite sex/male. The minimum frequency is 51 (10.2%) out of 500 men think that women wear short/fitted clothes because they want to flaunt their beauty and expect to be admired in a constructive way instead of getting sexually assaulted.

Figure 1 (a) shows that age group of 46 and older men have maximum frequency (90.20%) who thinks that women wear short/fitted clothes to attract opposite sex/male. 83.33 % boys of age group between 14 and 17 years old think the same as 46 and older age group of men. 12.41% men (minimum frequency) of age group between 18 and 25 years old think the same. Figure 1. (b) Shows that maximum frequency (95.95%) of men for those, whose qualification is less than high school, think that women wear short/fitted clothes to attract opposite sex/male. The Minimum frequency is 20.75% for graduate men who think the same. Also 58.97% Pg./PhD holder think that women wear short/fitted clothes to attract opposite sex/male.

Figure 1 (a)

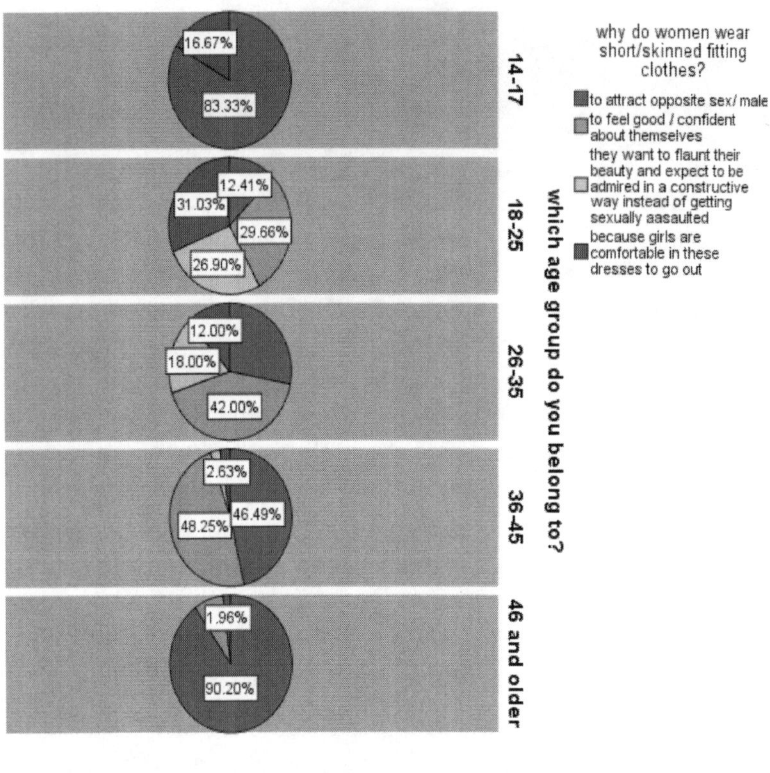

Figure 1 (b)

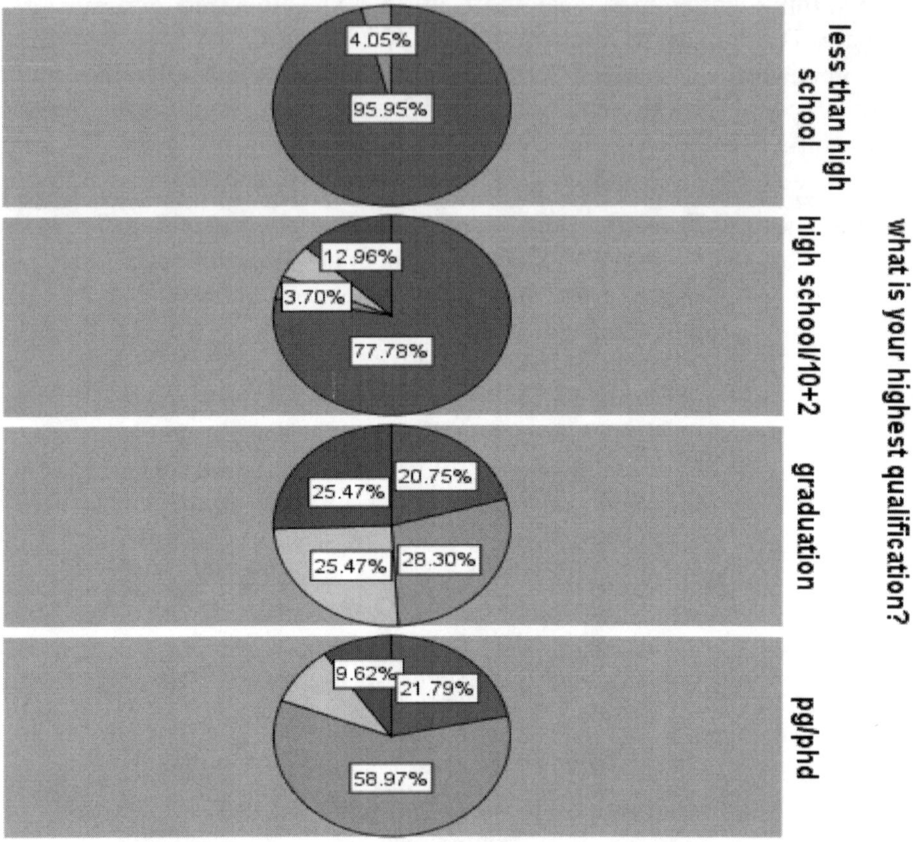

Table 2 shows that maximum frequency of men is 228 (45.6%). It means 228 out of 500 men think that women should not wear exposing dresses because it provokes men for sexual assault. The minimum frequency is 24 (4.8%), who think that girls should not wear exposing dresses because women in such dresses are not considered to be respectable. Eighty four men out of 500 think that these type of dresses are not in our culture. One hundred and sixty three men out of 500 think that men have no right to decide what women should wear or not. It should be their personal choice.

Figure 2 (a) shows that age group of 46 and older men have maximum frequency (82.35%), who thinks that women should not wear short/fitted clothes because it provokes men for sexual assault. Seventy five percent boys of age group between 14 and 17 years old think the same as 46 and older age group of men. Ten percent men (minimum frequency) of age group between 26 and 35 years old think the same.

Figure 2 (a)

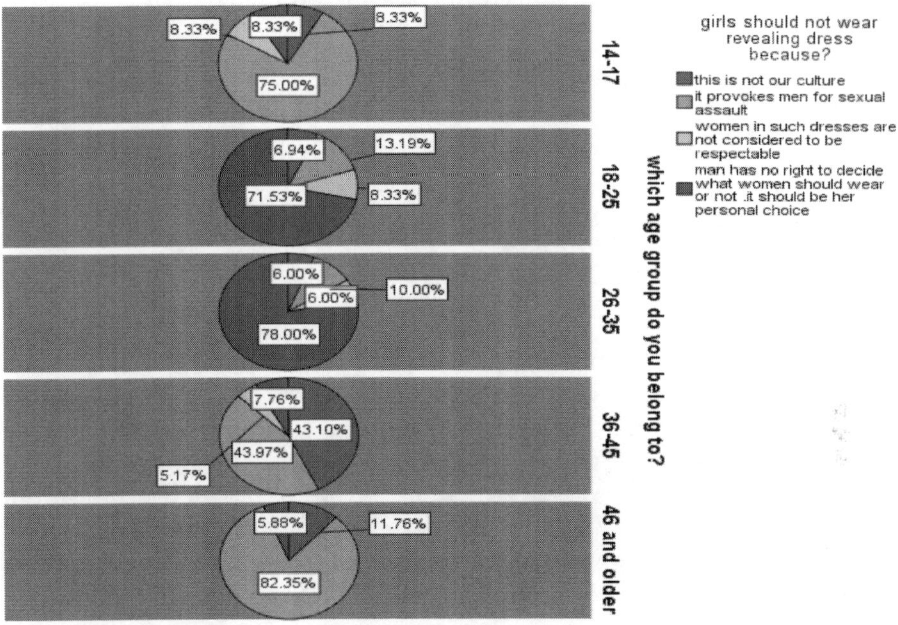

Figure 2(b) shows that maximum frequency (93.24%) of men for those whose qualification is less than high school who thinks that women should not wear short/fitted clothes because it provokes men for sexual assault. 79.63% men having high school/10+2 qualification think the same. 40.51% PG/PhD qualified men thinks that these types of dresses are not a part of our culture.

Figure 2(b)

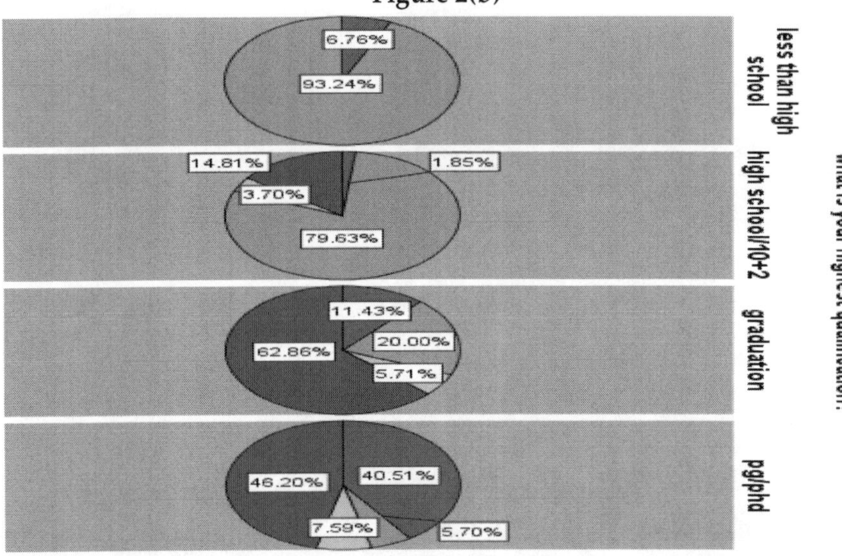

Table 3: Women ignoring conservative dress codes are at least partially responsible for sexual assault with them?

		Frequency	*Percent*	*Valid Percent*	*Cumulative Percent*
Valid	agree	99	19.8	19.9	19.9
	strongly agree	236	47.2	47.5	67.4
	disagree	85	17.0	17.1	84.5
	strongly disagree	76	15.2	15.3	99.8
	32	1	.2	.2	100.0
	Total	497	99.4	100.0	
Missing	System	3	.6		
Total		500	100.0		

Table 3 shows that maximum frequency is 236 (47.48%). It means 236 out of 500 men strongly agree that women ignoring conservative dress codes are at least partially responsible for sexual assault with them. Ninety-nine percent men agree that women ignoring conservative dress codes are at least partially responsible for their sexual assault. The minimum frequency is 76 (15.29%). It means only 76 out of 500 men completely disagree that women ignoring conservative dress codes are at least partially responsible for their sexual assault. 85 out of 500 disagree for same.

Figure 3 (a) shows that age group of 46 and older men have maximum frequency (88.24%) who strongly agree that women ignoring conservative dress codes are at least partially responsible for sexual assault with them. Sixty percent boys of age group between 14 and 17 years old strongly agree the same as 46 and older age group of men. Twelve percent men (minimum frequency) lie in the age group between 26 and 35 years old for strongly agree option.

Figure 3 (a)

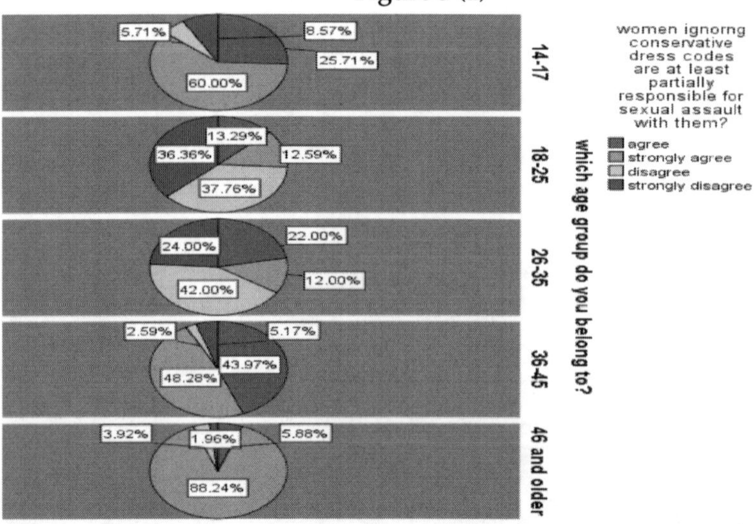

Figure 3(b) shows that maximum frequency of men (91.89%) for those whose qualification is less than high school strongly agree that women ignoring conservative dress codes are at least partially responsible for sexual assault with them. 79.25% men of high school/10+2 qualification strongly agree the same. 55.69% Post Graduate/PhD qualified men agree that women ignoring conservative dress codes are at least partially responsible for their sexual assault.

Figure 3(b)

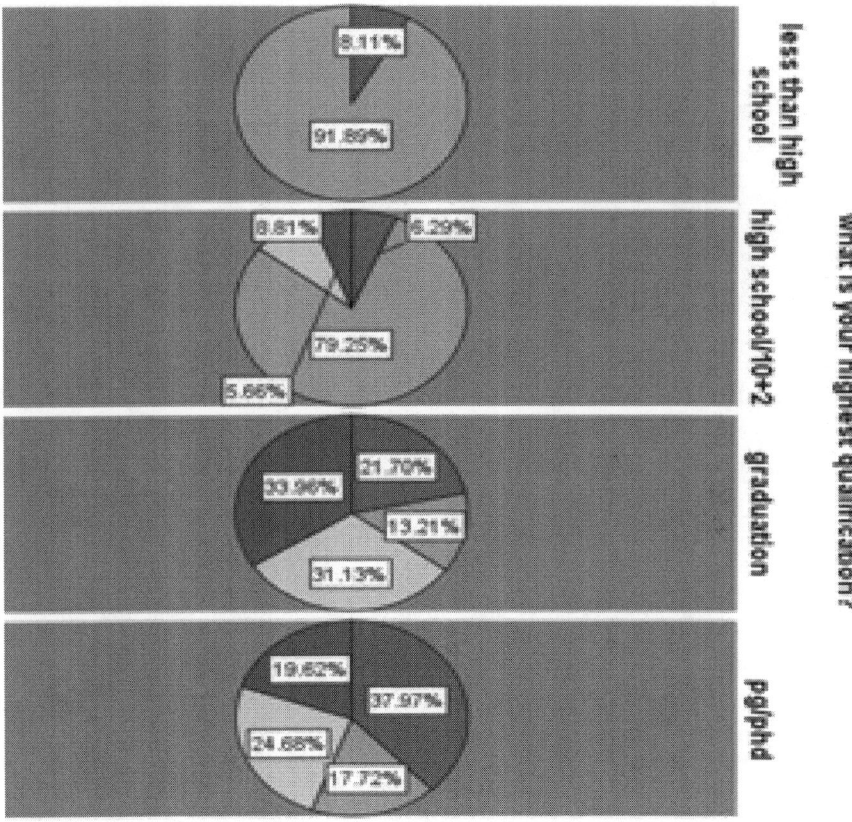

Findings and Discussions

Result shows that boys between 14 and 17 years old are conservative in their thinking. Most of them think if a woman wears any dresses except conservative garments have no dignity. They are considered to enjoy sexual assault hence can be approached for this. They think women wear modern attire to attract males. Frequency of this mind-set is going to decrease between the age of 18 and 35 years old men. But it gradually increases between the age group of 36 and 45 years old reach maximum after 45 and older ages.

If we take educational qualification as a parameter to check men's mind set, most of the narrow minded men are illiterate or less educated. But still today above 50%, well educated men think that women ignoring conservative dress codes are at least partially responsible for sexual assault with them. They think women wear modern attires to attract men.

CONCLUSION

Women in India are not treated equal to men. The data indicates that men assess the sexual availability of women through their dresses. They often pick up wrong cues as her dressing being suggestive of any sexual invitation. There is need to train the male mind to not judge a woman by her dress. Modern women like to wear different dresses and keep changing fashion rapidly. Perhaps, it may be due to higher income available to spend on clothing and more money available to spend on fashionable clothing. Clothing of women and sexuality are not co-related. Dressing up is about expressing herself and her joy through clothing.

Women have made rapid strides towards education, empowerment and freedom. Men have not been able to accept the drastic and rapid change that has already come about in the dressing of women. It is time for men to revisit this age-old thinking and change their outlook.

REFERENCES

Banarjee, J.N. (1956). The Development of Hindu Econography. Munshiram Monohalal Publication, Kolkata.

Barrios, O (1996). Unveiling and Subverting Hidden Meanings: The Sari as a Creative Tool in Designing a Woman's Identity in Shakuntala Boolell's "La femme enveloppée". Linguistics and Literature Studies 2(1): 16-28, 2014

P.R. Ghosh (2012). Western Women Should Not Wear the Indian Sari, February 2, 2012. Online available from http://www.ibtimes.com/articles/293861/20120206/indian-sari-fashion-western-women-bollywood.htm

E. Tarlo. Clothing Matters: Dress and Identity in India, University of Chicago Press, Chicago, 1996.

Lee, Y.Y., Beck, J.F (2010). "American women adoption of pants and the changing definition of femininity during world war 2", International Journal of Human Ecology, 11, 23-33

Foote, S. (1980). "Bloomers", Dress, 6, 1-12

Foote, S. (1989). "Challenging gender symbols", in C.B. Kidwell & W. Steele (Eds.), Men & women: Dressing thc part, pp. 144-157, Washington: Smithsonian Institution Press.

Purdah and Rural Housing in South Asia: A Literature Review. Created June 4, 2011. Online available from http://www.mcgill.ca/mchg/student/segregation/chapter3

Sharma, A. (2014). "Status of women: A socio-historical analysis in different ages of Indian society". Research Journal of Language, Literature and Humanities, Vol. 1(1), 10-14

Ahmed, Leila. Women and Gender in Islam: Historical Roots of a Modern Debate. New Haven: Yale University Press, 1992.

17

Status and Efforts of Women Education in 21st Century India

Ruchi Dubey, Payal Agarwal and Anamika Tiwari

ABSTRACT

Education is the backbone of not only a family, society, state, nation but for the whole world. Education does not mean enhancement in mere literacy rate but it is comprehensively related to qualitative and quantitative development of all the aspects of human beings. We can't imagine the complete vision of education by imparting it to a specific caste, creed, section, race, religion, region and gender, but to all. Today, the most important part of our society (girls and women) has lagged behind in the complete vision of educated India. Swami Vivekanand has aptly said, "There is no chance for the welfare of the world unless the condition of women is improved, it is not possible for a bird to fly on only one wing."

Education is the single most important factor to ensure gender quality and empowerment. However, many efforts have been made in this regard from primary to higher education and are still working towards equal and quality education. Since the year 2005 substantial progress has been achieved towards gender parity in education. But still a number of schemes and policies have yet to accomplish the target of 100%. For accomplishing the scheduled target and ensuring quality education, not only the government but the girls themselves will have to come forward to understand the significant role of education in their life and their responsibilities and duties towards the development of nation.

Keywords: *Status, efforts, women, education.*

INTRODUCTION

Education is the weapon in the hands of all the suppressed, minorities, deprived and the backward sub-sections of society, which enable them to prove their talent and capability to contribute for the development of the nation. The task of building of nation is not possible with the mere hand of one particular gender, i.e. male. It will be incomplete without the support of women. Earlier it was considered that males and females are the two wheels of a cart, but today the condition of one wheel is ignored and thus, the gender gap in all the phases of Census is clearly evident. On the other hand, 'women empowerment' has become a very fashionable and frequently used term, which invites several debates and discussions. It raises a striking question, that, why do women need empowerment when they have equal importance in all the walks of life. In order to define empowerment P.K.B. Nayar said, "Empowerment is an aid to help women to achieve equality with men or at least to reduce gender gap considerably". The government of India has tried to fully support education of girls through various schemes and policies. However, these lofty policies have not penetrated to the grass root level and much needs to be done. R. Govinda, Vice-Chancellor, National University of Education Planning and Administration (NUEPA), feels that though there are various policies in place, when it comes to implementation, there is a wide gap. According to the Census of 2011, the female literacy rate has increased up to 64.6% which is still less in comparison to male literacy, i.e. 80.9%. Thus, in order to throw light on rights and prestigious growth of women, year 2001 was dedicated to them as **Women Empowerment Year**. The condition of women education has been through many ups and downs from the Vedic period to the 21st-century India. This article presents an overview on women education as follows:

WOMEN EDUCATION IN VEDIC PERIOD

The history of female education in India has its roots in ancient Vedic period. Women had a place in society. They shared an equal position with their male counterpart and enjoyed a kind of liberty and respect that actually had societal sanctions. Some names come to mind like Ghosha, Lopamudra, Matreyi and Gargi, when talking about significant female figures of the Vedic Period.

WOMEN EDUCATION IN PRE-INDEPENDENT INDIA

In western India, Jyotiba Phule and his wife Savitri Bai became pioneers of female education when they started a school for girls in 1848 in Pune. Women's education was acknowledged in 1854 by Wood's Dispatch, a programme of East India Company. Gradually, after that, there was progress in female education, but it initially tended to focus on the primary level and was related to the richer sections of society. In 1878, the University of Calcutta became one of the first Universities to offer its Bachelor Degree programmes to women. Later, the overall literacy rate for women increased from 0.2% in 1882 to 6% in 1947.

WOMEN EDUCATION IN POST-INDEPENDENT INDIA

In pre-independent India, the University Education Commission recommended suggestions to improve the quality of education but stated against female education as, "Women's present education is entirely irrelevant to the life they have to lead. It is not only a waste but often a definite disability". In the post-independent India the female literacy rate was still very low at 8.9%. Thus, in 1958, a National Committee on Women education was appointed by the government. It recommended female education on the same footing as offered for boys. Further, a focus on girls' education was put in place by the National Policy on Education in 1986 followed by a Programme of Action in 1992.

WOMEN EDUCATION IN 21ST CENTURY INDIA

The 86th Constitutional Amendment Act, 2001, known as Sarva Shiksha Abhiyan, National Curriculum Framework in 2005 and the National Curriculum Framework for Teacher Education in 2010, have been path-breaking steps towards the growth of education, especially for females. These policies were complemented by other schemes such as National Programme for the Education of Girls at the Elementary level, Kasturba Gandhi Balika Vidyalaya Scheme, both ensuring inclusion and quality education for girls. The Mahila Samakhya Programme was launched in 10 states targeting marginalized sections of far-fetched women. Access to education was also facilitated by separate schools for girls, availability of open learning resources and materials, residential schooling, coaching facilities, scholarships, textbooks, uniforms and transport including bicycles. The Right of Children to Free and Compulsory Education (known as RTE) Act, 2010, is a new roadmap for gender equality in education in India. The government of India has established National Credit Fund for Women in 1993 for financial support to the developmental tasks of women empowerment. Some of the policies facilitating girls' education in 21st Century are as follows:

- **National Policy for the Empowerment of Women:** The programme was started in 2001 to bring about advancement, development and empowerment of women. It is specifically creating an environment through economic and social policies of enjoying human rights and fundamental freedom, equal access to participation and decision making, health care, quality education at all levels, career and vocational guidance, employment, equal remuneration, social security and aimed at elimination of all forms of discrimination against women.

- **Swayamsiddha:** A scheme for empowering the Indian women both socially and economically to enable them to live with dignity and self-reliance, launched by Central Government in July 12, 2001. Swayamsiddha merged the Indira Mahila Yojana (IMY) and Mahila Samriddhi Yojana (MSY). It not only educated women on their status, right and privileges but also generated awareness about women's health, nutrition, education, sanitation and hygiene.
- **Kishori Shakti Yojana (KSY):** It was started in the year 2001. It sought to empower adolescent girls, so as to enable them to take charge of their lives. The broad objectives of the scheme were to improve the nutritional, health and development status of adolescent girls, promote awareness of health, hygiene, nutrition and family care, link them to opportunities for learning life skills, going back to school, better understanding of their social environment and taking initiatives to become productive members of the society.
- **National Programme for Education of Girls at Elementary Level (NPEGEL):** This programme was launched in July 2003. It was an incentive to reach out to the girls, who the Sarva Shiksha Abhiyan (SSA) was not able to reach throughout the earlier schemes. The SSA called out to them, particularly the "hardest to reach girls". This scheme has covered 24 states in India. Under NPEGEL "Model Schools" have been set up to provide better opportunities to girls.
- **Kasturba Gandhi Balika Vidyalaya Scheme (KGBV):** This scheme was launched in July 2004, to provide education to girls at primary level who are unable to go to regular schools and 'out of school' girls in the 10+ age group. The schools that were set up have 100% reservations; 75% for backward class and 25% for BPL (below poverty line) females of rural areas with very low literacy level.
- **Rashtriya Madhyamik Shiksha Abhiyan (RMSA):** This is a centrally sponsored scheme of the Ministry of Human Resource Development, Government of India, launched in 2009, for the development of Secondary Education in public schools throughout India. One of the major objectives of the scheme is to remove gender, socio-economic and disability barriers.

- **Rajiv Gandhi Scheme for Empowerment of Adolescent Girls—SABLA:** It was started in November 2010 with the objective to improve the nutritional and health status of adolescent girls in the age group of 11 to 18 years and empower them by providing education in life skills, health and nutrition.
- **National Mission for Empowerment of Women:** This was a Centrally Sponsored scheme that was initiated in April 2011, for empowering women holistically. The salient features of the NMEW are poverty alleviation, economic empowerment, health, nutrition, gender budgeting, gender-based law enforcement, empowerment of marginalized groups, social empowerment and quality education.
- **Beti Bachao, Beti Padhao:** Prime Minister Narendra Modi launched the scheme on January 22, 2015, in Panipat (Haryana), with an initial corpus of Rs. 100 crore. The scheme has been launched in hundred districts across the country to make girls independent both socially and also financially through education.
- **Post-Graduate Indira Gandhi Scholarship for Single Girl Child for PG Programmes:** The scheme was launched in September 22, 2005, by Central Government of India in order to achieve and promote girls' education. University Grants Commission has introduced this scholarship for a girl child with an aim to compensate direct cost of girl's education in non-professional courses only.
- **Maulana Azad National Fellowship:** The fellowship was started by Central Government in 2003 for poor and talented girls of minority groups for higher education.
- **National Scheme of Incentives to Girls for Secondary Education:** The scheme was launched in the budget session of 2006–07, which provides a scholarship of Rs 3000 to the girls who have passed upper-primary and are being enrolled in secondary schools.
- **Scheme for construction and running of girls' hostel for students of secondary and higher secondary schools:** This is a Centrally sponsored scheme launched in 2008–09 and is being implemented since 2009–10 to set up a 100-bedded Girls' Hostel in each of 3479 Educationally Backward Blocks (EBBs) in the county. The main objective of the scheme is to retain the SC, ST, OBC, minority community and BPL girl child in a secondary school in case of long distance to school and lack of parents' financial affordability.

Despite all these efforts a large number of girls still remain outside the education system. According to Karin Hulshof, Indian representative in UNICEF, out of 81% girls joining school at the primary level, around 50% drop out at the secondary level because of factors such as child marriage, child labour, etc. "The Sarva Shiksha Abhiyan (SSA) and Right to Education (RTE) Act are tools that can empower the girl child. We need an effective delivery mechanism and have more gender-friendly classrooms," she said.

Table 1: Literacy Rates (in percentage)

Census Year	*Males*	*Females*
1951	27.2	8.9
1961	40.4	15.4
1971	46.0	22.0
1981	56.4	29.8
1991	54.1	39.3
2001	75.3	53.7
2011	80.9	64.6

1951–71: Age group 5 and above, 1981–2011: Age group 7 and above .

Data source: Educational Statistics at a Glance, Department of School Education and Literacy, MHRD, Government of India (website: mhrd.gov.in>statistics >ESG2016)

PROBLEMS AND STATUS OF GIRLS' EDUCATION IN THE 21ST CENTURY

The efforts of Indian government towards girls education are commendable, but the target of 100% enrolment, retention in schools and promotion is yet to be achieved. Girls' education is still facing some problems as:

- **Enrolment:** Enrolment of scheduled caste and scheduled tribe girls poses a greater challenge. Surveys, however, revealed that the participation of these disadvantaged girls in basic education has grown over the years. The overall gender gap in enrolment at the primary stage has dropped to 4.6 percentage points and at the upper primary level has reduced to 8.0 percentage points in 2005. With enrolment reaching at least 96% since 2009, and girls making up 56% of new students between 2007 and 2013. Upper primary and secondary schools' Gross Enrolment Ratio saw a rise of 13% and 17%, respectively in 2013–14 compared to 2007–08. The number of boys' enrolment in higher education has increased 13% and girls 21% since 2012–13. Number of female enrolments on per hundred males are as below:

Table 2: Number of females per hundred males enroled by stages of education

Level/Year	*Primary*	*Upper-Primary*	*Secondary*	*Senior Secondary*	*Higher Education*
1950-51	39	19	NA	15	13
1960-61	48	31	NA	26	21
1970-71	60	41	NA	33	28
1980-81	63	49	NA	45	36
1990-91	71	58	NA	49	46
2000-01	78	69	63	62	58
2005-06	87	81	73	72	62
2009-10	92	88	82	80	67
2014-15	93	95	91	90	85

NA= Not Available

Data Source: Education Statistics at a Glance, Department of School Education & Literacy, MHRD, Government of India. (website: mhrd.gpv.in>statistics> ESG2016).

- **Dropout:** Although the phenomenon of dropouts continue to be a serious problem in India's education scenario. The dropout rates in elementary education have been on the decline, more sharply in the case of girl education. Girls dropout rate in 2004–05 was lower than boys, at primary level, i.e. 25.42% compared to 31.81% for boys. Since 2000, girl's dropout rates have fallen by reduction of only 4.1 percentage points over the entire last decade (1990–2000). But according to the current data available in 2013–14, the average annual female dropout rate in primary level is 4.14 percentage points, in upper-primary 4.49 percentage points, in secondary 17.79 percentage points and in senior secondary 1.61 percentage points. Further, the condition of average annual SC, ST female student dropout is more pitiable. Level-wise Average Annual Dropout Rate is as below:

Table 3: Level-wise Average Annual Dropout Rate in School Education (2013-14) (in %)

Level	*Girls*		
	ALL	*SC*	*ST*
Primary	4.14	3.85	7.98
Upper Primary	4.49	5.04	8.85
Secondary	17.79	18.32	26.96
Senior Secondary	1.61	1.38	2.77

* Figures related to School Education are provisional.

Data Source: *Educational Statistics at a Glance,* Department of School Education & Literacy, MHRD, Government of India. (website: mhrd.gov.in>statistics> ESG2016)

- **Stagnation:** The situation inside the school is found that the repeat or repetition rates have been fast declining for girls. Two focused areas behind this trend are: 1) girls who enter the school system do not leave easily; and 2) school efficiency is gradually improving with girls completing the elementary cycle of education in lesser time. The number of out of school children have also been declining rapidly, from 32 million in 2001–02 to 7.5 million in 2006–07.
- **Promotion:** The promotion rate from primary to upper primary are also positive. The promotion rate has improved from 71.98 in 2003 to 80.64 in 2005. The promotion rates of girls (8.6 percentage points) have been higher than that of boys (7.65 percentage points). This has led to sharper decline in the gender gap in promotion rates from 4.03 percentage points to 3.02 percentage points. In the case of SC girls, the promotion rate has increased from 80% in 2004–05 to 83% in 2005–06 leaving a gender gap of 3 percentage points. The picture is comparable in the case of ST girls for whom the promotion rate has increased from 85% in 2004–05 to 88% in 2005–06 leaving a gender gap of 2 percentage points.

However, according to the data given by MHRD, the number of female enrolments in primary schools has reached at 629 lakhs; upper-primary at 327 lakhs; secondary at 182 lakhs; senior-secondary at 111 lakhs and higher education at 157 lakhs in 2014-15. The number of SC/ST female enrolment in primary school is recorded as 126 lakhs and 68 lakhs; upper-primary as 64 lakhs and 32 lakhs; secondary as 34 lakhs and 16 lakhs; senior-secondary as 20 lakhs and 7 lakhs; and higher education as 21 lakhs and 7 lakhs, respectively in 2014–15. The data shows high interest of girls in enrolment of the courses such as arts, science, commerce and education, whereas low interest in the courses like technology, engineering, business administration, computer application and law, in comparison to boys. MHRD reported the enrolment of boys as 89% whereas, girls only with 11% in higher education through Regular and Distance mode in 2014–15. The Gross Enrolment Ratio in higher education remains low at 23.6% in 2014–15. The current target is to increase GER to 25.2% in 2017–18 and further to 30% in 2020–21.

CONSTITUTIONAL PROVISIONS TO PROTECT WOMEN EDUCATION

The constitution of India not only grants equality to women but also empowers the state to adopt measures of positive discrimination in favour of women. In Article 15(1) on right to equality, provides no discrimination against any citizen on grounds only of religion, race, caste, sex, and place of birth or any of them. Article 15(3) grants the state to make any special provision in favour of women and children. Article 46 grants the state to promote with special care the educational and economic interests of the weaker sections of the people and to protect them from social injustice and all forms of exploitation.

Until 1976, education was a state subject. Since its transfer to the concurrent list by the 42nd Constitutional Amendment in 1976, the Central Government has played a more proactive role in this sector. Further, the 86th Constitutional Amendment Act, 2002 has made elementary education a fundamental right for children in the age group of 6–14 years. Thus, the amendments have laid the foundation for several Centrally sponsored schemes that had a distinct bearing on promoting education for girls.

CONCLUSION

Women occupy almost half of the population of India and represent half of the human resources. But it is unfortunate to say that there is a tendency to deny equal socio-economic opportunity for them. This neglecting attitude towards women is in all the aspects and particularly in the field of education. It is well known that education is the fundamental agent for the socio-economic development of any country. But equal access in the field of education had not been fairly treated. The importance of women's education is beautifully referred through the statement of philosopher-President and great educationist Dr. S. Radhakrishnan, "There cannot be educated people without educated women. If general education has to be limited to men or women, the opportunity should be given to women. From them it would most surely be passed on to the next generation." In the 21st century the importance of women education has been understood and a number of efforts are being made through government and non-government organizations. The effort and awareness for equal quality education is limited till primary level. The report says that 29% of children drop out before completing five years of primary school, and 43% before finishing upper primary schools; high school completion is only 42%. This ranks India among the top five nations for out-of-school children at the primary school age. Thus, to reach the set target not only organizations but individuals will also have to be aware and work responsibly to bring about quality education on ground for girls.

SUGGESTIONS FOR QUALITY ENHANCEMENT IN GIRLS' EDUCATION

1. The government of India must be sure to spend more on girls' education. Free and quality education for all and the provision of accessible schools for girls in every area of the country, will ensure that all the girls must gain equal access to education.
2. The infrastructure and quality of teaching in government schools should be supervised from time to time to stop the high dropout rates of marginalized sections of society, especially girls.
3. Efforts should be made to enhance the interest level of female students towards technology, engineering, business administration, computer applications and law.
4. Frame a non-traditional curriculum to enable them for present challenges.
5. Introduce flexible scholarships and fellowship schemes for both financially poor students and meritorious students to encourage women in secondary and higher education.
6. Design skill-oriented and professional higher education.
7. Increase the number of women teachers at all the levels of education.
8. Establish equal opportunity commission for all the stages of education.
9. Provide easy bank loan facilities for women students.
10. Lastly, the attitude of neglecting the education of women must be changed. Gender equality and women's empowerment must be promoted throughout the education system.

REFERENCES

1. Bhuyan, D. (2006). Empowerment of Indian Women: A Challenge of 21st Century. Orissa Review. Retrieved on 16 April 2017, from odisha.gov.in>jan2006>engpdf>.
2. Central Government Schemes for School Education, 2013. Reference Note by Parliament Library and Reference, Research, Documentation and Information Service (LARRDIS), No. 17, August 2013. Retrieved on 15 April 2017, from 164.100.47.134>intranet>
3. Educational Statistics at a Glance- 2014-15. Department of School Education & Literacy, Ministry of Human Resource Development, Government of India. Retrieved on 16 April 2017, from mhrd.gov.in>statistics>ESG2016-0
4. Female Education. Retrieved from https://en.m.wikipedia.org>wiki>
5. Gender Issues in Education, 2006. A Position Paper by National Council of Educational Research and Training. Retrieved on 15 April 2017, from epathshala.nic.in>doc>NCF>pdf

6. Girls Education in India: Achievements Since Independence, 2008. Department of School Educational Literacy, SSA, MHRD, Government of India. Retrieved on 16 April 2017, from ssa.nic.in>Notices
7. Important Constitutional and Legal Provisions For Women in India. Retrieved on 18 April 2017, from https://missionprahar.com>women-rights
8. Nath, S. (2014). Higher Education and Women Participation in India. *Journal of Business Management & Social Science Research (JMB&SSR)*, Vol. 3, No. 2, pp. 43–7. Retrieved on 17 April 2017, form www.borjournals.com>article>viewFile
9. Ramachandran, V. (2003). Gender Equality in Education in India. Paper Commissioned for the Education for All Global Monitoring Report 2003/4, The Leap to Equality. Retrieved on 16 April 2017, from unesdoc.unesco.org>images
10. Singh, S. (2015). Women Empowerment and Governmental Efforts. An article on Women Empowerment in the magazine Kurukshetra, No. 5, pp. 25–30.

18

Sustainable Development through Gender Equality in Education

Shiv Kumar Yadav

ABSTRACT

In the present globalised scenario, the concept of development has changed and most of the nations have agreed for sustainable development on Jan 2016, the 17 Sustainable Goals (SDGs) of the 2030 Agenda for Sustainable development adopted by world leaders in September 2015 at a Historic UN Summit.

Sustainable Development Goal 4 declares to ensure inclusive and equitable quality and education and promote lifelong learning opportunities for all. SDG 5 also declares to achieve gender equality and empower all women and girls.

To achieve these SDGs, education is the best weapon for all nations of the world. By providing good and quality education without gender discrimination; it can be achieved because, education is a human right in itself and an indispensable means of realizing other human rights.

The right to Education is protected under articles 13 and 14 of the International Convention on Economic, Social and Cultural Rights (ICESCR) which also enshrines a prohibition on discrimination based on sex both in law and in fact. To promote gender equality, states must target their efforts not only towards education itself, but also towards society's cultural and institutional frameworks and should reform the education system for equal opportunities for females and males.

This paper discusses how "education" can help in elimination of gender inequality and promote women's participation in the economy, and thus increase national capacity and achieve greater economic, social and cultural developments to meet the SDGs.

Keywords: *Sustainable development, Education, Gender Equality Human Right and inclusive Education.*

INTRODUCTION

> **"Sustainable development is development that meets the needs of the present without compromising the ability of future generations to meet their own needs"** —*Brundtland Report*

Sustainable Development Goals (SDGs) known as the global goals; are universal to end poverty, protect the planet and ensure that all people enjoy peace and prosperity. The concept of development has been changed and most of the nations have agreed for Sustainable Development, on January 2016, based on the 17 Sustainable Development Goals (SDGs) of the 2030 Agenda for Sustainable Development adopted by world leaders in September 2015 at a Historic UN Summit.

These 17 goals are based on the limited successes of the Millennium Development Goals, while including new areas such as climate change, economic inequality, gender equality, women empowerment, innovation, sustainable consumption, peace and justice.

According to UNDP Administrator, Helen Clark, "The SDGs provides us with a common plan and agenda to tackle some of the pressing challenges facing our world such as poverty, climate change and conflict."

Sustainable development recognizes that growth must be both inclusive and environmentally sound to reduce poverty and build shared prosperity for today's population and to continue to meet the needs of future generations. It must be efficient with resources and carefully planned to deliver immediate and long-term benefits for people, planet and prosperity.

Good and quality education must be provided for females and males to meet Sustainable Development through Gender equality. Gender equality between men and women, entails the concept that all human beings, both men and women are free to develop their personal abilities and make choices without the limitations set by stereotype, rigid gender roles and prejudices. There are 17 SDGs for 2030 agenda in which two goals are directly related to women empowerment and gender equality. **Sustainable Goal 4 declares to ensure inclusive and equitable quality education and promote lifelong learning opportunities for all. SDG 5 also declares to achieve gender equality and empower all women and girls.**

As Nelson Mandela had said, *"Education is the most powerful weapon which you can use to change the world."*

Education is the key to eliminating gender inequality, to reducing poverty, to creating a sustainable planet, to preventing deaths and illness, and to fostering peace and justice. Education is the new currency by which nations maintain economic competitiveness and global prosperity. Education is an investment, and one of the most critical investments we can make.

RIGHT TO EDUCATION FOR ELIMINATING GENDER INEQUALITY

Education is both a human right in itself and an indispensable means of realizing other human right. The right to education bridges the division of human rights into civil and political, economic, social and cultural development.

Educational inequality is a major infringement of the rights of women and girls, and an important barrier to social and economic development. The global struggle for universal education is nearly 61 years old. It was recognized as a right in the 1948 Universal Declaration on Human Rights (UDHR), which states, "Everybody has the right to education." The UDHR also declared that elementary education should be free and compulsory. These provisions were followed up by the UNESCO Convention against Discrimination in Education, adopted in 1960, which placed the right to education in a binding treaty for the first time. Under article 4 of the UNESCO Convention the right to free and compulsory education is guaranteed, and States parties "undertake...to formulate, develop and apply a national policy, which will tend to promote equality of opportunity and of treatment in the matter of education".

The right to education is protected comprehensively under articles 13 and 14 of the International Convention on Economic, Social and Cultural Rights (ICESCR), which also enshrines a prohibition on discrimination, based on sex, both in law and in fact. The two most recent conventions—CEDAW in 1979 and the Convention on the Rights of the Child (CRC in 1990)—contain the most comprehensive set of legally enforceable commitments concerning both rights to education and to gender equality. By mid-2003, some 173 countries had ratified CEDAW, whereas the CRC has been ratified by all the nations of the world with the exception of Somalia and the United States.

In the light of these above declarations and convocations, Indian government enacted ***The Right of Children to free and Compulsory Education Act, 2009 or Right to Education Act, 2009.*** This act assented to 26 August 2009 and commenced on 1 April 2010. This act describes the modalities of the importance of free and compulsory education for children between 6 and 14 in India under article 21(a) of the Indian constitution.

Now India has become one of the 135 countries to make education a fundamental right of every child when the act came into force on 1 April 2010.

GENDER-RELATED PROBLEMS IN EDUCATION

However, we cannot speak of gender-related problems in education in terms of access, students' enrolment or performance in the universities and colleges. There are still some areas where gender balance should be encouraged, like the representation of girls and women in science and mathematics; and to ensure that those already in scientific and research careers find their careers, prospects and rewards sufficiently satisfactory to keep them there. Gender inequalities in higher education and research have become an issue of growing policy concern since the late 1990s. Statistics and research have shown that gender equality has not been achieved in higher education quantitatively or qualitatively. This is so despite the fact that women have made great gains in higher education during the last decades. In the beginning of the 21st Century, women account for more than half of graduates in higher education throughout the world.

Despite this great potential for job creation and development, only those who can afford the new technologies, and have the skills to use them, will benefit, while the poor is being marginalized. Women make up the large majority of the poor worldwide; any strategy to increase their participation in the digital economy would increase national capacity and help raise the national standard of living. The large majority of women in developing countries are "employed" by the informal economy (street vendors or women working at home, for example handicrafts and sewing). Reaching these women will be the major challenge for policy makers. Among the key barriers faced by women are access to education, skills and training, access to the technologies themselves (both hardware and connectivity) and other constraints such as those related to knowledge of foreign languages (i.e. access to Internet content) or lack of financial resources to acquire access.

GENDER EQUALITY FOR SUSTAINABLE DEVELOPMENT

There have been many changes in India since the country gained its independence from Great Britain in 1947, the most impressive being the rise of the Indian economy. However, not all facets of Indian life have enjoyed the same advancement. Health, education and other human development issues have not seen the growth that the economy has enjoyed. India will not realize the full benefit of an improving economy until the lives of the Indian people improve. How can a country become an economic superpower when its people remain among the worlds' poorest?

The inequalities that exist among region, social class and gender prevent the growth of the Indian economy from improving the lives of many everyday Indian people. Nowhere is inequality more evident than in the lives of Indian women, and likewise, there is no sector more affected by the lack of improvement in social issues. Therefore, without eliminating these inequalities India cannot achieve SDGs.

The differences in the health, education and standards of behaviour between the men and women of India, all contribute to the impairment of women's ability. The continued perception that women are not fit for all types of jobs hinders women's ability to participate in the economy. The economic discrimination that the women of India suffer leads to a cycle of further discrimination in other areas and reinforces their low status.

The majority of women in India are doing tasks that are not recognized by Indian society as meaningful. Earlier, in the last Census, women and children who worked on family owned land or were self-employed working in either their home or family enterprises, were not considered employed. The majority of women work much longer hours than men, but much of their work is nurturing, and therefore not recognized as important. Even when women are contributing earnings, culturally their work is thought of as connected to their position as nurturer and therefore is not recognized as productive. Many of these women report in surveys that they are "housewives," even though they spend 14-16 hours a day earning an income.

Often, even when women are involved in income-producing activities outside the home, but their work remains invisible due to their low status. In the agricultural field, much of the work women do is pre and post-production, such as weeding, livestock rearing, and processing; and because economic value is placed on the actual output, the work is not seen as important.

Indian women are excluded from decision making from the time of their birth, in every aspect of their lives. It is therefore not surprising that this tradition carries over from the home and community to the national level. All over South Asia, powerful women leaders have reached the highest levels of national government, but the vast majorities of women are in poor health, illiterate, and are invisible in the economic accounting system. Women hold important positions in major political parties of the region, but these powerful positions have not necessarily produced positive results for the average woman living in this area of the world.

Changes in the way Indian society views women has changed to a certain extent as women have developed increased ability to participate in the economic growth of the country, enhanced through education and legislation. The low social status of women is seen in the homes and communities of India, and is reflected in Indian society as a whole. Only when women are valued in their homes and communities will the lives of women in India improve, and when the lives of Indian women improve, those of their families will improve also. The change in thinking must begin in the minds of Indian women themselves. When women begin to see themselves as powerful, change will begin. When India makes improvements in human development issues like health, education, and gender equality, the majority of people in India will begin to realize the benefits of an improved economy. Imagine the growth that would be seen if every citizen in the country was given the dream, the chance, and the right, to fully participate in the economy. Then India might truly become an economic superpower.

RECOMMENDATIONS ON GENDER EQUALITY IN EDUCATION

Education for all is important for three reasons. First, education is a right. Second, education enhances individual freedom. Third, education yields important development benefits.

There is indication of international commitment to gender equality in education, through international treaties for ratification by individual countries, which gives them legal weight, and political promises developed by international consensus to be a further stimulus to promote action.

Government of India has taken many steps for it but they are not enough for SDGs. NGOs also are playing important roles for employment of women and their education, but that is not enough. They have to make plans of action and execute them well.

Some suggestions for empowerment of the women that would meet SDGs are as follows:

- Government should make a plan of action for Gender Equality for empowerment of women.
- Non-formal Education should be given to rural women by joint efforts of Government and NGOs.
- Project Prodh Shiksha Abhiyan is a National level programme.

However, its implementation is not satisfactory. It seems to be limited only to the Literacy Mission. Now it should be redesigned and its goals should be wider as SDGs.

- In higher education such as engineering, medical, legal sector, women participation is less than men. So, we should eliminate its cause and promote girls for making career in these fields.
- For Gender Equality, it is suggested, we will have to change our point of views towards women. For this, Women Education should be a compulsory paper at undergraduate and postgraduate levels just like Environmental Education.
- Women Education should be a part of the curriculum and co-curriculum activities of higher secondary and secondary level.

INTERNATIONAL TREATIES

International treatise indicate commitment to non-discrimination in education with respect to gender. It commits states to economic measures for free primary education and financial support, educational and other forms of support for families, and support for teachers. One of the three instruments to make up the International Bill of Human Rights, this international treaty has limited coverage of gender and education.

POLITICAL AND SOCIAL PROMISES

The human rights of women and of the girl child are an inalienable, integral and indivisible part of universal human rights. As an agenda for action, the Platform seeks to promote and protect the full enjoyment of all human rights and the fundamental freedoms of all women throughout their lifecycle.

Its goal was to narrow the gender gap in primary and secondary education by 2005 and to ensure that by 2015, all children complete primary schooling, with girls and boys having equal access to all levels of education. Limited success has been achieved but some positive outcomes can be observed. This area of action aimed to address the need to change behaviours, attitudes, norms and values, which define and influence gender roles in society through education, the media, arts, culture and science in particular. Eliminating prejudices and stereotypes is paramount for the establishment of gender equality. In order to overcome stereotypes regarding gender roles in family and society, the following measures could be proposed.

Gender mainstreaming is different from previous approaches to equal opportunities, which focused mainly on the implementation of specific measures in favour of women. Although measures to promote women's rights are important, they are not sufficient to overcome structural inequalities in economic, social, political and family life. Gender mainstreaming thus entails fundamental transformation of the underlying paradigms of the sphere of education. It includes not only the activities of governments, but also those of schools, colleges and education institutions, and, where appropriate, those of NGOs and the private sector as well. Gender mainstreaming has to be implemented in co-operation with all social factors involved in combating poverty and social exclusion in the fields of employment, social protection, justice, education, health, public finances, economic policy, etc. Updating curricula, new teaching methods, the development of types of institutions, a new educational organization according to market economy principles, etc., all these aspects could be approached, taking into consideration the need for new definitions of the roles of women and men in societies, of private and public partnerships between men and women, of power structures in societies, etc.

CONCLUSIONS

Achieving sustainable goals through gender equality in education entails tackling gender ideologies that constrain enjoyment of the full array of positive freedoms that are valued in a rights and capabilities approach. This entails firstly putting women back into the picture as rights bearers and not deliverers of development, and extending our interest in how women's education impacts others, to assessing how education impacts women themselves. ICT and e-commerce offer substantial possibilities to improve the lives of women (and their families) in developing countries. While many examples exist of how women have used the new technologies to improve their businesses, create new businesses or find new employment opportunities, the large majority of women in developing countries are still excluded from the digital economy. Training and educating women in ICTs and e-commerce would enable women's participation and empowerment in the digital economy, and thus increase national capacity towards economic development and growth. Lastly, education and empowerment of women are the biggest means to achieve Sustainable Development Goals.

REFERENCES

1. Annual report—MHRD: mhrd.gov.in/sites/upload_files/mhrd/files/document-reports/AR2013-14.pdf, accessed on 18 April 2017.

2. Berta-Esteve-Volast (2007). *Gender discrimination and Growth: Theory and Evidence from India*, London: London School of Economics and Political Sciences.
3. Elementary Education | Government of India, Ministry of ... – MHRD: *mhrd.gov.in › School Education*, accessed on 18 April 2017.
4. educational statistics at a glance – MHRD *mhrd.gov.in/sites/upload_files/mhrd/files/statistics/ESG2016_0.pdf*, accessed on 18 April 2017.
5. Gender Equality in Education in India: A State Level Analysis: www.ijsrm.in/v4-i8/16%20ijsrm.pdf,accessed on 18 April 2017.
6. Gender equality – European Commission: ec.europa.eu/justice/gender-equality/, accessed on 18 April 2017.
7. Seguino, Stephanie (2006). "Gender Equality and Economic Growth: A Cross-Country Analysis", *World Development*, Vol. 28, No. 7, pp. 67–71.
8. Sunden, Annika and B. Surette (2008), "Gender Differences in the Allocation of Assets in Retirement Savings Plans", *American Economic Review*, Vol. 88, No. 2, pp. 207–11.
9. UNICEF Basic information and gender equality: http://www.unicef.org/girlseducation/index_statistics.html.
10. Velkoff, Victoria A. (1998). Women's Education in India. Report by the U.S. Dept. of Commerce, Washington: GPO.
11. http://www.census.gov/ipc/prod/wid-9801.pdf, accessed on 19 April 2017.
12. https://en.wikipedia.org/wiki/Sustainable_development, accessed on 19 April 2017.
13. www.un-documents.net/ocf-02.htm, accessed on 19 April 2017.
14. www.unesco.org/education/tlsf/mods/theme_a/mod02.html, accessed on 19 April 2017.
15. https://www.unicef.org/gender/,accessed on 20 April 2017.
16. United Nations: Gender equality and women's empowerment: mhrd.gov.in/sites/upload_files/mhrd/files/document.../Final_report_conf_0.pdfwww.un.org/sustainabledevelopment/gender-equality/,accessed on 20 April 2017.
17. UNESCO, Gender and Education for All: The Leap to Equality—Summary Report (2003) (hereinafter referred to as UNESCO Summary Report) at p. 1, available at http://www.efareport.unesco.org/.
18. Wilson, D. (2003). Human Rights: Promoting gender equality in and through education. Background paper for EFA GMR 2003/4.

19

Family Relationship and Gender Identity in Select Plays of Shakespeare

Kripashankar Verma

INTRODUCTION

When we talk about society, we directly or indirectly try to approach the initial need of its formation. This is a critical commonplace that to ensure the security or safety of some individuals it was perhaps assumed, that, to compromise on some aspects and interests common to a particular group of people. This could be one of the requirements that precipitated the formation of families and also gender roles and stereotypes.

Family may be considered the first society of human beings. Since, after birth the child has to pass the initial and important phase of life here. The members of the family are the members of the first society to him or her. This is the stage where the gender consciousness in the child is formed. He comes to know this is the father, this is the mother, etc. Besides, he or she later comes to know how the father is different from the mother.

When we think about some of the Shakespearean Plays, we observe that the playwright has given the family and its network of relationships a prominent place in his plays. He has not only kept this aspect in limelight, but if we look closely at the thematic concerns, we find that gender identity is also associated to the aforesaid aspect. For instance, *Othello, King Lear,* and a few others can be put to the analysis. Othello serves as an example to demonstrate the expectations of the Elizabethan Patriarchal Society, the practice of privileges in patriarchal marriages, and the suppression and repression of femininity.

A major interest of the feminist critics in English-speaking countries has been to reconstitute the ways we deal with literature in order to do justice to female points of view, concerns and values. One emphasis has been to alter the way a woman reads the literature of the past so as to make her not an acquiescent, but the "Resisting Reader"; that is one who resists the author's intentions and design in order, by a "revisionary rereading" to bring to light and to counter the covert sexual biases written in a literary work. The term 'resistance' is very important from the feminist point of view; since it is the predominant factor that exhibits women's sense of quest for identity in a patriarchal world.

In *The Taming of the Shrew*, Shakespeare's infamous 'shrew' Katherina voices a resistible imperative: women should resist. But what should be resisted, exactly? The authority of individual men—her father Baptista, her husband Petruchio—believe women should obey men? Patriarchal institutions—marriage, the family, education—prescribe and circumscribe what women can and cannot do? Or even demeaning conventions of representing women—including that of the 'shrew' of the play in which she appears—which have been a persistent feature of literature, art and theatre. And how should she resist? By violent opposition or separatism? By seeking place within the institutions from which women have been excluded? By changing the terms of representation itself? These questions anticipate the challenges posed by feminism, one of the most powerful movements in both political activism and literary criticism over the last century. Feminism, like Katherina, is broadly concerned with the possibility of female resistance: as Katherina thinks:

> *I see a woman may be made a fool*
> *If she had not a spirit to resist. (3.2)*

The Taming of the Shrew has always been the subject of much analytical and critical controversy almost from its inception. More recently, this controversy has tended to relate to a feminist reading of the play in general, and the final speech of Katherina in particular, as offensively misogynistic and patriarchal. Phyllis Rackin argues that "seen in the context of current anxieties, desires and beliefs, Shakespeare's play seems to prefigure the most oppressive modern assumptions about women and to validate these assumptions as timeless truths. Though Conall Morrison argues, "I find it gobsmacking that some people see the play as misogynistic, I believe that it is a moral tale. I believe 'do not be like this' and 'do not do this." But some of the critics stand against Morrison.

The feminist critics specifically take into review the long speech of Katherina in which she admits her submissive role as a wife to her husband:

> *... thy husband is thy lord, thy life, thy keeper*
> *Thy head, thy sovereign... (5.2)*

Further she keeps on advocating:

> *... and she is forward, peevish, sullen, sour*
> *And not obedient to his honest will,*
> *What is she but a foul contending rebel... (5.2)*

The different critics see this speech in different ways. Some of them see her as accepting the subordinate position in the patriarchal society while there are others also who refute this argument. Critically, four main theories have emerged in response to Katherina's speech:

1. It is sincere; Petruchio has tamed her.
2. It is sincere; but not because Petruchio has tamed her. Instead, she has fallen in love with him and accepted her role as a wife.
3. It is ironic; she is being sarcastic, pretending to have been tamed when in reality she has completely duped Petruchio into thinking he has tamed her.
4. It should not be read seriously or ironically; it is the part of the farcical nature of the play within the play.

A Critic who interpreted the final speech as sincere was George Bernard Shaw, who wrote in 1897:

> *"No man with any decency of feeling can sit it out in the company of a woman without being extremely ashamed of the lord-of-creation moral implied in the wager and the speech put into the woman's own mouth."*

If one accepts the interpretations of scholars like George Bernard Shaw and Duthie, the final scene must be interpreted literally; Katherina has been successfully tamed, and the speech is the outward manifestation of that process. It thus indicates Katherna has come to accept her newly submissive role to such an extent that she advocates the role for others. In this sense, the speech rationalizes, in both a political and sociological sense the submission of wives to husbands.

Elaine Showalter is one of the most influential feminist critics in the United States, her most widely read and studied essay is *Representing Ophelia: Women, Madness, and the Responsibilities of Feminist Criticism*. Here she sharply criticizes Jacques Lacan's point of view of calling Ophelia "an object Ophelia". Although Lacan starts his seminar on *Hamlet* by promising to speak of Ophelia, assuming his readers that he will be 'as good as my word'. Showalter laments that he is 'not as good as his word'. This is because he goes on to speak about Hamlet extensively, and when he does mention Ophelia, she merely says what Lacan calls "the object Ophelia"—that is the object of Hamlet's male desire. Showalter, by contrast, insists that feminists should be as good as their word and speak of Ophelia 'herself'. She thus signals her hostility to both the 'bait and switch' tactics of psychoanalysis (which she sees as patriarchal in its tendency to analyze woman only as objects in relations to male subjects) and the deferrals of deconstruction (which she regards as politically questionable, depriving woman of a voice with which to resist patriarchy).

Showalter does speak of Ophelia, but we see, it is not Ophelia we might expect. As Showalter concedes, Ophelia speaks very little in *Hamlet.* She appears in only five of the play's twenty scenes; her tragedy is not shared with the audience in soliloquies as Hamlet's is; what we know about her is largely due to what male characters tell us in a handful of unclear flashbacks. Despite Ophelia's relative marginality in *Hamlet*, she has commanded a disproportionate attention in a popular culture, from John Everett's and Millais' painting of drowned Ophelia (1852) to the Indigo girls' folk-rock album 'Swamp Ophelia' (1994). Confronting the tension between the paucity of information in *Hamlet* concerning Ophelia and the cultural fascination with her sexuality and madness, Showalter asks: what is feminism's responsibility toward her 'as character and as a woman'.

Showalter questions the value of French feminisms, for whom, 'Ophelia might confirm the impossibility of representing the feminine in patriarchal discourses as other than madness, incoherence, fluidity, or silence. In *Hamlet* we come across such sound that echoes Ophelia's speech.

For Showalter, recuperating Ophelia's 'nothing' is not an attractive option: 'to dissolve into a female symbolism of absence is to endorse our own marginality'.

Instead, Showalter argues that Ophelia does have a story of her own that feminist criticism can tell; it is neither her life story, nor her love story, nor Lacan's story, but rather the history of her representation. For Showalter, Ophelia's ninetieth and twentieth century iconography is partly licensed by the text of *Hamlet* itself. Whereas Hamlet's madness is presented as metaphysical, Ophelia's is seen as entirely feminine. Showalter notes how Ophelia's association with hysteria persisted well into the nineteenth century, coinciding with the birth of psychiatry. There is a category of feminist critics who share common consent over the following points of argument regarding Ophelia:

- Ophelia goes mad because males deny her a voice.
- Her mad songs articulate wisdom that transcends Claudius and Polonius' shallow platitudes.
- Her assessment of what males should be is sadly deficient in Denmark, and she knows it, but male brutality prevents a clear articulation.

In *Measure for Measure*, one would be hard put in the canon to find scenarios more brutal to women. Isabella's plight defines sexual harassment: have sex with me or your brother won't like the consequences, warns Angelo! When degrading and threatening Isabella, he mocks her with his male persona of impeccable virtue—"who will believe you?" he responds to her warnings of exposure. Expecting better behavior from Claudio yields no better results. After all pleads the prisoner, why would compromising your virtue matter if I am freed?

Interestingly Shakespeare portrays Isabella as the counterpart of Angelo. Although in a cloistered convent as a novice, she demands the rules be more strict.

What can a feminist reading reveal? The play is a comedy, although critics have remarked not much different in tone and expected outcome from the tragedies, but nonetheless its classification demands a happy ending, meaning opposites are reconciled and harmony restored.

From a feminist perspective, does that happen? The response is complicated. Isabella and Mariana ask the Duke/Friar to forgive Angelo. Naturally, the brutalization should never have occurred, but given the many Biblical allusions obviously including the title, forgiveness is universal, Shakespeare dramatizes, but denouement still remains difficult.

The Friar/Duke proposes to Isabella, but does she accept? If yes, a feminist reading might be that woman can remain safe only if men (Friar-church/Duke-state combined) grant them protection. If true, that may be a necessary condition legally, but hardly a sufficient one morally. Even today laws for rape favour men, implying the old misogynist premise that women seduce. Women are still at the mercy of what men dictate. The feminist critics, often, take in to account the various phases of women:

- Women as designed by sexuality
- Women as wives and mothers—property
- Women as promiscuous—prostitute
- Women as virgins and liberation
- Women as defined by passion
- Women as barred from having awareness

If Isabella refuses to marry thereby defying male authority, will she continue to enjoy the rights males have? Why did Shakespeare write the sonnets? Regardless of the "W.H." dilemma, the procreation sonnets are a plea for the young man to marry. Women, however, are not asked, they are told: defined by their passions. Women are still barred from knowledge. Their choices, circumscribed by males, remain either limited or non-existent. Morally, that will not do.

Othello can also be read from a feminist perspective. A feminist analysis of the play *Othello* allows us to judge the different social values and status of women in the Elizabethan society. *Othello* serves as an example to demonstrate the expectations of the Elizabethan patriarchal society, the practice of privileges in patriarchal marriages, and the suppression and repression of feminity. According to Elizabethan or Shakespearean society built upon renaissance beliefs, women, probably, were meant only to marry. As their single occupation, marriage, held massive responsibilities of house management and child rearing. Additionally, women were expected to be silent, chaste, and obedient to their husbands, brothers, and all men in general. Patriarchal rule justified women's subordination as the natural order because women were thought physiologically and psychologically inferior to men.

As we go through *Othello* we find that the women characters are presented according to this expectation of the Elizabethan society. There are only three women in *Othello*: Desdemona, Emilia, and Bianca. The way that these women behave and conduct themselves is undeniably linked to the ideological expectations of Shakespeare's Elizabethan society and to the patriarchal Venetian society that he creates.

Following the hearing of Brabantio's complaint and Othello's defence, the Duke eventually grants permission to Desdemona to accompany Othello to Cyprus. Othello speaks to his ensign, Iago, ironically describing him as a man of 'honesty and trust', informing the Duke that, 'To his conveyance I assign my wife' (1.3). Desdemona, as Othello's wife, is treated as his possession: he implies that she is a commodity to guarded and transported. This is, however, by no means peculiar to Othello: the first senator, wishing Othello well, concludes by hoping that he will 'use Desdemona well' (1.3). The 'Use' seems to connote the phrase 'look after', but also supports the Venetian expectation of women that they are to bow to the wills of their husbands who may utilize them as they wish. Moreover, the function of women within marriage is also delineated by Othello's words to Desdemona in Act II:

Come, my dear love,
The purchase made, the fruits are to ensue. (2.3)

Marriage is described as an act of 'purchase': a woman is bought by her husband, effectively as a favour, and is expected to fulfil his sexual desires in return for the privilege.

Iago's desire for revenge on Othello is, in part, dictated by his view of women as possessions. He believes that:

It is thought abroad that 'twixt my sheets,
He's done my office (1.3)

It suggests Iago's suspicion that Othello has slept with his wife Emilia. It could be argued, however, that Iago exhibits little love for his wife by insulting her in public and killing her, himself. It is simply the thought that:

... the lusty Moor
Hath leaped into my seat (2.1)

Driven mad with the thought that Othello has used a possession that belongs to him. Compounding this theory is the fact that Iago refers to his wife metaphorically in these two instances: she is his 'office' and his 'seat'; she is objectified and deprived of her humanity.

Moreover, in revenge for Othello's supposed act, Iago wishes to be 'evened with him, wife for wife' (II,I). By sleeping with Desdemona, he believes that they will then be equal. The feelings of Desdemona and Emilia are completely disregarded in his plotting. The women are merely the objects to be used in order to further his own desires. Although Iago is an extreme example, he nonetheless demonstrates, through his thinking, the fact that women, in both Elizabethan and Venetian society, are perceived as possessions, secondary to the lofty plans and desires of men.

Some modern feminist critics see Desdemona as a hideous embodiment of the downtrodden woman. Whether this is actually the case will be explored later in the paper. Desdemona herself declares that:

"I am obedient (3.3)

And continuing to obey Othello's orders from the early happy phase of their relationship through to the later stages of his jealous ravings. Even when he orders to Desdemona to go to her bed towards the end of Act IV, she still replies with submission 'I will, my lord' (IV, III). In her final breath she still remains true to her husband, saying:

"Commend me to my lord." (5.2)

She appears to have completely accepted her role as subordinate and obedient wife.

Arguably a much stronger character, Emilia also indicates that she is aware of her 'proper' role in society. When revealing Iago's conspiracy at the end of the play, she states that:

"It is proper I obey him, but not now." (5.2)

Although going on to betray her husband, she still feels the need to explain why she is deviating from the accepted behaviours. Bianca expresses a similar sentiment, consoling herself when Cassio spurns her by arguing that 'I must be circumstanced' (3.5): she feels compelled by the laws of society to be 'circumstanced'—'to put up with it'—implying that she has no other choice.

Society weighs heavily on the shoulders of these women; they feel that they must support the men and defend them, even if the actions of men are questionable. Brabantio's opinions of women appear to represent Venetian ideology. Speaking of Desdemona before she erred, he describes her as 'perfection', 'of spirit still and quiet', and 'A maiden never bold' (1.3).

By expressing these qualities of women in the masculine domain of the Venetian senate, Brabantio compounds and develops the traditional expectations of women in a patriarchal society. Moreover, when she marries Othello, going against his wishes, he describes her as erring 'Against all rules of nature'(I, III). Venetian society presents its own social beliefs as immutable laws of nature. It is 'natural' for women to be feminine and to do as their husbands and fathers tell them. It is unnatural for them to do anything else. This venetian concept was also an Elizabethan and pre-Elizabethan belief, and was widely understood by Shakespeare's audiences.

Today, feminists argue that it is not 'natural' for women to be 'feminine', that history has tried to camouflage its social expectations of women as part of the laws of nature. The women in *Othello,* however, are pre-feminism and seem to only compound the ideological expectations of what it is to be a woman through their own behaviour.

It is not to say, however, that the women of the play fail to question men at all. As Emilia talks to Desdemona at the end of Act IV, she is fairly damming in her opinion of men. In a speech reminiscent of Shylock's 'Hath not a Jew eyes', Emilia argues that women are no physically different to men:

Let husbands know,
Their wives sense like them; they see and smell,
And have their palates both for sweet and sour
As husbands have. (4.3)

She goes on to say that in addition to some identical physicalities, they also suffer from the same 'affections/desires for support, and frailty' (IV,III) as men. The only difference, Emilia implies, is mental: 'it is frailty that thus errs' (IV,III). This links of her earlier description of the appetite of mankind:

"They eat us hungerly, when they are full,
They belch us." (3.4)

Emilia suggests that men are brutish and simplistic, unable to control their desires with logical thought. This statement of Emilia reflects her own experience, and also clears how men look at women. It is perhaps ironic also because the actions of Iago and Othello confirm her arguments.

These opinions, however, are given to Desdemona in moments of privacy, Emilia does not express such opinions in the company of men. Ironically, it is Desdemona who exhibits some power in public, making powerful use of language when explaining to her father, in front of other Venetian senators:

And so much duty as my mother showed,
To you preferring you before her father,
So much I challenge, that I may profess
Due to Moor, my lord. (4.3)

It could be argued, however, that even in this instance, Desdemona still fails to assert herself: although she disagrees with her father, she couches this in terms of merely switching her 'duty' from father to husband. The issue of 'duty' itself remains unquestioned. This is because it is so ideologically embedded that women do not seem to consider any other possibility, other than, as this paper has shown, in private conversation to one another.

This is not to say, however, that women in *Othello* do not exhibit any sign of wielding power. Othello, when talking of his wife, often seems pre-occupied with the matters of flesh. Bemoaning the fact the he did not know earlier of his wife's supposed infidelity, Othello argues that he would have been happier:

If the general camp,
Pioneers and all, had tasted her sweet body,
So had I nothing known. (3.3)

He appears to be obsessed with Desdemona's sexuality. On the way to murder his wife, he states that:

> *Thy bed, lust stained,*
> *Shall with lust's blood be spotted. (5.1)*

The repetition of the word 'lust', combined with the associations of Desdemona's bed and the violent plosives and sibilants of this line, reflects and draws attention to Othello's preoccupation with sensual matters. Though he seems to have drooped in sexual jealousy, yet his mind can be read without being biased.

All three women of the play are accused of prostitution and inappropriate sexual conduct, yet it appears that none of them are guilty. As male society falls apart in Cyprus, its constituent members seem to vent their spleen and anger by labelling all of the female characters 'whore'. When things go wrong, it appears to be acceptable for men to blame the women.

The patriarchal society presented in the play, moulded on the ideology of Elizabethan England, seems to put women firmly in their place. Men consider women to be possessions, who ought to remain submissive and meek at all times. The only power that women do seem to be able to wield—their sexual power—is considered to be an 'evil' which must be resisted by the men in society. Men seem free to be able to refer to women as 'whores' and get away with it. The language that Shakespeare gives to his female characters suggests that they have internalized society's expectations of them, believing this to be 'natural'.

REFERENCES

1. Abrams, M.H. (2012). *A Glossary of Literary Terms*, Delhi: Cengage Learning India Private Limited.
2. Carolyn Ruth Swift Lenz, Carolyn and Grume Gayle and Neely Carol Thomas. *The Woman's Part: Feminist Criticism of Shakespeare,* Urbana, Chicago.
3. Hamilton, Shron (1943). *Shakespeare's Daughters.* North Carolina:Mcfarland Company Inc Publishers.
4. Harrish, Jonathan Gill (2010). *Shakespeare and Literary Theory.*Oxford University Press.
5. Knight, Wilson (2001). *The Wheel of Fire: Interpretations of Shakespearean Tragedy.* New York: Routledge Classics.
6. McCurdy, Harold Grier (1953). *The Personality of Shakespeare.* New Haven: Yale University Press.
7. Raleigh, Walter. *Shakespeare.* Great Britain: R/R Clark Limited, Edinburgh.

20

Depiction of Women Characters in an Indian Novelist's Perspective with Special Reference to '*A Time to Be Happy*' and '*Storm in Chandigarh*'

Hira Bose

ABSTRACT

This paper focuses on two novels by Nayantara Sahgal (1927) namely, 'A Time to be Happy' *and* 'Storm in Chandigarh'. *The author was born to a mother, who abandoned the stereotype image by becoming the first woman cabinet minister in the world and India's ambassador in the UN, and a father who believed in women's equality, Nayantara Sahgal inherited their traits of individuality and love of freedom. Once she became aware of the inferior status of women and being a rebel she protested. Her women represent that class which is newly becoming aware of the biased attitude of society. They tend to assert their individuality by challenging the taboos and destructive social norms. The position of women has changed drastically in Post-Independent India. Women novelists writing in English attempt to project women as the central figure and seem to succeed in presenting the predicament of women most effectively. The works of Nayantara Sahgal have given a distinct dimension to the image of woman in family and society. In most of her writings, she tried her best to free the female mentality from the age-long control of male domination.*

A novel is said to be a genre, generated and sustained by the middle class in Europe in the eighteenth century to incorporate the values of their class as against the feudal values of the epic or romance. The Protagonist of the novel has to make a choice which is distinctly his own. But this concept of individualism can also be related to the new social mobility that industrialization made possible, displacing man from his secure traditional niche making him realize the unique potential of each human being including himself, outside social hierarchy. The novel came into existence in India in the second half of the nineteenth century. This was roughly a generation after Macauley's *Minute* decreed English a language of higher education, exposing an entire class of urban Indian writers to British narrative models. It may be noted that from the very beginning the English novel seemed the genre somewhat favourable to women. Jane Austen, George Eliot, the Brontes, Mrs. Gaskell, Dorothy Richardson and Virginia Woolf are the women novelists who made significant contributions to the English novel. The English "gentleman" of the eighteenth century did not think very highly of the new genre that came to be called novel. It was dismissed as something unworthy of a refined man's attention. However, it became very popular with women and went on to have a significant impact on gender relations and issues in the modern world. Terry Eagleton states: "In the end, the English novel would wreak its vengeance on those who dismissed it as fit for females by producing some magnificent portrayals of women, from Clarissa Harlowe and Emma Woodhouse to Molly Bloom and Mrs. Ramsey. It also produced some distinguished female exponents of the art". In a similar vein, early Indian novelists of the nineteenth century portrayed strong and positive women characters in their novel. It may be noted that During the Vedic age women were considered equal to men. They composed Vedic hymns and participated in the learned discussion with the man. Gargi, Ghosala, Apala, Maitreyi, are some of the women of this type. Widows were allowed to marry. Later on the position of women deteriorated. They became a victim of male domination in our male-dominated society

The concept of woman is one who remains chaste, faithful, moderate, polite and sincere to her husband in her whole life even after being crushed. According to Virginia Woolf, a 'woman' has to be the perfect 'angel in the house' (*Profession for Women and Writing*, 59). In the nineteenth century, when Renaissance came to India, intellectuals of the period concentrated on the emancipation of women. People like Iswar Chandra Vidyasagar and Annie Besant Margaret Cousin and Sarojini Naidu carried on the good works of Raja Rammohan Roy and fought for the women's sake and her sovereignty.

In the twentieth century, the spirit of nationalism held sway in India. The period from 1930s to 1940s was momentous both in the history of Indian nationalism and in the history of Indian novel in English. Caught between sometimes complementary and sometimes opposing claims of home and the world, the novelists of the 1930s and 1940s owed their inspiration and the conditions for their emergence to two contexts: the social and political upheavals of the Gandhian whirlwind and the era of late modernism in Europe. Concerns of women were broadly speaking overshadowed at that time. With some exceptions like R.K. Narayan's *Guide* that has a strong woman character, fiction of this period did not concern with woman on the specific issues.

In the next two decades, i.e. 1950s and 1960s, after independence the dominant concern of literature was character development and psychological depth, often considered with a sense of the alienated individual, dissatisfied with modern life. The idealism of independence was also waning as various problems began to surface in free India. It may be that this sense of alienation reflects the situation of the Indian writers in English in the 1950s and 1960s. The theme of alienation takes on a special edge in the numerous novels published by women in the period such as Kamala Markandaya, Ruth Prawer Jhabvala, Nayantara Shagal and Anita Desai.

This paper focuses on two novels by Nayantara Sahgal (1927) born to a mother, who abandoned the stereotype image by becoming the first woman cabinet minister in the world and India's ambassador in the UN, and a father who believed in women's equality, Nayantara Sahgal inherited their traits of individuality and love of freedom. Once she became aware of the inferior status of women and being a rebel she protested. Her women represent that class which is newly becoming aware of the biased attitude of society. They tend to assert their individuality by challenging the taboos and destructive social norms. The position of women has changed drastically in Post-Independent India. Women novelists writing in English attempt to project women as the central figure and seem to succeed in presenting the predicament of women most effectively. The works of Nayantara Sahgal have given a distinct dimension to the image of woman in family and society. In most of her writings, she tried her best to free the female mentality from the age-long control of male domination.

Nayantara Sahgal is one of those women writers who are against dehumanization of women, against their subjection by men and against treating them as mere possession. Maya in the novel *A Time to Be Happy* (1975) is the predecessor of Mrs. Sahgal's women protagonists who are the victims of the male-dominated society. She is a woman who is not willing to submerge her individuality. As she is brought up in a nationalist family, she wants to join the Congress as a volunteer and serve the nation. She is a sensitive woman who is not interested in having ornaments and embellishments and always wears a plain sari of same nondescript colour.

But Harish her husband is always interested to walk on the path of the British. There is a big communication gap between her and her officer husband. As the Deputy collector of Lucknow, he is interested in throwing parties to the rich and going to the club. Being different from his wife in temperament, attitude and outlook, he used to neglect his wife all the time and punish his wife with isolation. For Maya, marriage was doomed from the very beginning, owing to the antithetical personalities of her husband and herself.

> *She had the cool purity of the Eucalyptus, as compared with his extravagant gulmohar, she was the mirror smooth lake to his rushing waterfall. (A Time to Be Happy, 39)*

Maya is the pioneer of the women character in Nayantara Sahgal's novels. Her dreams of sovereignty and freedom take her to the villages to serve for the nation. She is not satisfied to be the shadow of her husband. She is a woman with her own dignity and self-respect which motivates her not only to live life of a shadow but as an individual or as an entity.

Finally, Maya finds out that she can easily communicate with the narrator and they are in love. But she cannot think of a divorce. She never tries to escape into extramarital arms and the narrator cannot express love for her as both of them have tremendous belief in the indissolubility of the marriage. It takes a long time for the narrator to regain the ground and to conduct himself with her in a usual way.

In the novel *Storm in Chandigarh* (1988), Saroj represents for the first time that a woman can enjoy her selfhood and find out a way of her own if she wants. Her marriage fails because of her honesty and simplicity. Being brought up in an atmosphere of freedom, love and trust, she is married to Inder Mehra who has everything to make life comfortable but who is possessive, jealous and a typical male chauvinist. What Saroj values most is people should talk to each other frankly and life being easier because of it. She tells her husband all about her past, but repents for it all through her life. Inder who had no problem about having sex with other women either before marriage or after, feels shocked and his jealousy is roused.

Actually in Inder's world there is no question of self-expression for women. It's not what Saroj hides from him that is troubling him but what she does not hide becomes the conflict between them. He treated Saroj brutally and considers her a sinner. Inder would punish her and often torture her physically and mentally. Ironically enough, Inder who takes such a stern view of his wife's innocence never gives any explanation for his own extramarital relationship with another man's wife. Saroj tried her level best to enjoy her womanhood within the bondage of marriage. As in the traditional concept of marriage she was taught to get involved in the bondage of marriage but did not get the same response from her husband. She turns her interest towards her children and also towards her flowers. Even she gets satisfaction bearing a child. As a modern woman Saroj wants to live like a friend but not like a slave to her husband. Inder thinks that he is cheated by his wife. For Saroj, emotional involvement is more important that the sexual relationship. In spite of her belief in truth, individuality and commitment, Saroj thinks of a divorce only when she is practically kicked off from the world of her husband. By that time Vishal Dubey came into her life as a friend who helped her to become free from a conventional happy married life. Vishal Dubey who befriended Saroj taught her to respect herself and enjoy her sovereignty; being suffocated in all the money and comforts of life Saroj was, at last, able to search a way of sovereignty with the help of Vishal Dubey. Vishal's consolation to Saroj was practically the suggestion of Sahgal herself:

> it was life's precious obligation to rebel and humanity's right to be free, to choose from the best light it could see, not necessary the long-accepted light (*Storm in Chandigarh* 173).

Sahgal's woman protagonist struggle against antagonist forces which threaten to ruin their attempts of emancipation, but they are not necessarily against men. Maya in the novel *A Time to be Happy* and Saroj in the novel *Storm in Chandigarh* were able to search a way of sovereignty with the help of the narrator and Vishal Dubey. As Nayantara Sahgal is an Indian novelist, she knows the Indian psyche and social set-up; besides her personal experiences also helped her to look upon the character in Indian perspective. She never loses faith in the institution of marriage nor she denies the existence of man in a woman's life. Rather her characters having being exploited by their husbands, want solution, with the help of another understanding man. Sahgal's vision is to create a new world which will be based on equality, sharing and harmony between the sexes.

REFERENCES

1. Eagleton, Terry. *The English Novel: An Introduction*. New Delhi: Atlantic, 2004.
2. Mukherjee, Meenakshi. "The Beginnings of the Indian Novel". *A Concise History of Indian Literature in English*. A.K. Mehrotra (ed.). Ranikhet: Permanent Black, 2008.
3. Mukherjee, Meenakshi. *Realism and Reality: The Novel and Society in India*. Delhi: OUP, 1985.
4. Sahgal, Nayantara. *A Time to Be Happy*, New Delhi: Sterling, 1975.
5. Sahgal, Nayantara. *Storm in Chandigarh*, New Delhi: Penguin, 1988.
6. Woolf, Virginia. *Profession for Women and Writing*. London: WP, 1979.

21

Gender Bias in Vijay Tendulkar's *Silence! The Court Is In Session*

Laxmi Prasad Anuragi

ABSTRACT

Vijay Tendulkar (1928–2008) is a leading, outstanding contemporary Indian playwright in Marathi. He has significant contribution to the contemporary Indian Marathi theatre along with Badal Sarcar, Habib Tanvir, Girish Karnad and Mohan Rakesh. Tendulkar has mastered different genres of literature like essays, short stories, criticism, screen play writing and drama. This paper aims to study gender bias in a patriarchal set-up with social reference to the famous Indian playwright Vijay Tendulkar's book Silence! The Court Is In Session. *In the play, Miss Leela Benare is a young, intelligent, educated, and economically independent woman who wants to live a life of her own but she is not allowed to do that. Moreover, her private matters are disgracefully discussed publicly and society uses every ploy to crush her life. The play has depicted the difficulty of a young woman, who is a victim of the male-dominated society. Tendulkar has criticized the follies prevailing in the society. The play carries all the vitalities of contemporary life. It focuses on the human mind and detects the ugliness in it. In the play, cruelty is exhibited through the system of law courts and is centred on the tragic story of Miss Benare, the protagonist of the play who becomes the victim of patriarchal society for her act of adultery. It is not only the tragic story of Benare, but it is the story of every woman in society whether it is rural or urban. The play is a satire against rigid society, custom, orthodoxy and the social ills of the middle class society.* Silence! The Court Is In Session *presents a play within a play where Benare as the accused is tried for an imaginary crime of infanticide. Though the trial is conducted in a game-like and non-serious manner, it exposes the past life of Benare and authenticates the feeling of superiority. It also deals with the mental state of educated woman in a traditionally male-dominated Indian society. Tendulkar attacks them ironically and satirically throughout the play. If India has to progress in a sustained manner, it is necessary that gender bias should be removed in the society and women should be treated as equal.*

Keywords: *Women, exploitation, gender bias, discrimination, trauma, ploy.*

Vijay Tendulkar spent his early childhood in Bombay. His father Dhondopant was a clerk and ran a small publishing house. He was an actor and director as well. His mother's name was Susheela and he had two elder siblings, Raghunath, and a sister Leela. The family was literature oriented and his interaction with books encouraged Tendulkar to take up writing in the future. Tendulkar did not get a formal education of play writing from any institution. There were no courses available as well. He learned by a sheer trial-and-error method. He got this earliest lesson in theatre in his home itself. His father and brother used to write plays and also acted in them. They used to take young Vijay for rehearsals. Vijay felt amused as well as puzzled to see men playing female parts. Tendulkar tells Gauri Ramnarayan in an interview, *'From the time I was four year old, I was taken to those rehearsals, and they were a kind of magic show for me. That's where I saw living person change into characters. At that time women's roles were played by men. Imagine my amazement when I saw some of actors suddenly changing their voice and movements to become women. They did not wear Saris, but in some mysterious way their pants and shirts stopped identifying them as men. I often fell asleep in the middle of those rehearsals. I suppose father carried me home. All I know that I woke up in my bed to the next morning.'* Tendulkar through his plays gave voice to the oppression of an individual in conventional social codes. His plays present a fictional reality in which the reality of life assumes a new significance and were based on his own observation of life from newspapers, reports, incidents narrated to him.

My contention is that gender bias has to be destroyed if our society and country has to make sustained and sustainable development and this I would like to prove with help of Vijay Tendulkar's play *Silence! The Court Is In Session*, written in Marathi (*Shantata! Court ChaluAahe*) based on a short story (novel) *Die Panne* (traps) by Friedrich Durrenmatt in 1956 and translated into English by Priya Adarkar. It was presented on the stage for first time in 1967, and has been translated into several languages and adopted by various theatre groups over the years. The play is social satire on middle class society. It was a phenomenon of the 1960s and the first significant modern Indian play that centred on woman as protagonist and victim, with its heroine Miss Leela Benare who is a school teacher by profession, not at an acquiescent receiving end, but at a point of conflict whereas aggressive-transgressor of sexual mores of her community. She challenges the executors of power in absentia. It is the part of Tendulkar's dramatic strategy that Benare's immediate persecutors in the play are as powerless as she, and all their exertions to cut Benare down to size are more about striving after power than a real exercise of power. In fact, to a considerable length it reflects the individual powerlessness of each of her assailants, grabbing every opportunity to expose or humiliate another, and ganging up only to attack Miss Benare. In the process exposing their own powerlessness and their desperate need to assume a presence of power in the collective! And yet the invisible presence of power ruling or dominating over all of them is subtly woven into the scheme with reference to the networking for forces and operations manoeuvring to throw Benare out of her job as punishment for her sin. Tendulkar concentrates on painting these aspects with unsettling compassion in his plays which revolve around some contemporary ideas, events or issues and continues to pose more questions than offering easy and comfortable solutions. This has elevated the work above a mere 'happening' social melo-drama. This work is rooted in his deep compassion and respect for human life—a life which was a social reality of Post-Colonial India. *"Feministic ideology which pits women in direct encounter with chauvinistic male oppression, finds its full and free expression."* (N.S. Dharan in his article: "Gynocentrism in *Silence! The Court Is In Session* and *kamala*").

Silence! The Court Is In Session is based on a grave social problem of unmarried motherhood of Miss Leela Benare and men's attitude towards her. Benare loves life and is full of spirit and very proud of her performance as a teacher and feels that her life is her own and no one has the right to interfere. It is a quest for reality and feminine identity broadly in a patriarchal society. In the play, Tendulkar has depicted the predicament of a young woman who is a victim of a male-dominated society. Miss Leela Benare is a member of this theatre group, whereas the other members are Mr. Kashikar, Babu Rokde, Sukhatme, Karnik, Prof. Damle, etc.

Gender bias is one of the outstanding issues in the play, *Silence! The Court Is In Session,* of Vijay Tendulkar. He saw social conflict, violence, discrimination and sex characterize Indian middle class society. The social, political, economical power and conflicts concerned with these lead to bias. The middle class people feel insecure but they crave for power and the result is bias. There are various types of bias or aggression: physical, psychological, sexual and social. This generates disillusionment and also bias. But ultimately his characters come to realize the futility of life and sex. The middle class society is reflected in the plays of Mohan Rakesh, Badal Sircar, Girish Karnad and Vijay Tendulkar. Tendulkar throws light on a woman's victimization due to men's lust and prejudice. At the age of fifteen Miss Benare is molested by her own maternal uncle and she was innocent and her impulses were natural. Her maternal uncle was a mature person and she was drawn by her uncle in this affair purposely. However, her disillusionment in love, in winning a man through her body leads her to realizing its inevitable futility. She experiences physical, sexual and psychological trauma. Benare is continuously subjected to torture and humiliation by the members of the theatre group acting against her.

Another cause of such bias is the frustration of these characters in their life. Except Benare no one has an individuality and no one is self-reliant. The frustration leads these characters to bias and surprisingly enough, all this is done in the name of a game. The most serious charge is that Benare has a love affair with Prof. Damle and she has surrendered her body to him and is pregnant. The characters go on attacking her. They declare her *"a sinful cancer on the body of society"* and blame her for being pregnant. She is a slur on motherhood and she is sentenced to kill her infant child, but in fact Benare loves it as any legitimate mother does. She decides to give birth to the baby. In the play, the court orders her to kill the baby before its birth. Benare is prosecuted for the crime which she has not committed and the court is to do the same. The prosecution's logic is based on morality and social value and not on the legal ground. Benare is victim of the social atrocities. There is an abortive attempt to commit suicide by Benare. Bias in the play operates at two levels: verbal and physical. In the patriarchal society men are given the right to do injustice to women. Benare is sinned more than her sinning. Mr. Kashikar is of the opinion that in order to avoid the immorality in the society, the old-fashioned child marriage system should be introduced and recommends that the girls should be married off before puberty. Some incidents of physical violence or bias take place in the play. The door being locked from behind and Benare's banging the door to go away from the court and the process by which she is forced to remain inside is the example of physical bias or violence she was subjected to. This is a powerful commentary on a society with heavy patriarchal bias that makes justice impossible. In this play, we find how Miss Benare becomes the victim of her male counterparts. Miss Benare is presented as an extraordinary and crucial character in the play. She is a thirty-four-year old middle class woman. Her admiration for her profession is shown when she says to Samant:

> *I never had been behind with my lesson! Exercises correct on time too, not a bit of...Room for disapproval, I don't give an inch of it to anyone! (Silence! The Court IsIn Session, 04).*

Further, Tendulkar throws light on the character of Benare:

> Conversation between Benare and Samant,
>
> BENARE. *I am soul of seriousness: But I don't see why one should play,* we should sing! If we can if they will let us, we should dance too! Should Not have any false modesty or dignity or care for anyone! I mean it.
>
> When your life is over, do you think anyone say, Samant? Do you think them?
>
> Will?
>
> SAMANT. *You are quite right: The great sage Tukaram said ... at least*
>
> I think it was him.
>
> BENARE. *Forget about the sage Tukaram. I say it – I, Leela Beanare am a living* woman, I say it from my own experience. Life is not meant for anyone else. It's your own life. It must be. It is a very important thing. Every moment, every bit of it is precious ... (Silence! The Court Is In Session, 08).

They form a group to torture Benare. She is charged as a licentious woman, who is always ready to sell her body. She is even charged to share an illicit relationship with her maternal uncle; she explains the way in which she was abused by her own maternal uncle at the age of just fourteen. Benare says:

> *Why, I was hardly fourteen! I didn't even know what sin was, I didn't! I insisted on marriage. So I could live my beautiful lovely dreams Openly ... But all of them ... my mother too were against it, and My brave man turned trial and ran. (Silence ... 74)*

When she remembers her uncle she says:

> *Life is a poisonous snake that bites itself. Life is a betrayal, life is a fraud, and life is drug. Life is drudgery ... life is a dreadful thing ... (Silence ... 75)*

The judge Mr. Kashikar orders Benare to abort her child. According to him, to have the child without marriage is against the tradition of Indian culture. She screamed to this:

> *No! No! No! I won't let you do it. I won't let it happen, I won't let it happen. (Silence ... 76)*

The actual play was scheduled to be staged at night. The characters wanted to rehearse the drama, a mock trail, and also use it as an opportunity to dig up Leela Benare's past life. Babu Rokde, Ponkshe, Karnik, and Samant appeared as witness for the trial against Benare.

Samant was forced to accept and act as the fourth witness in the play on behalf of Prof. Damle. Sukhatme suggested that the theatre artists make Miss Benare an accused in the mock trial. She has to perform the role of a woman who is indicted of infanticide. Mr. Kashikar played the role of the judge. Benare was accused by the judge of 'The mock law court' as:

> *Prisoner Benare under section No. 302 of the Indian penal code,*
> *You are accused of the crime of infanticide (foeticide). Are you*
> *Guilty or not guilty of a fore mentioned crime ... ? (Silence ... 25)*

Benare replied:

> *I don't like your word at all: infanticide ... infanticide: why don't you accuse me instead of snatching public property ... ? I plead not guilty.*
> *I could not kill even a cockroach. I am scared to do it how could I kill a new born child ...? (Silence ... 29, 30)*

Mr. Kashikar quoted a Sanskrit proverb:

> *"Mother and the motherland both are even higher than heaven" (Silence ... 30).*

Sukhatme was playing the role of counsel of defense and counsel for the crown. He added:

> *Considering this what would we respectable citizens say if any woman was to take the life of delicate bundle of joy she has born, we would say, there could be no baser or more devilish thing on the evidence that the prisoner has done this same vile dead (Silence ... 31)*

The character of Miss Benare also reminds us of the Ibsen's heroine Nora in *The Doll House*: Nora abandons her children and her husband due to the annoyance and dominance created by her husband. She questions the male dominating society and finds her escape. According to Arundhati Banerjee, *"Benare's monologue is reminiscent of Nora's declaration of independence"* (Banerjee 40). Mrs. Kashikar does not help the helpless Miss Benare in the court in spite of being a woman. She is against Miss Benare because she is a conventional Indian housewife who has accepted all the norms framed by the society. She accepted the role of a woman as a beautiful flower to be decorated in a flower pot with no existence of her own. Benare, on the other hand was a progressive contemporary woman. She was psychologically tortured but was still ravenous to search for her existence.

CONCLUSION

To conclude, we can say that Vijay Tendulkar is a playwright of world stature. His plays match the artistic and thematic richness of any of the great dramatists of the world. I tried to look into the social aspects and continuous struggle between the members of the theatre group like Miss Leela Benare and other characters and shows how the Indian middle class society was out to gain and maintain power over one another. Power is not, for Tendulkar, something embodied in authoritative leaders, privileged classes, monarchs and patriarchs only; it is a tendency of men and women to overcome each other in every human relationship. Be it MANU's LAWS, which divided Indian society on caste and gender bias or recently acquired democratic political set up and newly emergent Indian middle class and its morality, Indian society kept on nourishing inequalities remained divided between those who posses power and those who stayed powerless. The play *Silence! The Court Is In Session* exposes the hypocrisies of the male-dominated society. It discusses some of the petty middle class moralities and the position of a single woman, Miss Leela Benare, in the male-dominated society. The woman illustrates the endeavours of a woman to gain financial liberation and her decision to remain unmarried for a pretty long time are negatively dubbed as her immoral rebellion and waywardness by her male counterparts. The jealousy of the failed middle class members of her society plots her entrapment and tries to silence her natural lust for life. The play is a treatise on moral slavery and middle class obsession of controlling the social weakling. The present paper has attempted to present a critique of the society, Tendulkar portrays in his *Silence! The Court Is In session*. The paper has tried to point out the fault lines of Indian society which make it fraught with bias or violence—psychological as well as physical. In this study, the protagonist (Miss Benare) suffers from social and moral pangs. The readers and the audience find the story very influential.

REFERENCES

1. Tendulkar, Vijay (1978). *Silence! The Court Is In Session*. Trans. Priya Adarkar. Calcutta: Oxford University Press.
2. Dharan, N.S. (1999). *The Play of Vijay Tendulkar: Creative Book*. New Delhi.
3. Gulati, Varun. (22 Feb 2015). *Silence! The Court Is In session: Social Criticism and Individual Tragedy*.
4. http://www.languageinindia.com/aug2007/gulatitendulkar.html

   Tendulkar, Vijay. (1974). *Preface to RaatraanilItar Ekankika*. 2nd Edition Continental Publication, Pune.

   Banerjee, Arundhati (2006). *Introduction: Five Plays*. Oxford India Paperbacks. New Delhi.
7. Woolf, Virginia (1929). *A Room of One's Own*. London: The Hogarth Press.

22

Gender Inequality and Representation of Women in the Works of V.S. Naipaul

Lav Kumar

ABSTRACT

This article examines how the presentation of women characters has evolved in V.S. Naipaul's fiction. The influence of the father is evident in the initial phase of the writer's career and this is reflected in his delineation of the women characters. The article examines, if there has been any change in the arena of influence of the female characters which is restricted to the private sphere in the initial phase of writing. The role of the women characters in the narrative, progression of events as well as their influence on the growth, action and development of the main character has also been examined. A distinct change that corresponds with the progression of time is noticeable in both the arenas.

Naipaul has been accused of being a misogynist by his critics and although women have never been the central characters in his novels the labelling is erroneous. Talking about his first three novels, Helen Pyne Timothy says that Naipaul's presentation of female characters is "extremely harsh, moralistic and judgmental". Gillian Dooley writes that, "The women in Naipaul's first three novels seldom have an existence independent from men, while there are some men who seem reasonably independent of women." Naipaul's initial three novels namely, The Mystic Masseur, The Suffrage of Elvira, and Miguel Street, abound in the depiction of interpersonal violence directed towards women. In his initial novels Naipaul describes this violence as a normal occurrence in the society he is depicting. While it is tempting to label the writer as being indifferent to the plight of women in the society, this is a misplaced criticism. Naipaul is a writer who refuses to be drawn into the battles that are not his. Another aspect that influences the presentation of the female characters in his novels is the influence of his father on Naipaul as a writer. Patrick French says that, "In his own presentation of the past, Vido would concentrate subsequently on the virtues of his father, with the result that Ma's voice can be hard to hear." If we examine his books a little closer it becomes apparent that the voice of his father may be the first voice that is audible to the reader but the strength of the women is lurking just beneath the surface. They can be heard by any reader willing to listen. The voice comes through to a discerning reader, and it would not be an exaggeration to say that the main character is primarily influenced by the women in his life. Examining the delineation of violence that is a daily occurrence in the lives of the female characters that he is depicting, Dooley writes, "He shows neither approval nor disapproval of what was, in the world in which he grew up, a fact of life." For the writer to have taken a different stand point would have led to a different kind of presentation which would have been at variance with the lived reality of the people whose lives, he in his stories is dealing with. If it seems he is being unsympathetic to the violence that women are being subjected to, he is depicting the indifference of the society being inhabited by these characters. Dooley says that: An unprejudiced reading of Naipaul suggests that his reputation as a misogynist is based merely on two or three characters, and a few incidents, principally from the three novels of the 1970s. The total impression of his wider work is much more complex. He does from time to time portray misogyny in his characters: Jimmy in *Guerrillas and Bobby in a Free State* are probably misogynists, but this does not mean that Naipaul shares their views of women, especially since he clearly disapproves of their behavior and attitudes in every other respect. In this article an attempt will be made to see if there is any significant difference in Naipaul's presentation of women in his seminal text *A House for Mr Biswas*, as compared to the world he portrays in *Half a Life and Magic Seeds*. The aim is to examine, if there has been any change in his approach, or does it fundamentally remain the same. Does the arena of influence of the female characters change, or does the force they exert on the scheme of the narrative remain unchanged. The novels being considered here have been selected based on the passage of time between their writing. While *A House for Mr Biswas* was published in 1961, the other two were written in 2001 and 2004 respectively. Although there is a time gap of more than forty years between them, but Naipaul had become established as a mature writer with a profound understanding of the complexities of human nature with its flaws and complexities with the publication of *A House for Mr. Biswas*. Landeg, White says that this novel "was the first to reveal his full abilities." White goes on to add that, "all Naipaul's important ideas have been present in embryo from the start—but the relevance has steadily widened." Now, if we look at the setting of the two novels the time in which they are set progresses gradually. In *A House for Mr Biswas* the setting is of the time around the Second World War, both preceding and succeeding it, and is limited to the immigrant Indian Trinidadian community. Most of the action in *Half a Life* is located in the post-colonial India and Europe and colonial Africa; the writer has broadened his arena both in terms of the world he covers as well as the range of characters. *Magic Seeds* begins where *Half a Life* ends in terms of chronological depiction of time. The canvas is also wide in terms of it covering both independent India that has to some extent moved beyond the colonial legacy and modern-day England grappling with the post-colonial setup. To compare the two worlds we will examine how the sphere of influence changes, if the range and growth of the female characters remains stagnant or has it evolved to become more encompassing. The wide array of female characters that appear in these novels will be examined to see the similarities and differences in approach if any. Similarly the arena of influence of these female characters and the roles they play in the narrative progression of events as well as their influence on the growth, action and development of the main character will be examined. Now in the first novel that we are considering, we find, that it abounds with strong female characters, in the form of Tara and Mrs Tulsi. They are both strong women in a patriarchal Indian set up who are pushing the boundaries in their own way. They have a major influence on the progression of events in the novel. From the time of the death of Mr. Biswas the main protagonists' father, it is the actions of the women in his life that controls his life events. Another aspect that is interesting in Naipaul's depiction of these two strong women is the pretence of the male in control that they create. For Tara, it is her husband Ajodha, and for Mrs. Tulsi it is her sister's husband Seth. It is evident from the very onset that Seth is just a front to keep up the pretence, especially when dealing with the workforce in the fields, or prospective sons-in-law, or when a show of brute strength is required. Seth's symbolic strength and lack of acumen first becomes evident when Mrs. Tulsi starts living in Port of Spain for Owad's education. At a later stage when she breaks away from him, he and his so-called acumen to do business are exposed to be false. He fails in one venture after another. Mr. Biswas on a chance stop over at Hanuman House notices the change that has overtaken Seth's fortune. Seth, "had been charged with wounding and insulting behaviour, and had lost much local support. His skills appeared to have left him as well. He had tried to burn one of his old lorries and had been caught and charged with conspiracy." In contrast things start unravelling for Mrs. Tulsi, because she has lost interest in the running of the house, but whenever she wants to assert herself, she is successful. This is evident when she relocates her family to Short Hills. Even reluctant members like Mr. Biswas, are made a part of this move. The handing over of the running of the Tulsi household and finances to Owad is not a sign of weakness, but a long-term desire that she fulfills; the withdrawal is voluntary. It is a mother passing on the legacy of the father to a willing son. Now when we move on to his last two novels the similarity is evident in the unsavoury and scathing language that is used in depicting Willie's mother by her father. This is similar to the language that is used by Mr Biswas, when it comes to Mrs. Tulsi, and at times even his wife Shama. But as we move on to the next generation of strong women Naipaul presents to us the character of Ana, an out and out positive persona. She is described in positive terms whether physically or otherwise. Her power is not emasculating but enriching. The only time Willie is shown to feel secure and fulfilled is in her presence. At no other stage in his life earlier or later is he able to achieve this feeling of security and fulfilment again. He tells his sister Sarojini, "I loved her ... for the luck and liberation she had brought me, the undoing of fear, the granting to me of full manhood." *A House for Mr Biswas* portrays a world which abounds in numerous female characters that are uneducated, financially dependent as well as powerless. Mr. Biswas's mother Bipti, his sister Dehuti, the Tulsi daughters both married and widowed all fall in this category. Shama in spite of being intelligent and not being subjected to any physical abuse is powerless in stopping Mr. Biswas from making some of the mistakes that are the cause of his failure in running the business at The Chase or in the purchase of the house at Sikkim Street. *Half a Life* also has women who are uneducated and powerless but they are not meek. In the African world that Naipaul portrays with its poverty and prostitutes, we have Ana's African maid, Julio's daughter, as a representative of this exploited female figure who strikes back at the world with all she has. The writer in the European setting presents to us characters who might be poor but not necessarily weak. Whether it is June, Percy's girlfriend, or any other female figure, she is not meek or weak. Willie's mother and Sarojini might be ugly but they are both fighters, proactive females-a complete contrast to Willie. Moving on to the first half of *Magic Seeds* we find that women are relegated to the background with the exception of Sarojini. In the characters of the professor's wife, daughter and maid we have nameless faceless characters that are not even shadows in the world they occupy. It seems as if in the Indian set up Naipaul's women are conspicuous by their absence. Their absence is striking, whether it is the city, the villages or the guerrilla movement, the writer presents us with no women characters worth mentioning. One or two very minor female presences are alluded to, but no one name stands out or can be recalled by the reader in the part of the novel that is set in India. This is a major contrast from his novel *A House for Mr. Biswas*. The only woman who is present throughout this narrative space is his sister Sarojini who can hardly be categorized as a traditional Indian woman. We come across the women characters when the narrative shifts to England. The women presented at this stage are delineated without any sympathy, they are flawed characters and the writer seems to be putting the blame for their plight squarely on their doorstep. Whether it is Perdita, or Roger's girlfriend from the community houses, or the other women of the community houses, Naipaul presents a very unflattering commentary. It is difficult to sympathize with these women as opposed to his women of the earlier two novels. They are shown to be users who have no appreciation of any relationships, they are portrayed as selfish and negligent mothers caught up in fulfilling their own desires. They are a contrast to the women of *A House for Mr. Biswas* where we do not have one bad mother, none intentional at least. They might be strict and flawed but they always try to do the best they can. Whether it is the widows or Bipti or Dehuti or even the indomitable Mrs Tulsi, the interests of the children are shown to be of paramount importance to them. *A House for Mr. Biswas* also has some unexplored aspects that are present in his later novels. The first is the presentation of strong independent women who are not fully fleshed out as well as presented in a harsh light. The first to fall in this category would be Shaker's wife Dorothy. The sisters are shown to present a negative picture of her, but Naipaul brings out the jealousy behind this portrayal to debunk this presentation as inherently flawed. The fears are their own. She is the first example of, if not positive, then at least, benign presence. Her advent on the scene does not displace the sisters hold in the house as they fear and is the underlying cause of their antagonism. Naipaul shows that it is Owad, their brother, who is finally responsible for the loss of the protective Tulsi house. Naipaul also presents to us Owad's wife as the educated modern woman of the changed world. Here again the negative sentiments of the sisters which were earlier endorsed by Owad are proven to be born out of jealousy and fear. In this novel, Naipaul presents these two modern women who are both educated and independent, they are present as an idea that we will find developed in later novels. The second aspect that becomes evident in this novel is the focus on education of both the male and female child as essential. Naipaul goes a step further and presents the reader with the character of Savi; she is shown to have been in the shadow of her younger brother Anand in the initial stages of her life. A child who suddenly morphs into the saviour of the Biswas family, she takes over the responsibility of the family at a stage where but for her arrival on the scene things could have turned out very differently for Mr Biswas's household. There is no negative commentary surrounding her character, in fact she is shown to dethrone Anand in her father's mind. Her father had always envisaged Anand as the prodigal son who will help the family out of the quagmire of powerlessness and poverty. Naipaul writes, "Savi returned and Mr Biswas welcomed her as if she were herself and Anand combined. Savi got a job, at a bigger salary than Mr Biswas could ever have got". This is shown to happen in a span of almost two pages and the event is not discussed in detail or given a lot of narrative space. Another aspect that is present in its nascent stage in this novel is the presence of the women in the public sphere. It is shown to be a new phenomenon and is an emerging trend. Naipaul presents to us the character of Miss Logie, his boss at the Community Welfare Department. Naipaul describes her as "a tall energetic woman in late middle age. She was not pompous or aggressive ... She had the graces ... She also had the attraction of novelty." Naipaul presents her in a positive light with hardly any flaws of character or blemishes.

In her we find a representative of the new emerging breed of women who exerted their influence outside the personal sphere. A beginning of this trend is presented in a positive light with Savi taking over the responsibilities of the house once Mr. Biswas is no longer able to work. A major progression that is evident when we compare the novels is the absence of any mention of sexual relationships in *A House for Mr. Biswas*. There is no explicit mention of it and it is only alluded to within the confines of marital relationship. In contrast to this in his last two novels when Naipaul is depicting the African and European setting the presentation of sexual relationships is a major component of the male–female relationships. They are not confined to the marital sphere. Naipaul presents extramarital affairs and prostitutes and casual sex as a norm in these set ups. But here again when it comes to this element of male female relationship it is absent in the part of the novel set in India. Whether it is the relationship between Willie's father and his mother in *Half a Life* or the Indian characters present in *Magic Seeds* the absence of even a hint of this aspect is absent. The passage of time does not affect his presentation. Willie's sexual encounters are shown to have occurred outside of the Indian setting. It is as if in some ways the world has remained unchanged on the Indian subcontinent in the authors mind. The three novels have some elements that are present in a greater or lesser degree right from the beginning. The end of mutual antagonism between the male and female characters as symbolized by the relationship of Mr. Biswas and his wife Shama, that is reached at the end of *A House for Mr. Biswas* happens much earlier in his latter novels. The acceptance of the female life force as essential by Willie, the main protagonist happens much earlier and much more clearly in his latter novels. It helps him to finally accept himself as the person he is and feel fulfilled.

REFERENCES

1. Dooley, Gillian. "Naipaul's Women". *South Asian Review* 26.1 (2005). pp. 88–103.
2. —. *V.S. Naipaul: Man and Writer.* Columbia: University of South Carolina Press, 2006.
3. French, Patrick. *The World is What It is: The Authorized Biography of V.S. Naipaul.* 2008. London: Picador, 2009.
4. Naipaul, V. S. *A House for Mr. Biswas*. 1961. London: Picador, 2003.
5. —.*Half a Life*. 2001. London: Picador, 2002.
6. —.*Magic Seeds*. 2004. London: Picador, 2005.
7. Pyne-Timothy, Helen. "Women and Sexuality in the Later Novels of V. S. Naipaul". World Literature Written in English 25.2 (1985): pp. 298–306.
8. White, Landeg. *V.S. Naipaul A Critical Introduction*. London: Macmillan, 1975.

23

Role of Women in Society and their Contributions With Special Reference to Kamla Markandaya's *Nectar In A Sieve*

C. Blessy and Priyanka Singh

ABSTRACT

Women are important part in our Society. The modern society has started recognizing the individual identity of women. She is believed to have her aspiration, abilities and qualities as a man does and it is also agreed that she should have the right opportunities to develop her faculties and to express them according to her own choice. A "strong" woman knows how to keep her life in order. Even with tears in her eyes, she still manages to say, 'I'm Fine', with a smile.

Kamala Markandaya had great hopes for India. Her most famous novel, Nectar in a Sieve, *tells the story of a woman who faced incredible hardships yet never ceased to dream of a better life.* Nectar, *which takes its title from a poem by Samuel Coleridge, is typical of Markandaya's forward-thinking perspective.* Nectar in a Sieve *is anchored by a strong female character. The protagonist's optimism serves dual purposes. It allows Markandaya the writer to imagine a better future both for the characters and the country.*

"When women are empowered and can claim their rights and access to land, leadership, opportunities and choices, economies grow, food security is enhanced and prospects are improved for current and future generations".

—*Michelle Bachelet,* Under-Secretary-General and Executive Director of UN Women

INTRODUCTION

Women who were the most dormant part of India's population have now become active participants in all walks of life. Till now, they were only a unit of the family organization. Now, women are becoming not only a significant unit of the society but are also influencing the course of social change in society. Kamala Markandaya's *Nectar in a Sieve* portrays its optimistic woman character as an ideal sufferer and nurturer. "The cause of her suffering springs mainly from poverty and natural calamity. The women are from the rural sections of society. They are the daughters of the soil and have inherited age-old traditions which they do not question. Their courage lies in meek or at times cheerful way of facing poverty or calamity". She faces a lot of hardships. She demonstrated her true character each time she overcame one of her problems.

Rukmani the protagonist and narrator in the novel is a simple peasant woman whose persistent battle has been against poverty. The younger daughter of a village headman, she marries Nathan, a landless tenant farmer, at the age of twelve. The dwindling financial position of Rukmani's father forces him to marry her off to a tenant. Her sisters Shanta, Padmini and Thangam were married in a befitting manner, but as luck would have it the headman is no longer rich and is of no consequence; hence Rukmani with neither beauty, nor dowry is given away to Nathan a tenant farmer. Poverty and starvation stalk the threshold of the couple from the beginning of their married life. When Rukmani comes to live with Nathan, his house images her withered future,

> *"Across the doorway a garland of mango leaves, symbol of happiness and good fortune, dry now and rattling in the breeze".*

Rukmani accepts her adversity calmly and reveals her stoic acceptance of the inevitable. In her relationship with her husband she learns the values of mutual love, understanding, respect, acceptance, and adjustment. Both Rukmani and her husband lead a simple and contented life with the barest necessities such as food, clothes and shelter. Nathan was a poor peasant in every sense of the word. He possessed a very small hut:

> *Two rooms, one a sort of storehouse for grain the other for everything else. A third had been begun but was unfinished, the mud walls were not more than half a foot high.*

Rukmani seems to conform to the established image of a woman personified in the mythical figures of Sita and Savitri who silently bear all hardships and remain devoted to their husbands. Born of the village headman and married to a tenant farmer below her family status, her good soul speaks of her husband as one "who was poor in everything but in love and care for me". She feels proud of him as he is efficient in farming, in maintaining the household single-handedly and he is also a loving husband. Rukmani begets her first child and sheds, "tears of weakness and disappointment; for what woman wants a girl for her first-born?" She knows that irrational conventions and anachronistic traditions decry a female offspring. As a typical village farmer, Nathan also believes in the notion of the superiority of a male child. After the birth of Ira he was not happy as he should be, since Ira was a girl.

Rukmani and her daughter Ira display suffering throughout the novel. Rukmani works hard and is devoted to her gentle husband. She endures blow after blow from life: poverty, famine, the divorce of her barren daughter, the deaths of her sons, her daughter's prostitution, and finally her husband's death. She accepts the blow and moves on in life. In addition, when her son Raja is murdered, even her thoughts do not express rebellion. She moves from numbness to grief, thinking,

> *"For this I have given you birth, my son, that you should lie at the end at my feet with ashes in your face and coldness in your limbs and yourself departed without trace."*

Then she begins to wash the corpse and prepare it for burial. When two officials from the tannery, where Raja was killed, come three days later to try to bully her into saying they have no responsibility, she tells them what they want to hear, thinking,

> *"What compensation is there for death? I felt confused, I did not know what they were getting at."*

When the officials turn to leave, she realizes that one of the men feels "shame and misery" and tries to make him feel better: "You should not care", I said very softly to him alone. "It does not matter". Her goodness and inner strength prevent her from becoming hard and bitter.

Yet although Rukmani's general submissiveness may appear a weakness to Western readers, from another point of view she has incredible strength. These two views, which represent conflicting Western and Eastern values, explicitly appear in *Nectar in a Sieve.* Rukmani confronts the Western doctor, Kenny, who urges,

> *"You must cry out if you want help. It is no use whatsoever to suffer in silence. Who will succour the drowning man if he does not clamour for his life?"*

In response, Rukmani thinks, "Want is our companion from birth to death, familiar as the seasons or the earth, varying only in degree. What profit to bewail that which has always been and cannot change?"

But Kenny, the Westerner, believes that, "there is no grandeur in want, or endurance." In contrast, Rukmani, the Indian woman, sees suffering as good for the spirit and endurance as a necessity, because she cannot change her situation. Looking at Rukmani only from the Western point of view leads one to misunderstand her character and the values that sustain her. The Western viewpoint equally misjudges the ideal of the devoted wife.

Rukmani in her trials of penury comes out successfully. Whether it was showing compassion to those less fortunate than her, persevering for the sake of herself and family, or adapting to a new livelihood, Rukmani overcomes all of the difficulty. Rukmani exhibits her true character of compassion, perseverance, and adaptability to changing circumstances each time problems faced her. She frequently acted out of her compassion with many characters. Rukmani even exercised her compassion to Kunthi during a period of hardship and famine in her village.

Rukmani, the mother figure, symbolizes the mother earth. The earth is the life-giver, the supporter, the sustainer, the nourisher and even more, the healer as it is the positive, sustaining force of life. The mother Earth is omnipresent with outstretched arms to welcome each and every one. While commenting on the noble quality of the stoic endurance of Rukmani, Deepti Pandey observes:

> *"Rukmani in Nectar in a Sieve is the Mother Earth. Her integrity is never on the brink of collapse. On the face of all calamities, she unfolds her lap to take in everything and everybody around her. She is the eternal mother figure." (Pandey 29)*

CONCLUSION

Rukmani's sufferings form a queue and they multiply with the advancement of time but fail to crush her spirits or to shake her faith in the basic human values. Having faced the biggest blow of her husband's death, she comes back to her village with a renewed faith in an adopted son Puli and reconciles to life, which is in store for her.

Arundhati Chatterjee describes the character of Rukmani accurately: *"She is the eternal mother bound by love and affection to her hearth and home. Biologically, she is the receiver giving birth to human beings. Emotionally, philosophically and spiritually too she is the absorber who imbibes everything that comes her way—joy, happiness, hardship, poverty, loss, pain, suffering—Nectar as well as poison. Her journey from home to her husband's house is her journey to motherhood"* (Chatterjee, 1987). Everything that crosses her path is sieved through her kind, simple, tolerant, understanding, sympathetic and loving self.

Women can help the society in various ways. They can engage in social activities and work for the betterment of the society. Young educated girls can get engaged in a profession of their choice. The world cannot grow at a good pace unless women come forward and take initiative for the development works. They can contribute significantly in the field of health care. Education among women will also improve the level of sanitation and hygiene. As a mother, her role in the development of the emotional psychological aspect of the newborn child has also been very significant. She was not only the creator and maintainer of her child but an educator and disciplinarian as well. An empowered and financially independent woman may not have to go through the sufferings of Rukmani.

Woman is now an important instrument of social change. The extent of women's participation in various professions and in the workings of the society are thus the measures of social change in India.

REFERENCES

1. Chatterjee, Arundhanti. "Rukmani, The Mother Figure in *Nectar in a Sieve"*. *Studies in Indian Fiction in English*, Ed. G.S. Balramaghupta. Gulbarga: IIWL Publishers, 1987. Print.
2. http://www.importantindia.com/20500/importance-of-women-in-our-society/
3. Markandaya, Kamala, (1956), *Nectar in a sieve*, Jaico Publishing House.
4. Pandey, Deepti. *Feminism in The Novels Of Kamala Markandaya*. Varanasi: MPASVOM. Publication, 2013.
5. Parmeshwaran, Uma. *A Study of Representative Indo-English Novelists*. New Delhi: Vikas, 1976.
6. Rao, Narayana. K.S. "Love, Sex, Marriage and Morality in Kamala Markandaya's Novels." *The Osmania Journal of English Studies*, 10 (1973).
7. Shirwadkar, Meena. *Image of Woman in the Indo-Anglian Novel*. New Delhi: Sterling Publishers Private Limited, 1979.
8. Shiv K. Kumar, " Tradition and change in the novels of Kamala Markandaya", *Kakatiya Journal of English Studies*, Vol. III, 1979.
9. Shukla, Rajesh. *Multiculturalism in Indian Fiction in English*. Jaipur: Ritu Publications, 2014. Print.

24

Companionate Marriage and Women's Equality in the Pioneering Tamil Novel

Ashish Alexander

ABSTRACT

The rise of novel in the nineteenth-century India was more than a mere literary event. It marked the emergence of individualism, arrival of modernity and, particularly, the change in the status of Indian women. The novel not only recorded the changes in the status of women that appeared in the wake of modernism and Westernization, but was used by the novelists to further the cause of reform. It is no coincidence that all the earliest novels in various Indian languages were centered on a woman protagonist. The first Tamil novel The Life and Times of Pratapa Mudaliar *(1879) by Samuel Vedanayagam Pillai is a tribute to the image of an ideal woman. Despite the fact that the novel is named after the male protagonist, it is the woman protagonist who is presented as a model individual to both the male and female readers. This paper argues that, notwithstanding its simple story line and mellow sentimentalism, this pioneering Tamil novel breaks new ground in the representation of women characters and projects the idea of "new woman" on the imaginative landscape of the emerging Indian nation. It challenges the traditional roles and images of women and is able to present radical ideas about women emancipation in a non-confrontational manner.*

Keywords: *women in literature, early Indian novel, Tamil literature, post-colonialism, gender*

INTRODUCTION

In his classic study *The Rise of the Novel*, Ian Watt sets out to establish that there are "enduring connections between the distinctive literary qualities of the novel and those of the society in which it began and flourished". Watt states that the eighteenth-century English society had a wave of specific changes sweeping over it—and among the most prominent ones was the change in the status of women. He later remarks that, "The rise of the novel, then, would seem to be connected with the much greater freedom of women in modern society, a freedom which, especially as regards marriage, was achieved earlier and more completely in England than elsewhere" (Chapter 5). Novel has often been called the most democratic of art forms. Unlike the more "classic" forms of literature, such as epics, tragedies and lyric poetry—all of which required education and training in classical languages—novel was the genre closest to the lived life of common men and women in the eighteenth century, when English novel reached a state of maturity. Not only were women a major constituent of the reading public, women began to compose their own narratives and novels. This was not only a remarkable literary event but a significant milestone in women/human history. Watt, very minutely, studies the social-economic and cultural changes that impacted the change in the status of women which then became the warp and woof of many of the earliest novels. The rise of individualism, especially "economic individualism" and redefining of family as "conjugal" family, "formed by the voluntary union of two individuals" (Watt, Chapter 5) has been a key element in shaping the English novel. In Watt's estimation, the loosely constructed prose narratives that had prevailed till the middle of the seventeenth century made way for the novel proper when Samuel Richardson wrote Pamela in 1740. The plot of this immensely popular book made man–woman relationship an abiding theme of the English novel.

It was this kind of novel that came to be a model for most Indian writers who began attempting novel writing in English or their native languages, nearly a century and a half later. This is how Meenakshi Mukherjee sums up the situation and assesses its impact on Indian writers:

> The depiction of love and courtship was a *major concern* of English novelists of the eighteenth and nineteenth centuries. Around the time the novel emerged in English, the relationship between the sexes was undergoing a change. The concept of romantic love was displacing that of the courtly love and marriage was slowly becoming a *matter of individual choice rather than familial obligation.* (69, emphases added)

Here Mukherjee is echoing the analysis of Watt and she states how, that significantly impacted novel writing in India.

> In late nineteenth-century India not only were conventions of marriage restrictive, even social intercourse between the sexes was not common in upper classes. Where girls were married off by parents before puberty, there was very little scope for emotional relationships of the kind depicted in the English novel which the educated Indian enjoyed reading. (70)

Mukherjee underlined the dilemma of the Indian novelist who wished to write a novel in the manner of the models he/she had studied, namely, English novels, but found the prevalent social situations completely alien to the task of novel writing.

In the chapter titled "Women in a New Genre" in her seminal book *Realism and Reality*, Meenakshi Mukherjee discusses four of the earliest novels written in four different Indian languages, each of them written by a male author but the protagonist of each of these novels was a woman. Mukherjee observes that, "of the four only one ends traditionally and happily with a marriage. *Indulekha*, unusually for its time, depicts romantic love in a contemporary situation between two young persons and ends in a marriage that combines individual fulfillment, social sanction and material benefit." Indian writers, thus, faced a challenge—how to write a novel in a society that hasn't experienced growth and evolution of social relationships as seen in England. The position of Indian woman had nothing to write home about in the nineteenth century. This prompted many Indian writers to situate their ideal and extraordinary Indian women in the distant past or in the religiously inclined community novels—a literary strategy successfully employed by pioneering writers who wrote historical novels such as Bankim Chandra Chatterjee (1838–1894) in Bengali and Bhai Vir Singh (1872–1957) in Punjabi. But the problem of writing a realistic novel persisted because "the two axes on which formal realism of the western variety rests", namely, "present time and ordinary life" (Mukherjee, 72) had to form the basis of the Indian novel's plot and structure, too.

Some Indian writers solved that problem on the basis of, it might be argued, sheer optimism. They were not merely writers, writing for a living (Ebeling, 248) but reformers hoping to bring a change in the society. One such writer was Samuel Vedanayagam Pillai (1826–1889).

WOMEN'S EQUALITY AND COMPASSIONATE MARRIAGE IN SAMUEL VEDANAYAGAM PILLAI'S NOVEL

Samuel Vedanayagam Pillai is generally considered to be the father of the Tamil novel. He started his professional career as a clerk in the East India

Company in 1848. A man of literary sensibilities, young Samuel published his first book *Nitinul* ("The Book of Right Conduct"), a collection of six hundred poems on moral issues, in 1857. In 1869 he published another collection of poems *Penmati malai* ("The Garland of Female Wisdom") and an essay "Pen Kalvi" ("Women's Education"). Both the poems and the essay were published in one volume. In the preface, Vedanayagam says:

> *One of the crying evils of the land being the degradation to which females are subjected in their domestic and social life, the writer has dwelt at some length on this evil, and has endeavoured to convince the reader, by facts and illustrations, by a reference to the old shastras, etc. of the right that the softer sex of our land have to be treated by their husbands, etc. with greater kindness and regard than what, by the pernicious custom of this country, fall to their lot.* (quoted. in Ebeling 246; emphasis in the original)

It is instructive to note from this quote that the reason for the "degradation" of women, according to Vedanayagam, was the treatment meted out to them by their families, particularly by the husbands. And, he wrote another essay *Pen manam* (Women's Dignity) in 1870, the aim of which again was to ensure "respect due to them, and the manner in which they should be treated" (Ebeling 247). When one studies the literary career of Samuel Vedanayagam Pillai, his abiding concern was the rejuvenation of Tamil culture and the nineteenth-century Tamil society. Proficient in English, he chose to write in Tamil, introduced prose writing, worked towards establishing religious harmony in the society and produced works with unflinching ethical themes and content. All his concerns finally converged in his novel that he published in 1879—*Prathapa Mudaliar Charithram.*

The novel has a first-person narrative and the story is told by principal character Pratapa Mudliar. Pratapa Mudaliar's grandfather was a Dewan of a Muslim Nawab. Pratapa's father inherited large property, wealth and assets, and simply enjoyed them. The novel pokes fun at the aristocratic class, and mildly chides it for its self-indulgent and carefree manner. In the manner of the earliest English novelists, Vedanayagam has a comic approach to his subject matter, as one critic remarks: "It is obvious that Vedanayakam Pillai was not inspired by the English romantics like Sir Walter Scott or the Gothics like Ann Radclyffe but by English comedians like Henry Fielding and William Thackeray...the Tamil author's desperate attempt to bring out ironically the comic aspects of life as lived by the Tamilians is quite obvious on every page in the novel" (Satyan 80–81). But exposing the follies and foibles of the upper strata of the society was not the only, or even the primary aim of the author. His primary objective was to ensure respect and regard for the women in the Tamil society and thereby point towards possibility of an ideal marriage and conjugal bliss. So while, Pratapa finds the comic and ridiculous in every situation and every character, including himself, there are two characters in the novel for whom he has nothing but utmost respect—his mother Sundari Anni and his wife Gnanambal. In fact, in the English preface that he wrote for his Tamil novel, the author states:

> *... the principal personages who play important parts in this novel are the hero's mother Sundara Anni and his wife Gnanamabal, both being ladies of high birth and fortune, with every accomplishment both personal and mental, and endowed with every estimable quality that could adorn the female sex. The father and the father-in-law of the hero are types of uneducated native gentlemen in high life, with all their eccentricities and singularities of character. They are, however, made by the gentle artifices of Sundara Anni and Gnanambal, to exhibit traits of talent and good feelings, and to perform praiseworthy acts. (quoted in Sundaram 27)*

Going by this extensive quote from the preface, it may not be wrong to say that this novel doesn't have a hero but two heroines—one major and other minor, the wife and the mother respectively. Instead of resorting to the patronising attitude of men trying to "improve" the status of women, Samuel Pillai, reverses the equation and creates situations where women, *through their example*, make men "perform praiseworthy acts". There are two peculiar things in this choice of the author. First, he took an immense risk in making women—especially a young wife—the protagonists and centre of didactic teaching in a patriarchal culture; patriarchal both in the senses of being dominated by men and being always subservient to the elderly and the aged. Sundari Anni, the mother of Pratap, is clearly shown to have more wits and wisdom around her than both Pratap's father (the male head) as well as Pratap's grandmother (the elderly and all-powerful Indian mother-in-law). Second, the novel fiercely states that if women are given equal opportunities to study and cultivate themselves, they are equal to men in all regards. Both these ideas went against the most cherished ideals of the dominant culture.

As Pratap recounts his life, he is quick to mention one of the most decisive influences on his life had been that of his mother, and that was regarding his education. Pratap's father was least interested in whether his son learnt anything or not. His grandmother thought that only the poor needed to learn as they must seek employment—heirs of the erstwhile Dewans need not be subjected to discipline and demands of education. The mother Sundari Anni, goes against such "conventional" wisdom and ensures that her son receives proper education. She, in fact, is the first teacher that Pratap has. The nature of the ideal woman was further elucidated in Gnanambal, who becomes the fellow pupil of Pratapa and eventually his wife.

Fellow students, Pratapa and Gnanambal grow together, and we are made aware of innate goodness, courage and wisdom of Gnanambal—the meaning of her very name is "wise woman".[1] The focus of the novel, despite the episodic nature of the plot, is the conjugal relationship, the married life of Pratapa and Gnanambal. It was an ideal marriage because it was a union based on mutual love and respect between two adults and not a marriage arranged in childhood by the parents to fulfil some religious or social duty.

The idea of companionate marriage, thus, was at the heart of the novel. Pratapa's and Gnanambal's marriage was ideal, but the author is careful to show that this was more an exception than a rule. The real conditions prevailing in the Tamil society of that time were made such union, the idea of companionate marriage, an unattainable goal. The story of Andachi Ammal in chapter sixteen illustrates that. A young woman shares how her mother-in-law and sister-in-law destroyed her married life. The idea of a man and woman happily married, it seems, was a threat to the cultural and domestic order. Andachi ammal says that after her marriage, her mother-in-law had gone to her sister-in-law, who had lost her husband, and she says, "This was the happiest time of our lives, and my husband and I came very close" (Vedanayakam 73-74). When the mother and daughter returned, Andachi says, "my husband and I were deeply engrossed in the delight of each other's company". However, this sense of companionship was deeply resented by the mother-in-law, and there was the following exchange between the mother and the son:

> My mother-in-law said to her son, I was married to your father for twenty years and during all that time, I didn't speak even two words to him. And here you are talking to the girl who swallowed your sister's husband no sooner than she stepped here.
>
> Confused, he said, How can my wife be blamed for that? And it was my wife I was talking with, not some other woman. (74)

But the husband had broken a strict cultural code and this brought a series of disciplinary measures against the erring couple. First, the servants were banished and the daughter-in-law was made to do all household work. Second, the sister-in-law and mother-in-law took turns to sleep outside the husband's house lest the wife should stealthily go in the room and have at least a conversation with her husband. Finally, as the hapless wife recounted: ""My mother-in-law and sister-in-law began to bring prostitutes to the house frequently and tried their best to lure my husband" (75).

The author, however, is conscious of efforts by some men to forcefully modernize their wives and family and coerce them into companionate marriage. The previous narrative could be juxtaposed with the one concerning a young Brahmin boy Ananthiah, whose poor father wanted him to learn both English and Tamil. But Ananthiah completely disregarded Tamil and sought to become an Englishmen. With only a surface knowledge of European culture, he gave himself over to life of hedonism. Since he had no access to the society of the Englishmen, he kept company of the "cooks and butlers of the British and poor Anglo Indians" (Vedanayakam 126). He sought to extend the "English" influence to his family by trying "to get his wife and other women of his family to converse and move freely with strange men as he did with the womenfolk of his new-found friends" (126). The wife, we are told, tried stopping him from this foolish behaviour but her efforts "met with little success". When Ananthiah fell into bad times, his wife and children who had been "tutored by him in the principles of hedonism" left him. One implication of this episode is that husbands must learn from wisdom of wives in matters of social decorum. This fits well with the author's intention of making husbands respect and regard their wives.

Pratapa's and Gnanambal's marriage finds the perfect mean between the two situations discussed above. A monogamous marriage of consenting adults for life-long union based on mutual love, respect and sacrifice was the author's prescription for the cultural shortcomings.

The other important element that Samuel Vedanayagam adds in this book is that the women in companionate marriage are not supposed to be limited to domestic sphere. They are as capable as men in matters of governance outside the four walls of the home. Very early in the novel, we are told that Sundari Anni is able to manage the estate of her husband.[2] The last section of the novel narrates how Gnanambal rules over a city as its king, in a male disguise. This part of the novel runs counter to the criticism of postcolonial critics who claim that the nineteenth-century companionate marriage tends to limit the woman to the domestic sphere. Gananmbal proves to be the most able administrator, inspired by highest ideals of justice. Later, she is joined by her husband and both, in disguise, look after the kingdom. The story could have ended here. But the author's idea of a companionate marriage in normal and realistic circumstances would then have to be abandoned. The fantasy must make way for realism.

The novel ends with both Sundari Anni and Gnanambal being felicitated by Queen Victoria herself for their accomplishments.

CONCLUSION

Nineteenth century in India was a period of immense changes sweeping over the Indian subcontinent. The cultural life of the country came under the sway of new notions of individual, society and social relationships. In literature, new characters and stories were emerging. The realist mode of depicting the lives of common men and women was nothing less than revolutionary, as it had been in Europe a century or so earlier.[3] It had a peculiarly significant impact on the lives of women. The image of women created in these new realistic novels allowed the emergence of a confident, self-respecting and empowered woman.

NOTES

1 With notable exceptions of Hana Catherine Mullens (1826–1861), and probably, Krupabai Sattianadhan (1862–1894), all the pioneering Indian novelists were men.

2 "*Indira* by Bankimchandra Chatterji (Bengali; 1873; revised edn. 1893); *Indulekha* by O. Chandu Menon (Malayalam; 1888); *Pan Lakshyant Kon Gheto* by Harinarayan Apte (Marathi; 1890); and *Umrao Jan Ada* by Mirza Mohammad Hadi Ruswa (Urdu; 1899)" (Mukherjee 70).

3 Different spellings of the author's name are in vogue. The English translation of his novel published by Katha mentions the name of the author as Mayuram Vedanayakam Pillai. His first name *Samuel*, has been replaced by the name of the district (Mayuram) where he served as a *munsiff*. This paper uses the actual first name *Samuel* and traditional spellings for the middle name *Vedanayagam* (with a "g"), which is closer to the Tamil pronunciation.

4 Or as the novel translates it, "goddess of wisdom".

5 "Since my father took no interest in running our estates, my mother assumed this entire responsibility, and so could not spare even a minute for me. My grandmother and father therefore decided to take charge of my studies, which led to disastrous results" (13).

6 "The realist novel represents one of the great revolutionary cultural forms of human history. In the domain of culture, it has something like the importance of steam-power or electricity in the material realm, or of democracy in the political sphere" (Eagleton 19).

REFERENCES

1. Eagleton, Terry. *The English Novel: An Introduction*. Blackwell, 2004.
2. Ebeling, Sascha. Afterword. *The Life and Times of Pratapa Mudaliar* by Mayuram Vedanayakam Pillai, translated by Meenakshi Tyagarajan, Katha, 2005, pp. 239–268.
3. Mukherjee, Meenakshi. *Realism and Reality: The Novel and Society in India*. OUP, 1985.

4. Satyan, R. "Three Pioneer Indian Novelists". *Indian Literature*, vol. 24, no. 4, Jul.–Aug., 1981, pp. 78–84. *JSTOR*, www.jstor.org/stable/23330211.
5. Sundaram, S. Sivapatha. "Pioneers of the Tamil Novel: New Discoveries". *Indian Literature*, vol. 21, no. 4, Jul.–Aug. 1978, pp. 25–39. *JSTOR*, www.jstor.org/stable/24158230.
6. Vedanayakam Pillai, Mayuram. *The Life and Times of Pratapa Mudaliar*, translated by Meenakshi Tyagarajan, Katha, 2005.
7. Watt, Ian. *The Rise of the Novel: Studies in Defoe, Richardson and Fielding*. Pimlico/Random House, 2000. *Kindle E-book*.

SECTION 5

SUSTAINABLE DEVELOPMENT THROUGH WOMEN ENTREPRENEURSHIP AND WOMEN FRIENDLY MANAGEMENT PRACTICES

25

Work–life Balance Initiatives in Indian Public Sector Banks:

Employees' Perspective

Shefali Nandan

ABSTRACT

Work–life balance (WLB) is about helping employees in maintaining healthy, rewarding lifestyles that will, in turn, lead to improvements in productivity and performance. Nature of workforce is changing as the number of 'dual-career families' are increasing. Family commitments and personal aspirations are as important to these workers as work responsibilities. Thus, it is important for organizations today to take initiatives for helping employees achieve work–life balance. Due to increasing competition, public sector organizations in India, like their private sector counterparts, are adopting innovative practices in managing their human resource, to get a competitive edge. This empirical research was undertaken with the objective to study the employees' perception regarding initiatives taken for work–life balance by public sector banks in India. Data was collected from six public sector banks in India through structured questionnaire, using convenience sampling. Exploratory factor analysis was used to identify the factors perceived to be contributing to work–life balance of employees. Three factors were found to constitute WLB initiatives in public sector banks, which in their order of importance are: time to fulfil personal commitments, support of senior officials, and manageable workload. The study provides an insight to academicians and policy makers in banks and other organizations into the needs of today's employees and initiatives taken in public sector banks for work–life balance. Other organizations may adopt these practices or innovate methods taking cue from these practices, for helping employees attain work–life balance and hence improve their job satisfaction and organisational productivity.

INTRODUCTION

The changing social patterns have resulted in many changes in lifestyles of people. They have to manage personal responsibilities as well as organisational work responsibilities. Work–life balance is a two-way process that has consideration of the needs of employees as well as those of employers (Lewis, 2000). Work–life balance practices are aimed at encouraging employers to adopt such initiatives and culture as can help their employees achieve a better balance between the demands of employers and those of personal life. The concept of work–life balance is based on the notion that work–life priorities and personal life priorities should not be seen as competing elements, but as complementary aspects of life. This can be realized by adopting an approach that is "conceptualised as a two-way process involving a consideration of the needs of employees as well as those of employers" (Lewis, 2000, p.105). Though hygiene factors (such as basic compensation and safety) are important for employees but studies show that work–life balance strategies attract employees during recruitment.

In 1999, a wide study of PriceWaterhouse Coopers covering students from 11 countries found work–life harmony to be the most important career goal. Research has also indicated that employees of organisations with work–life programmes are less likely to leave the job as compared to employees of other organizations. Since women usually prefer to combine work and family, WLB practices help employers to retain valued female employees. In other words, work–life strategy would help employers retain talented and valued employees thus saving the costs related to recruitment, interviewing and training. Work–life balance issues are common in today's work scenario as numerous employees feel overwhelmed by an imbalanced life that becomes obvious with symptoms like depression, stress due to responsibilities, lack of energy and enthusiasm for daily activities, etc.

Many public sector and private sector organizations in India are becoming aware of the importance of helping employees attain Work–life balance and are adopting strategies to achieve the same. This study was undertaken to find out practices of Work–life balance in Indian Public sector banks.

LITERATURE REVIEW

Different researchers have explained differently as to what constitutes work–life balance practice. Estes & Michael (2005) have given a broad definition of work–life balance practice that includes organizational support for dependent care, flexible work options, and family or personal leave. According to this definition these practices include flexible work hours (e.g. flexitime and compressed work week, working from home, job sharing), family leave programs (e.g. parental leave, adoption leave, compassionate leave), on-site childcare, and financial and/or informational assistance with childcare and eldercare services.

According to Roehling et al., (in Busby and James (ed.), 2011, p. 42) work–family conflict may be defined as "the direct result of incompatible pressures from an individual's work and family roles", and we may anticipate that levels of work–life conflict will vary with national, individual and family circumstances. Work–life conflicts exist when the time for work and personal/family activities becomes diffused. This occurs in the situation of having too many things to do and too little time in which to do them (Greenhaus & Beutell, 1985; Voydanoff, 2005) This work–life conflict can originate both in the home or in the work environment (Frone, Yardley, & Markel, 1997). But since work schedules tend to be less flexible than personal schedules (Eagle, Miles, & Icenogle, 1997) work is more likely the cause of work–life conflicts (Greenhaus & Parasuraman, 1999).

Career opportunities, in the form of prospects for advancement within an organization or more generally in one's chosen field, are impacted by family commitments. The use of flexible working practices by employers designed to assist employees to balance their work and home and the desire for a balanced lifestyle between work and family also affects decisions to change jobs or accept a geographical transfer. Moreover it can help to shape employees' intentions to change an organization or an entire career. In fact young people's occupational choices are influenced by the way in which they prioritize their work and family roles, and that they tend to place a high value on both work and family rather than on one or the other (Smithson, 1999).

Increasing workloads have pressurised employees to demonstrate their commitment to work in more obvious ways (Ishaya and Ayman, 2008). Consequently, a larger part of them have tended to be present at their workplace for longer periods of time, thereby reducing the time for which they are available at home. The Internet and mobile phones have made it possible for the organizations to keep in constant touch with the employees both during the day and at night (Morgan 2003). This has further intensified the work demands on employees and consequently there are growing reports of stress and work imbalance (Bhagwagar, 2009). The extended family, even in India, is slowly disappearing (Patel 2005). Small nuclear families have come to stay, where both the spouses go to work. In addition, there are an increasing number of single parent households due to increase in divorces (Amato et al., 2003). Jenkins (2000) observes that issues like child rearing, the need to balance multiple roles, etc., have consequences on health and family relationships. Basic economic pressures and the cyclical tight labour market throughout the last two decades drove these work–life initiatives as corporations increased efforts to attract, motivate and retain employees. High turnover has huge cost implications.

Unsupportive workplaces lead to spillover from jobs into employee's personal lives which, regardless of the quantity of work–life programs, limits the effect of such programs on job performance (Bond, Galinsky and Swanberg, 1998). Research has identified certain characteristics of corporations that correlate with having work–life programs, such as size of the organization and percentage of women in executive positions (Galinsky and Bond, 1998).

Cultural norms and values are fast facing the changes like women entrants in workforce, both parents working, single-parent homes, etc., resulting in intensification of the need to integrate work and family life as a part of everyday reality and a bitter one too. The new global economy, with its focus on full-time availability and long work hours, only worsens the problem generated by the lag in the organizations of paid works, as if workers were without personal interests or domestic care concerns (Roehling, Roehling and Moen, 2001). The disadvantages associated with work–life imbalances are numerous and impact both employee and employer. For the employee, consequences can have a negative impact on "work and life satisfaction, on wellbeing, mental health, physical health and on individual performance in organizations," as identified by O'Driscoll in 1996 (Guest, 2001).

WLB efforts could be of two types: policies designed to provide care services (information and referral services, financing of child care or elder care, etc.) and those designed to create more flexible work arrangements (flexible schedules that permit flexible starting and quitting times, telecommuting, compressed workweeks, job sharing, etc.).

Early studies showed that availability of day care (Youngblood and Chambers-Cook, 1984; Milkovich and Gomez, 1976) increased retention rates in the short term.

WLB practices are beneficial for employers as they affect several employee attitudes. Baltes et al. (1999) reported a significant relationship between flexible scheduling and employee outcomes, such as, job satisfaction, satisfaction with scheduling. Several studies have found that when employees have supervisors who support work–family balance, job satisfaction is higher and work–family conflict is lower (Bowen, 1998; Carlson and Perrewe, 1999; Greenberger et al., 1989; Thomas and Ganster, 1995). Work–life balance practices do not necessarily influence levels of employee work–life conflict, but improve organizational performance by the way of reduced overheads in the case of employees working from home, improved productivity among employees working at their peak hours, or social exchange processes arising from perceptions of organizational support (e.g., Allen, 2001; Apgar, 1998; Shepard, Clifton, & Kruse, 1996).

RESEARCH METHODOLOGY

As per the Report of the committee on HR issues of Public Sector Banks, (June 2010), HR has been a neglected area and is not seen as a priority. In fact, there has been an absence of innovations in HR that may lead to risks, in future. Therefore, HR requires a fundamental transformation in Public Sector Banks. This study was conducted to get an insight into the level of work–life balance in the public sector banks in India as not many studies have been conducted on this aspect.

Sources of data: Both the sources of data have been used for the study, i.e. Primary source and secondary source. Primary data has been collected through interviews, and structured questionnaire. Secondary data has been collected through books, magazines, journals and Internet.

Sample: The data has been collected from the employees of Public Sector Banks in eastern Uttar Pradesh. The Public Sector banks that have been approached for the data collection include—Punjab National Bank, Bank of India, State Bank of India, Central Bank of India, Bank of Baroda, Vijaya Bank. It includes the employees of Public sector banks of the Top Management level, Middle Management level, Lower Management level and Non-managerial cadre. The sample size is 100 and sampling method is convenience sampling.

Research Instrument: Structured questionnaire has been used which is divided into 2 parts. First part is related to demographic profile of respondents and the second part contains the variables to study the perception. These variables were measured on a five-point Likert scale ranging from 'strongly agree' to 'strongly disagree' where 1–strongly agree, 2–agree, 3–neither agree nor disagree, 4–disagree, 5–strongly disagree. Statistical methods used was factor analysis.

FINDINGS AND ANALYSIS

Demographic Profile

23% respondents were females, while 77% were males. Majority of the respondents surveyed were married (69%) whereas the remaining 31% of the respondents were single. Most of the respondent were of the age group of 26–35 years (34%), followed by the age group of 36–45 years (21%). Twenty per cent respondents belonged to the age group 46–55 years. Age group of 18–25 had a share of 17% and the age group 56 and above accounted only for 8% of total respondents.

Most of the respondents, i.e. 40% have 5–6 members in their family followed by 37% with 3–4 members. Further, 12% have 3–4 members, 11% have 1–2 family members.

Most of the respondents belonged to the non-managerial cadre, i.e. 48%. Both the lower management and middle management level had a participation of 22%. Top management accounted for 8% of the respondents.

About 39% of the respondents have a work experience upto 5 years. Twenty-four per cent had a work experience of more than 20 years; 16% of the respondents had a work experience of 5–10 years; 12% have a work experience of 15–20 years and the remaining 9% had a work experience of 10–15 years.

Factor analysis was conducted to reduce the items into meaningful factors which resulted in 7 factors and their reliability was calculated. Certain items were deleted to increase the reliability of factors. The Kaiser-Meyer-Ohlin (KMO) measure of sample adequacy and Bartlett's Test of Sphericity were applied to measure inter-correlation of data, and thereby the appropriateness of factor analysis. The KMO measure of sample adequacy yielded a value of 0.728, which is above the acceptable value of 0.500, and Bartlett's test of sphericity indicates that the correlations between variables are statistically significant (Table 1).

Table 1: KMO and Bartlett's Test

Kaiser-Meyer-Olkin Measure of Sampling Adequacy	.728
Bartlett's Test of Sphericity Approx. Chi-Square	968.211
Df	351
Sig.	.000

The appropriateness of application of factor analysis is, therefore, justified. Extraction method was Principal Component Analysis and Rotation Method was Varimax with Kaiser normalization.

To determine the number of components, only the Eigen values greater than or equal to 1 were considered (Kaiser, 1960). On examination of the rotated component matrix, the following were observed: The factor analysis resulted in seven factors; the items which displayed cross-loadings, were deleted.

The factor loading of the variables, reliability coefficient (Cronbach alpha), and percent of variation explained by the factors are shown in Table 2). Factors with reliability less than .6 were rejected. Thus, four factors were rejected. The most important factor was found to be 'Time to fulfil personal commitments', since percent of variation explained by this factor are respectively 0.626 and 23.196. This factor consists of 7 variables which are as: (1) My organization provides flexitiming that helps in managing work–life balance, (2) I am satisfied with the number of hours I have to

Table 2: Factor loadings, reliability and variance explained

Factor	*Variable*	*Factor Loading*	*Reliability coefficient*	*Variance explained*
Time to fulfil personal commitments	My organization provides flexitiming that helps in managing work–life balance.	.722	.0.772	23.196
	I am satisfied with the number of hours I have to work in a day.	697		
	I get time for entertainment	.616		
	I am able to spend considerable time with my family.	582		
Support of senior officials	My superior has a concern for my personal problems.	.856	0.790	10.419
	I get counseling from my superiors whenever required.	.754		
	Family get-togethers are organized by organization.	.572		
	I am able to give time to fulfil my social commitments.	.498		
	My organization has taken good initiatives to help employees manage their personal lives	.495		
Balanced work load	I feel tired and depressed because of my work.	0.806	0.727	6.648
	I am able to manage the stress arising out of work.	0.656		
	I get enough time for sleep and maintaining a healthy life style.	.530		

work in a day, (3) I get time for entertainment, (4) I am able to spend considerable time with my family, (5) I am able to take time off my work whenever required to meet the requirements of my children's school, (6) I am able to take care of my elderly dependents satisfactorily along with my work, (7) I get sufficient time to eat and enjoy my food. This factor has a reliability coefficient of 0.772.

The second factor identified is 'Role of senior officials' which consists of 5 variables which are as: (1) My superior has a concern for my personal problems, (2) I get counseling from my superiors whenever required, (3) Family get-togethers are organized by organization, (4) I am able to give time to fulfil my social commitments, (5) My organization has taken good initiatives to help employees manage their personal lives. This factor has a reliability coefficient of 0.790. The percent variation explained by this factor is 10.419.

The third factor is "manageable work load" with Eigen value of 1.795. It consists of 3 variables which are as: (1) I feel tired and depressed because of my work, (2) I am able to manage the stress arising out of work, (3) I get enough time for sleep and maintaining a healthy lifestyle. This factor has a reliability coefficient of 0.727. The percent variation explained by this factor is 6.648.

CONCLUSION

The research conducted to study the factors affecting the employees perception of work–life balance in public sector banks resulted in 3 factors, which in their order of importance are: (1) Time to fulfil personal commitments, (2) Role of senior officials, and (3) Balanced Work load.

An individual has commitments to his family as well as to his job, and hence he needs to appropriately allocate his time for different activities so that he can enjoy his sleep, food, family and job thus maintaining a work–life balance. The flexible work hours provided by the organisations help the employees carry out their responsibilities with ease and with comfort.

Senior officials are the major drivers of the work–life balance. Their positive attitude towards the employees' problems and their ability to empathize with them can help the employees to maintain a work–life balance. Initiatives by senior officials in terms of counseling and regular dialogues can guide the employees through the turbulent times.

As technological changes continue to occur at a rapid pace, it necessitates the employers to make their employees consistently updated with existing and new technologies. Also a drive to be a dominant player makes the employers push their employees to put in more effort. This increases the workload of the employees which becomes a cause of stress among the employees. As the workload increases stress level of the employees increases which can result in loss in productivity of the organisation and employee turnover.

These three factors broadly highlight the factors constituting Work–life balance, as perceived by employees in public sector banks in India. This study can be of use to the policy makers in public sector banks, who can keep in mind these factors while designing their policies for the employees. These can serve as some indicators for private sector banks as well.

Above all, there have been few studies related to work–life balance in Public Sector Banks. This study attempts to give useful insight into the work–life balance initiatives in the Public Sector Banks from employees' perspective. Other organizations taking cue from the findings of the study, may also adopt WLB practices for helping employees attain work–life balance and hence improve their job satisfaction and organizational productivity.

In future researches, WLB practices in private banks may also be studied and a comparison may be made of the employee perceptions in public sector and private sector banks.

REFERENCES

Allen, T.D. (2001). Family-supportive work environments: The role of organizational perceptions. *Journal of Vocational Behavior*, 58:414–35.

Amato, P.R., D.R. Johnson, A. Booth, and S. J. Rogers. 2003. Continuity and change in marital quality between 1980 and 2000. *Journal of Marriage and Family*, 65 (1):1–11.

Apgar, M. (1998). The alternative workplace: Changing where and how people work. *Harvard Business Review*, 76: 121–36.

Bowen, G. (1998). Effects of leader support in the work unit on the relationship between work spillover and family adaptation. *Journal of Family and Economic Issues*, 19: 25–52.

Bhagwagar, H. 2009. Need for workplace counseling in India. http://prod.bolohealth.com/healthzones/21-total-health/article/165-needfor-workplace-counseling-in-india

Baltes, B.B., T.E. Briggs, J.W. Huff, J.A. Wright, and G.A. Neuman. 1999. "Flexible and Compressed Workweek Schedules: A Meta-Analysis of Their Effects on Work-Related Criteria," *Journal of Applied Psychology*, 84(4):496–513.

Bond, J.T., E. Galinsky and J. Swanberg. 1998. The 1997 national study of the changing workforce, No.2. New York: Families and Work Institute

Busby, N and James, G (ed.) (2011). *Families, Care-Giving and Paid Work: Challenging Labour Law in the 21st Century*, Edward Elgar Publishing, p. 42.

Carlson, D. and P. Perrewe (1999). The role of social support in the stressor-strain relationship: and examination of work-family conflict. *Journal of Management*, 25: 513–40.

Eagle, B.W., Miles, E.W., & Icenogle, M.L. (1997). Interrole conflicts and the permeability of work and family domains: Are there gender differences? *Journal of Vocational Behavior*, 50(2): 168–84.

Estes, S.B., & Michael, J. (2005). Work-family policies and gender inequality at work: A Sloan Work and Family Encyclopedia entry. Retrieved from http://wfnetwork.bc.edu/encyclopedia_entry.php?id=1230&area=All.

Frone, M.R., Yardley, J.K., and Markel, K.S. (1997), Developing and testing an integrative model of the work–family interface, *Journal of Vocational Behavior*, 50: 145–67

Galinsky, E. and J.T. Bond (1998). *The 1998 business work-life study*. New York: Families and Work Institute.

Greenhaus, J.H., & Beutell, N.J. (1985). Sources of conflict between work and family roles. *Academy of Management Review*, 10: 76–88. 29

Greenberger, E., W. Goldberg, W. Hamill, R. O'Neil, and C. Payne (1989). Contributions of a supportive work environment to parents' well-being and orientation to work. *American Journal of Community Psychology*, 17:755–83.

Greenhaus, J.H., & Parasuraman, S. (1999). "Research on work, family, and gender: Current status and future directions". In G.N. Powell (Ed.), *Handbook of Gender and Work. Thousand*, Oaks, CA: Sage. pp. 391–412.

Guest, D.E. (2001). *Perspectives on the Study of Work-Life Balance*. Retrieved March 10, 2012 from http://www.ucm.es/info/Psyap/enop/guest.htm

Ishaya, N., and R. Ayman (2008). *Predicting Work-family Conflict via Perceived Involvement and Overload*, Boston, MA: American Psychological Association.

Kaiser, H. F. (1960). The application of electronic computers to factor analysis. *Educational and Psychological Measurement*, 20:141–151. Retrieved March 13, 2012

Lewis, J. 2000. Employers, lone parents and the work-life balance. Sheffi-eld: Department for Work and Pensions.

Milkovich, G. T., & Gomez, L. R. (1976). Day care and selected employee work behaviors. *Academy of Management Journal*, 19(1): 111–15.

Morgan, H. 2003. "The challenges of a global marketplace". In M. Goldsmith, R. Gandossy, and M. Effron (Ed.) *Human resources in the 21st century*, New York: Wiley.

Patel, T. 2005. *The family in India: Structure and practice*. New Delhi: Sage.

Roehling, P.V., Roehling, M.V., & Moen, P. (2001). The relationship between worklife policies and practices and employee loyalty: A life course perspective. *Journal of Family and Economic Issues*, 22(2): 141–70.

Shepard, E., T. Clifton and D. Kruse (1996). Flexible work hours and productivity. *Industrial Relations* 35: 123–39.

Smithson, J. (1999). Equal choices, different futures: Young adults talk about work and family expectations. *Psychology of Women Section Review*, 1, 43–57.

Thomas, L. and D. C. Ganster (1995). Impact of family-supportive work variables on work-family conflict and strain: A control perspective. *Journal of Applied Psychology* 80: 6–15.

Voydanoff, P. (2005). Toward a conceptualization of perceived work family fit and balance: A demand and resources approach. *Journal of Marriage and Family*, 67, 822–36

Youngblood, S., & Chambers-Cook, K. (1984). Child care assistance can improve employee attitudes and behavior. *Personnel Administrator*, 29, 45–47.

26

Problems and Prospects of Women Entrepreneurship in India:

A Study of Allahabad District in Uttar Pradesh

Keshav Shyam and Ekta Verma

ABSTRACT

Women Entrepreneurship is a phenomenon for helping women to achieve financial autonomy, a form of activism for women's rights that holds positive implications for family well-being, community viability and national prosperity. The aim of the study is to analyse the socio-economic profile, educational and family background of women entrepreneurs, reasons for initiating a business, factors for problems and success and to suggest the strategies for further development of women. The methodology adopted is an exploratory research design in which a structured questionnaire is devised and administered among 80 women entrepreneurs. The statistical tools such as simple percentages, weighted score analysis, chi-square test are used to analyse the data. The findings reveal that Allahabad district is in dire need of upliftment of women entrepreneurs and encouragement in the business. Entrepreneurship as women workforce is promptly available to exploit the unexpected dimension of business ventures.

Keywords: *Women Entrepreneurs, Business, Equity, Economic Development.*

INTRODUCTION

Economic development of the country essentially means a process by which the per capita income of that country changes upward over a period of time. Entrepreneurship plays a vital role in economic development through creation of utilities and generation of employment within a short period. The impetus for entrepreneurial ventures had come from industrialization in the developed nations by setting up large-scale, technological, and sophisticated industries investing huge capital. Particularly, among the Asian countries, the concept of huge capital-intensive industry has not only failed to solve their economic problems but also triggered off a spate of human and social problems. Stagnation of economy, widening inequality, staggering unemployment and under-employment and a volley of socio-cultural problems associated with urbanization plagued the Asian counties when they attempted to transplant Euro-American concept of Entrepreneurship in their countries. This experience has led these countries to follow the policy of encouraging individual small-scale ventures. It has been accepted that entrepreneurship is an economic venture by which that lot of the people can be changed upward within a short period of time especially from the point of view of employment generation. Like other developing countries India has been endowed with abundant natural, biological and human resources. Technical progress of a country alone cannot lead to economic development unless the technology is used by the entrepreneurs.

An entrepreneur organizes and puts to use capital, labour and technology. It is true that an entrepreneur is an agent of economic development of a country. Therefore, entrepreneurial awareness among the people in general and educated in particular is perhaps an urgent need. In India entrepreneurship will lead to generate more income, reduce the acute problem of unemployment, minimize the incidence of poverty, reduce the regional imbalance and increase the export trade and reduce the balance of payments to the possible extent.

Women in traditional societies are still confined to the four walls of home, children and family rituals. In a male-dominated society, women are not equally treated by the partners. Women are dynamic and dependable workers, who work without pay for 12 to 14 hours a day round the year, and yet are given the humiliating status of being subordinate. Most of the women, not only in India but throughout the world are associated with these kinds of jobs. To grant the equality status to the women, India by the law has remained counter-balanced with social prejudices due to their self factors like lack of education, and lack of effective opportunity for employment. In spite of marked progress, Indian women have remained the nation's greatest untapped resources.

Despite all the hurdles, modern Indian women have realized that their neglected power is at the core of their backwardness and hence they have taken the great step of empowering themselves with the available resources to make their own decisions. Also women have recognized their importance and the role they have to play in the economic development of the nation which leads to their economic self-reliance. Today, women are at a historical compulsion to revise and redefine their values and roles at home and outside. The future belongs only to those who with assurance could shake hands with the widening global economy and adapt themselves to the faster pace of technological changes.

The organized sector in India, which employs an estimated 19 per cent of the total workforce, accounts for only an estimated 6 per cent of the female workers (Iyer, 1991). This means that 94 per cent of the female workforces are engaged in various informal sectors or in household activities. These informal activities include subsistence farming, petty trading and hawking, through wage employment in unregulated small enterprises or home-based contract work for larger formal sector firms to ownership of small business.

The word 'entrepreneur' first appeared in the French language at the beginning of 16th century and was applied to leaders of military expeditions. ***Richard Cantillon***, the first person who introduced the term, 'entrepreneur' to mean "an agent who buys means of production at certain prices in order to combine them into a product, which he is going to sell at prices that are uncertain at the moment at which he commits himself to his costs".

Entrepreneurs are a specialized group of people who bear risks and deal with uncertainty and if a women takes the same uncertain risk of initiating a business, sustaining it and successfully running it by contributing to the nation's economic development in the form of capital formation, improvement in per capita income and balanced regional development, then she is the real '***undertaker of the business***' and a successful women entrepreneur. (Knight)

According to the Government of India, a women entrepreneur is defined as, "***an enterprise owned, controlled by a women having a minimum of financial interest of 51 per cent of capital and giving at least 51 per cent of employment generated in the enterprise to women***".

It is estimated that presently women entrepreneurs are about 10 per cent of the total entrepreneurs in India. It is also clear that this percentage is growing every year. If prevailing trends continue, it is not unlikely that in another five years, women will comprise 20 per cent of the entrepreneurial force in India (Sahai, 2005).

MOTIVATIONAL FACTORS FOR WOMEN ENTREPRENEURSHIP

In recent years there has been a lot of debate in the print and electronic media, parliament and other forums about the development of entrepreneurship amongst women. Due to various cultural and social reasons, women in different parts of India have different motives, aspirations, social status, needs and urges. Varied motivation needs and interests plunge in women entrepreneurs for establishing an enterprise. The most dominant motives are fulfilment of ambition and pursuits of own interests is evident in almost all women entrepreneurs.

Factors that largely contribute to making women to be entrepreneurs include:

1. economic needs (to earn money);
2. as a challenge to satisfy some of their personality needs (power, achievement and novel experience);
3. educated women utilizing their knowledge;
4. family occupation (second generation entrepreneurs); and
5. as a leisure time activity.

The assessment of business management skill is essential for every women entrepreneur before she starts her business as it provides the knowledge of one's strengths and weaknesses. Management skills required for women entrepreneurs:

1. Finance securing capital.
2. Dealing with people (especially with trade unions), Management development and training.
3. Marketing/Sales—Marketing research, Product promotion and selling.
4. Idea generating, Product innovation.
5. Business Operations, Inventory, Production, and Day-to-Day operations.
6. Organizing and planning Business strategy, Organization structure policies, etc.

A woman of a challenging attitude, firm determination, ambitious goals will certainly manage her enterprise successfully. Such women are confident of their abilities to deal with problems, believe that hard work is a sure ingredient to success in entrepreneurial ventures. Below is a profile of successful women entrepreneurs:

1. High need for achievement;
2. Commitment of conviction;

3. Capacity to analyze;
4. Risk taking;
5. Initiative and independence;
6. Hopeful about future and search for environment; and
7. High personnel efficiency.

Success depends on one's ability to prove the best by putting more efforts to succeed. Though women have the traits of being an entrepreneur, such as achievement-oriented, responsible, moderate risk factor, success-oriented, energetic, forward looking, organized, still the number of women entering entrepreneurship is very low. The turnout of women entrepreneurs is minimum because a women is given lower status in the society. Though women are considered as weaker gender physically, mentally they are more capable and alert in managing things. Over the ages women have been managing houses and small finances in their best possible way. Women understand management techniques and they adopt them quickly with utmost sincerity and honesty. The Government's role is also utmost important in the enhancement of women status in all sectors and walks of life. Effective strategies and policies are being formulated and implemented to achieve this end.

BARRIERS OF WOMEN ENTREPRENEURSHIP

In India women entrepreneurs are not free from problems in managing their units. They are facing a number of problems from internal as well as external environment. Women are not getting any encouragement from their family members as well as the government. They are facing multifarious problems like:

- Severe competition from the units which are managed by male entrepreneurs.
- Non-availability of raw material. The prices of raw material is also high.
- Access to financial support is a big problem to the women entrepreneurs.
- Women entrepreneurs are facing problems of managerial deficiency.
- Technical know-how is another problem to the women entrepreneurs.
- Women entrepreneurs have lesser economic and social risk bearing capacity.
- Inferiority complex among women is a great barrier to the women entrepreneurs.
- Lack of specialized training to the women particularly in rural areas.

- Lack of sufficient infrastructure facilities is also discouraging the women to enter in the industrial sector in general and cooperative sector in particular.
- Lack of proper encouragement from the government by the way of special incentive packages exclusively for the women entrepreneurs.

LITERATURE REVIEW

In his study, *Small Business Opportunities for Women in Jamaica,* Nelson (1991) revealed that women were concentrated in businesses which required the least capital outlay or an extension of household activities. The study also revealed that women entrepreneurs were dependent on their business to maintain their homes and support their families.

Sikha Sahai (2005), has highlighted that presently women comprise about 10 per cent of the total entrepreneurs in India. It is clear that this percentage is growing every year. If prevailing trends continue, it is not unlikely that in another five years, women will comprise 20 per cent of the entrepreneurial force in India.

Lall & Sahai (2008), conducted a comparative assessment of multi-dimensional issues & challenges of women entrepreneurship and family business. The study identified Psychographic variables like, degree of commitment, entrepreneurial challenges & future plan for expansion, based on demographic variables. Through stratified random sampling & convenience sampling the data have been collected from women entrepreneurs working in urban area of Lucknow. The study identified business owner's characteristics as self-perception, self-esteem, entrepreneurial intensity & operational problem for future plans for growth & expansion. The study suggested that there has been a considerable growth in number of women opting to work in family owned business.

Tambunan (2009), carried out a study on recent developments of women entrepreneurs in Asian developing countries. The study focused mainly on women entrepreneurs in small and medium enterprises based on data analysis and review of recent key literature. This study found that in Asian developing countries SMEs are gaining overwhelming importance; more than 95% of all firms in all sectors on average per country. The study also depicted the fact that representation of women entrepreneurs in this region is relatively low due to factors like low level of education, lack of capital and cultural or religious constraints. However, the study revealed that most of the women entrepreneurs in SMEs are from the category of forced entrepreneurs seeking for better family incomes.

STATEMENT OF THE PROBLEM

Entrepreneurship development among women has picked up momentum in recent years. Several factors contributed to this phenomenon. The policies of the Central and State Governments in the matter of industrial development have undergone sweeping changes in the recent past, particularly in the post-liberalization era. A series of measures, conferring a wide variety of special concessions, subsidies, incentives, rebates, reliefs are enunciated. With an objective of rendering the requisite financial, technical, managerial, marketing, information and infrastructural, etc., support and guidance to the existing and prospective women entrepreneurs, liberal financial assistance has been made available under various employment programmes. The contributions made by the institutions, organizations and government departments are indeed commendable and are primarily responsible for accelerating the process and the movement of women entrepreneurship development in India. It is true that laudable efforts have been made in recent years for the development of women entrepreneurship in India, but the irony of the situation is that several women entrepreneurs have their grievances and have been through harrowing episodes. Several of the women entrepreneurs, who have set up industrial and commercial units with great optimism, are not able to achieve all their targeted goals. It is all because of plethora of problems they are confronted with in the course of promotion and development of their units. Several of these units have not been able to achieve the desired levels of operational efficiency and economic viability. With this backdrop the present paper purports to identify the problems and prospects of women entrepreneurs in Allahabad district.

OBJECTIVES OF THE STUDY

1. To analyze the socio-economic profile, educational and family background of women entrepreneurs in Allahabad district.
2. To identify the reasons that made the women entrepreneurs in Allahabad district to start the business enterprises.
3. To ascertain the factors responsible for success of women entrepreneurs in Allahabad district.
4. To study the problems faced by the women entrepreneurs in Allahabad district.
5. To examine prospects of women entrepreneurs in Allahabad district.
6. To suggest strategies for further development of women entrepreneurship in Allahabad district.

METHODOLOGY FOR THE STUDY

In view of the objectives of the study listed above, an exploratory research design has been adopted. To study the problems and prospects of women entrepreneurs in Allahabad district, a structured questionnaire covering different aspects of women entrepreneurs was devised and administered among the sample women entrepreneurs.

SOURCES OF DATA

This study includes the collection of data from both primary and secondary sources. The primary data has been collected by conducting a survey among the sample women entrepreneurs with the help of a well-structured questionnaire. The secondary data has been compiled from various published books, magazines, research projects, research papers and articles, etc.

SAMPLE FRAME

There are more than 500 women entrepreneurs in Allahabad district. A detailed study of such large number of women entrepreneurs is a herculean task for an individual researcher. Therefore, to keep the inquiry within manageable and reliable limits, a sample of 80 women entrepreneurs in the district across the business concerns like Garments, Parlours and Health Club, Food, Retail, School, Marketing and Advertising, Paper and Ceramics, Leather, Engineering and Electronics, Real estate, miscellaneous, etc., was taken as the sample by using the stratified sampling method.

HYPOTHESIS

1. **H01**: There is close association between the marital status of women and their entry into business.
2. **H02**: The religion and caste of the women entrepreneurs and their participation in the business are dependent on each other.
3. **H03**: Qualification of the respondents and their efforts to get jobs before entering into business are dependent on each other.
4. **H04**: There is no significant variation between the nature of family and its influence on the women's participation in business.
5. **H05**: The spirit of women entrepreneurs and Government support/assistance are dependent on each other.

TOOLS FOR DATA ANALYSIS

The data collected for the study has been analyzed logically and meaningfully to arrive at logical and meaningful conclusions. The statistical tools, viz. simple percentages, weighted score analysis, ÷2 test are used.

LIMITATIONS OF THE STUDY

The study of women entrepreneurs' perception had to be carried under two major limitations. One of them was the small size of the selected sample. A sample of 80 women entrepreneurs appears to be inadequate to draw generalizations on the issues involved. However, considering the inhibiting factors that the researcher had to encounter, the present sample size appeared to be the best possible alternative under the circumstances. Secondly, an elaborate questionnaire was used consisting many questions to elicit the women entrepreneurs responses on various aspects; the respondents did not answer all the questions and some questions had to be left out of the analysis.

DATA ANALYSIS AND INTERPRETATION

General Profile of Respondents

The general profile of the sample respondent women entrepreneurs is given in Table 1. From the data provided, the following inferences may be drawn.

(a) Out of the 80 respondent women entrepreneurs taken for the study, 20 per cent belonged to the age group of 25-34 years, 48.75 per cent belonged to 35- 44 years, 17.5 per cent belonged to 45-54 years and 13.75 belonged to 55+ year's age.

(b) Twenty-per cent of the respondents belonged to general community, 35 per cent belonged to backward community, 33.75 per cent belonged to most backward community and only 6.25 per cent of them belonged to SC/ST community.

(c) Regarding the marital status 75 per cent are married, 16.25 per cent are unmarried, 7.5 per cent were divorced and 1.25 per cent were widowedd. Among the sample respondents, 10 per cent are illiterates, 27.50 per cent have studied up to 10th standard, 36.25 per cent are graduates, 16.25 per cent are post-graduates and 10.00 per cent are technically qualified.

(d) Regarding the family type 80 per cent of the women entrepreneurs are from nuclear families and 20 per cent of them are from joint families.

(e) Fifty per cent of the respondents are first generation entrepreneurs, 40 per cent of them got that position from their parents and only 10 per cent of them have their in-laws as entrepreneurs.

(f) Eighty per cent of the respondents had the previous experience and only 20 per cent are fresher's.

(g) Fifty per cent of the respondents received manual help from their family members, 20 per cent of them have received advisory support and 30 per cent of them have received financial support.

(h) Only 20 per cent of the respondents spent up to 4 hours towards their business, 40 per cent of them from 4 to 8 hours, 30 per cent of them from 8 to 12 hours and 10 per cent of them spent more than 12 hours.

(i) Among the respondents, 40 per cent run the business in rural area and 60 per cent run in urban areas.

(j) Regarding ownership, 66 per cent of them have 100% self-owned firms and 33 per cent of them have partnership firms.

(k) About financial assistance, 15 per cent of the respondents have received soft loans, 70 per cent have enjoyed the subsidy and 15 per cent have received power concession.

Table 1: General Profile of Sample Women Entrepreneurs

Particulars	*Classification*	*No. of Respondents*	*Percentage to total*
Age (Years)	25–34	16	
	35–44	39	20.00
	45–54	14	48.75
	55 +	11	17.50
Community	Forward	20	
	Backward	28	25.00
	Most Backward	27	35.00
	SC/ST	5	33.75
Marital Status	Married	60	75.00
	Unmarried	13	16.25
	Divorced	6	7.5
	Widow	1	1.25
Educational Qualifications	Illiterate	8	10.00
	Up to 10th Standard	8	27.50
	Under Graduation	22	36.25
	Post Graduation	29	16.25
	Technical Education	13	10.00
Family Type	Nuclear Family	64	80.00
	Joint Family	16	20.00
Category of Women Entre-preneurship	First Generation Entrepreneurs	40	50.00
	Parents as Entrepreneurs	32	40.00
	In-laws as Entrepreneurs	8	10.00

Particulars	*Classification*	*No. of Respondents*	*Percentage to total*
Experience as Women Entrepreneur	Yes	64	80.00
	No	16	20.00
Form of Family Help	Manual Help	40	50.00
	Advisory Support	16	20.00
	Financial Support	24	30.00
Time Spent Up to	4 hours	16	20.00
	4–8 hours	32	40.00
	8–12 hours	24	30.00
	More than 12 hours	8	10.00
Location	Rural	32	40.00
	Urban	48	60.00
Ownership 100%	Self-owned	53	66.00
	Partnership	47	33.00
Forms of Financial Assistance	Soft Loan	12	20.00
	Subsidy	56	40.00
	Power Concession	12	30.00

Source: Compiled from the Questionnaire administered to the sample respondent women entrepreneurs

Marital Status of Women and their Entry into Business

The information relating to marital status of the respondent women entrepreneurs and its effect in entering into business is provided in Table 2. The survey results have proved that the majority of the married women (76 per cent) were stepped into business. This indicates that women have succeeded in breaking the traditional barricades of living within four walls after the marriage.

H01: There is close association between the marital status of women and their entry into business.

Table 2: Marital Status of Women and their Entry into Business

Marital Status	*Participation in Business*		*Total*
	Affected	*Not Affected*	
Married	34 (55.74)	27 (44.26)	61 (76.00)
Unmarried	17 (89.50)	2 (10.50)	19 (24.00)
Total	51	29	N = 80

χ^2 calculated value = 7.43

For $\nu = 1, \chi^2$

0.05 = 3.841 (at 1 degrees of freedom and 5% level of significance)

χ^2 calculated value $>\chi^2$ 0.05 at 5% level of significance

Note: Figures in parenthesis represents percentages to total.

Source: Compiled from the Questionnaire administered to the sample respondent women entrepreneurs.

Since the calculated value is higher than the table value, the null hypothesis is rejected. That is to say, marital status of the women entrepreneurs has direct influence on their business career. Another important finding of the study is that, family members had also encouraged the decision of taking part in services sector like opening parlour, tailoring shop, apparel shop, and departmental stores, photocopy centres next to her doorstep or within their locality. This clearly indicates that women get social security as well as generate surplus income by working close to the house and the family members.

Selection of Industries by Women Entrepreneurs

The traditional belief about the women enterprises around the 3 Ps of kitchen, i.e. papad, pickles, and powders (spices) were not found in the sample entrepreneurs. Rather, they have broken away from the beaten tracks and are exploring new avenues of economic participation.

Table 3 presents data relating to the type of enterprises chosen by the sample women entrepreneurs. It is observed from the table that the women entrepreneurs in the sample are engaged in diverse activities. As many as 78.50 per cent of them are engaged in traditional business activities like garments, food products and processing, parlours and health clubs, leather works, wood works, etc. The remaining were engaged in retail outlets (8.75 per cent), maintaining schools (2.50 per cent), oil and rice mills (3.75 per cent) marketing and advertising (1.25 per cent), engineering and electronics (2.50 percent) and the remaining are in real estate (2.50 per cent) respectively.

Table 3: Selection of Industries by Women Entrepreneurs (Type of Enterprises)

Type of Enterprise	*No. of Respondents*	*Percentage to total*
Garments	23	28.75
Food Products and Processing	27	33.75
Parlours and Health Club	5	6.25
Retail outlets	7	8.75
Schools	2	2.50
Oil and Rice Mills	3	3.75
Marketing and Advertising	1	1.25
Paper, Ceramics, Leather works, etc.	4	5.00
Wood works	4	5.00
Engineering and Electronics.	2	2.50
Real estate	2	2.50
Total	80	100.00

Source: Compiled from the Questionnaire administered to the sample respondent women entrepreneurs.

Religion-wise Participation of Women in Business

In a democratic country like India, religion plays an important role in all the activities, particularly, in business sector. The survey results shows that over 81 per cent of the women entrepreneurs were of Hindu religion, 12.50 per cent of the women entrepreneurs were of Christian religion and the remaining 6 per cent were Muslim women, who have dared to cross all the religious boundaries to stand unique in the front line of business.

H02: The religion of the women entrepreneurs and their participation in the business are dependent each other.

Table 4: Religion-wise Participation of Women in Business

Religion of Women Entrepreneurs	*Affected*	*Not Affected*	*Total*
Hindus	36 (55.40)	29 (44.60)	65 (81.25)
Muslims	4 (80.00)	1 (20.00)	5 (6.25)
Christians	8 (80.00)	2 (20.00)	10 (12.50)
Total	48	32	N = 80

χ^2 calculated value = 3.07
For $\nu = 2$, χ^2
0.05 = 5.992 (at 2 degrees of freedom and 5% level of significance)
χ^2 calculated value $<\chi^2$
0.05 at 5% level of significance

Note: Figures in parenthesis represents percentages to total.

Source: Compiled from the Questionnaire administered to the sample respondent women entrepreneurs.

As the calculated value of chi-square is lesser than the table value, the null hypothesis is accepted. That is, the religion of the entrepreneur will not have influence on the women to participate in business and their growth.

Size of Investment in Women Enterprises

The women entrepreneurs often complain about the availability of funds from financial institutions and their access to funds. The study reveals that the size of funds used in women enterprises are very small and are provided from their own sources. Data relating to investment are given in Table 2.5. It is observed from the table that most of the units have a very little asset base. Forty per cent of the units have a total investment including working capital less than 1 lakh and 68.75 per cent of the units are operating from rented accommodations. The investment in plant and machinery and other fixed assets is less than 1 lakh in case of 67.50 per cent of the units, while 77.50 per cent of the units have working capital less than 1 lakh. Only 21.25 per cent of the units invested 5 lakhs or more in land and building, while 36.50 per cent of the total units in this range.

Table 5: Size of Investment in Women Enterprises (in Lakhs)

Size of Investment	*Land & Building*	*Plant and Mech. and Other FAs'*	*Working Capital*	*Total*
Below 1.0	2	54 (67.50)	62 (77.50)	32 (40.00)
1.0 to 5.0	6	9 (11.25)	5 (6.25)	19 (23.75)
1.0 to 10	6	8 (10.00)	5 (6.25)	11 (13.75)
10 to 20	8	5 (6.25)	5 (6.25)	8 (10.00)
20 and above	3	4 (5.00)	3 (3.75)	10 (12.50)
Total	**25**	**80**	**80**	**80**

*Rest 55 units are operating from rented accommodation

Note: Figures in parenthesis represents percentages to total.

Source: Compiled from the Questionnaire administered to the sample respondent women entrepreneurs.

Motivational Aspects of Women Entrepreneurs

One of the important problems which most of the working women including the entrepreneurs face is the long working hours and the absence from the home. But, most of the women entrepreneurs in our sample reveal that they got good support from their family members and hence are living happily with their husbands and children. A significant fact emerged from the survey, that is thc women entrepreneurs possessed adequate skills and strong motivation and run their units. The basic sources of motivation and the responses of the women entrepreneurs are presented in Table 6. It is observed from the table that earning money was the predominant motive for 44.58 per cent of the respondents. It is implied from this motive that they want to be financially independent. It is followed by the desire to become independent (24.80 per cent), to prove oneself (18.54 per cent), status (5.42 per cent), utilization of one's skill and knowledge (3.54 per cent) and previous job satisfaction (3.12 per cent). Several studies have indicated that the desire to be independent is the predominant motive to take up some gainful activities, but in the present study earning more money is the predominant motivating factor. It is mainly due to the economic pressure of the family on them.

Push and Pull Factors of Women Entrepreneurship

Another important problem that the study has addressed is how the women become entrepreneurs. To explain this process, the study has identified some situational factors which prompt them to be entrepreneurs. The responses of the sample entrepreneurs are presented in Table 7. It is observed from the table that first five factors are conducive for the

Table 6: Sources of Entrepreneurial Motivation

Motives	*No. of Respondents*			*Weighted Score*	*Rating (Per cent)*	*Rank*
	No. One	*No. Two*	*No. Three*			
Desire to be Independent	21	18	20	119	24.80	2
To prove oneself	15	15	14	89	18.54	3
Status	5	2	7	26	5.42	4
Earning more money	33	40	35	214	44.58	1
Previous Job dissatisfaction	2	3	3	15	3.12	6
Utilization of one's skill	4	2	1	17	3.54	5

Source: Compiled from the Questionnaire administered to the sample respondent women entrepreneurs.

enterprise creation and hence considered to be positive push and pull factors, while the last two are negative factors which force somebody to be an entrepreneur. The most important factor considered by the respondents for entrepreneurship is the attractive source of income (67.50 per cent), followed by the inspiration and support from the family members (58.75 per cent). The respondents think that the unemployment and unsuitable working conditions are the compelling factors to take up this profession. The inner feeling of doing something better (competencies) associated with previous experience (15.00 per cent) prompts some of them to be entrepreneurs.

Table 7: Push and Pull Factors of Women Entrepreneurship

Factors	*No. of Respondents*	*Percentage to total*
Attractive sources of Income	54	67.50
Education	18	22.50
Family Support	47	58.75
Government policies and incentives	18	22.50
Competencies and experience	12	15.00
Unable to find suitable employment	27	33.75
Unsuitable working environment	15	18.75

Source: Compiled from the Questionnaire administered to the sample respondent women entrepreneurs.

Respondents' pre-entrepreneurship efforts for getting job

The data relating to job attempts made by the respondents before establishing the enterprise is provided in Table 8. Majority (74 per cent) of the respondents did not try for any jobs and the rest of them (26 per cent) made an attempt to get some job either in government sector or in private sector, but were not successful. As a result they started their own enterprise. The following hypothesis was put to test in this regard.

H03: Qualification of the respondents and their efforts to get job before entering into business are dependent on each other.

Table 8: Efforts Made by the Respondents for Getting other Jobs

Respondents	*Job attempts made before establishing own enterprise*		*Total*
Qualification	*Attempted*	*Not Attempted*	
Up to 10th Standard	1 (16.67)	5 (83.33)	6
Under Graduation	15 (34.10)	29 (65.90)	44
Post Graduation	8 (32.00)	17 (68.00)	25
Technical Education	2 (40.00	3 (60.00)	5
Total	21 (26.25)	59 (73.75)	N = 80

χ^2 calculated value = 3.22
For $\nu = 3$, χ^2
0.05 = 7.81 (at 3 degrees of freedom and 5% level of significance).
χ^2 calculated value $<\chi^2$
0.05 at 5% level of significance.
Note: Figures in parenthesis represents percentages to total.
Source: Compiled from the Questionnaire administered to the sample respondent women entrepreneurs.

The calculated value of chi-square is lesser than the table value; hence, the null hypothesis is accepted. This indicates that the qualification of the respondents and their efforts to get any other private or government job has not influenced them to start their own enterprises.

Nature of Family and its Influence on Women Entrepreneurship

The nature of family to which women entrepreneurs belongs is depicted in Table 9. It is observed from the table that 58.75 per cent of the respondent women entrepreneurs belong to nuclear family and only 41.25 per cent of them belongs to joint family. The following hypothesis was put to test in this regard.

H04: There is no significant variation between the nature of family and its influence on the women's participation in business.

The calculated value is more than the table value. Therefore, the null hypothesis is rejected. That is, the nature of the family whether it is nuclear or a joint family, influenced in decision making of women regarding her entry into business. Another important finding from the study is that the women entrepreneurs from joint family faced acute problem; they were over strained by working at both the sides, managing both business and family; they had the problem of cooperation from other family members, difference of opinion due to age differences, etc.

Table 9: Nature of Family as an Influencing Factor on Women's Participation

Nature of Family	*Influencing factor on women's participation*		*Total*
	Yes	*No*	
Nuclear Family	28 (59.60)	19 (40.40)	47 (58.75)
Joint Family	28 (84.84)	5 (15.16	33 (41.25)
Total	56	24	N = 80

χ^2 calculated value = 6.12
For ν = 1, χ^2
0.05 = 3.841 (at 1 degrees of freedom and 5% level of significance)
χ^2 calculated value >χ^2
0.05 at 5% level of significance

Note: Figures in parenthesis represents percentages to total.

Source: Compiled from the Questionnaire administered to the sample respondent women entrepreneurs.

Respondents received financial support from the Government

It is necessary to understand that government institutions are coming forward to extend financial support to women entrepreneurs. The information relating to this aspect is presented in Table 10. The survey shows that only 20 per cent (16) of respondents got finance from government agencies, like, UPSFC, DRDA, Commercial banks, etc. 80 per cent of the respondents have not received any such support from government agencies and they depend on their own contribution, from their family members, etc. A hypothesis has been put to test and the following results were drawn.

H05: The spirit of women entrepreneurs and Government support/ assistance are dependent each other.

Table 10: The Spirit of Women Entrepreneurs and Government Support/Assistance

Received Govt. support/assistance	*Entrepreneurial Spirit*		*Total*
	Affected	*Not affected*	
Received	10 (62.50)	6 (37.50)	16 (20.00)
Not Received	14 (22.00)	50 (78.00)	64 (80.00
Total	24	56	N = 80

χ^2 calculated value = 9.14
For ν = 1, χ^2
0.05 = 3.841 (at 1 degrees of freedom and 5% level of significance)
χ^2 calculated value >χ^2
0.05 at 5% level of significance

Note: Figures in parenthesis represents percentages to total.

Source: Compiled from the Questionnaire administered to the sample respondent women entrepreneurs.

The calculated value of chi-square is greater than the calculated value and, hence, the null hypothesis has to be rejected. That means the support and assistance by the government acted as a motivating factor to the women for venturing into the business world.

Sources of Finance to Women Entrepreneurs

Finance is the basic input for any activity and it forms the basis for all key inputs, viz. labour, material, machinery, etc. The data relating to financial sources of respondent women entrepreneurs is depicted in Table 11. The table reveals that 45 per cent of the respondents have their self-owned sources of funds, 40 per cent of them have taken bank loan, 10 per cent of them have depend on the support by spouse/family, and only 5 per cent of them have other sources of finance. Therefore, for majority of the respondents self-owned funds constitute the major source of finance.

Table 11: Sources of Finance to Women Entrepreneurs

Sources of finance	*No. of Respondents*	*Percentage to total*
Self-owned funds	36	45.00
Support by Spouse/family	8	10.00
Bank Borrowings	32	40.00
Other Sources	4	5.00
Total	80	100.00

Source: Compiled from the Questionnaire administered to the sample respondent women entrepreneurs.

Employment in Selected Women Enterprises

Manpower constitutes the most significant input factor along with other resources, viz., capital, machinery, material, methods, etc. The data relating to the manpower employed in the selected women enterprises in given in Table 12. It is observed from the table that 70 per cent of the units were employing 3 to 5 workers, 12 per cent of the units were employing 6 to 10 workers, 8 per cent of the units had 11 to 20 workers and only 10 per cent had more than 21 workers. On an average, sample enterprises employed 7 full time workers.

Table 12: Total Employment in Selected Women Enterprises in Allahabad District (2016-17)

Employment (No. of Persons	*No. of Enterprises*	*Percentage to total*
3 to 5	56	70.00
6 to 10	10	12.00
11 to 20	6	8.00
21 and above	8	10.00
Average Employment	7	

Source: Compiled from the Questionnaire administered to the sample respondent women entrepreneurs.

Annual Turnover of sample Women Enterprises

The annual turnover of the selected women enterprises for the financial year 2011-12 is depicted in Table 13. It is observed from the table that 16 per cent of the enterprises have the turnover below ₹ 1 lakh, 46 per cent of the enterprises have ₹ 1 to 10 lakhs, 23 per cent of the enterprises have ₹ 10 to 20 lakhs, 10 per cent of the enterprises have ₹ 20 to 30 lakhs and only 5 per cent of the enterprises have the turnover of above ₹ 30 lakhs. The mean annual turnover of the selected enterprises was ₹ 13.50 lakhs.

Table 13: Total Annual Turnover of Selected Women Enterprises in Allahabad District (2011-12)

Turnover (Rs. in lakhs)	*No. of Enterprises*	*Percentage to total*
Below 1.0	13	16.00
1.0 to 10.0	37	46.00
10.0 to 20.0	18	23.00
20.0 to 30.0	8	10.00
30.0 and above	4	5.00
Average Turnover	13.50 lakhs	

Source: Compiled from the Questionnaire administered to the sample respondent women entrepreneurs.

Net Profit of sample Women Enterprises

Net profit is the difference between total revenue and expenditure. The data concerning the net profit of the selected women enterprises for the financial year 2011-12 is depicted in Table 14. Thirty-six per cent of the units had incurred loss during the year. The net profit of 36 per cent of units was below 1 lakh while it was more than, 5 lakhs in case of 4 per cent of units. The average net profit was 1.02 lakhs. The net profit was high in service enterprises. Most of the manufacturing enterprises incurred loss during the year.

Table 14: Net Profit of Selected Women Enterprises in Allahabad District (2016-17)

Net Profit (Rs. in lakhs)	*No. of Enterprises*	*Percentage to total*
Loss above 1.0	8	10.00
Loss below 1.0	21	26.00
Profit below 1.0	29	36.00
Profit 1.0 to 5.0	21	26.00
Above 5.0	3	4.00
Total	80	100.00
Average Profit	1.02 lakhs	

Source: Compiled from the Questionnaire administered to the sample respondent women entrepreneurs.

Challenges Faced by the Respondent Women Entrepreneurs

Indian society is characterized by male chauvinism on account of which talented and energetic Indian women cut notice in high-flying business activities which are traditionally dominated by men. The conventions and traditions prevalent in our society are not favourable for women to set up business units and if they enter this field they may have to eat the humble pie because of non-cooperation and meddlesome attitude of our society. The data relating to the challenges faced by the respondents is depicted in Table 15.

Table 15: Problems of Selected Women Entrepreneurs

Nature of the Problem	*No. of respondents*	*Percentage to total*
Power problem	16	20.00
Technical/management assistance	13	16.25
Financial problem	19	23.75
Manpower/human resources problem	9	11.25
Problem of marketing their products	11	13.75
Problem of availability of raw materials	4	5.00
Penetrating competition	2	2.50
Constraints in mobility	2	2.50
Lack of proper training on innovative business	2	2.50
Poor support from family members	2	2.50
Total	1 80	100.00

Source: Compiled from the Questionnaire administered to the sample respondent women entrepreneurs.

It is observed from the above table that the majority of the respondents (23.75 per cent) have struggled due to financial problem, while 20 per cent of them have struggled due to power problem, 16.25 per cent of them have faced technical/management assistance problem, 13.75 per cent of the respondents have highlighted the problem of marketing their products, 11.25 per cent of them have expressed the problem of manpower/human resources, 5 per cent of the respondents have expressed the problem of availability of raw materials and only a few respondents (2.5 per cent) faced the problems like penetrating competition, constraints in mobility, lack of proper training on innovative business practices and poor support from family members.

SUGGESTIONS

In the light of interaction with the sample respondents and the foregoing analysis of data, the researcher has offered the following suggestions for the betterment of women entrepreneurs in general and in Allahabad district in particular:

1. Free training on technical aspects, marketing and financial management should be offered. Further, women entrepreneurs are advised to undergo some HR training conducted by SMEs. This would help them to acquire knowledge of emerging HR policies and practices, which in turn, causes for cordial relations with the employees.
2. Proper co-ordination between executives of promotional agencies and viable entrepreneurs must be promoted.
3. In the modern market era (liberalization, privatization and globalization), the entrepreneurs should attend to trade fairs and exhibitions to acquire more knowledge on the recent trends and developments at the national and international level.
4. The State Financial Institutions, District Industries Centres (DICs), Association of Women Entrepreneurs, Organizations like FICCI, CII, NABARD, SIDBI, etc. could set up guidance cells for women entrepreneurs.
5. Rural women entrepreneurs should be given liberty to choose their business activity. This creates interest in the entrepreneur and attracts her commitment.
6. A most striking problem among majority of the entrepreneurs is the 'finance'. Estimation of financial requirements and assistance by the government agencies is unrealistic. Apart from providing concessional financial assistance to the entrepreneurs in rural areas, more important is providing sufficient finance to run their business operations.
7. To promote women entrepreneurs effectively, integration of governments supporting agencies, in providing inputs and marketing of finished products, is necessary.
8. Adequate data regarding marketing situation should be made available to the women entrepreneurs.
9. Adequate follow-up support to the women entrepreneurs.
10. The government should ensure speedy change from traditional occupation to modern business enterprises in order to take the maximum advantage of the new market conditions and available new technology.
11. The government should make planned efforts to inculcate the spirit of entrepreneurship among women through many incentives and developmental programmes.

12. Last but not least is the family support for women entrepreneurs. Family support boosts the morale and confidence in them and gives strength to fight various problems.

If the suggestions offered above are implemented, no doubt, the women entrepreneurship in the district will take a new path and will create sound employment and self-sufficiency, and the country will become the most entrepreneurial country.

CONCLUSION

The present study is based on the problems and prospects of women entrepreneurship in Allahabad District of Uttar Pradesh. Women are said to be the backbone of any economy special with regard to the developing economies, but in factual terms they are considered to be the non asset of the economy. It is in this context that the research paper tends to present the causes that led to the growth of entrepreneurs. The major factors were desire for independence, income, skill development, etc. The study further reveals that the sample entrepreneurs are facing constrains like finances, lack of family support, power shortage, management skills etc. In order to develop women entrepreneurs in the area of study, it is pertinent for the government to take initiatives in providing financial assistance, technical training, and create an environment whereby women entrepreneurs feel motivated in initiating and exploiting potential resources.

REFERENCES

1. Aldrich, H (ed.)1989, "Networking among Women Entrepreneurs", in *Women owned Businesses* G. Hagan, and D. Sexton (ed.), New York: Praeger.
2. Azad, G.Z, *Development of Entrepreneurship Among Indian Women*, SEDME, 16(3), 1989.
3. Baporikar, N., 2007, *Entrepreneurship Development & Project Management*, Himalaya Publication House.
4. Bhanushali, C.G., 1960, *Entrepreneurship Development*, Bombay: Himalaya Publishing House.
5. Bowen, Donald D. & Hirsch Robert D 1986, "The Female Entrepreneur: A career Development Perspective", *Academy of Management Review*, Vol. 11,
6. Buttner, E.H., and Moore, D.P., 1997 "Women's Organization Exodus to Entrepreneurship: Self-Reported Motivations and Correlates with Success", *Journal of Small Business Management.*
7. Collerette, P and Aubry, P. "Socio-Economic Evolution of Women Business Owners in Quebec", *Journal of Business Ethics.*
8. Damwad, 2007, Women Entrepreneurship – A Nordic Perspective, Nordic Innovation Centre.
9. Desai, V., 1996, *Dynamics of Entrepreneurial & Development & Management* Himalaya Publishing House, Fourth Edition, Reprint.

10. Dhameja S.K., 2002, Women Entrepreneurs: Opportunities, Performance and Problems, Deep Publisher (P) Ltd., New Delhi.
11. Gordon E. & Natarajan K.: 2007 Entrepreneurship Development – Himalaya Publication House, Second Revised edition.
12. Kaplan, E., 1988 *Women Entrepreneurs: Constructing a Framework to Examine Venture Success and Failure,* Frontiers of Entrepreneurship Research.
13. Kumar, A. 2004, "Financing Pattern of Enterprises Owned by Women Entrepreneurs", *The Indian Journal of Commerce,* Vol. 57, No. 2.
14. Maria John S., Jeyabalan R., Krishnamurthy S. (eds.), 2004, *Rural Women Entrepreneurship,* Discovery Publishing House, New Delhi.
15. Mathivanan, S., Selvakumar, M., "A Study on Socio-Economic Background and Status of Women Entrepreneurs in Small Scale Industries", *Indian Journal of Marketing.*
16. O' Meally-Nelson, B., 1995, *Small Business Opportunities for Women in Jamaica,* SEDME, Vol.18, No.1.
17. Raheem A. 2006, "Role of SHGs", *Yojana,* Vol. 50,
18. Renuka V., 2001, Opportunities and challenges for women in business, India Together, Online Report, Civil Society Information Exchange Pvt. Ltd.
19. Saxena, A., 2005, *Entrepreneurship: Motivation, Performance and Rewards,* New Delhi: Deep and Deep Publications.
20. Sextan, D., Kent, C. 1985, *Female Executives and Entrepreneurs: Preliminary Comparison,* "Frontiers of Entrepreneurship Research",
21. Sheetal, S. 2006, "Educated Women, Powered Women", *Yojana,* Vol. 50, No.12,

27

Emerging Human Resource Practices with Respect to Women Employees at Workplace

Amita Maxwell, Archana Chandra and Sarita Maxwell

ABSTRACT

This paper gives an overview of the various challenges and issues faced by women employees at workplaces and factors affecting their work-life balance. The present paper aims to highlight, measures and policies supporting women progression at the workplace, and the need for the entire industry to come together to provide opportunities and support required for their successful career advancement within the corporate sector across various industry verticals. This paper aims at understanding the key human resource practices and organizational policy changes with respect to employment of women workers and exploring the changing scenario at workplace as more and more organizations are developing new ways of engagement and harnessing the productivity of women employee as it has been proven through various research studies that there is positive relationship between human resource practices and women employee's performance which means human resource practices increases the productivity of women employees.

Keywords: *work-life balance, role conflict, human resource policies for women, emerging HR practices.*

INTRODUCTION

Career and growth are the most important factors in life. Women are considered to play the role of a perfect homemaker since time immemorial. Looking from the point of view of different religions or the Vedic period of Indian history, we find a woman being depicted as somebody who manages the affairs of the family, confined to the four walls of the house, where she is supposed to play her best role. Her identity is marked to this and non-existing in the outer boundaries or outside realm. This role depiction of women since ages and the perception of society have completely undermined the personality of women. The biggest challenge for women is how to balance the demands of family and career and the struggle between two conflicting roles of mother versus manager has always created role conflict and work-life balance. Most of the women are now coming forward to work in order to support their family. This change is now natural and dynamic due to change of environment and economic conditions. The literature identifies the various aspects such as career advancement, work stress, career aspiration, work-family conflict and family-work conflict, child care in context with work-life balance and its practices. This paper aims at identifying factors affecting work-life balance of women employees, exploring the key human resource practices and policy changes with respect to employment of women workers and the changing scenario at work place. The various sources identified for the present paper comprise of journals, articles, reports and Internet resources.

LITERATURE REVIEW

Vijaya Mani (2013) has revealed the major factors influencing the Work-Life Balance of women professionals in India such as role conflict, lack of recognition, organizational politics, gender discrimination, elderly and children care issues, quality of health, problems in time management and lack of proper social support.

Heather S. McMillan et al. (2011) suggested that the individual harmony and its effects have developed a new harmony based on conflict and enrichment.

Kumari K. Thriveni et al. (2012) have studied and analyzed the significant relationship between the demographic variables and WLB.

Shalini and Bhawna (2012) reported in their study, quality of work life is being used by the organizations as a strategic tool to attract and retain the employees and more importantly to help them to maintain work-life balance with equal attention on performance and commitment at work.

N. Krishna Reddy et al. (2010) concluded that the married women employees indeed experience Work Family Conflict (WFC) while attempting to balance their work and family lives. Thus, Organization needs to formulate guidelines for the management of WFCs since they are related to job satisfaction and performance of the employees.

Niharika and Supriya (2010) have studied the work-based factors and family-related factors that are considered to contribute to work-life balance. Work-based factors are flexi time, option to work part time and freedom to work from home and the family related factors are child care facility and flexibility to take care of emergencies at home is more prevalent than family-work conflict (family interfering with work) though both can occur. However, regardless of the direction of causation, when one domain is discordant with another domain, the result is conflict and increased stress on the individual. Attribution theory states that there are internal and external explanations for work family and family-work conflict.

Amita Singh (2010) suggested that flexi time, home working, child care facilities, option to work part time are facilities that need to be introduced and recommended for building a supportive work environment in the IT sector in India.

Mathew and Pachanatham (2009) stated that the women workforce in India was mainly employed in non-managerial, subordinate or low-profile positions in the past. At present they occupy almost all categories of positions in the workplace. These changes in work culture have added to women's duties and responsibilities to their family as well as to society.

On the basis of literature review it can be stated that women employees do experience work-life imbalances and conflict resulting into low productivity of women employees at workplace and this becomes a hurdle for their progress in terms of career advancement or growth in the organizational hierarchy.

MOTHER VERSUS MANAGER CONFLICT

Role of women in all spheres of life can be seen in the 21st century. Women's dilemma has always been centred on the dual role, which she plays in society and which leads to role conflict. Her first priority is always to play the role of the best homemaker and second her role relates to her career or professional life where also she wants to excel and deliver her best. In today's world there are numerous examples of great women entrepreneurs, business women, women playing significant roles and successful in professions like banking, teaching, medical science, lawyers, etc.; women are cutting across all classes. "*Women really are more than just homemakers. Today the working young women appear to be as ambitious as men when it comes to eagerness to climb the career ladder, and 26 percent women contribute even more towards family income than their husbands,*" (General Manager corporate communications at the Yash Birla Group).

Compared and contrasted with the role of homemaker which most women play in the real world, Maslow's Need Hierarchy Theory may be understood differently for a homemaker. Maslow's hierarchy of needs pyramid can be reversed for a homemaker.

The American motivation psychologist, Abraham H. Maslow developed the hierarchy of needs consisting of five hierarchic classes. According to Maslow, people are motivated by unsatisfied needs. The needs, listed from basic (lowest-earliest) to most complex (highest-latest).

Maslow's hierarchy of needs theory can be summarized as follows:

- Human beings have wants and desires which influence their behavior. Only unsatisfied needs influence behavior, satisfied needs do not.
- Needs are arranged in order of importance to human life, from the basic to the complex.
- The person advances to the next level of needs only after the lower level need is at leastminimally satisfied.

Physiological needs comprise of the most basic of Maslow's needs. Physiological needs refer to the need for food, water, and other biological needs. These needs relate to the survival and maintenance of human life. Safety Needs: Once physiological needs are satisfied, the next level of need to be satisfied is safety or security needs. These needs find expression in such desires as economic security and protection from physical dangers. Social needs: On the next level up, social needs refer to the need to bond with other human beings, be loved, and form lasting attachments with others. Esteem needs: The satisfaction of social needs makes esteem needs more salient. Esteem need refers to the desire to be respected by one's

Figure 1: Maslow's Hierarchy of Needs

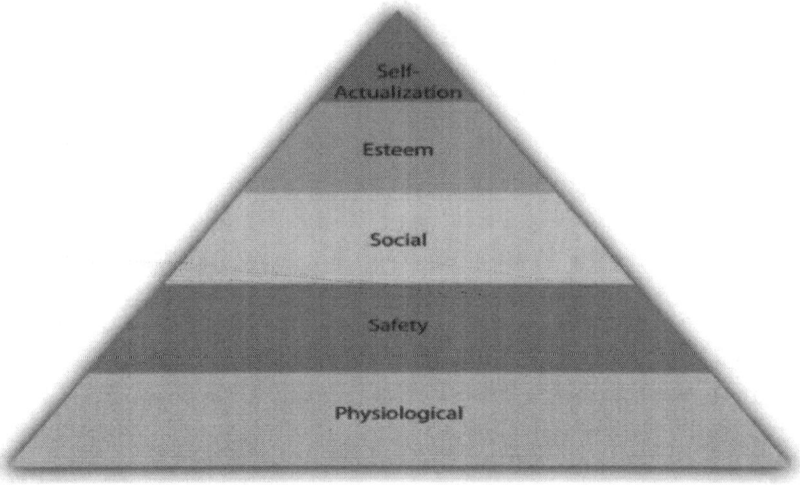

peers, feel important, and be appreciated. These needs refer to self-esteem and self-respect. They include such needs which indicate self-confidence, achievement, competence, knowledge and independence.

Self-actualization needs: Finally, at the highest level of the hierarchy, the need for self-actualization refers to "becoming all one is capable of becoming". This need manifests itself by the desire to acquire new skills, take on new challenges, and behave in a way that will lead to the attainment of one's life goals.

Self-actualization and ***esteem needs*** that are shown at the top of the pyramid constituting most complex, highest-level need. However this need must be placed at the lowest level of the pyramid for a homemaker, as this level represents the culmination of all the lower, intermediate, and higher level needs of human beings. In other words, the final step under the need hierarchy model is the need for self-actualization. This refers to fulfilment whereas a homemaker dedicates all her effort towards fulfilment of the basic needs, like physiological, safety and security of her family which constitutes her spouse, elders in the family and children. She manages a very important unit, i.e. household and does micro management where she plays an important role of sometimes a boss, a manager, HR personnel, financial management or consultant but still her contribution is not added to the GDP of the nation and her contributions go unaccounted for.

As stated above women are seen playing different roles successfully in diverse areas we can say that the line between mother and manager is getting blurred in today's world irrespective of country, religion and traditions. Today women are trying to integrate and merge both roles in such a way that they are successful homemakers as well as leading professionals in whichever area they serve by maintaining work-life balance. They are no more referred to as weaker vessels confined to homes as they have the potential, and in all developed nations of the world an active role of women is seen in the active workforce and India is no exception to this.

Today women are leading some of the most innovative and important Indian tech companies. With thousands of people reporting to them, these women are a force to reckon with in business. Here is a new emerging segment of women CEOs at large IT companies—Vanitha Narayanan is the Managing Director of IBM India Private Limited, and the Regional General Manager for India/South Asia, Neelam Dhawan is the Managing Director of Hewlett-Packard India, Kumud Srinivasan is responsible for general management of Intel's operations in India and many more. The new breed of female tech CEO is here to stay and only bound to grow in number.

THE CHANGING SCENARIO AT WORKPLACE

Women professionals are moving up the corporate ranks and managing homes as well. To a large extent HR policy in India has undergone a lot of change to benefit a woman employee and in turn help a woman give her best as it's a tough act for working women to balance home and work. HR fraternity at large has grown to be very sensitive to the fact that a majority of the workforce consists of women. A woman has to balance multiple arenas like home, work and growing children's needs. More and more companies are fast adapting their policies to suit the requirement of women and help provide various options. As per a research study based on *Impact of Human Resource Practices on Female Employees Performance in Karachi, Pakistan* (Nadeem M, Ahmad R, Ahmad N, Abdullah M, 2015) it was concluded that HR policies and practices are very important for all the employees working in the organization. Women workers should be encouraged because they are participating equally. Results show that there is a positive relationship between human resource practices and women employee performance which means human resource practices increases the productivity of the women employees. Human resource practices should be flexible for women employees because their responsibilities differ in nature and HR practices affect them differently. In view of the above study we can suggest that organizations need to look at women employee from a different perspective.

Daniel Jebasingh, of Consim Info Ltd, agrees that HR policies are becoming friendlier in Indian companies and claims, *"We are one of the very few companies in India with an in-house counselor who helps women cope with stress and generally maintain a good work life balance."* Mondelez, the parent company of multinational confectionary subsidiary Cadbury, has two mentoring programmes for women. The *'My Mentor'* program is a self-paced 12-week program to augment the key competencies of senior high potential women at the organization. There are also *'mentoring circles'* which is a collection of mentoring relationships that meets on a regular basis for an agreed period of time.

Investment banking firm Goldman Sachs understood the pain of the new mothers of leaving their toddlers under unreliable supervision and coming to work. Therefore, they started an on-site corporate office creche in London where the parents could leave their kids at the child care centre and work without any stress.

In America, Apple offers huge amounts to women employees who wish to *freeze their eggs*. The reason being that women can focus on progressing in their careers. This may however be the most disruptive ways of career advancement. Facebook has also introduced this policy. Egg freezing technology gives women the option to climb the career ladder and have a family later in life and allows women greater freedom and flexibility.

Bhattacharya, head of the SBI bank's investment banking arm SBI Caps, made a provision of a *sabbatical of up to 6 years* for women with a cap of 5% of employees going on such long unpaid leaves at a given time. At SBI, a woman can take an unpaid leave of up to 13 months for child birth, she said, adding that other events like the child's secondary examinations and elderly falling sick also require time-off.

KEY POLICY CHANGES

Key human resource policy changes that could be implemented to ensure inclusion and participation of women at workplace are as follows:

1. **Telecommuting and Hot desking:** Many companies don't have a flexible work hour policy. This sometimes leads women to leave the organization because they can't balance work and home. Having a more flexible work hour policy will support not just women but everyone to balance work and home more effectively. They are now working on web top rather than desktop to take advantage of online collaboration, hotdesking and telecommuting or tele-working. Unfortunately few employers allow to telecommute. Companies are now moving and encouraging employees towards flexible HR practices like hot desk (sharing work or workstations between office workers, working on any work station in office and work from home).
2. **Sabbatical:** Companies must have policies that allow employees to take a break and have a mechanism for them to come back to an appropriate role at the end of the break.
3. **Paternity leave:** In India, the lack of a paternity leave policy forces men to be more hands-off when they become parents. Companies should make paternity leave mandatory, to ensure that men play an equal role in supporting the family.
4. **Gender diversity:** To make a better impact on gender diversity in India, we definitely need to make it a priority for the entire organization, not just top management or HR. The value that

diversity drives in organizations needs to be better articulated and that is a bigger issue to address. It is important for the top management to make gender equality and diversity a part of their goals, and equally as important as their business and financial goals. They need to build a culture that not only hires women candidates, but also ensures that they are paid and promoted as per their capabilities. Encouraging and taking deliberate action to include women on their board and have them lead global teams will also have a large impact on gender equality. Nestle India's MD, Suresh Narayanan, urged companies to treat diversity at workplaces as a top management priority and not just as a human resource gimmick.

5. **Post-work break-stigma:** There are several social and professional stigmas associated with women getting back to work post breaks. Internal and external issues that play a crucial role in prohibiting women from getting back to work post a sabbatical. External issues refer to the lack of suitable opportunities to return to the workforce. Often companies don't invest time and effort in training a woman with the new skills once she returns from a break. That often acts as a deterrent for both women to apply and companies to recruit. There are also strong stereotypes that these women will need more flexibility, take more breaks, take more leaves, etc. These generalized assumptions often make managers rethink hiring women who have been on career breaks. Whereas internal issues would mean women often carry a sense of internal stigma that stops them from returning to work or being successful after they come back.
6. **Mentoring**: Many companies are adopting active diversity policies to support women balance their family and professional responsibilities. Companies are framing policies to help retain talented women. They also provide mentoring and coaching support to their high potential women employees to groom them to be potential directors.

Promoting women-friendly HR policies, flexible work schedules, fast-track programmes and mentoring are steps to encourage more women to forge ahead in their careers. Companies should create strong policies for 'back-to-work moms' and 'work-from-home women'. Out of the 1,456 companies listed on National Stock Exchange, only 490 have a woman Director on their board, National Stock Exchange.

KEY HR PRACTICES FOR WOMEN AT WORKPLACE

1. HR policies that support healthy work family balance support women. Subsidized child care, back-up child care, flexi-time, telecommuting, paid health care and paid family leave are all popular benefits. Companies that win awards as **best places to work** illustrate the types of programs that are valued:
   - Flexible working hours; 80% allow employees to telecommute some or all of the time.
   - All progressive companies offer a lactation room for new mothers, and more than 90% offer child care resources, referral and lactation support services.
   - Some offer onsite child care centers.
2. *Working Mother*, a magazine, notes that best companies are training managers to better oversee the work-life concerns of their employees and support flexible work arrangements. That's critical, because just having good policies on the books isn't enough to foster a truly flexible environment that accommodates work and family demands. According to a report by the American Psychological Association (APA), a study of employees whose company had onsite child care showed that having a supportive supervisor reduced their levels of both work/family conflict and absenteeism whereas use of the onsite care alone did not. "It's a much deeper issue than just providing more benefit programs."
3. Randstad, the second largest HR services and staffing company in the world ($22.0 billion global provider of HR services) emphasizes on women participation at workplace.
   - Randstad's survey showed how important a factor it is for a company to have women in positions of leadership when it comes to their prospective employees.
   - According to Randstad US Employee Engagement Index study, equal pay, more visible female leadership, and more family-friendly work policies are among the most beneficial ways in which companies can help women advance.
4. For Volkswagen, family-friendly human resources policies are a key attribute of an attractive employer. Volkswagen intends to increase the proportion of women in the company in a sustainable way. Volkswagen aims to attract female students at an early stage. This increased proportion of qualified women joining the company will enable to steadily lift the proportion of female executives in the coming years.

i. To increase the proportion of women in management, it embarks on the cross-brand *Management Mentoring Program*, designed to support women on the way to management positions. In addition, Volkswagen offers the "Compass" program to specifically encourage women with high potential in their decision to aim for a career in management.
ii. In addition to hiring and supporting talented female employees, Volkswagen is working continuously to improve its employees work-life balance which includes flexible part-time and shift models or teleworking arrangements.
iii. Another step towards becoming a family-friendly company is the constant expansion of a range of childcare options. The Volkswagen Group has had positive experiences with near-site childcare in Germany and abroad. There are plans to expand childcare options at other locations as well.

5. The *Report on Women and IT Scorecard India by National Association of Software and Services Companies (NASSCOM) and The Open University (UK)* said the number of firms with over 20% women at senior level is expected to touch nearly 60% this year. Policies and practices like flexible working hours, parental leave and anti-harassment have helped in bringing more women into India's IT sector. In 2017, it is estimated that the number of firms that have more than 20% women at senior level will increase to nearly 60%, and nearly 51% of firms will have more than 20% of women at C-suite level (top executive level), according to the report.

The Indian IT sector is heading in a right way towards recruiting and retaining more women in leadership roles. The efforts of companies and stakeholders have been a contributing factor in achieving the growth in the number of women in India's IT sector.

Furthermore, specific HR policies and practices such as conveyance, flexible working hours, parental leave, anti-harassment, healthcare, and an emphasis on recognizing and supporting women needs have led to a positive trend, according to the report.

CONCLUSION

Human resource practices should be flexible for women employees because they are different in nature and human resource practices affect them differently in order to work freely and effectively. Conducive working conditions and overall environment at a workplace is important for women workers in an organization. Special attention and sensitivity is required in making human resource policies of the organizations. Organizations should provide a facilitating and stress-free environment within the organizational boundaries. If organizations provide stress-free environment, comfortable working conditions, flexible working hours, etc., the productivity of the women employees can be increased as seen in the developed countries. The key issues identified in the present paper regarding role conflict and work-life balance with respect to women employees as she plays both the roles of home maker as well as a professional should be incorporated in the human resource policies and plans right at the stage of recruitment and throughout the entire career advancement and growth phase of a women employee. The key HR practices being adopted by corporate should become benchmark practices and innovative practices as women employees positively contribute towards organizational productivity. The research studies have also proved that human resource practices are positively correlated with the productivity and performance of employees which means human resource practices affect the employees of the organization. Many corporates have started introducing women-friendly policies, like flexible working hours, telecommuting, teleworking, hotdesking, childcare facilities, sabbatical, special mentoring programmes, etc., in order to retain and encourage women participation at workplace.

REFERENCES

1. Anakwe, UP, 2002 "Human Resource Management Practices in Nigeria: Challenges and Insights", *The International Journal of Human Resource Management 13*: 1042-1059.
2. Baruch Y, Rosenstein E, 1992, "Career planning and managing in high tech organizations", *International Journal of Human Resource Management* 3: 477-496.
3. Boxall P, Macky K., 2009, "Research and theory on high-performance work systems: progressing the high involvement stream", *Human Resource Management Journal 19*: 3-23.
4. Conway, E., 2004, "Relating career stage to attitudes towards HR practices and commitment: Evidence of interaction effects", *European Journal of Work and Organizational Psychology 13*: 417-446.
5. Hakim, C., 2006, "Women, Career and Work Life preferences", *British Journal of Guidance and Counselling* 2006; 34(3).
6. Kuvaas, B., 2008, "An exploration of how the employee-organization relationship affects the linkage between perception of developmental human resource practices and employee outcomes". *Journal of Management Studies 45*: 1-25.
7. Mani, V., 2013, "Work Life Balance and Women Professionals", *Global Journal of Management and Business Research Interdisciplinary* 13(5).
8. Shiva. G., 2013, "A study on Work Family Balance and Challenges faced by

working women", *IOSR Journal of Business and Management*, 14(5): 1-4.

9. Nadeem M, Ahmad R, Ahmad N, Abdullah M (2015), Impact of Human Resource Practices on Female Employees Performance in Karachi Pakistan. *Business Economics Journal*. doi:10.4172/2151-6219.1000147.
10. Poole, M., Jenkins, G., 1997, "Responsibilities for Human Resource Management practices in the modern enterprise", *Personnel Review 26*: 333-356.
11. Sheel, S., Khosla, Sindhwani, B. et al., 2012, "Quality of Work life, employee performance and career growth opportunities", *Zenith International Journal of Multidisciplinary Research*, 2(2): 13-21.
12. Singh A., 2010 A study on the perception of work life balance policies among software professionals, *IUP Journal of Management Research*, Hyderabad 2010; 9(2): 51-29.
13. Singh, S., 2013, *Work Life Balance: A Literature Review, Global Journal of Commerce & Management Perspective*, 2(3): 84-91.

28

Gender Equality through Women Entrepreneurship:
Recent Trends and Tendencies in India

H.K. Singh, Vineet Kumar Maurya and Veenita Singh

ABSTRACT

The educated Indian women have to go a long way to achieve equal rights and position because traditions are deep rooted in Indian society where the sociological set up has been a male dominated one. Despite all the social hurdles, Indian women stand tall from the rest of the crowd and are applauded for their achievements in their respective field. In today's world, women entrepreneurs are playing a very vital role and they have become an important part of the global business environment and it's really important for the sustained economic development and social progress. In India, though women are playing a key role in the society, but still their entrepreneurial ability has not been properly tapped due to the unequal status of women in the society. The main purpose of this paper is to find out the status of women entrepreneurs in India. The present paper endeavours to study the concept of women entrepreneur—Reasons women become entrepreneurs; reasons for slow progress of women entrepreneurs in India; suggestions for the growth of women entrepreneurs; schemes for promotion and development of women entrepreneurship in India.

Keywords: *Gender Equality and Women Empowerment.*

INTRODUCTION

'Women Entrepreneur' refers to those women who commence and operate a business venture. Like male entrepreneurs a women entrepreneur has many functions. They should explore the prospects of starting new enterprise, undertake risks, introduce new innovations, coordinate, administer and control business and provide effective leadership in all aspects of business. Government of India has described women enterprise as an enterprise/venture owned and controlled by women having at least financial interest of 51% of the capital and giving at least 51% of employment generated in the organization to women.

Women Entrepreneurs are highly increasing in the economies of almost all countries. The hidden business potentials of women have been increasing with the growing sensitivity to the role and economic status in the society. The knowledge, skill and compliance in business are the core reasons for women to come forward into business ventures. Women entrepreneurs engage in business due to push and pull factors which give confidence to women to have a self-sufficient occupation and enable them to stand on their feet. Desire for independent decision-making in life and career is the key inspiration that insists on defining 'Women Entrepreneur' as a person who accepts challenging roles to meet her personal desires that also turnout to be economically independent. An aspiration to do something positive is an integral quality of entrepreneurial women, who are competent of contributing values in both family and social life. With the popularization of media, women are conscious of their own qualities, rights and also the work situations. The stereotypical thinking is on the decline and women are ahead in all lines of business, where earlier they were not venturing. In fact they are immensely successful in conventional and unconventional fields and serve as motivation to other women.

OBJECTIVES OF THE STUDY

The objectives of the present study are as follows:

- To find out the factors which encourage women to become entrepreneurs
- To study the support given by the government and banks to women entrepreneurs.
- To examine the challenges faced by women entrepreneurs.

REASONS WHY WOMEN BECOME ENTREPRENEURS

Self-esteem, recognition, financial independence and ambitions are the key drivers for women to become entrepreneurs. Sometimes, women choose such career paths for proving their potential and caliber in order to achieve self- satisfaction. However, dismal economic conditions of the family arising out of unemployment in the family and divorce can compel women into entrepreneurial activities. The days have gone when women were confined within the boundaries of their houses. Now women are found in every line of business. The entry of women into business in India is an extension of their normal home activities. But with the spread of education and passage of time women started shifting from doing work at home or in the kitchen to a business venture. Skill, knowledge and adaptability in business are the main reasons for women to emerge into business ventures. Women Entrepreneur are women who accept challenging roles to meet their personal needs and become economically independent. A strong desire to do something positive is an inbuilt quality of entrepreneurial women, who is capable of contributing values in both family and social life. With the advent of media, women are aware of their own capabilities and rights and also the work options. The challenges and opportunities provided to the women of digital era are growing rapidly and the job seekers are turning into job creators. Many women start a business due to several reasons, like occurrence of a traumatic event, such as divorce; discrimination at work due to pregnancy; need to support the family financially, work–life balance in doing your own work; the health of a family member; or economic reasons such as a layoff. A new talent pool of women entrepreneurs is emerging today, as more women opt to leave the corporate world to chart their own destinies. They are growing as designers, interior decorators, exporters, publishers, garment manufacturers and still exploring new avenues of economic participation.

CONSTRAINTS IN THE PATH OF WOMEN ENTREPRENEURSHIP

Highly educated, talented and professionally qualified women should be encouraged for running their own business, rather than relying on wage service jobs. The uncharted talents of young women can be acknowledged and used for various types of industries to increase the yield in the business sector. A desirable environment is necessary for every woman to inculcate entrepreneurial values and involve greatly in business dealings. But women in India are faced by many problems to progress in their professional life or in business. A few problems can be detailed as follows:

Lack of Self-Confidence: In India women have lack of self-confidence in their strength and ability. The family members and the society are unwilling to support or encourage their (women's) professional growth. To a certain degree, this situation is improving with Indian women but there still needs to be an incredible change to boost the rate of growth in women entrepreneurship.

Socio-Cultural Barriers: Family and personal obligations often work as a great barrier for succeeding in the women's entrepreneurship venture. Only few women are capable of managing both home and business efficiently, giving sufficient time to perform all their responsibilities based on priorities.

Risks Related to Market: Tough competition in the market and lack of mobility of women make them dependent on middlemen. Many business women find it very difficult to capture the market share and popularise their products and get them accepted by customers. They are often not fully aware of the changing market conditions and hence are unable to take advantage of or utilize the potential of media and Internet effectively.

Mobility Constraints: Women in India have to face lot of restrictions with respect to their mobility as our conservative society still restricts women from travelling to far off places or out of the city or country. Though women faced lots of problems on being mobile as they pursued their entrepreneurial activities, there has been a recent change in that issue with growing awareness and safer mobility options.

Business Administration Knowledge: Women must be educated and trained specifically and continuously to acquire the skills and understanding of the required functional areas of a business venture. This will enable them to excel in their entrepreneurial venture, learn leadership skills, improve decision making, and develop good business skills.

Financial Assistance: Most of the women, especially in rural areas, are not aware about the financial assistance provided by various institutions. The efforts taken for women entrepreneurs may not reach the entrepreneurs in rural and backward areas.

Training Programs: Depending upon the needs, duration, skill and the purpose of an entrepreneur there are various workshops and training programs available through the social & welfare association. Such kinds of programs are helpful to new and young entrepreneurs who desire to start a small- and medium-sized business independently.

SCHEMES FOR PROMOTION AND DEVELOPMENT OF WOMEN ENTREPRENEURS IN INDIA

1. **Trade Related Entrepreneurship Assistance and Development (TREAD) scheme for women:** This scheme provides women with proper trade related training, information and counselling along with extension activities related to various trades, products, services, etc. Besides, Government Grant also provides up to 30% of the total

project cost as appraised by lending institutions, which would finance the remaining 70% as loan Assistance to applicant women. It mostly helps poor and usually illiterate/semi-literate women to get started on their business.

2. **Standup India:** The Stand up India Scheme is aimed at promoting entrepreneurship among SC/ST and women by giving loans in the range of Rs.10 lakh to Rs.1 crore for setting up a new enterprises. SCs/STs and women entrepreneurs who avail loan would be given a RuPay Debit Card for withdrawal, besides comprehensive support like pre-loan training, facilitating loan, factoring and marketing. There would be a Rs.10,000 crore refinance window through Small Industries Development Bank of India (SIDBI) and the National Credit Guarantee Trustee Company Ltd (NCGTC) will create a corpus of Rs.5,000 crore.

3. **Bhartiya Mahila Bank Schemes:**

   A. **BMB Shringaar** – Loan For Beauty Parlour/Saloon/Spa
      - For assisting women to establish their own parlour.
      - For purchase/construction of shop purchase of tools and equipment, meeting day-to-day expenses of business.
      - Collateral free to be covered under CGTMSE
      - Tie up with Naturals, CavinKare and Lakme ltd.
      - Loan repayment in 7 years
      - Age of applicant min 20 years and max 60 years.

   B. **BMB Annapurna Loan** – Food Catering
      - For assisting women to establish food catering unit for selling tiffin/lunch packs
      - Nature of loan: Term Loan
      - Age of applicant min 18 years and max 60 years
      - Collateral Free to be covered under CGTMSE
      - Loan repayment in 3 years

   C. **BMB Parvarish**: Loan For Day Care Centre
      - To assist women to establish Child day care centre, for purchase of utensils, equipment etc
      - Collateral Free to be covered under CGTMSE
      - Loan repayment in 5 years
      - Age of applicant min 21 years and max 55 years

4. **State Industrial and Development Bank of India (SIDBI)** has introduced the following schemes to assist the women entrepreneurs. These schemes are:

   - Mahila Udyam Nidhi

- Micro Credit Scheme for Women
- MahilaVikas Nidhi
- Women Entrepreneurial Development Programmes
- Marketing Development Fund for Women

6. **Other Banks Schemes**

   A. **State Bank of Mysore:** SBM has two schemes for women entrepreneurs, the Annapurna Scheme and the Stree Shakti package. **Annapurna Scheme**—This scheme is designed for women who wish to establish food catering units, and offers loans up to Rs 50,000 for this purpose. The loan can be used to purchase kitchen essentials, gas connections, raw materials, etc., and has a repayment period of 3 years. **Stree Shakti**—Loans under this scheme can be availed by women entrepreneurs who have undergone EDP training. Loans up to Rs 50 lakh can be availed under this plan, with lower interest rates applicable for higher amounts.

   B. **Oriental Bank of Commerce**: Oriental Bank of Commerce has two schemes designed for self-employed women and those who are keen on setting up a beauty parlour/saloon.

      Scheme for Beauty parlours/boutiques—This scheme aims to promote entrepreneurial spirit among women, and offers loans up to Rs 10 lakh to set up a saloon, boutique, tailoring centre or beauty parlour. The loan amount can be used to meet any expenditure associated with setting up such a centre and for daily expenses.

      Scheme for self-employed women—This loan can be utilised to purchase fixed assets to enhance or start a business. The maximum loan amount is limited to Rs 5 lakh, with a repayment period ranging between 5 and 7 years.

   C. **Bank of Baroda**: Bank of Baroda offers one loan scheme for women entrepreneurs, the **Akshaya Mahila Athik Sahay Yojna (AMASY),** designed to help women reach their business dreams without having to worry about finances. This loan can be availed by women who are engaged in or wish to establish a business in retail trade, cottage industries and/or allied agricultural activities.

   D. **Dena Bank**: Dena Bank offers an exclusive scheme to aid female entrepreneurs, providing them sufficient financial help to build an enterprise. Loans can be availed as per RBI directions, with the amount varying according to the sector in which a woman wishes to establish a venture. This loan can be used for agriculture, MSMEs, education, housing and retail trade. Borrowers are also eligible for a special interest rate which is 0.25% lower than prevailing rates.

E. **Tamilnadu Mercantile Bank Limited**: TMB offers a loan designed for women entrepreneurs, the Mahalir Loan. This loan can be used to finance any business, with loans upto Rs 10 lakh available. The loan can be repaid within 7 years, with the interest rate depending on the quantum of loan.

F. **Punjab National Bank**: PNB offers 5 different schemes for women entrepreneurs, each one targeting a specific population.
PNB Mahila Samridhi Yojana: This scheme was launched to provide financial assistance to women who wish to set up boutiques, beauty parlours, cyber cafes, Xerox stores, telephone booths, etc.
PNB Mahila Udyam Nidhi Scheme: This scheme aims to reduce the gap in equity, helping women set up new ventures in the small scale sector or enhance their current undertakings.
PNB Scheme for Financing Crèches: This scheme aims to provide financial assistance to women who are keen on setting up crèches. The loan can be used to purchase the necessary materials and to meet any recurring expenditure.
PNB Mahila Sashaktikaran Abhiyan: This scheme provides credit to women who intend to establish small and micro enterprises in the non-farm sector, offering fee waiver and lower interest rate.
PNB Kalyani Card Scheme: This scheme provides loans for women engaged in agricultural, farm or non-farm activities.

SUGGESTIONS

- Awareness programmes should be conducted on a mass scale with the intention of creating awareness among women about the various areas to conduct business.
- The financial institutions should lend their hand to provide more working capital assistance both for small-scale ventures and large-scale ventures.
- Government should recognize the successful or growing women entrepreneurs and award them. This recognition and publicity will motivate other women entrepreneurs.

CONCLUSIONS

Empowering women entrepreneurs is crucial for achieving the goals of sustainable development and the bottlenecks hindering their growth must be reduced to enable full participation in the business. Moreover, training programs newsletters, mentoring, trade fairs and exhibitions also can be sources for entrepreneurial development. As a result, the desired outcomes of the business are quickly achieved and more of remunerative business opportunities are found. Therefore promoting entrepreneurship among Indian women is certainly a short-cut to rapid economic growth and development. Let us try to eradicate all kinds of gender bias and thus allow 'women' to be great entrepreneurs at par with men.

REFERENCES

1. http://www.dcmsme.gov.in/schemes/treadwomen.htm
2. https://smallb.sidbi.in/%20/fund-your-business%20/additional-benefits-msmes%20/women-entrepreneurship
3. http://shodhganga.inflibnet.ac.in/bitstream/10603/6775/12/12_chapter%201.pdf
4. Dr. Vijayakumar, A. and Jayachitra, S., *Women Entrepreneurs In India—Emerging Issues and Challenges*, International Journal of Development Research, Vol. 3, Issue, 04, April 2013, pp.12–17
5. Meenu Goyal and Jay Prakash, "Women Entrepreneurship in India-Problems and Prospects", *International Journal of Multidisciplinary Research* Vol. 1, Issue 5, September 2011, ISSN 2231 5780.
6. Shikha Mahajan, "Women Entrepreneurship in India", *Global Journal of Management and Business Studies*. ISSN 2248-9878 Vol. 3, Number 10 (2013), pp. 1143-1148. © Research India Publications http://www.ripublication.com/gjmbs.htm

29

Challenges Faced by Female Entrepreneurs in Eastern Region of Ghana

Archana Chandra and George Sarpong

DEFINING AN ENTREPRENEUR AND ENTREPRENEURSHIP

The theory of "entrepreneurship" has been widely used in commerce, academia and in daily conversation of ordinary people. Defining the term "entrepreneurship" is challenging as its meaning varies according to scholars and practitioners, thus there is a lack of an agreed definition of the theory (Gartner, 1990). The term entrepreneur originated from the French word "entreprendre" signifying "to undertake" in old French; and was first used in 1852 (Porfeli, 2009). The definitions of entrepreneurship and entrepreneur in literature are very diverse and vary as they include human attempts to commerce a new product or service (Jennings, 1994). As Jalbert (2000) agrees with the above statement and explains: entrepreneurship exists from a person's "creative spirit into long-term business owner, job creation and economic security" (Jalbert, 2000).

Additionally, Schumpeter (1934) and Hisrich *et al.* (2008) describes entrepreneurs as innovators. That is, a person who introduces a unique idea or something new within the economy. Such innovations may be the creation of new products, a process of production and the organisation of the industry (Dzisi, 2008). Being an innovator can be difficult at times as it does not only involve the ability to develop and conceptualize an idea, but also the capability to understand the forces at work within the environment the person is working in. Other interpretations of entrepreneur is that, they "add value" by acquiring and utilizing available resources to generate products and services satisfying customers and marketers (Butler, 2003). In so doing, they are risk-takers as Richard Cantillon (1755) stressed that they are arbitrageurs who conduct all exchanges and bear the risk as a result from buying at certain prices and selling at uncertain prices (Cantillon, 1755). The phrase illustrates that entrepreneurs can buy their products at certain prices but when selling, they sell at ambiguous prices as it changes due to the request of the consumer whose needs and wants are being satisfied. More so, entrepreneurship involves individuals who operate their own ventures by innovating and creating their own products and means of productions and accepting the risk involved. The process of creating such new ideas, taking and accepting the risks involved is referred to as entrepreneurship (Hisrich *et al.*, 2008). Both men and women become entrepreneurs. Though, this research concentrates on female entrepreneurs. The word "female" is an adjective describing an individual who is a woman or girl as both are nouns; the words female and woman are used alternatively, like the words man and male, which are used interchangeably.

LITERATURE ON FEMALE ENTREPRENEURS

Public perception and history would propose that entrepreneurship is naturally the field of businessmen. As in most countries, a significant amount of businesses are owned by men (Dzisi, 2008). Indeed, women are still the minority in the business world, who have exhibited entrepreneurial potential and are an important resource in economic growth. In agreement to the above statement, women entrepreneurs can influence positive economic growth because employment will be created, standard of living improved as income increases. Though in Ghana, most women are within the private informal sector of the economy and do not partake in economic development and growth since they are not supported by the government and/or support systems (Drine & Grach, 2010). The role of women in societies has triggered a lot of controversy as well as their participation in economic activities. The main argument is that the role of women is restricted in the home and with children and should play a subordinate role in the economy and in public affairs; while the other argument is against the mentioned point (Amu, 2004). We agree with the latter as women tend to influence economic growth especially in the 21st century. Besides, Leavitt (1971) too agrees with the latter pointing that the most significant role of a woman is her ability to participate in economic life and control over the property and products she creates (Amu, 2004). Women have always been in business mainly in the agricultural and service sector of the economy with few in the manufacturing. Examples would be women who established private food stores or restaurants, beauty spots or parlours and private schools mainly "crèche" as in the case of Little Scholars in Old Estate, Koforidua. These examples illustrate the women entrepreneurs utilizing "problem-solving strategies to manage transpiring issue, deal with multiple activities, form team, organise resources *and* develop organizations" (Dzisi, 2008).

Currently, women entrepreneurs are on the rise and have increased over the past decades due to structural change. The upsurge of women entrepreneurs is part of the societal, political and economic change occurring around the globe as more are in the workforce, in businesses and commencing businesses (Fielden & Davidson, 2005). Moreover, women are getting married later because they are becoming independent, socially and financially, owing to the acquired education in modern Accra, Ghana. Increase in education was reflected in the results of the 2000 census which was supported by the Ghana Living Standard Survey Four (GLSS4). The report demonstrated the change in number of adults who attended school in urban areas, in which about 87.8 percent of adults were males, while 74 percent were females. Though, this has changed significantly as is evident in the recent statistics in the GLSS5 report where school attendance for females in urban area has gone up to 93.4 percent as represented in Table 5.1. The percent of adults attending school rose to 19.4 percent from the year 2000 to 2008. In general, women entrepreneur is the creation by entrepreneurial women of new ventures in which they recognize an opportunity, make use of it, develop and grow a business successfully by accepting the risk involved (Dzisi, 2008). Such creativity provides employment and improves the standard of living as income increases.

CHALLENGES FACED BY FEMALE ENTREPRENEURS

Women entrepreneurs influence the economic growth of a country by providing jobs, increase income and the standard of living through the innovation, development and production of products that satisfy the needs of the population, and in so doing it provides them self-satisfaction, flexibility and independence. Nonetheless, these women face some obstacles before reaching their goals, such as their financial and psychological independence. Female entrepreneurs differ from their male counterparts as they encounter more problems as indicated by Jalbert (2000) and Saffu and Manu (2004). Research illustrates that men face less challenges than women especially with finance, education and management skills. Firms owned and managed by men had more sophisticated planning compared to females and they survive and grow from medium- to large-scale enterprises because they are literate and have access to credit and credit facilities since the societal norms are more in tune with them (Dovi, 2006).

SOCIAL-CULTURAL CONSTRAINTS

Female entrepreneurs face some challenges like the socio-cultural situation in certain societies impedes the development and growth of female's owning or operating a business. Most females find it difficult to start and operate their business because they deal with their traditionally ascribed roles, i.e. mainly being at home. Ghana being a democratic country that exercises the free market economy has lingering patriarchy in its system especially where women are of concern (Amu, 2004). Having lingering patriarchy is sometimes detrimental to women's economic and social position, in that their economic and social prosperity are lower than men and/or is non-existent at all (Parish & Willis, 1993). This provides men the opportunity to capture newer high-paying jobs and open their own businesses with little or no obstacles. Contrastingly, women and women entrepreneurs are confronted with challenges in starting and developing their businesses because they are expected to be dependent on family members and husbands as they are to remain at home. Women are perceived to be those whose domain is the home and its related tasks and can in no way perform outside or help in the growth of the economy, reducing their self-esteem as they are made to believed that they are inferior to men and can therefore cannot stand up for themselves (Amu, 2004). Due to these ideologies on women, they have difficulties in starting, developing and growing their own businesses as they lack the motivation from the men and the society to do so.

LACK OF ACCESS TO CREDIT

Access to financial resources such as cash and assets of the business is a critical success factor of a business (Bygrave, 1992). Obtaining financial resources such as loans or credit is one of the major problems that female entrepreneurs in Ghana combat with. Financial resources that are injected into the business are attainable from sources like personal savings, family members, venture capital funds, government programs and banks.

Though, it is difficult to attain most of the time because of various complications and formalities for the business and the owner (Dzisi, 2008). Particularly, women entrepreneurs in Ghana lack access to finance from banks and other formal institutions due to gender-related issues as reported by the *Daily Graphic* (2003). Further, they are disadvantaged in acquiring finances since women have less experience and equity than men in the business; they are discriminated against by lenders on the basis of gender, nature and/or size of the business. With banks for instance, they often provide services to large- and medium-sized companies to the disadvantage of small-scale enterprises which comprises mainly of women. Women-owned businesses are generally small preventing banks to provide them financial resources since small-scale enterprises are regarded to be riskier than large scale enterprises to invest in (Verheul & Thurik, 2000). In relation to the inaccessibility of finance, women face high interest rates and huge collaterals which are needed for the acquisition and repayment of the loans (Amu, 2004). For example, banks in Ghana insist on land property as collaterals make it hard for women since the control and ownership of land is often with the male members of the family (Bokei-Doku Areetey, 2000). The inaccessibility of land becomes complicated for women to open and operate their own enterprise as they only use land for agricultural purposes (Bokei-Doku Areetey, 2000).

Moreover, women in Ghana do not have land as compared to the males due to customary laws that are developed traditionally by the members of the society. The land tenure system and its administration is intertwined in a complicated web of family and tribe holdings where land is held in trust by the leaders of the family or tribe who most often are men (Amu, 2004). Women entrepreneurs in Ghana are faced with these problems because men are seen as the natural leaders (Duncan, 2004). Though in Ghana, there are Constitutional provisions protecting the right of women as well as other groups of society with regards to land in Article 35(1) (Amu, 2004). Besides, women entrepreneurs in Ghana continue to have limitations regarding finance due to high interest rates. Interest rates are high as it is an instrument used to curb inflation rates in the country. Women are very risk averse and will not take loans that have 30 percent interest on them (Dovi, 2006). Interest rates continue to rise in Ghana and as reported on the Ghana Web (2010); the country has one of the highest interest rates in the continent and the second highest in the world after Brazil (Ofosu-Appiah, 2010). For example, banks such as Standard Chartered were charging an interest of 29.5 percent on loans in the year 2010. Having such high interest rates on loans drives away entrepreneurs, especially females since they are not high risk-takers.

LACK OF EDUCATION AND INFORMATION

Women and men in Ghana play equal roles in the economic production of the country; women compared to males experience greater poverty, lower literacy rates especially at tertiary levels thus have less or limited knowledge on financial literacy for bookkeeping (Roomi and Parrott, 2008). This is because gender has been identified in research as the major role in creating barriers; and due to limited education and financial skills, women tend not to have control over their income as they allow other members of the family or skilled individuals to record their finances (Dovi, 2006). Over the years, girls were not educated because they were believed to be a "waste of" resources since they would eventually be married off.

Nevertheless, attitudes towards the girl-child education are positive as more parents are educating female members as they believe that they deserve the same opportunities as the males. The literacy rate for the female members of the society has increased in the last eight years because they are now enrolled in schools. This has increased the literacy rate of adult females for age 15 and above from 46 percent in 2000 to 59.6 percent in 2008 within the urban areas (GSS, 2008).

Table 1 illustrates the changes in female literacy in Koforidua and other urban areas.

Table 1: Locality Gender Koforidua Other Urban Area All

Male	88.3	75.1	79.7
Female	73.7	53	59.6
Total	80.8	63.2	69

From the figures above, adult literacy rates by gender and locality (percent) Educational level of females in Koforidua has increased, though females still have high illiteracy rates compared to their male counterparts which remain significantly low. For instance, 6 in every 10 men are literate while 4 in every 10 women are literate (GSS, 2008). Due to such educational barriers, female entrepreneurs concentrate less in skill and knowledge based industry which puts them in the informal private sector employment and self-employment in the informal sector (GSS, 2008). Ghana has sufficient human capital especially with women and it requires harnessing and in which governments and parents invest in the form of education. Low educational level impedes the growth of the business owned by women because less information is available regarding facilities that may benefit the business and themselves. More so, in order for women entrepreneurs to succeed economically, one needs to position herself to benefit or take advantage of the information available on new technology, existing and new markets opportunities so as to move ahead in business (Amu, 2004). Although some women may have access to certain business sensitive information, most women in Ghana are limited to most of the available information.

OTHER CONSTRAINTS

Furthermore, these entrepreneurs are unable to expand because they lack coordinated support, cheap and long-term credit and sufficient access to new technologies as well; have poor infrastructure, low capacity and sometimes obstructive government policies (Dovi, 2006). Reasons such as these make about 80 per cent of women-owned businesses in Ghana trapped at the "micro" level. Though they experience these issues, women become entrepreneurs to be liberated. Jalbert (2000) who focused on women entrepreneurs in the global economy observed that cultural and social traditions play an important role in determining who within the society becomes an entrepreneur.

Women entrepreneurs in Ghana are very common but are predominantly in the informal sector because they lack technological skills, internal and external support, as well as absence of self-sustaining governmental intervention (De Groot, 2001). Besides, they often lack managerial skills and support systems, are less educated, and have lower financial literacy (De Geus, 2010). This affects the performance of female entrepreneurs limiting them to the informal sector. The informal sector includes the service and manufacturing sector such as having local restaurants, salons, bakery, dress making, manufacturing of beads and local fabrics.

Moreover, women start businesses to avoid and eliminate gender, societal and generic imbalances because they become more independent, "achieve job satisfaction, attain personal accomplishment and become economically self-sufficient" (Jalbert, 2000). Being an entrepreneur enables individuals be it a male or female economic security.

CONCLUSION

Though the extant research suggests many similarities among male and female entrepreneurs, there are sufficient differences to warrant discussion and special attention in the classroom.

Some of the most salient issues that young women need to be better informed about include:

- The need for business-relevant education and the importance of business and managerial experience.
- The fact that personal decisions about timing and commitment to the business currently play a greater role in women's entrepreneurial choices than they do for men. So too, do issues of work and family balance.
- The relationship between personal considerations and women's choices of industry, growth aspirations, access to capital, and long-term financial success.

It is important to raise these issues early and to present them as choices rather than destiny. The use of teaching materials that feature women entrepreneurs in a greater variety of industries and with high growth aspirations can expand the horizons and stimulate aspirations of women students while broadening the perspectives of their male colleagues who are likely to be their future spouses, bankers, investors, and employees. Multiple ways to expand business experiences can also be considered, including programs of personal coaching and mentoring. Training programs to address specific tasks and skills can address not only increased expertise, but also enhance levels of self-confidence. A broader education can also help young women understand their unique situation regarding historical, economic, ethnic, legal and religious contexts (Oppedisano, 2003).

As the enrolment of women in business schools continue to increase, we can provide these young women with the tools and skills so important to success in entrepreneurial venturing. The payoffs will come at the individual, the firm, and the community level.

REFERENCES

Amu, N. J. (2004). *The Role of Women in Ghana's Economy*. Accra: Federich Ebert Foundation.

Aryee, R. (2011). Challenges Faced by Female Entrepreneurs in Accra, Ghana. (I. Cham, Interviewer)

Bediako, G. (2008). Ghana Living Standard Survey Report of the Fifth Round (Glss5). Accra. Ghana Statistical Service.

Bortei-Doku, A. (2000). "The participation of women in the Ghanaian economy" in Aryeetey, E., et al., (eds). *Economic reforms in Ghana: The miracle and the mirage,* Oxford: James Curry.

Butler, J. (2003). *New Perspectives on Women Entrepreneurs,* Greenwich: Connecticut, Information Age Publishing Inc.

Cantillon, R. (1755). Essai Sur la Nature du Commerce en Genera, 1931, edited and translated by H. Higgs, London: Macmillan.

De Geus, A. (2010). Women Entrepreneurship: An asset for society and economy. Retrieved December 24, 23, from http://www.oecd.org/dataoecd/60/43/46249649.pdf

De Groot, T.U. (2001). Women Entrepreneurship Development in Selected African Countries. Vienna: United Nations Industrial Development Organisation.

Dovi, E. (2006). Tapping women's entrepreneurship in Ghana: Access to credit, technology vital for breaking into manufacturing. Africa Renewal, United Nations, p. 12.

Drine, I., &Grach, M. (2010). Supporting Women Entrepreneurs in Tunisia. Helsinki: United Nations University—World Institute for Development Economics Research. (Amu, 2004).

Duncan, B. A. (2004). *Women in Agriculture in Ghana*. Published by Friederich Ebert Foundation Ghana.

Dzisi, S. (2008). Women Entrepreneurs in Small and Medium Enterprises (SMEs) in Ghana. Victoria: Swinburne University of Technology. Retrieved January 21, 2011, from http://www.unece.org/gender/documents/Overview.pd Estes, V. (1999). Women & business development: Promoting.

Fielden, S. & Davidson, M. (2005). I*nternational Handbook of Women and Small Business entrepreneurship*, Northampton, MA: Edward Elgar Publishing Limited.

Gartner, W.B. (1990). "What are we talking about when we talk about entrepreneurship?" *Journal of Business Venturing*, Vol. 5, No.1, pp.15- 28.

Hisrich, R.D., Peters, M.P., Shepherd, D.A. (2008). Entrepreneurship. 7th Ed. Boston, MA: McGraw-Hill.

Jalbert, S. E. (2000). Women Entrepreneurs in the Global Economy. Retrieved 25.3.17

Ofosu-Appiah (2010) https://www.ghanaweb.com/GhanaHomePage/NewsArchive/Government-Must-Tackle-Seriously-This-Outrageous-Interest-Rates-196522, Feature Article of Wednesday, 3 November

Porfeli (2009). Origins of Entrepreneur. Retrieved December 24, 2010, from Entrepreneur Media, inc. http://www.entrepreneur.com/tradejournals/article/196723352.html

Saffu, K., & Manu, T. (2003). Strategic capabilities of Ghanaian female business owners and the performance of their ventures. Accra, Ghana.

Schumpeter, J.A. (1934). The Theory of Economic Development, Cambridge, MA: Harvard University Press.

Verheul, I & Thurik, A.R. (2000). "Start-up Capital: Does Gender Matter?" *Small Business Economics*, Vol.16, pp.329–45

30

College Entrepreneurship and Gender Equality

Kalpana Sinha

India has the world's fastest growing startup ecosystem as per NASSCOM startup ecosystem report of 2015. With over $5 billion worth of investment in 2015 and three to four startups emerging every day, India is poised to secure the third position in the world in terms of the number of startups, 4200 startups and growing at a rate of 40%. Their statistics on the demography of the ecosystem says that 72% of the founders are young, less than 35 years old; however, the gender breakup of these startups is 91% male and 9% female entrepreneurs.

Similarly, the 2015 Female Entrepreneurship Index (FEI) that seeks to identify the conditions that enable the flourishing of high potential female entrepreneurs analyzed 77 countries to measure entrepreneurial environment ecosystem and individual aspirations. It scored India at 70th rank below Egypt and Ghana!

An earlier study by the sixth economic census 2013, released by ministry of statistics and programme implementation also presented a worrisome picture of the status of women entrepreneurs in India. The survey shows that women constitute only 13.76% of the total entrepreneurs, i.e., 8.05 million out of the 58.5 million entrepreneurs. These establishments in total provided employment to 13.45 million people. Thus the average employment per establishment for women-owned establishments was a meagre 1.67.

The Indian Government is fiercely pushing Entrepreneurship through many new policy initiatives and programmes. It has woken to the serious challenge of finding jobs for a growing population. According to labour ministry data, around 1 million people enter the workforce in India every month. At any given point, around 30 million students are pursuing higher education in India. As such it has targeted the academic institutes to play an imperative role in shaping the start up movement of the nation. Since women and girls represent half of India's population and therefore half of its potential, successive Governments have been launching various schemes for women entrepreneurs but there are few takers.

This brings up some important issues that need to be raised, whether entrepreneurship education in institutes of higher learning will empower females and reduce the gender gap in entrepreneurship? What is the gender equality we are seeing on campuses where various agencies like National Entrepreneurship Networks (NEN), The Indus Entrepreneur (TiE) have been actively promoting entrepreneurship? What further measures are required to close this gender gap?

Entrepreneurship education prepares people to become responsible and enterprising individuals. It helps people develop the skills, knowledge and networks necessary to achieve the goals they set out for themselves and realise their dreams. It empowers them to spot opportunities, leverage resources, create solutions and start ventures.

Student start-ups have started to contribute towards market expansion and job creation in some NEN member institutes. Since most of the student owned start-ups have evolved from technology courses instead of other liberal studies or social sciences disciplines, the percentage of female-owned students' startup has remained negligible.

However, institutes that have been promoting Entrepreneurship education have seen a definite improvement in the awareness and 'entrepreneurial spirit and culture' to support start-ups. Though the awareness of opportunity is high in NEN supported Institutions but the ability to act on opportunity is low especially for girls. This is particularly true in those cases where the students have taken educational loans. For female students the desire to act on these opportunities get further constraints due to their risk-averse nature, cultural biases, lawlessness, women safety and security issues.

Launching a successful venture requires the potential entrepreneur to have the necessary start-up skills (Papagiannidis and Li, 2005). The 'Perception of Skills' of the female students is high in these institutes as they believe they have the necessary skills to start a business, but in reality, they often lack a more complex level of skills needed to grow a business to the next level of size and sophistication. Hence, further education and mentoring will play a vital role in teaching and developing entrepreneurial skills and building networks.

The lack of awareness about various startup support schemes, funding agencies, complex legal frameworks and processes further closes the mindset of spirited girls to look at entrepreneurship as a viable career opportunity. This gets further compounded by dismally low personal level networking with the entrepreneurial community by female students as can be seen from the percentage of female students with LinkedIn profiles. Networking is critical for entrepreneurs, particularly female entrepreneurs (Klyver and Terjesen, 2007) and institutes must highlight its importance and train their female students on effective networking skills.

To create awareness we must first become aware ourselves. Faculty is the fulcrum on which the success of the entire entrepreneurship education is based. Most of the educators engaged in entrepreneurship education have purely academic background, lack enthusiasm, self-motivation and training in entrepreneurship. Their mandate is to complete the University designed course within the stipulated time, with little innovation and creativity. This makes them least impactful. It has been seen that as the interest of the students heightens in creating startups their queries also become piercing. Since the faculty lacks knowledge and experience they douse any enthusiasm and entrepreneurial spark of the students. Selection of faculty who is passionate, proactive and willing to learn is of paramount importance. This needs to be followed by training the trainers in new pedagogy, discovery learning, curriculum development and design so that they make the students do entrepreneurship rather than teach entrepreneurship. Since Entrepreneurship is an integrated subject, cooperative and collaborative teaching that involves educators, investors, bankers, entrepreneurs, practitioners, etc., working in tandem to lead, instruct and mentor groups of female students will be more fruitful.

The Entrepreneurial ecosystem becomes robust by creating entrepreneurial infrastructure on campus. These include an entrepreneurship Cell (E-Cell), campus company program, formal mentoring unit, Entrepreneurship Development Cell (EDC), Incubation and innovation centres. An entrepreneurship Cell or E-Cell is an organisation run by students to practice and promote entrepreneurship in their campus communities. They are committed and driven to thinking and acting entrepreneurially and to explore entrepreneurship as a career option and a way of life. The objective of an E-Cell is to help create the Entrepreneurial Leaders of tomorrow—leading/starting companies. Entrepreneurial leaders are focused on opportunities and value creation and have the necessary knowledge, skills and networks to be highly successful. These leaders will positively impact the economic growth and nurture the entrepreneurial ecosystem of the nation. Motivating female students to be part of this E-Cell will have a direct and positive impact on the numbers of female entrepreneurs in the economy.

Providing an enabling environment where students can start ventures on campus will give confidence to think big and work on real problems. The campus company program has to be institutionalised and credits assigned for people who take it up. In many engineering campuses students do projects for academic purposes only. If proper selection of topics based on need gap analysis is done then workable solutions would be developed and startups with a little handholding would naturally emerge.

Having an incubator on campus and encouraging students to visit and interact with the startups makes them more aware about the informal and progressive startup culture. A healthy interaction and a personal visit also changes many misconceptions about risky nature of startups. Having more female entrepreneurs talks on campus also provides role models to the students to emulate, change perception and increase their aspiration. As a British documentary maker summarised this perfectly: "If she does not see it, she can't be it' or 'If she can see it, she can be it.'"

Encouraging female students to take internship or live project with startup run by women entrepreneurs will also increase their awareness and knowledge about leadership and the enigmatic startup world.

The biggest hurdle to start a venture is availability of funds. Despite various schemes being launched by the Government under such as 'Pradhan Mantri Micro Units Development and Refinance Agency Limited (MUDRA)' with an initial corpus of Rs. 20,000 crore to extend benefits to around 10 lakhs SMEs, there is little awareness about its registration process, eligibility criterion and so on, amongst the students especially for Shishu or Kishor categories of loans. Another deterrent of these schemes is the personal guarantee to be given for these loans and the high rate of interest charged by the banks. Since the success rate of startup is dismally low even the interested students are not willing to add on to the burden of their parents. Entrepreneurs are new age patriots who take various types of risks to create jobs, achieve economic success and financial security, hence they need to be supported compassionately with minimum hurdles.

Some issues are deep-rooted and require a systemic overhaul of thinking. Creating an enabling environment at a macro level for females to take up the daunting path of entrepreneurship also includes, enforcing strict compliance of Sexual Harassment of Women at Workplace (Prevention, Prohibition and Redressal) Act 2013, on campus and in all organisations, faster redressal of cases in crime against women, improving law and order situation in the country, sensitising parents to the importance of entrepreneurship and fostering positive race, class and gender dynamics in class.

All great accomplishments are the accumulation of countless seemingly small actions. Only by creating a pipeline of budding female entrepreneurs, well rounded with a wide array of talent at the grass root academic level can this gender gap in startups be reduced.

REFERENCES

1. The Female Entrepreneurship Index (FEI), An analysis of the conditions that foster high-potential female entrepreneurship Produced at the Global Entrepreneurship and Development Institute by Siri Terjesen and Ainsley Lloyd.
2. NASSCOM startup ecosystem report of 2015.
3. The sixth economic census 2013-14 of Government of India.
4. Klyver, K., and Terjesen, S. (2007). 'Gender differences in entrepreneurial networking: A process perspective,' *Women in Management Review.*
5. Papagiannidis, S. and F. Li (2005). 'Skills brokerage: A new model for business startups in the networked economy', *European Management Journal*, 23(4): 471-482.
6. United Nations Development Programme, Human Development Reports 2016, Table 5: Gender Inequality Index.

31

Financial Planning: Women and Investment Decisions in Indian Perspective

Nidhi Khanna, Shubham Kesharwani and Somya Arora

ABSTRACT

It has been observed that although it is imperative that women should be given equal power to take financial decisions as taken by men, yet many Indian women are facing more than a few cultural, financial, psychological and physical barriers that are creating hindrances in becoming financially aware. A study commissioned by a large fund house reported that about 77 per cent of working women in India depend on their fathers or spouses to make investment decisions for them. Of the other 23 per cent, 18 per cent are single working women. "Most women are only informed of investment decisions already taken or are, at best, joint decision makers... The main reason why women don't take investment decisions is that they are safety-oriented and reluctant to take risk," the report noted. An unforeseen event can completely turn a family's fortunes topsy-turvy and lack of knowledge of financial matters may make things worse. Financial services industry observers pointed that the proportion of sole decision-makers among working women is significantly higher among the single, divorced and widowed ones. The intention of the research is to investigate the impact of self-confidence, traits and risk level of women behaviour on financial and investment decision making power in India.

Keywords: *Financial investment, unforeseen event, psychological barrier.*

Women have been suppressed under custom and law for which man was responsible and in the shaping of which she had no hand. Woman has as much right to shape her own destiny as man has to shape his. It is up to men to see that they enable them to realize their full status and play their part as equal of men. —Mahatma Gandhi

INTRODUCTION

The empowerment of women occurs when women are involved in decision making, which leads to their better access to resources, and therefore improved socio-economic status. In recent years, gender equality and women's empowerment have been recognized as crucial to the health and socio-economic development of an entire country, and not just individual families. This is evident in the fact that promotion of gender equality and empowering women is one of the stepping stones of development. We have seen that education and employment together lead to increased participation of women in various household, financial decisions with decreased occurrences of domestic violence. Our study also suggests that older women have greater say in household decisions than younger women. This is keeping in line with the nature of joint family system in India wherein the wife of the head of the family has more decision making power. And also more urban, educated, and working women participate in these decisions. This may be due to greater awareness of their rights and duties.

There are certain factors that are positively related to their participation in family decision-making, such as:

1) Women's access to resources, 2) women's socio-economic status, 3) women's ages, 4) women's responsibilities, 5) women's education, and 6) Women's perception of their role.

Today's family structure is changing and these changes are also visible in the structure of Indian families. Men have accepted that it is difficult to live without women's participation. Hence men delegate part of their decision-making power in the family to women. Delegating part of decision-making to the women at home can develop women responsibility.

OBJECTIVES OF THE STUDY

1. To find out the risk appetite of women investors.
2. To find out the barriers for lack of awareness among women in financial and investment decisions.
3. To point out the reasons why women need financial planning.
4. To point out the role of government in economic empowerment of women in India.
5. To make suggestions and recommendations for economic empowerment of women.

Why it is that men are overwhelmingly more likely to be in charge of a family's savings and investments?

In India, most public discourses on women focus on their safety. However, when we dig deeply, many of the issues boil down to empowerment in an everyday sense, and one of the issues underlying empowerment is often money.

- The obvious problem here can be that women in general earn less than men, often a lot less. However, that's just one part of it. There are other dimensions to this.
- Even when women earn well, and even when they belong to allied where there is no overt discrimination, they are less likely to be managing their own money, their savings and their investments. Leaving out those who are in a financial profession, it seems that investment is something that women just don't do. There are men who seek advice for their finances and there are men who ask on behalf of themselves and their spouses. However, there are practically never any women who seek advice for their own finances, and absolutely never any who ask for advice for their family's finances and investments.
- Women are looked at as great spenders rather than investors. When on a shopping spree, women should remember that a smart investment of their funds scores high over an attractive deal.
- This state of things wouldn't come as a surprise to anyone but we need to pause and question it a little deeply. What exactly is the reason? The obvious answer is that in families, it's the men who manage savings and investments. But that simply restates the problem in different words.
- Though women are believed to be gifted with better reasoning and foresightedness than the male counterparts, they are still afraid to venture into financial markets presuming that they might fail and will be ridiculed. In the process, they forget that this holds equally true with men too.
- Lack of private transport and reliance on public transport for many women on low incomes make attending courses, or even getting to banks, a time consuming and frustrating event.
- Stakeholders have noted a range of literacy, numeracy and technological literacy barriers among the women they represent. These include low levels of literacy and numeracy and lack of skills to access information on the Internet.

- The jargon and often technical language used by financial institutions particularly a problem for many of the women attending the focus groups. These problems were compounded by the lack of English literacy among the women.
- The working women see the cost of some financial services as a critical barrier to accessing financial information. Exclusion from education programs or financial literacy services because of an inability to pay, is a significant issue to be considered when designing or implementing programs.

Why Women should take Charge of their Finances?

- **Changing demographics**: Women can be single, widowed or divorced. They are solely responsible for their own financial independence.
- **Time off for raising children:** Many expectant mothers wish to take a time off over and above their maternity leaves in order to raise their children, but can't do so due to financial commitments. Hence, a proper planning on creating a 'time-off' corpus can help them to do this
- **Medical reasons**: Fighting diseases can wipe out a family's savings. Women should plan proactively to build a health fund.
- **Financial contribution of women to their families:** Today, more of the daughters are evolving as contributors to the family finances. Women, by participating in financial decisions, can become trendsetters by continuing to be an asset to their own family even after marriage
- **More life to live:** In old age, women largely depend financially on their spouses. But, with life expectancy of women being higher than men, it is advisable to put in place a separate retirement planning for themselves

GOVERNMENT SCHEMES FOR ECONOMIC EMPOWERMENT OF WOMEN IN INDIA

The following schemes at present are aiming at women empowerment and gender equality in India:

1. Child Development Integrated Services (ICDS) (1975)
2. Rajiv Gandhi Scheme for Empowerment of Adolescent Girls (RGSEAG) (2010)
3. The Rajiv Gandhi National Crèche Scheme for Children of Working Mothers

4. Integrated Child Protection Scheme (ICPS) (2009-10)
5. Support to Training and Employment Programme for Women (STEP)
6. Dhanalakshmi (2008)
7. Short Stay Homes
8. Swadhar
9. Ujjawala (2007)
10. Scheme for Gender Budgeting (XI Plan)
11. National Mission for Empowerment of Women
12. Rashtriya Mahila Kosh (1993)
13. Rajiv Gandhi National Crèche Scheme (2006)
14. Sukanya Samridhi Account (2015)
15. Beti Bachao Beti Padhao (2015)

SUGGESTIONS TO INCREASE WOMEN PARTICIPATION IN FINANCIAL AND INVESTMENT DECISION

- Increasing the participation of women in the workforce, the quality of work allotted to them and their contributions to GDP are indicators of the extent of women being mainstreamed into the economy.
- Gender wage gap across rural and urban, agriculture and non-agriculture jobs, regular and casual employment should be addressed. Ensuring pay parity, low level of confidence with respect to work are critical subjects for insecurity in women particularly in the informal employment.
- Financial inclusion of women needs to be universalized so that women gain a financial identity, have access to financial services such as saving services, insurance, pension schemes, aimed towards poor women special financial literacy programmes for poor women must be organized.
- Women undertake the bulk of unpaid care work, such as looking after and educating children, looking after older family members, caring for the sick, preparing food, cleaning and collecting water and fuel, etc. This burden of unpaid work undermines women participation in the economy. Recognizing women's unpaid work in terms of economic and social value, household surveys should be undertaken to assess monetary value of work.

CONCLUSION

Empowering women with economic opportunity, educating them to the benefits of investment is not only the right thing to do but it is the smartest thing to do. Sustainable business, powered by smart investment by women folk is expected to result in higher economic development. Today, women have more power and earning potential than ever before. When they are graduating with more college degrees than men and are climbing up the ranks in nearly every industry, then they surely have the ability to sharpen their skills in building wealth. At the same time, man has an equal responsibility to let his wife/daughter/sister/mother take part in financial decision making.

REFERENCES

1. www.thehindu.com, retrieved April 2017
2. http://www.sida.se/contentassets/e21f4c7bf63941999a7214ce37fc8f88/womens-economic empowerment-key-issue, retrieved April 2017
3. https://www.valueresearchonline.com/story/h2_storyview.asp?str=22334&&utm_medium=vro.in, retrieved April 2017
4. https://www.worldwidejournals.com/indian-journal-of-applied-research-, retrieved April, 2017 (IJAR)/file.php?val=January_2015_1420092610__83.pdf, retrieved April 2017
5. http://wcd.nic.in/sites/default/files/draft%20national%20policy%20for%20women%202016_0.pdf, retrieved April 2017
6. http://www.investmentyogi.com/financial-planning-for-empowerment-of-women-in-india/, retrieved April 2017
7. https://www.worldwidejournals.com/indian-journal-of-applied-research-, retrieved April, 2017 (IJAR)/file.php?val=January_2015_1420092610__83.pdf, retrieved April 2017

32

Role of Social Media Platforms in the Sustenance of Businesses: A Study of Women Entrepreneurs

Deependra Sharma and Amrita Grewal

ABSTRACT

Purpose: *This study aims to explore how the women entrepreneurs have used social media platforms as a marketing tool for the sustenance of their businesses.*

Methodology: *This study adopts a qualitative approach based on extensive review of literature available on women entrepreneurs and social media platforms and personal interviews of women entrepreneurs of Gurgaon.*

Findings: *Social media platforms have created a new generation of women entrepreneurs, allowing their businesses to be set up and be promoted with a very low cost, giving everyone an equal opportunity to succeed.*

Implications: *The study's findings have important implications for policymakers and practitioners charged with promoting growth of female entrepreneurial ventures. It also provides insights to women entrepreneurs who wish to start their own ventures.*

Keywords: social media platforms, women entrepreneurs

INTRODUCTION

The vision of "Make in India" launched by the Prime Minister of India Mr. Narendra Modi on 25th September 2014 is an initiative taken to encourage multinational as well as national companies to manufacture their products in India. It has set a benchmark of increased independence on oneself as a nation than dependency on others. It has two-fold benefit; it of course will make us the hub of manufacturing by attracting Foreign Direct Investment but more importantly it will focus on job creation and skill enhancement. Similar initiatives have been started by states on the sidelines with an objective to create a business-friendly atmosphere.

Riding on the euphoria of *Make in India,* is the importance of encouraging entrepreneurship to fulfil the vision. As per the data available in India there are a total of 198.74 lakh entrepreneurs: 18.06 lakhs are women and 179.74 are men, 0.93 are unrecorded (MSME, GOI, 2006-07). These figures present in itself an abundance of opportunity for encouraging entrepreneurship.

This research report looks at the role of social media platforms in the sustenance of the business with special reference to women entrepreneurs.

WOMEN ENTREPRENEURS IN INDIA

> *"To call woman the weaker sex is a libel, it is man's injustice to woman. If by strength is meant brute strength, then, indeed, woman is less brute than man. If by strength is meant moral power, then woman is immeasurably man's superior"...* ***—Mahatma Gandhi***

> *"Women who innovate, initiate or adopt business actively are called women entrepreneurs."* ***—J. Schumpeter***

> *"Women entrepreneurship is based on women participation in equity and employment of a business enterprise."* ***—Ruhani J. Alice***

Entrepreneurship for women can create new economic opportunities not only for women but also help in overall growth of the nation by the upliftment of women and reducing poverty.

The sixth economic census, released by ministry of statistics and programme implementation, presents a worrisome picture of the status of women entrepreneurs in the country. (MOSPI, GOI. [n.d.])

- The survey shows that women constitute only 13.76% of the total entrepreneurs, i.e. 8.05 million out of the 58.5 million entrepreneurs.
- These establishments in total, owned by females, provide employment to 13.45 million people.
- Another revelation is that out of these entrepreneurs, 2.76 million women (34.3% of the total entrepreneurs) work in agriculture sector whereas 5.29 million females (65.7% of the total entrepreneurs) work in non-agricultural sectors.

- In the agriculture, livestock dominates (with a share of 31.6%) among all other farming activities.
- Among the non-agricultural activities owned by women entrepreneurs, manufacturing and retail trade are dominant ones with corresponding percentages being 29.8% and 17.8% respectively.
- Out of the total establishments under women entrepreneurs, percentage share of various social and religious groups OBC: 40.60%, SC: 12.18%, ST: 6.97% and Others (40.25%); Hindus: 65.6%, Muslim: 12.84% and Christian: 5.2%.
- Among the states, the largest share in number of establishments under women entrepreneurship is of Tamil Nadu (13.51%) followed by Kerala (11.35%), Andhra Pradesh (10.56%), West Bengal (10.33%) and Maharashtra (8.25%).
- Average employment per establishment for women-owned establishments is 1.67.

According to the World Economic Forum's (WEF) Global Gender Gap Report 2014, Indian women spent an average of 352 minutes per day on unpaid work while men spent just 52. If we consider the overall workforce, India doesn't rank as a leading country in the world—113th out of 135—when it comes to the gender gap while women entrepreneurs constitute only 10 percent of the total number of entrepreneurs in the country.

In fact, a 2015 study done by BNP Paribas showed that India had the maximum number of women entrepreneurs in percentage terms at 49%. But, the Female Entrepreneurship Index (FEI) released in 2015 by The Global Entrepreneurship and Development Institute (GEDI) reached a very different conclusion. It ranked India at 70 out of 77 countries. Countries like Saudi Arabia and Egypt had better rankings than India. The FEI ranking is significant because it does not consider the number of women entrepreneurs, but ranks a country based on the favourable conditions it provides for female entrepreneurship (KStart, 2016).

WEB 2.0 MOMPRENEURS

Mothers in India have emerged as a force to reckon with in every possible field and are forging ahead with confidence.

Women have entered sectors which are prominently male dominated and have had success in the same. Most of these women entrepreneurs have gained experience in corporate jobs and have applied the same learnings in their business as well. Most of these women who take up ventures are in their mid-30s and wish to live their lives on their own terms. It is time to pave the way for 'mompreneurs'.

Going by the recent trends, the 'mompreneur' is here to stay. The share of female entrepreneurs in India is showing a healthy growth of 71 per cent per year. This comes as a welcome relief after the World Economic Forum ranked India at the 131st position in the list of economic participation and opportunity of women among 135 countries.

As per the current study conducted by the Women's Web Women and Entrepreneurship in India 2012 study: (Singh, A.V., 2012)

- A significant chunk (58%) of entrepreneurs had started their businesses between the ages of 20 and 30; interestingly, 25% had started up even before turning 25, that is, probably before holding a job or a very short time after holding one.
- Bangalore led all other in the presence of women entrepreneurs, while as expected other metros such as Chennai, Mumbai, NCR, Hyderabad and Pune accounted for the bulk of the rest.
- Professional services, IT/ITES, apparel/accessories and food & beverages are the four major sectors in which women own businesses (59% of those surveyed).
- The majority of women-owned businesses are micro-enterprises or small/mid-sized businesses, with 73% reporting a revenue of under Rs.10,00,000 (Rs. Ten lakh or One million) in the last financial year. Corresponding to this, the majority had under 5 employees (71%).
- Sixty per cent of women entrepreneurs started their business with a capital of under Rs.1,00,000, and personal funds and savings were used to start the business in a majority of cases.
- As for support in their entrepreneurial journey, besides friends and family (the top choices), the growing importance of the entrepreneurial community is reflected in the fact that 26% mentioned other entrepreneurs and entrepreneur groups and 23% also mentioned mentors and advisors.

Some of the successful mompreneurs who have been able to cut across the stereotype and make a place for themselves in a predominantly male diaspora are: (Singh, 2012)

1. Nidhi Agarwal: **Kaaryah—Online Women's Apparel Store**
2. Richa Kar: **Zivame—Online Lingerie Store**
3. Sairee Chahal: **Founder—Sheroes**
4. KanikaTekriwal: **Co-Founder—JetSetGo**

5. Rashi Choudhary: **Co-Founder—LocalBanya**
6. Masoom Minawala: **Founder—Style Fiesta**
7. Priyanka Gupta: **Founder and CEO—IndiaBookStore.net & Vivilio**
8. Ishita Anand: **Co-Founder, BitGiving**
9. Nandini Rathi: **Co-Founder, Betaout**
10. Upma Arora and Arti Bareja: **Co-Founders, Dhaba Lane**

If women started growth-oriented businesses at the same rate as men in the next two years millions more jobs would be created (Aidis et al., 2015)

SOCIAL MEDIA (WEB 2.0)

Social networking service (also social networking site, SNS or social media) is an online platform that is used by people to build social networks or social relations with other people who share similar personal or career interests, activities, backgrounds or real-life connections.

Social network services can be split into three types: socializing social network services are primarily for socializing with existing friends (e.g. Facebook); networking social network services are primarily for non-social interpersonal communication (e.g. LinkedIn, a career and employment-oriented site); and social navigation social network services are primarily for helping users to find specific information or resources (e.g. Goodreads for books). A study reveals that India has recorded the world's largest growth in terms of social media users in 2013.

A survey (Duggan et al., 2013) found that 73% of the adults in the US use social networking sites. A study (Duggan et al., 2016) shows that 85% of people aged 18 to 34 use social networking sites for their purchase decision making. While over 65% of people aged 55 and over rely on word of mouth.

According to Jody Nimetz, author of Marketing Jive, there are five major uses for businesses and social media: to create brand awareness, as an online reputation management tool, for recruiting, to learn about new technologies and competitors, and as a lead generation tool to intercept potential prospects. These companies are able to drive traffic to their own online sites while encouraging their consumers and clients to have discussions on how to improve or change products or services.

A study shows (Duggan et al., 2016) that 79% now use Facebook, more than double the share that uses Twitter (24%), Pinterest (31%), Instagram (32%) or LinkedIn (29%).

A study by public relation firm Burson-Marsteller shows that 86% of 100 largest companies on the Fortune 500 list use at least one of the social media sites such as Facebook, Twitter, YouTube or blogs, and 28% of them use all four platforms.

RESEARCH OBJECTIVES

Considering the literature that is available we understand that social media and SNS are becoming a key tool to for a company's branding as well as for continued relationship building, product innovations, reach. Moreover, to some extent business are using social media also for crowd funding to meet their financial needs.

As per the report of Global Women Entrepreneur Leaders-2015 (Aidis et al., 2015) states that the main challenge for Indian women entrepreneurs is not starting a business but sustaining and scaling it up. Where we understand and take that social platforms help boost the initial phase of a business, however, to continually engage in the medium to achieve the objective through all the stages of a business is what is imperative.

There is not much research done in India regarding understanding the role of social media platforms in helping women entrepreneurs sustain their businesses, which was the reason this qualitative research was undertaken to expand and develop the knowledge base related to women entrepreneurs and social media platforms acting as a tool to help sustain and grow business.

The research paper looks at therefore answering the following research questions:

1. Do women entrepreneurs believe social media platforms are a useful marketing tool to help sustain their business?
2. How women business owners are using social media platforms to help in business sustainability?

LITERATURE REVIEW

According to Ukpere et al. (2014), the study of Social Media Platforms and their impact in determining the financial success of the women entrepreneurs globally has been widely observed and quite vital to the new generation of gender based ventures that are digitally driven through the use of technology. This technological development helps women to adapt and utilise Social Media platforms in promoting the creation of a new revolution of modern digital entrepreneurial culture. It can be seen from how this new technological wave drives the changing of the female society from a technologically challenged to a technologically savvy one by providing ample of opportunities that are made available by the use of Social Media Platforms and the Internet.

REVIEW OF DATASET

Key Words	*No. of documents Extracted*	*Journals*
Social media, women enterpreneurs	26	Most articles published in reputed Journals, conference papers, articles
Social media platforms and women entrepreneurs	10	Journal of Small Business and Enterprise; Development, Education, Business and Society: Contemporary Middle Eastern Issues; Mediterranean Journal of Social Sciences; International Journal of Multidisciplinary Research

According to Henar (2012), it is found that social networking is a cheap and easy method of advertising and gives all entrepreneurs a better chance of reaching their target market and, thereby, succeeding in their ventures. With the rise in the use of social networking, entrepreneurs can now target their markets using online social networks. Social networking web sites allow businesses to introduce their products to specific market segments, with low expense, and with a low chances of failure.

According to Shabbir et al. (2016), social media applications in the present time have become highly efficient and effective tools for small business entrepreneurs and normally all small business use social media platform for the advertising and publicity of their products and services, they make fan pages for the followers and they warmly welcome the suggestions and opinions which help in improving their business.

Based on the study done by Ukpere et al. (2014), women micro-entrepreneurs are proactively using the social networks to advertise their goods and services and then make use of this mobile technology, which work for them in terms of client payments and banking. This special feature offered by the social media as a mobile application where the users can manage their accounts from mobile phone and only need basic literacy to operate the phone provide them another reason to use this platform. Due to the fact that the system does not rely on any physical infrastructure such as phone wires and is accessible to a large segment of the population (Elder and Rashid, 2009 as cited in Mbogo, 2010: 164) gives them another point to embrace this opportunity as well.

According to Razak et al. (2016), the information shared on web sites are related to businesses and act as a marketing tool, to help raise brand awareness and helps to make connection and online networking with customers, dealers partners and investors. It is also a medium for business transaction and more. Thus, Facebook is the most used and preferred by most of the women entrepreneurs compared to other social media networks, such as Twitter, Instagram and even their own website.

As per the study conducted by Niiya (2016) where they established that entrepreneurs who actively expanded their social networks achieve higher business growth. They also brought out through their study that social competency and active networking are both related to business growth.

PERSONAL INTERVIEWS

As part of trying to understand the role of social media in helping sustaining businesses, three women entrepreneurs were interviewed from the Gurgaon region. The entrepreneurs who were interviewed were actively using social media platforms.

Two interviews were conducted at the office sites of the entrepreneurs and one interview was conducted over the phone due to logistic issues.

The business profiles were as follows (the names of businesses and entrepreneurs have been kept confidential)

1. XYZ Boutique and Tailoring shop: The business was operational for the last 4 years. It initially started with one employee and has grown to add 3 employees. It is located in a populated colony in a upper middle class locality.
2. ABC Bakery is a home establishment. It is operational for the last 6 years. It is a one-man shop situated in a densely populated residential area.
3. PQR online company has been operational for the last 5 years. It focuses its efforts on conducting seminars, discussions, trainings and open houses on issues related to sustainable living.

There was no questionnaire prepared, however there were leading questions which helped guide the interview. The standard interview questions were as follows:

- When did you start your business?
- When did you start using social media for business purposes?
- Have you seen any benefits?
- What challenges did you face?
- Did you experience any substantial jump in the business?

FINDINGS OF THE INTERVIEWS

1. The entrepreneurs are comfortable using the various social networking sites. They find Facebook posts and WhatsApp as the two most beneficial social networking services (SNS).
2. The benefits of SNS are felt most while establishing a business as it is the first tool used for promotion and reach. It helps build their customer base, however, only those with a larger social circle are the ones who are able to reach many.
3. Currently the use of social media is only restricted to getting customer orders, payment receipts and promotion of branding. Except for one of them who engages actively on the social media platforms.
4. They do not regularly post on their Facebook pages as they feel they lack the skill set to actively engage on the platform.
5. Social media sites/services have certainly made it easier to build customer base, as it works a lot on referrals.
6. They especially mentioned e-wallet is the technology that they are finding useful as through this they are being able to break barriers, where customers are ordering online and payment happens online. Hence it has made the business more efficient.
7. Each entrepreneur felt that probably there is more to offer on social media, however they find themselves a little ill-equipped to understand the full potential of the medium.
8. Initial investment is primarily for setting up the business. Social media has made marketing easier even for a layman. When earlier you would have to get pamphlets printed and distributed which in itself involved cost.

FINDINGS

Social Media tools have a lot to offer to women entrepreneurs in terms of encouraging and assisting indirect sales, while the most vital of all the tools is enabling the brand awareness and customer base.

Social Media platforms have also encouraged and resulted in women entrepreneurs forming forums for advice and networking that make expert advice available promptly, at the same time making use of the same for interacting with existing as well as prospective clientele.

Social Media has facilitated women entrepreneurs to create relationships and build trust, leading to concrete and positive interactions.

Presence on social media outlets are crucial and important, since the resulting factor is improved capability of meeting people and grow one's client-base.

Undoubtedly, online social networking web sites such as Facebook have created a new generation of entrepreneurs, allowing their businesses to be set up and be promoted with a very low cost, giving everyone an equal opportunity to succeed.

The women entrepreneurs can choose their target market segments through social media, more effectively and can enable display advertising and social discussions which could eventually lead to higher customer base and help in sustaining their business.

Women entrepreneurs must realize that merely obtaining technology and adopting digital platforms will not grow their practices, however, it is only when they practically play an active role in engaging with these platforms and spaces that these tools can enhance their growth and expansion. Women must be taught how to embrace and incorporate technology into their businesses so that the future women entrepreneurs can follow suit.

All these findings support that indeed the rise of social media platforms have made the process and motivation of starting a business more viable due to easy access and low cost. They provide opportunities through technology to cut across geographical boundaries and expand businesses to other markets as well. Social media platforms also provide opportunity to enter into foreign markets with reduced marketing and logistics cost, especially due to e-wallets and e-marketing. Hence it can be said that social media platforms are no longer about building social networks, but about increased customer base, low marketing cost, efficient payment system, possibility to enter into foreign markets all ways of ensuring continued business growth.

Significance of Study and Scope for Future Research: The significance of this study is that, not much research is available for women entrepreneurs in India and their use of social media platforms. Women entrepreneurship and social media are both mushrooming at this age. It makes it an interesting study to note how one effects the other. There is scope for future research to be done on women entrepreneurs in the I tier cities and in II tier cities in India and their understanding and ability to use social media platforms as an effective marketing tool in their businesses.

Limitations: There is no actual tool that is available to measure the benefit of the social media platform in sustaining business. It is merely based on qualitative research. Hence there is scope for further research where quantitative variables can be developed to measure the benefit of social media platforms in sustaining businesses.

CONCLUSION

The use of technology by women entrepreneurs has been seen as a very positive step in the right direction. Social Networking Sites are being used not only as a social platform but as a tool for expanding the reach of businesses. With appropriate training being given to women entrepreneurs as to its full potential, it will possibly be seen as one which not only helps establish a business but plays an important role in expanding and sustaining a business. This type of development through which women adapt and utilise Social Media platforms promotes the creation of a new revolution of modern digital entrepreneurial culture, where opportunities are made available by the use of Social Media Platforms and the Internet.

REFERENCES

1. Ukpre, C.L., Slabbert, A.D., & Ukpre, W.I. (2014). The Relevance of Modern Technology Usage on the Business Ventures of Kenyan Women Entrepreneurs. *Mediterranean Journal of Social Sciences, 5(10),* 58-66. Doi:10.5901/ mjss.2014.v5n10p58
2. Ukpre, C.L., Slabbert, A.D., & Ukpre, W.I. (2014). Rising Trend in Social Media Usage by Women Entrepreneurs across the Globe to Unlock Their Potentials for Business Success. *Mediterranean Journal of Social Sciences, 5(10),* 551-559. Doi:10.5901/mjss.2014.v5n10p551
3. Melissa, E., Hamidati, A., Saraswati, M.S., & Flor, A.G. (2013). Investigating the Potentials of Social Media to Support Women Entrepreneurship in Indonesian Urban Areas. ICTD 2013, Dec 07-10 2013, Cape Town, South Africa. http:// dx.doi.org/10.1145/2517899.2517921
4. Rosenbaum, G.O. (2017). Female entrepreneurial networks and foreign market entry. *Journal of Small Business and Enterprise Development*, Vol. 24, Iss 1, pp. 119–135. Permanent link to this document: http://dx.doi.org/10.1108/JSBED-07-2016-0113
5. Henari, J.I.T. (2012). Entrepreneurial success, using online social networking: evaluation. *Education, Business and Society: Contemporary Middle Eastern Issues*, Vol. 5, Iss 1, pp. 47-62 Permanent link to this document: http://dx.doi.org/10.1108/ 17537981211225853
6. Razak, N.A., & Jah, N.J.A. (2016). Online Writing Strategies in Social Media for Women Entrepreneurs. ICWC 2016, Selangor, Malaysia. Retrieved from *ejournal.ukm.my/ebangi/article/viewFile/16081/5011*
7. Cesaroni, F.M., Demartini, P., & Paoloni, P. (2016). Women in business and social media: state of the art and research agenda. IFKAD proceeding 2016. Retrieved from https://www.researchgate.net/publication/309721973

8. Niiya, Y. & Taji, Noriko (2016). Social Competency and Social Networks as Predictors of Business Growth in Japanese IT and Web Startups. See discussions, stats, and author profiles for this publication at https://www.researchgate.net/publication/307568828
9. Shabbir, M.S., Ghazi, M.S., & Mehmood, A.R. (2016). Impact of Social Media Applications on Small Business Entrepreneurs. *Arabian Journal of Business and Management Review*, 6 (3), 1000203. DOI: 10.4172/2223-5833.1000203
10. Paoloni, P. & Dumay, J.C. (2015). The relational capital of micro-enterprises run by women: the startup phase, *VINE*, Vol. 45, Iss 2, pp. 172-197 Permanent link to this document: http://dx.doi.org/10.1108/VINE-01-2014-0003
11. Melissa, E., Hamidati, A., Saraswati, M.S., & Flor, A.G., The Internet and Indonesian Women Entrepreneurs: Examining the Impact of Social Media on Women Empowerment. DOI:10.1007/978-981-287-381-1_11. See discussions, stats, and author profiles for this publication at: https://www.researchgate.net/publication/283594389
12. Nieva, F.O. (2015). Social women entrepreneurship in the Kingdom of Saudi Arabia. *Journal of Global Entrepreneurship Research (2015) 5:11*.DOI 10.1186/s40497-015-0028-5
13. Aidis, R. et al. (2015). Global Women Entrepreneur Leaders Scorecard. Retrieved from *https://www.dell.com/.../documents~2015-gwel-scorecard-executive-summary.pdf*
14. Goyal, M. & Parkash, J. (2011). Women Entrepreneurship in India-problems and prospects. *International Journal of Multidisciplinary Research*, Vol. 1, Issue 5, pp. 196-207, September 2011, ISSN 2231 5780
15. MOSPI, GOI. (n.d.) Sixth Economic census. Retrieved on 13 Apr 2017 from URL: http://mospi.nic.in/. See more at- http://www.governancenow.com/news/regular-story/fact-sheet-women-entrepreneurs-in-india#sthash.ZbTKrYPd.dpuf
16. K. Start. (2016). Survey on Women Entrepreneurs. Retrieved on 13th April 2017 from *https://yourstory.com/2016/04/kstart-women-entrepreneurship-survey/*
17. Singh, A. V., (2012). Women and Entrepreneurship in India. Retrieved on 13th April 2017 from http://www.womensweb.in/articles/women-entrepreneur ship-in-india/
18. MSME, GOI. (2006-2007) Fourth All India Census of MSME: Unregistered Sector. Retrieved on 13th April 2017 from URL:http://dcmsme.gov.in/publications/Final%20Report%20of%20Fourth%20All%20India%20Census%20of%20MSME%20Unregistered%20Sector%202006-07.pdf
19. WEF. 2014. The Global Gender Gap Report. *World Economic Forum*. ISBN 92-95044-38-X
20. ISBN 978-92-95044-38-8. Retrieved on 13th April 2017 from URL:
21. http://www3.weforum.org/docs/GGGR14/GGGR_CompleteReport_2014.pdf
22. BNP PARIBAS. 2016. The emergence of the "millennipreneur". *2016 bnpparibas*
23. *global entrepreneur report*. Retrieved on 13th April 2017 from URL: https://cdn-actus.bnpparibas.com/files/upload/2015/11/04/docs/ataglance.pdf
24. Duggan, M., & Smith, A. (2013) Social media update 2013. *Pew Research Centre. URL*:http://www.pewinternet.org/2013/12/30/social-media-update-2013/
25. Greenwood, S., Perrin, A. & Duggan, M. (2016) Social media update 2016 *Pew Research Centre*, URL: http://assets.pewresearch.org/wp-content/uploads/sites/14/2016/11/10132827/PI_2016.11.11_Social-Media-Update_FINAL.pdf

33

The Cultural Tools of Women Empowerment:

How Advertising has Changed to Become a Medium of Social Transformation!

Aditi Hajela

ABSTRACT

Various studies have delved into the difference in portrayal of men and women in advertising and how such portrayal influences the society's outlook towards gender equality and stereotypes. With globalization, products and services have proliferated, and consumers have become more diverse and savvy. Accordingly, competition among firms and changing technologies have influenced advertising in terms of both its content and, as we will argue, its purpose. We study the portrayal of women in advertisements and conduct a qualitative longitudinal analysis of advertising in different countries at various stages of economic development. We find that paradigms of gender representation and equality have indeed undergone changes and that advertising in developing economies provides a potent medium of social communication. The role of advertising in promoting the empowerment and parity of women makes it an important cultural tool for sustainable development.

Secondary data was used for this study. Relevant articles from newspapers and business magazines, research papers from journals and the internet were studied and qualitatively analyzed.

INTRODUCTION

Led by the United Nations (UN), a set of 17 Global Goals were adopted by member countries as part of the agenda for 2030 Sustainable

Development Goals.[1] Of the 17 Goals, Goal 5 is 'Gender Equality': to achieve gender equality and empower all women and girls and put an end to discrimination against them.[2] Although, there have been serious efforts in this direction for some years now by various countries and organisations, a lot more needs to be done. The discrimination against women is both social and economic and hence, the mindset of the society at large needs to change. Advertising, through its positive portrayal of men and women in various media, can be an immensely useful tool in sustainable development, as it has had a great influence on people on largely all aspects of their lives. There have been exhaustive and growing studies on gender representation in advertising.

Since it can be so powerful, at a time when advertising was in its infancy, President Calvin Coolidge had remarked:

> *"Advertising is the most potent influence in adapting and changing the habits and modes of life affecting what we eat, what we wear, and the work and play of a whole nation."*

For a long time adverts blatantly promoted gender stereotypes, however that seems to be slowly changing. This is an attempt to study the portrayal of women in advertisements and conduct a qualitative longitudinal analysis of advertising at various stages of economic development and see advertising as a potent medium of social communication. One finds that paradigms of gender representation and equality have indeed undergone changes—from obvious gender stereotyping to being more progressive and empowering.

STEREOTYPING IN ADVERTISING

Gender stereotyping in advertising has existed from the beginning. Women are associated with home and body product adverts while men are associated with services, technological and automotive product advertisements. There was clear compartmentalization of gender roles in them. As mentioned in the introduction, advertising plays a powerful role in influencing the psyche of the society. Such biased portrayal reinforces stereotypes in the society. Amongst the studies on gender stereotyping in advertisement two views emerged—'Mirror' and 'Mould'.

MIRROR AND MOULD

'Mirror' proposition says that advertisements reflect what is already there in society, rather than causing some external effect on society. Advertisements depict the views and cultural beliefs of the prevalent times.

The stereotypes in advertising, they say, are the reflection of the stereotypes present in the society, thereby indicating that advertising does not really influence people at large.[3]

The 'Mould' view says that advertising attempts to influence society by targeting the mindset of a segment to promote their products. Gradually, and with effective repetitions, the mindset becomes the social norm.[3] For example, women for the longest time were shown as either homemakers or sex objects whereas men were shown in positions of power and decision-making. When depicted repeatedly in several adverts, this stereotype gets reinforced and women are often relegated to being just that.

AFFECTIVE CONDITIONING

Advertising helps people transfer their feelings of being warm and happy to things which have little to do with happiness. *Coca-Cola* has nothing to do with joy or smiles or equality, but somehow it is associated with all those things. This transfer of our feelings from one set of items to another is called *affective conditioning*.[4] And so, a cream or a car could mean the difference between women at home or office, as mothers or as doctors.

Advertising, in the absence of suitable social policies, can make a significant impression on audiences from a very young age, right into adulthood.

CHANGING REPRESENTATION OF WOMEN IN ADVERTISING

In the late 1980s and early 1990s Aunt Jemima and Betty Crocker were one of the most visible and popular adverts representing women in their role of home-makers with food-related products. Since then, gender portrayal had undergone a considerable change. By the 1990s, women were shown to be working professionals alongwith their role as home-makers. In the 21st century, advertising truly started to break some of the gender stereotypes—enter 'Femvertising'.

BREAKING STEREOTYPES

Femvertising

'Femvertising' is defined by SheKnows Media, which awards one winner in the category annually, as "advertising that employs pro-female talent, messages and imagery to empower women and girls. Simply put, it is pro-female messaging within advertisements. It became known in 2004 with

Dove's "Real Beauty" campaign, but has gained widespread currency in recent times.[5]

Some of the ad campaigns on various media that are helping break gender stereotypes and empower women:

- **Always' #likeagirl**—The **Always** campaign points out how phrases such as *'Like a girl'* are pejorative and actually relate to negative stereotypes. Then **Always** goes on to break them by telling that 'Like a girl' should never be used like an insult but as a fact.
- **Tanishq**—One of Tanishq's ad campaigns shows a dark-skinned woman as the protagonist of the ad. The ad breaks several stereotypes—those of skin colour, remarriage, motherhood.
- **JC Penny's #hereiam**—The ad features several plus-sized women. The message is not to glorify obesity but to convey that plus-sized women should be comfortable in their own skin.
- **Girls who code 'Why girls can't code?'**—Girls who code is a not for profit organization that tries to dispel the notion that girls are not as tech savvy as boys in their video.
- **Bournvita**—This commercial shows a young girl training to be a boxer. The mother is stands by her daughter as she goes through the grind.

These were some of the examples of empowering ad campaigns in recent times. There are several others. The need to portray real women and authenticity is being recognized more and more. In a survey done by SheKnows, 91 percent of respondents believe that how women are portrayed in advertising has a direct impact on girls' self-esteem, and 94 percent thought depicting women as sex symbols is harmful. 51 percent of women voted that they like pro-female ads because it helped break down gender-equality barriers, and 71 percent of respondents think brands should be responsible for using advertising to promote positive messages to women and girls.[6]

CONCLUSION

Gender equality is not only a fundamental human right, but is essential to a progressive, happy, and sustainable world. When a women is empowered, has access to education, health-care, is able to have career aspirations, it will have a multiplier effect on the world at large, as Mr. Antonio Guterres, Secretary General, United Nations has said:

> "...Healthy, educated and empowered women, children and adolescents can drive the transformation we need for a better future."

Through its Goal 5 of achieving sustainable development through gender equality, it targets to:

> "Providing women and girls with equal access to education, health care, decent work, and representation in political and economic decision-making processes will fuel sustainable economies and benefit societies and humanity at large. Enhance the use of enabling technology, in particular information and communications technology, to promote the empowerment of women."[7]

While ads are being less stereotypical, there is still a long way to go when it comes to the representation of women on screen and in print. Marketers can influence and help remove biases, promote greater equality and help achieve the above goals by breaking stereotypical barriers in the society through advertising.

A PROMISING CHANGE

Products targeted at one and all are now using women not just as their mascots, but as the symbols of all people, from all walks of life. The hope is that women will support products, services and businesses that support women. The hope from men is that they too will now pay less attention to the brands who demean and objectify women—whether on magazine pages, billboards or on TV screen.

Also it is heartening to know that vital positions in advertising are being occupied by women now, enabling them to wield major influence on concepts of ad campaigns, giving hope that portrayal of women in advertising would see more positive images of women and help in making the world a better place by changing mental attitudes and biases towards men and women.

REFERENCES

1. http://www.un.org/sustainabledevelopment/sustainable-development-goals/ Femvertising Accessed on March, 2017,
2. http://www.undp.org/content/undp/en/home/sustainable-development-goals/goal-5-gender-equality.html, Accessed on March, 2017
3. Eisend, M. (2010). A meta-analysis of gender roles in advertising. Journal of the Academy of Marketing Science, 38(4), 418-440; cited by Adrian Furnham in https://www.psychologytoday.com/blog/sideways-view/201604/are-men-and-women-portrayed-differently-in-tv-ads
4. Art Markman, August 31, 2010. What advertising does do?—https://www.psychologytoday.com/blog/ulterior-motives/201008/what-does-advertising-do
5. Renae Hurlbutt, March 10, 2017. Femvertising: What is it and How to do it well;

https://spark.adobe.com/blog/2017/03/10/femvertising-what-is-it-and-how-to-do-it-well/

6. Nina Bahadur, October 3, 2014. 'Femvertising' Ads Are Empowering Women—And Making Money For Brands; http://www.huffingtonpost.com/2014/10/02/femvertising-advertising-empowering-women_n_5921000.html
7. http://www.un.org/sustainabledevelopment/gender-equality/, Accessed on March, 2017.

Index